About This Book

Why Is This Topic Important?

Sales professionals provide the cash flow that keeps a company healthy and growing. Yet too many of them are either untrained or are using sales approaches that were developed thirty to forty years ago. Add to this the concern that buyers are more savvy than ever, and leaders of sales teams must always look at the latest information on what really works today in selling. Sales executives, managers, and training team members can together create potent sales training that offers a clear competitive advantage in their market.

What Can You Achieve with This Book?

This book is actually a working resource of best practices in sales training. It is a tool kit for helping trainers, consultants, and sales managers improve the performance of each member of the selling team. The ultimate purpose of this book is to help senior sales executives and their internal or external training partners to redesign existing training. The book includes stories and humor to set up each learning module. There are learning activities to help salespeople practice, then adapt new behaviors that lead to increased revenue for both the individual and the company. The stories can be used to reinforce learning after the fact by putting them in email reminders or publishing them as articles in corporate newsletters. Sales trainers will find the exercises to be an excellent addition to their knowledge and experience as they build better training programs for their organizations.

How Is This Book Organized?

The opening section, Preparing the Sales Pro to Sell, gives a definition of world class sales professionals and reinforces the critical need to adopt and implement a selling system. Part Two, Training the Sales Pro to Sell, offers all the pieces of the sales puzzle, the key elements of a great selling system. Part Three, Training the Sales Pro to Improve Performance, covers individual practices and behaviors for a salesperson that increase the power of the system. Finally, a structure is given to re-create your existing training experience. This includes key concerns as well as some insights on the option of buying, as opposed to designing your sales training.

About Pfeiffer

Pfeiffer serves the professional development and hands-on resource needs of training and human resource practitioners and gives them products to do their jobs better. We deliver proven ideas and solutions from experts in HR development and HR management, and we offer effective and customizable tools to improve workplace performance. From novice to seasoned professional, Pfeiffer is the source you can trust to make yourself and your organization more successful.

Essential Knowledge Pfeiffer produces insightful, practical, and comprehensive materials on topics that matter the most to training and HR professionals. Our Essential Knowledge resources translate the expertise of seasoned professionals into practical, how-to guidance on critical workplace issues and problems. These resources are supported by case studies, worksheets, and job aids and are frequently supplemented with CD-ROMs, websites, and other means of making the content easier to read, understand, and use.

Essential Tools Pfeiffer's Essential Tools resources save time and expense by offering proven, ready-to-use materials—including exercises, activities, games, instruments, and assessments—for use during a training or team-learning event. These resources are frequently offered in looseleaf or CD-ROM format to facilitate copying and customization of the material.

Pfeiffer also recognizes the remarkable power of new technologies in expanding the reach and effectiveness of training. While e-hype has often created whizbang solutions in search of a problem, we are dedicated to bringing convenience and enhancements to proven training solutions. All our e-tools comply with rigorous functionality standards. The most appropriate technology wrapped around essential content yields the perfect solution for today's on-the-go trainers and human resource professionals.

Pfeiffer
www.pfeiffer.com   *Essential resources for training and HR professionals*

About the American Society for Training & Development

The American Society for Training & Development (ASTD) is the world's largest professional association dedicated to the training and development field. In more than 100 countries, ASTD's members work in organizations of all sizes, in the private and public sectors, as independent consultants, and as suppliers. Members connect locally in 130 U.S. chapters and with 30 international partners.

ASTD started in 1943 and in recent years has widened the profession's focus to align learning and performance to organizational results and is a sought-after voice on critical public policy issues. For more information, visit www.astd.org.

Dedication

Are you inspired by people who build you up or those that did you wrong?

To Jerry S, who fired me from my first selling job almost 30 years ago. Some clients had flown into Chicago from New York during a terrible snowstorm. They had to make a decision quickly, then run back to the airport. I used my boss's office (he was at lunch) for an impromptu meeting where I finalized the sale. Jerry returned and was more angry at my breaking a rule than doing a deal. "You disobeyed me by using my office to close a sale. It is now 2:35 p.m. and you are no longer employed here." I walked to the door and stopped, my hand on the handle. I then refused to leave, telling him, "I am the best performer you have and asking me to go is a bad decision." He stared at me and said, "Okay, get back to work. Just don't tell anyone we had this conversation." Thanks, Jerry, for letting me close you on continuing in this career.

To Ron C, my basketball coach, who said I'd never play beyond high school. Now, decades after playing four years of college ball, I've had the opportunity to represent the United States in World Masters Competition, winning three gold medals (so far). Thanks, Ron, for pushing me to prove you wrong. The sport has also taught me a lesson I take into my profession every day that I sell.

I hate losing more than I enjoy winning.

Now to those who build me up.

I'm inspired by the barn owl who's hooting outside my bedroom window at night. And, during the day, the woodpecker that's hammering away at the house, looking for food (don't tell my wife about the woodpecker; she's embarrassed he's damaging the property). Why these birds? Nature has a way of revealing itself in a spectacular array of variety. Colors, shapes, and sounds. On the ground, in the air, in the sea (if you've never scuba dived, you're missing something special). And that variety is exactly what we see in people across this planet. As a sales pro, I appreciate individual uniqueness and continue to learn to adjust to get in synch with everyone I meet.

But mostly I'm inspired by and dedicate this work to my Princess Bride, Wendy, with whom I constantly celebrate our marriage by arguing – who is smarter – me for marrying her, or her for marrying me?

You can divide the world into people who make good decisions and those that don't. You made a great decision to pick up this book. I trust you'll recognize the wisdom of that decision and use this tool to improve the performance of your sales team, as well as your career.

Dan Seidman, Barrington, IL

DAN SEIDMAN

THE ULTIMATE GUIDE TO SALES
Training

Potent Tactics to Accelerate Sales Performance

Pfeiffer
A Wiley Imprint
www.pfeiffer.com

Published by Jossey-Bass

A Wiley Imprint

One Montgomery Street, Suite 1200, San Francisco, CA 94104-4594—www.josseybass.com

Library of Congress Cataloging-in-Publication Data
Seidman, Dan.
  The Ultimate Guide to Sales Training : potent tactics to accelerate sales performance / Dan Seidman.
     p. cm.
   Includes bibliographical references and index.
  ISBN 978-0-470-90000-0 (pbk.); 978-1-118-16054-1 (ebk.); 978-1-118-16055-8 (ebk.); 978-1-118-16056-5 (ebk.)
  1. Selling. 2. Sales management. I. Title.
  HF5438.25.S4358 2012
  658.3'1245–dc23

                                                  2011039743

FIRST EDITION

PB Printing 10 9 8 7 6 5 4 3 2 1

Contents

Part Three: Training the Sales Pro to Improve Performance   **267**

Part Four: Re-Creating Your Training Experience: Key Concerns   **405**

Foreword

It's about time! I've waited in line at banks, clothing stores, restaurants, and more. As the president and CEO of Sales & Marketing Executives International (www. SMEI.org), I spend an inordinate amount of time on airplanes and standing in security lines and boarding lines. You know the feeling. Some things are worth waiting for; others just aren't.

The Ultimate Guide to Sales Training was well worth the wait. You are holding in your hand a comprehensive work that will serve as an advanced GPS navigation system for serious sales professionals.

SMEI was born from what were called "sales managers' clubs" in the 1880s. Then in 1935, IBM Founder Thomas Watson, Sr., and other visionaries brought these clubs together to form a network of sales and marketing executives. Within fifteen years, groups from more than forty countries began to participate in this movement to draw off the collective brainpower of professionals in a wide variety of industries. It's still happening today—only now we've added formal certification programs whereby sales professionals can prove their commitment to the selling profession by validating their understanding of and application to selling. They can choose to do this either as salespeople or as sales executives.

Dan Seidman's systematic approach to sales training has covered all the key elements that have formed the foundation of an elite sales approach since the beginning of these clubs. In my work with SMEI, I travel across the globe visiting these salespeople, executives, and entrepreneurs. They are hungry to attain the highest levels of performance.

Prior to writing this foreword, I spoke in four cities in China, the capital of Vietnam, then flew to Washington, D.C. Now I will use this book to cover all the critical pieces of the sales puzzle. Each chapter includes exercises to anchor the reader's learning. Each chapter kicks off the learning moment with a sales war story, a humorous anecdote, even a joke. Any one of these chapters just might be the piece that plugs the gap in your team's performance.

And Dan's done something else quite unique. For each piece of the sales puzzle, he identifies a concept that trainers, managers, and sales professionals can use to help training moments stick in their brains. My favorite was *Great Sales Pros Can Predict the Future*. In the chapter called The Ultimate Objection-Handling Tool, this concept is used to help companies remove the biggest bottleneck that occurs during sales dialogues—buyer resistance. If you put the concepts in this book into practice, buyer resistance will no longer be an issue for you, because you will not only have anticipated every objection possible (*predict the future*), but you'll use Dan's strategies to come up with dozens of responses for any possible objection. Why so many? This idea is brilliant as well. You need so many possibilities because each person on your team must "find his or her voice" and react to resistance in a manner consistent with his or her own personality and style.

The Ultimate Objection-Handling Tool was the training Dan chose to present when I invited him to Puerto Rico this past fall, where he spoke at our Sales & Marketing Executives International Conference. He stayed an extra day to train the Blue Cross/Blue Shield organization that handles insurance for this territory. The objection-handling tool alone is a significant contribution to our profession. Imagine using it, as Dan suggests, to create a book of responses to resistance. Rookies come aboard and immediately brainstorm each type of objection and prepare for it. You'll significantly shorten their learning curve and speed them toward success, because you will have taught them to *predict the future*.

Dan also introduces a phrase I found both a bit disturbing and comforting: *We are in the before and after business. If there is not a distinct difference between learners' behavior—after they've encountered our training—we have failed.*

- I find that disturbing because it points out that the *real* focus of our sales training should be on changing behavior, adopting new language skills, and practicing techniques that improve performance, which it often is not.

- I find it comforting because it means that great sales training *can* improve performance by changing behavior. There is no better way to quantify the value of good sales training than to see an increase in revenue.

There are so many other highlights from this book that I'll just point out a few that are critical for sales executives and designers of training programs.

- Dan identifies the number 1 problem sales pros face—chasing poor prospects. To counter this, he provides a detailed strategy for qualifying and disqualifying buyers as quickly as possible.

- Dan reminds us that sales professionals have been told to take charge of each sales call, but we can't really control anyone. However, we can take charge of the dialogue and virtually eliminate the buyer's ability to end the meeting with an "I'll think it over and get back to you."

- There's a monstrous-sized section of lead generation ideas, which I won't go into.

- And Dan presents a distinct way to debrief sales calls. If a manager isn't available, salespeople can critique and improve their own skills by debriefing themselves. What a concept!

- Dan even discusses presentation skills training and reminds us that we need to evoke emotion in our sales calls to motivate buyers to buy.

You can work through this book front to back, or bounce around, using specific chapters to fix gaps in your team's performance. You will even find a very cool CAT scan diagnostic tool that you can use to analyze your existing training.

Dan is truly earning the title "Trainer to the World's Sales Trainers."

The Ultimate Guide to Sales Training is a work that will have global impact in the sales field, and I look forward to seeing that it is available in multiple languages wherever I travel around our planet.

I trust you will also find plenty of "aha" moments as you read and that this book will inspire you to look seriously at *how* you train as well as *what* you build into your training.

Willis Turner
CAE CSE, President and CEO
Sales & Marketing Executives International
www.SMEI.org

Preface

Weird Sales Training Experience

I'm working with a client and partway through the morning's sales training I do a "confession session" where reps share their most embarrassing moments.

It's a very funny time. Colleagues who have known one another for a decade or more are shocked to find out some of the stupid things their peers have done in their selling infancy.

We take a break, and as everyone rushes off to eat, drink, phone, text, etc., the cartoon (pictured here) is still up on the screen.

A woman walks up and barks loudly: "I am very offended by that image."

"What? You are?" I'm shocked. Then people start to gather in as they hear the energy in her voice.

"Yes, it is very obvious that that man is looking up her skirt."

"Are you serious?" I ask. Her lips tighten as she nods.

Then silence as everyone peers closely at the cartoon picture.

A man says, "But he has no eyes!"

She glares at him and retorts, "He is looking up her skirt and it is very offensive."

I'm shocked and struggle with whether to make a witty comment or a sarcastic one, then resign myself to . . .

"I'll have to get that guy a male psychologist."

Here's the thought for you sales training pros.

What kind of baggage is she bringing into the training? I've been training for more than twenty years and continue to be entertained and, at times, shocked by what's residing in the heads inside the room. Once I offered a theoretical story about distinctions between moms' and dads' nurturing behavior and a woman said, "My father would never speak like that!" Whoa, lady. It's an example. And now that you bring that up, I'm probably glad you and I don't share the same father.

In the real world, outside the classroom, we still deal with this as well when we sell. What kind of baggage do your learners and their prospects bring to the selling world? Everyone's experience embeds these concerns, this baggage, into their brains. This focus (and I hope your fascination) with seeing how different everyone is in our selling world will help you better train those who sell for a living.

I love this diversity of personalities and decision-making styles and company cultures. It's really a reflection of the wildly unique world in which we live. For anyone who travels, you can't ignore the variety in clothing, architecture, and the differences in geography—on land, flying above it, even scuba diving beneath the ocean. Because of this diversity, I'm always surprised that so many sales reps sell everyone as if they are all alike.

It's because of this diversity that there are three things on which you'll want to focus throughout your *Ultimate Sales Training* learning experience. *The Ultimate Guide to Sales Training* will help your learners celebrate and profit from embracing the diversity through the use of training techniques that:

- Build Mental Flexibility
- Anchor Concepts for Easy Recall
- Encourage Behavioral Change

Build Mental Flexibility

Many of the best salespeople have the brainpower and skill to adjust to a variety of buying situations. This includes adjusting conversations to deal with distinct prospect personalities. It also includes those prospects' varied corporate buying procedures. Classic systems theory states that the individual or organization with the most options will be in control. He or she will have the flexibility to respond to change. For example, think of companies that migrated from building mechanical to digital tools—like cameras. Your job is to offer a wide variety of those options in each sales setting (opening dialogues, objection handling, closing techniques). This is so that each rep can find what he or she is most comfortable saying and doing. In essence, we will help them find themselves as sales professionals. This is also why this *Ultimate Guide to Sales Training* is so large. You have plenty of choices to offer your wide, wild variety of reps, who in turn will use them to handle their wide, wild variety of buyers.

Anchor Concepts for Easy Recall

Each module should have a phrase reps can learn to anchor what's being trained. It's easy to do follow-up coaching by referring to that phrase when a rep gets stuck. Here's an example: *Great Sales Pros Can Predict the Future!* This is taught in The Ultimate Objection-Handling Tool chapter. In order to predict the future, we must anticipate every form of resistance that a buyer can offer. Every business has half dozen objections that cause the most trouble for sales team members. Not any longer. You will now prepare your pros with multiple responses to each objection. We can calmly, confidently respond and keep from being stonewalled at this point in the sales process. So start today to use concepts for each piece of the training puzzle. By the way, this is one of my favorite elements I add when I'm invited to redesign existing sales training programs. It's a powerful way to stamp learning onto the pages of a sales rep's brain. We'll cover this in some detail later in the book.

Encourage Behavioral Change

We are in the before and after business. If there is not a distinct difference between learners' behavior—after they've encountered our training—we have failed. Sorry to sound like I'm coming from the dark side of selling. But all the learning, fun, good experience, and head knowledge that come with training are useless if our reps don't go out and do things differently. Your job and mine is to help learners adapt new language and behavior. This book represents a rich resource of the best practices from sales training and psychologically sound persuasion principles from across the planet. Get your men and women to practice in training, then go into the field and put these concepts into play.

One final thought before you dive in.

I'd wish you good luck navigating this tool, but I love the old catchphrase that says, "The harder I work, the luckier I get." So instead I'll wish you lots of learning, hard work, and, most importantly, changed behavior for yourself and your sales pros.

Dan Seidman
Barrington, Illinois
January 2012

Chapter 1

How to Use This Sales Training Resource for Optimal Results

CHAPTER OVERVIEW

Who Can Benefit from This Book

Complex vs. Simple Sales

Book Structure and Approach

What This Book Is Not

How Training Pros Prepare to Train Sales Pros

Quick Sales Training Preparation Tips

Teach Concepts to Sales Pros

Who Can Benefit from This Book

A wide variety of sales professionals will own and utilize this book. In recognition of that, it has been designed to accommodate:

1. **Serious trainers**, who can immediately build programs off each chapter
2. **Sales managers**, who might want to use stories and tips to run weekly sales meetings
3. **Senior sales or human resource executives**, who want to redesign existing training to incorporate the latest and best practices so that they see an increase in revenue (additional strategies on this are in Chapter 30)
4. **Entrepreneurs**, who are hiring experienced or rookie reps and need some focus on key elements of the sales process to ensure a greater measure of selling success
5. **Sales professionals**, who are hungry for new ideas they can apply to improve personal performance

The next sections will cover the structure of the book, how training pros prepare to train sales pros, my unique spin on anchoring learning (which is to teach *concepts* using an anchoring phrase attached to each lesson), and what this book is *not* useful for.

Complex vs. Simple Sales

It might or might not be important to note the distinctions between these two basic sales scenarios.

Let's look at some of the unique characteristics of a *complex* selling environment. Then read on to find out how the training elements in this book apply. You might be a bit surprised at how little it matters whether we're training complex or simple/transactional sales professionals.

- Complex sales are often attained at the C-suite level. Sales professionals and their team must be perceived as peers of the C-suite decision-makers.
- They require multiple calls over time, designating the value of these solutions, as buying parties must commit to investing in the process as well. So we have a much longer sales cycle.

- There are most often both teams of decision-makers as well as teams of sales pros. This involvement of stakeholders includes highly valuable and highly critical work from support personnel on both sides of the table. A good example of this is the classic Miller Heiman approach, which designates buyers by the acronym *CUTE*. Decision-makers can be leaders who represent each of the *CUTE* pieces of the selling puzzle. They can encompass a Coach (or internal advocate or champion), Users (those in the buyer's company who are working with the solution on a regular basis), Technical buyers (often involved in approving and implementing solutions to match existing systems), and Economic buyer(s) who ultimately approves and/or signs the check to acquire the solution. Each of these groups is represented by an executive looking out for the best interests of his or her department or team.

- Implementation can be complex for the buying organization.

- Deep research is often required on prospects as well as competitors. Because of this, support personnel are critical to the sales process. Also, research is undertaken during sales dialogues through masterful questioning, a key component to gathering data before presenting a solution.

- Solutions are often custom-designed for each buyer. Because of this, a total solution can negate pricing differentiation and give an advantage over competing offers. Return on investment (ROI) can therefore be defined in a variety of ways. Because of this, quantifying solutions becomes critical to attaining a successful complex sale.

- Ongoing relationships are often a component of complex sales, which means the selling organization will often assign account managers to provide ongoing help for the buyer.

- Organizations that understand the politics of a buyer's situation can gain additional advantage in the proposal process.

- Request for Proposals (RFPs) are often requested by the buyer to formalize the relationship and give the sales organization a seat at the table to begin selling the opportunity.

- Because of the formal contract-based relationship, negotiation becomes a critical part of the sales process.

- Deep understanding of a prospect's decision-making criteria can impact either negatively or positively on the solution(s) being created and offered.

And what we have just described about complex sales is much less complex than are international solutions in today's global selling environment.

Many of the bullet points above are not trainable elements for a salesperson, but descriptive of the selling relationship. The traits of complex sellers are described below.

Great complex sellers are masterful with words. They present well and are perceived as peers by C-suite stakeholders. They ask superb questions. They gain commitment from buying teams. They collaborate powerfully with their own team to craft solutions that are so desirable to the buyers that a YES becomes inevitable.

I really look at this handbook of sales training best practices as a book of language skills. Here's where, within these pages, you can train the sales pro who has to master a complex sale.

Look at the list of chapters below that are focused on learning strategies; then check out the most critical things upon which you can focus.

Chapter 3—The Many, Many Values of a Selling System

Chapter 4—Competitive Intelligence and Prospect Research

Chapter 5—Potent Communication Skills

Chapter 6—Buyers' Behavior and Decision-Making Strategy

Chapter 7—Potent Proposals

Chapter 8—Pre-Work for the Sales Call

Chapter 9—Establishing Rapport

Chapter 10—Prospecting

Chapter 11—Opening the First Meeting

Chapter 12—Qualifying and Disqualifying Prospects

Chapter 13—Bypassing Gatekeepers

Chapter 14—Power Questions

Chapter 15—Practicing Listening Skills

What's most critical? Chapter 20, Debriefing the Call.

A salesperson who is already in a role that requires managing complex sales probably has enough experience, insights, and assistance to get to the table. It's the coaching along the way that moves the company's offering into position to close the complex sale.

This is about adjusting, tweaking, going back to your stakeholders (finance, operations, engineering, manufacturing, technical leaders), and gaining concessions and adjustments to your firm's offerings. You need a deep, detailed debriefing to continue to advance the opportunity.

While writing this, I went back to the Foreword of Jeff Thull's outstanding book, *Mastering the Complex Sale* (2nd ed.; 2010). Wayne Hutchinson, a vice president of Shell International, relays this dialogue on Thull's contribution to his company's increase in sales performance between 2004 and 2009:

We asked, "What's the business value of our anticorrosion tool?"

"Business value? It doesn't make money. It eliminates corrosion in the processing room in a refinery or chemical plant."

"Sure, but what happens in the absence of this tool? What happens if you don't eliminate corrosion in the processing room?"

"Well, eventually there will probably be a fire or an explosion."

"If that happened, what would be the consequences—what would it cost the customer?"

The value-hypothesis lights began to flicker on.

Interesting that Hutchinson chose, out of all the outstanding impact from Thull's work, a re-framing of language to highlight his key learning.

You will see this, as well, in the latest offering to sales professionals, a fascinating work titled *Sales Chaos* by Brian Lambert and Tim Ohai (2011). The authors present potent language choices throughout the book.

So complex sale or transactional sale, your teams will gain outstanding skills by adopting the ideas from *The Ultimate Guide to Sales Training*.

Book Structure and Approach

Each chapter includes an explanation of the strategy being discussed. You then will read a description of how this piece of the selling puzzle improves sales professionals' performance.

A *story* then presents a scenario where the concept is applied. Apart from stories, I've used jokes, odd news items, research—almost anything to quickly capture attention and illustrate the point of the chapter. The power of storytelling is a huge asset to the training environment. My original sales training brand was built from a collection of more than six hundred selling blunders, which I used to teach salespeople. If you are intrigued by the use of stories, odd news items, and more to offer tips to your reps, have a look at over three hundred examples, often using hilarious personal tales, at www.SalesAutopsy.com/blog (Figure 1.1). I encourage you to

Figure 1.1. www.SalesAutopsy.com

model this approach for any internal publications to the team, whether you touch them by email, newsletter, or audio recording.

Embedded within each training module is a *concept,* a phrase that is offered to anchor the learning. This is key, as it helps give focus to the learning. The simple phrase is easy to revisit. It can even serve as a catchphrase for your sales pros to repeat when they're asked: "What is the reason this module is important to your sales lives?" Because this element is so important to embedding information into reps' brains, a detailed explanation of the use of concepts is included later in this chapter. *Training content* follows, including an *exercise* to reinforce and practice the learning.

This structure, *Story, Concept, Content, Exercise,* is so simple I use it for even short sales meetings.

Here's a quick sample lesson on the topic of buyers.

Buyers

The sheriff says to the outlaw, "I'll give you a fair chance. We'll step off ten paces and you fire at the count of three."

The men pace off, the sheriff shouts, "One, two"—then he suddenly spins and fires.

The dying outlaw says, "I thought you said to fire on three."

The sheriff said, "That was your number. Mine was two."

When you're selling, did you ever notice that your buyer's timing is never quite in sync with yours? Not on the same page? Not working with the same number?

For example, as sales pros we prefer urgency and a quick decision. As buyers we're often fairly cautious, slow, even methodical, before making our choice.

So shame on us, when we sell, that we are surprised by buyers who won't give us a clue how soon they're deciding what to decide. Our ability to get in the head of the buyer, to understand his or her perspective, his or her view of the sales process is critical to selling success. Today's training module will focus on the value of seeing life from the view of the buyer.

Buyers, Cont'd

Exercise

Discuss and/or write down what you think is going on in a buyer's head when you sit with him or her. Then list on a piece of paper or a flip chart, in contrast, what you might be thinking.

Reponses might include:

- *Buyer's Perspective*—This person is here to sell me. I will probably offer some limited information, but her questions will reveal whether she really cares about what I need here or whether she's just here to sell, regardless of what I really want or need.

- *Salesperson's Perspective*—I hope this person is the one making the decision. And we're a bit more expensive than other options, so I sure hope that their budget is broad enough to embrace our solutions. If I can get certain questions answered (honestly!), I'll be in good shape to sell this firm.

Notice how the only thing both people have in common is uncertainty about the other person's intentions. Buyers often want to make the safest decision they can and they need to trust the seller early on in order to advance the conversation closer to the close.

If a salesperson doesn't have a clear understanding of the buyer's feelings, intentions, and decision-making process, the two of them could end up in voicemail jail after the call—never again connecting with one another.

There you have, in about four hundred words, a quick lesson on buyers. This can be used to later reinforce that actual training. Also, from a writing standpoint, notice the technique of tying the lesson, in the final words, back into the story. We had an outlaw and a sheriff, and the wrap-up warns about ending up in voicemail "jail."

In conclusion, the massive amount of content you have in your hands right now should help you feel that you're in the happy hunting grounds of sales training. This book can be used informally by pulling a chapter out to focus on, or formally, by breaking down a chapter and working with reps over sixty to ninety days until they get the ideas, adapt them, and show results.

What This Book Is Not

The Ultimate Guide to Sales Training is not a step-by-step "cookbook" that will guarantee you a highly motivated, successful sales team if you simply follow a formula or methodology or a certain training template. Offering such a guarantee is not practical, nor would it be truthful. Your role as a trainer or sales executive is to translate the strategies and techniques into a training environment in which your facilitators can help your sales pros adopt the learning, then put it into play— changing behavior in order to increase revenue—so that the company receives a return on the sales training investment. This book offers a broad and ultimately useful tool for a wider audience as well, which includes sales training and development professionals; sales managers; entrepreneurs who double as sales executives and managers, and coaches or mentors. This large group of sales professionals, who are charged with performance improvement, are always seeking personal or one-on-one tools and exercises to better the knowledge, skills, abilities, and attitudes of the selling staff. And for you sales pros who are brave enough to buy a book that's this dense with strategies: I applaud your desire to improve on your own or to gain the knowledge to someday be able to run your own sales force.

You might not be a true training professional where your role, full-time, is facilitating programs for the selling team. You might fall into another category of user. Let's look at the various roles of individuals and groups who could have this book in hand, and how they can best use it to improve sales performance for their firms.

- *Sales training professionals.* You get this book. It has new content, which will be refreshing to use and could have a huge impact on your team's performance. Just keep your focus on the endgame of *changed behavior*. It's not knowledge transfer (what good is a smart salesperson who doesn't put ideas into play?). Make sure your facilitation skills are outstanding and have fun, going to work right away. You might look at this detailed resource as an opportunity to connect with upper-level management and sell the idea to lead the charge on a newly rejuvenated sales system. There's a lot here, Have fun and pay close attention to the use of *concepts* for anchoring learning.

- *Sales managers.* If you're managing a team, you might have some training experience, but what you probably have little of is *time*. So focus on key pieces of the sales process puzzle. These include making sure your sales pros do a great job of qualifying and disqualifying prospects (Chapter 12). Help them to craft a powerful opening conversation (Chapter 11). Have each develop power questions (Chapter 14). See that the team creates responses to resistance by utilizing the unique and potent Ultimate Objection-Handling Tool (Chapter 16). Finally, you should become an expert at doing a thorough debriefing (Chapter 20) in order to correct and redirect your sellers' focus on skills and behaviors during sales calls. If time really is an issue, just use the exercises as they're designed and hold that team's feet to the fire in order to make sure that they are changing their behavior so that they improve performance.

- *Entrepreneurs who oversee sales teams.* As you seek to grow your organization, you'll find that all the masterful marketing in your world will not come to fruition without selling skills to convert prospects into clients and customers. How well do you understand the steps in the selling process? How well can you sell yourself? How well will you manage, encourage, and coach your salespeople until you can hire someone to fill that role? This book can form the foundation of your company's selling system. Find someone you trust to work through it, with your guidance, and create and name your sales methodology.

- *Coaches and mentors.* You work in a more relaxed atmosphere than those formal training sessions or sales managers' meetings. Take your time to work through the most important elements in this book. I'm assuming you'll do some assessment prior to coaching, in order to identify what areas of the sales process are key to helping your client or salesperson. So focus on strengthening strengths and managing weaknesses.

- *Senior sales executives.* Do you have the latest best practices built into your corporate selling methodology? It's time to redesign. Within these pages you will find strategies to embolden your selling team, whether they are approaching buyers with the simplest, most basic transactional offerings or whether your team is creating the most complex products, services, or processes imaginable. Pay close attention to the key elements of the selling process (Training the Sales Pro to Sell, Chapters 9 through 22). Get feedback from your managers, sales professionals, even trusted clients, to identify what areas need work or need to be re-worked. Then put a team together to re-craft your existing sales training.

- *Sales professionals.* Brave soul! What area of your sales life could use improvement? Find a sturdy desk upon which to set this book and set to work learning how to better yourself. Here's a special tip I offer at every keynote and sales training experience I facilitate: Go find someone to teach what you've just learned. The best learners become teachers as soon as they adopt new ideas. With whom will you choose to share this? You will also create accountability to put your newly adapted ideas into practice (we'll continue to revisit the idea of behavior change).

Now, let's look at how trainers (and those of you filling that role) can get ready to work with sales improvement content, based on level of experience, within the training profession.

How Training Pros Prepare to Train Sale Pros

There's an old story about a golf pro and an amateur (in our telling, he's also a sales rep). They are on the driving range before a big charity tournament. The amateur is on his third bucket of balls, nervous about embarrassing himself in front of the pros, his peers, even potential clients who might be at the award ceremony. His pro partner casually walks up to the practice tee with a driver over his shoulder. He reaches into a pocket, pulls out five balls, and drops them on the mat. He lines up the first ball, hits it, and 90 seconds later has finished smacking the other four. He turns to head back to the clubhouse.

The sales rep is stunned. "Excuse me, but is that it? Is that your whole warm-up routine?"

The pro smiles and says, "Rick, if you didn't bring it with you, you're not going to find it here."

If you didn't bring it with you, you're not going to find it here.

What message does that statement send to you about getting ready for your big event—the training experience?

To me, it's this: The number one practice that you as a training pro can engage in is the *prepare* to train. This includes each of these three typical individuals who fall into sales trainer roles.

1. New trainer hires with no sales experience and no training background

2. Skilled trainers who have no experience or clear understanding of the real world of selling

3. Salespeople who are moved into training roles with little or no training experience

The fourth category is, obviously, skilled, experienced trainers who have solid sales backgrounds. So if you fit that profile, pay attention as well.

Quick Sales Training Preparation Tips

1. New Trainer Hires, No Sales Experience

First, you should know that this animal really exists and is not in danger of extinction. Over the past ten years working with the American Society for Training and Development (ASTD), I have encountered dozens of trainers who tell me they handle things like diversity or new software applications and add, "I do some sales training as well." This includes mature businessmen and -women as well as students, fresh out of college. You think sales reps have to have thick skin to sell? You'd better be thicker-skinned to train 'em. If you're a rookie, here are some things you can do to enhance your image:

- Get the language of selling down, so you don't stumble over concepts and strategies. This includes industry, corporate, and cultural terminology.

- Get in the car or on the phone! About twenty-five years ago I experienced a very unusual week of training. As a recruiter who was going to work placing sales reps in the medical field, I was given an out-of-state Yellow Pages phone book and told to begin making sixty calls a day to sales managers and HR people who hired advertising reps. The company knew I was going to screw up and encounter lots of objections that were new to me. They preferred I do it away from my backyard and away from my actual prospects. And getting beat up over three hundred phone calls offered an amazingly deep dunking into the selling of recruitment services. Although I always wondered—and never got a good answer—whether my practice work was just screwing up the image of the actual ad recruitment people in the major city where my Yellow Pages came from. So if you had a difficult time selling recruiting in Boston during the 1980s, I apologize.

Let me know how I can make it up to you. The point of all this is that trainers who lack sales experience need to actually sell in order to best relate to learners.

- Know all your content cold. Few things are worse for learners than to have the instructor read out of a book. Years back I was reviewing sales training for a major credit card company and was shocked to see a young woman reading from a manual for a full eight-hour day of training. She clearly was unfamiliar with the content. I told the national sales manager that she was insane to have that person working with salespeople (when people pay you enough for your advice, sometimes your comments are only affirming their greatest fears). The problem actually resided with the sales training vendor. This firm was equally at fault and proved good at fooling a buyer into buying sales training content, without worrying about the experience of effectively administering it.

- Have *great* facilitation skills. Sales audiences are as tough as you'll find anywhere. You'd better be able to banter and have fun and, at times, be able to stand up to someone who questions your credibility with comments like: "Look, you've probably read more sales books and had more training than I've had bowel movements. But you're probably here because you don't apply all those things that you could have—to make you (and the company) more money. So just as you'd take money from a buyer you wouldn't date or marry, I expect you to tolerate my youth or inexperience, focus on the content, and put it into play." Now I'm not suggesting you antagonize your learners. But I bet you'd get a laugh and tons of respect for saying something like this with a BIG smile on your face. Remember most of all that making a classroom a safe place for everyone is a key function of the trainer. So be cautious. But I guarantee you can say and do things with sales trainers that you can't do with other employees in other roles. For loads of great information on presenting, see Chapter 18.

2. Skilled Trainers, No Sales Experience

- Get the language of selling down (see previous comments).

- Know all your content cold (see previous comments).

- Get in the car or on the phone (see previous comments).

- Acquire a clear understanding of a learning environment.

- Use your facilitation experience, and please avoid lecturing.

- Feel free to briefly embed success stories of your own that support teaching points. In fact, you might have encountered a wide variety of salespeople over the years, so pointing to your experience as a buyer can enhance credibility with a group of sales reps.

3. **Salespeople, No Training Experience**

- Play off your sales experience by tying stories of your own to each training piece. Salespeople love war stories, and your ability to share them to support teaching points is powerful.

- Focus on the learners first; they are really here to get better, not necessarily to judge or even enjoy their trainer. In other words, don't be tempted to get carried away regaling everyone with your experience and success stories.

- Know all your content cold (see previous comments).

- Get *great* facilitation skills (see previous comments).

For each of these three types of trainers, it is mandatory to go to train-the-trainer training. This could cover platform/performing/facilitation skills as well as design skills. This is fine because it is highly valuable to understand how and why training programs are crafted to be most effective in the classroom.

The premier organization that provides this training, as well as a variety of certifications for anyone who trains for a living, is Langevin Learning Services (www.langevin.com/). Find local workshops listed at their website to see how quickly you can enhance your ability to facilitate a great training experience for your company's sales professionals.

4. **Sales Training Professionals**

You'll notice some very unique content in this encyclopedia-sized manual. So whether you are using training handed to you, or redesigning and embedding new content into your company's new sales system, enjoy the new knowledge, exercises, and responses you'll obtain when you facilitate these techniques and strategies. And when you develop your own exercises and have noteworthy experiences and feedback from the training, let me know about it at Dan@GotInfluenceInc.com.

Teach Concepts to Sales Pros

This is a key to really reinforcing learning with your sales professionals.

A *concept* is an idea derived from a specific occurrence. To use this in training, you back off from a teaching moment, a story, or lesson, and create a simple idea. This is offered to learners in order to anchor each session's key point.

To use concepts most effectively, you'll want to teach your team the key to each module by stating the purpose of the session. You'll then summarize it by offering a "phrase that pays." This is a snapshot of the concept you want them to remember. Do this and you'll anchor learning in a deeper way than having them just learn and practice specific techniques.

Here's an example. Many reps work hard to spend time presenting their solutions to an individual who is not the true decision-maker. Tony Parinello is the sales guru who built his reputation on teaching reps to make sure you sell to VITO, the very important top officer. In his best-selling book, *Getting to VITO* (2005), he talks about "Seemore." This person isn't VITO. He or she is someone who always wants to see more of everything—you, presentations, phone conversations. You know this person, the man or woman who believes he or she serves the company as a conduit to the decision-maker. But that doesn't serve you in helping to sell your products or services to this person's organization.

As you help reps learn to avoid these time-wasters, the concept would be this:

You cannot get a NO from someone who can't give you a YES!

Your "phrase that pays" would be:

Who's really in charge?

This succinctly addresses the need to invest your selling time into the person who can say YES and see that you are handed a check. When you wrap up each module, make sure that your reps can state the phrase that pays in order to keep their focus on the bottom line of the day's learning.

This concept becomes doubly powerful after the training experience in coaching and managing reps. A simple reminder of this phrase can serve to both gently guide sales reps back on track when they are wasting time or as a harsh reminder (based on how you motivate each individual) that you won't tolerate their time-wasting. So they must get back to finding the person who is really in charge.

I learned the power of concepts when I worked with Dr. Edward De Bono, the world's leading expert on creativity (with more than seventy books under his belt). His concept extraction strategy is brilliant. Check out his works at www.debonoconsulting.com/lateral-thinking-alternatives.asp.

Many years ago, as De Bono's sole sales rep in the United States, I went through all certification training. I then began to call on corporate executives who had major problem-solving issues or wanted to develop new products. Fascinating work, as you'll see from the example that follows.

Here's how Dr. De Bono uses concept extraction to solve a problem:

Let's say we have a glass of water; we cannot touch the glass ourselves but need to remove the water.

One person suggests pouring rocks into the glass, forcing the water out. What is the concept behind this? Displacement. What are other forms of displacement? You could dangle a balloon in, then blow it up.

Another person suggests using an air hose to blast the water out. The concept? Energy. Another energy alternative? Evaporate the liquid using the energy of heat with a bright light or heat underneath—to turn liquid to gas.

A third suggestion might be placing fabric/sponge in the glass, from which we extract the concept of absorption.

And on we go. We can now solve our problems or build our new products from any of these points forward. This actually becomes kind of fun to do. De Bono's work has been embraced with global acclaim. I was amazed to find that Edward used his success to buy islands. You read that right. The man owns four islands around the world. I mention this here because the next chapter encourages you to talk with your reps about what success really means and how attaining world class sales status can enable them to buy things that they feel great about and that can wow others.

(By the way, ask me in person sometime about how I honored this prestigious, internationally acclaimed authority on business creativity by playing a very funny practical joke on him. I point this out for one simple reason: sales pros should be having fun throughout their normal workday. This profession is tough and can be both rewarding and discouraging—the typical low closing ratios mean your sales-people have negative results 80 to 90 percent of their careers. So having fun is a beautiful way to blow off steam and reduce the stress.)

Concepts should be your secret weapon to anchor learning throughout a training program. Here are five of my favorites:

1. *Great selling pros can predict the future!* Once you've developed a potent response to every objection you could possibly encounter, you'll have no surprises on a sales call. The trick is to confidently and casually respond to resistance in a way that you know will advance the sale.

2. *Perspective.* Learn to look at things from the buyer's point of view. This one's easy. How can you teach it? Is there a story you can use? I have a game I taught my kids that teaches perspective. This completely transforms how they interact with others. Your ability to see things through the eyes of others is a powerful skill to own.

3. *Who do you compete with?* Everyone's first guess is themselves. Next guess is the cheapest source. But the answer is a great jumping-off point for training and selling the value of training. Want the answer? Email me at Dan@GotInfluenceInc.com.

4. *Number one problem sales pros face.* The answer is *they chase poor prospects.* So how do you help them focus on who's worth attending to and who they should ignore? This is easy; everyone has a nightmare story about hunting a big client where nothing materialized. I did a keynote at a major sales conference (REMAX) where I asked for these stories and gathered amazing disasters, time-wasters, energy-wasters, and lost sales revenue. All these people could have been working with qualified buyers, but had no specific strategy to qualify or disqualify. The "winner" of the event actually chased a buyer for ten and a half years before realizing he wasn't going to buy.

5. *If you can't measure it, you can't manage it!* Thank you, late, great Peter Drucker for this. This one's simple: Know your numbers! If a rep is

making forty phone calls a day and earning $60,000, bump that to fifty calls and she earns $75,000. What if she handles her top objection more effectively and the closing ratio goes up, too? Measure to manage.

You will find the use of concepts in this book in Parts Two and Three, where you'll be working directly with the sales team members to improve performance. It's possible to have multiple concepts in some modules. Find what works best for your organization and use it.

In conclusion, I encourage you to pay close attention to concepts. Create your own phrase that pays, or better yet, have the team you're training help to create one per group. People have stronger ties to ideas they've personally built.

Let's now get into the meat of *The Ultimate Guide to Sales Training.*

Part One

Preparing the Sales Pro to Sell

Part One reveals the foundational elements of great selling. These include how world class sales pros distinguish themselves from mediocre salespeople, the value of adopting a selling system, competitive intelligence, communication skills, buyer behavior, potent proposal design, and pre-work for sales calls.

Chapter 2

What Makes a World Class Sales Pro
Selling the Value

Selling the Value of a Selling Career

What's the real value of success in a selling career?

> *Rob is a friend of mine and he can sell. He is the number one investment advisor for a national firm and works in a bank.*
>
> *He was a bit nervous when the bank changed hands. But the surprise he received on day one was completely unexpected. The new president called Rob into his office on the first morning after the buyout.*

"Rob, I'm happy to meet you and appreciate what you've done in our community for many years, but there's a bit of a problem with the money you make. Do you realize your earnings are significantly more, almost double, what most bank presidents make? I just want you to know there will probably be some adjustments to your base and commissions."

Rob, positive and upbeat, smiled broadly and said, "Nice to meet you. My community (notice he chose not to say 'our') is where I've grown up and where my family has had a successful business for many generations. My clients are really neighbors and friends who trust me with their money. The day my compensation changes, I will go down the street, with 100 percent of my clients, and serve them there. No hard feelings, but my income has nothing to do with yours. I'm simply rewarded for doing my job quite well. I really do wish you good luck in your new role here."

He stands, shakes hands, and goes back to work.

The next day, to the president's credit, Rob receives an apology and is informed that he is a treasured staff member whom the company hopes will stay on board for many more years.

Because of Rob's success in selling, he held his ground, held onto his high earnings, and holds onto his customers. Rob also does spectacular trips with his wife (and at times, family) to exotic locations around the planet. He is rewarded for his skill. He also rewards himself with cool toys to drive and wear and play with.

Imagine Your Future as a World Class Sales Pro

Aside from, and along with the cash, you could:

- Live on the beach, in the mountains, the downtown of your favorite city.
- Vacation in those places you've dreamed about.
- Drive the car of your dreams.
- Buy the toys and tools you read about and see others using.
- What will you wear, where will you play? Who will you share it with?

Great sales pros have choices that mediocre reps do not.

EXERCISE 2.1. Daydreaming

SETUP: In this exercise your learners will cast a vision for themselves as to how they will handle the success of significantly improving selling performance. Create a document with this list of questions. Your salespeople will want to keep this handy to remind them what they're working toward. This is similar to goal setting, but give permission for them to be creative and have fun with their wish lists.

You have begun to attain all the earnings you could possibly desire.

- What will you do with the money?
- Where will you go?
- What will you buy to wear, drive, live in, play with?
- Who will you share it with?
- When will you make your big purchase, your big trip?
- How will you manage your money?

The purpose of this training is to move you from wherever you are today to attaining the status of a world class selling professional. To get there you need to obtain key skills and characteristics. Here's a baker's dozen of those we'll cover in this comprehensive training experience, including:

1. The ability to refuse to chase poor prospects. As you'll learn, the number one problem sales reps face is that they do pursue bad buyers for too long, losing time, energy, and money in the process. (QUALIFYING AND DISQUALIFYING PROSPECTS, Chapter 12)

2. The skill to sell differently, depending on the buyer. Mental flexibility means you can change your language to fit the buyer's style. This includes a simple alternative to the traditional feature/benefit sales approach. (SOLUTION- VERSUS CONSEQUENCE-CENTERED SELLING, Chapter 17)

3. Recognizing that opening is more critical than closing. If you don't open with strength and skill, you will never get close to the close. A specific technique for beginning your buyer relationship is a big adjustment that top sales pros have already made. (OPENING THE FIRST MEETING, Chapter 11)

EXERCISE 2.1.   Daydreaming, Cont'd

4. Healthy heads. This is rarely taught in training. Great sales pros deal well with adversity, have resilience, are optimistic, have solid self-talk, don't procrastinate, are good goal setters, and more. (MENTAL HEALTH FOR SALES PROS, Chapter 28)

5. Phenomenal focus. They plan and manage their day with precision, not letting others control their time. They also manage their energy well, indicating the value of health and productivity throughout the whole selling day. (DAILY PERFORMANCE TIPS, Chapter 23)

6. Adapting a system. This is huge and a few quick highlights include (a) knowing when to walk away from a sale, (b) no surprises in the selling process, and (c) the ability to take charge (not control!) of buyer/seller conversations. (THE MANY, MANY VALUES OF A SELLING SYSTEM, Chapter 3)

7. *Great* communication skills. Utilize power questions, employ great listening, smoothly respond to objections with good language choices, deal with email, voicemail, and much more. (POTENT COMMUNICATION SKILLS, Chapter 5)

8. Referrals. We talk about this all the time, but few make the request a regular practice. There is no better lead than one from a client. When will you build it into your daily dialogues? (PROSPECTING, Chapter 10)

9. Predicting the future. This is a critical concept that distinguishes this training tool from others. Great sales pros are never surprised by objections (although they might act that way to the buyer!). They are prepared, with multiple responses, to smoothly work past the resistance and advance the sale. (THE ULTIMATE OBJECTION-HANDLING TOOL, Chapter 16)

10. Knowing when to close. Will you use one technique or twenty to finalize the sale? (CLOSING, Chapter 19)

11. Getting past gatekeepers. Nothing snuffs the life out of a sales opportunity faster than a non-decision-maker who blocks your access to the money. (BYPASSING GATEKEEPERS, Chapter 13)

EXERCISE 2.1. Daydreaming, Cont'd

12. A career commitment to constant learning. This means they are hungry to absorb new ideas, to keep growing, apart from what the company has to offer. (YOUR SALES PROS NEED TO WORK ON THIS ON THEIR OWN)

13. Knowing that, if they can't measure it, they can't manage it. Thank you to the late, great Peter Drucker for helping the selling world to recognize the value of knowing your numbers. (KNOW YOUR NUMBERS, Chapter 24)

The purpose of summarizing this training tool and pointing to identifiers of world class sales pros is to help your learners catch a vision of what they can be, as well as to hint at some of the new learning they'll need to attain to get there.

An exercise to have them select what information is relevant to each individual is a good way to reinforce their investment in learning.

EXERCISE 2.2. Skills Ranking

SETUP: In this exercise trainees will analyze, then check off, the level of their perceived skill at handling each of the thirteen items listed above.

Make a checklist of the thirteen items above. Are your skills in each . . .

a. Great

b. Just okay

c. In need of help

While research says to play to your strengths, every sales professional needs to have a strong ability to manage each of these key focal points of his or her sales life.

EXERCISE 2.3. Prioritization and Accountability

SETUP: This training experience is about improving your sales performance by adjusting your behavior to emulate world class sales pros. So let's now re-visit our checklist and prioritize which of these elements we want to work on first.

Prioritize which you need to attend to by writing the items above in order from 1 to 13.

EXERCISE 2.3. Prioritization and Accountability, Cont'd

1.

2.

3.

4.

5.

6.

7.

8.

9.

10.

11.

12.

13.

I will start with [write the first item here]: _____

I will start working, personally, on this date [write date here]: _____

I will ask [write name] _____ to be my accountability partner. This means he or she will check in with me to see that I'm putting this key element into play. I will schedule a time to regularly connect with my accountability partner and will ask my partner to also randomly check in with me by email, text message, or phone call.

Next, identify when your first selection becomes a part of your regular sales practices; then repeat this prioritization and accountability exercise with a date to begin work on the second item, and so on.

Please remember to thank your partner often and in many ways. He or she shares your success, and great sales pros are grateful for others who contribute to that success (including their buyers!).

Creating accountability, as well as adopting mentors, are two key approaches to accelerating the learning curve toward greater selling success. Additional details can be found in Chapter 25 on mentors.

Chapter 3

The Many, Many Values of a Selling System

Calling on a Colossal Company

Tom's big client shrinks on contact.

Leo Burnett is one of the largest ad agencies in the world. So when a woman called from there, I thought my low-income days of selling party planning services were over. One big client like that could keep me in new suits for years.

She wanted to hear about our offerings on the phone, but I insisted that I see her in person. After a few minutes of hard selling, I convinced her that a meeting was best. There was no way I was going to miss the opportunity to get face-to-face with a company that hosts huge parties as a major part of its business!

I drove into downtown Chicago, paid a ridiculous amount of money for parking, and was led to the woman's office.

"That's it!" she cried, pointing to a picture in my picture book of party options. She was pointing at a single photo of a clown.

"That's exactly what I want for my four-year-old's birthday."

She was not a corporate client after all. She wasn't even a high-level decision-maker for the company. I blew a half-day on a call that was no more fruitful than the smallest sale I could possibly make.

Tom shared this story when I was keynoting a sales event. He brought it up because I was talking about the value of a systematic best practices approach to identifying best prospects. As you'll learn later, qualifying and disqualifying are key identifiers of truly professional salespeople.

By understanding each element of the sales process and creating a systematic approach to each, you will, simply put, make more money. Now I'm not suggesting each of you become robotic in managing your relationships. Everyone should have the creativity to let his or her individual personality shine forth while selling. But you do want to understand selling as a system, because of this potent fact:

Great sales professionals can predict the future.

Once you understand each piece of the sales puzzle and can know what is going to happen next, you're set in sales.

I really believe that to attain world class status in selling, you just have to be able to anticipate everything that could possibly happen in your prospect interactions and prepare potent responses to each. Here's one example:

Every business offering encounters, on average, six objections. Once your company has identified those and determined multiple responses to each one, you are ready to meet prospect resistance head on, with no fear of surprise. And, so . . .

Great Sales Professionals Can Predict the Future

In The Ultimate Objection-Handling Tool in Chapter 16, this phrase serves as the concept or "phrase that pays." There you'll see that your company will want multiple responses to each objection so that members of your sales team can use the ones they're most comfortable with and that match their personalities and styles. This is what we call "finding your voice."

Here's how that works. You're running a meeting on handling objections and Rick says, "When I get resistance to our price, I say, 'That's okay; our best clients had those exact concerns before their companies said yes to us as well.'"

Abbie says, "That's a good response. I've never heard that before. But I wouldn't feel comfortable saying that. It isn't me. But what Josh suggested earlier sounds more like me, 'When you say it's too much money, how much too much do you mean?'"

You build your book of responses to all your objections and are prepared to deal with them confidently and professionally. Of course, your reps have to have the ability to sound spontaneous when they hear the objection. And you want to take the time to deal with every objection encountered, not just the top six.

The concept of *predicting the future* is the basis for all systems, anywhere. So it can really be seen as the foundational concept of sales training itself. The best example of this concept is a franchise organization where a book (often rather large) is handed to the business owner and he or she is shown exactly how to systematically manage every single facet of his or her work life. This is exactly why franchises have an astounding 92 percent success rate five years after startup, whereas an independent business's rate is only 23 percent. In a nutshell, you are four times more likely to succeed with a franchise than by winging it with a solo startup! That's the value of following a system.

This systematic franchise manual approach to managing a business is clearly evident in every facet of a major corporation as well.

EXERCISE 3.1. Using Systems for Sales Success

SETUP: For this exercise you need to think about how you or your company currently use systems. [Note to trainer: There are two different questions from which you can choose. One involves personal awareness of one's own systems. The second covers a company's use of systems to manage its business.]

What systems have you used or had access to so far in your day, *before* you got to work?

EXERCISE 3.1.   Using Systems for Sales Success, Cont'd

Answers might include:

- Cooking breakfast, where an oven uses a system to generate heat.
- Brushing my teeth the same way every time to optimize cleanliness.
- Using water that has a plumbing system working in the background.
- Driving the car, which has serious systems, both mechanical and digital, to run the vehicle.
- Lighting has rules that govern it, stemming from electricity.
- Physical laws, like gravity, etc.

What systems are in use in your company? Hint: think in terms of departments.

Answers might include any of the following systems.

Human Resources

There is no more valuable asset to a firm than its employees. The use of pre-hiring assessments ensures the best match for company culture, job roles, and more. What could be more systems-oriented than a test form filled with questions that help the company know whether a person is a match or not?

The HR department also handles legal issues, benefits administration, and training. Each of these systematically follows an if/then work flow formula. If an employee behavior is X, company response is Y. A benefits manual is a clear, detailed system on how to work through any situation when the staff person may have access to a benefit. Training should be methodically developed to obtain a change in behavior in order to prove its worth to the organization (if you're unsure of programs' abilities to do this, go to The CAT Scan Diagnostic Tool described later in the book).

For an employee, a career path is a flow, a system. In fact, companies without clearly identifiable career paths have trouble retaining staff, who will make their own opportunities by moving on and out of the firm.

You get the picture. There are systems within systems, embedded in the best practices of any HR department.

EXERCISE 3.1.   Using Systems for Sales Success, Cont'd

Information Systems

Hardware/computers and software? This is the best example of the value of structure and systems in this list. Have you ever seen the source code of a program?
Tens of millions of lines deal with any possible if/then scenario. This whole department operates on mathematical principles. Even the data made available to you
through your CRM is searchable by fields like name, address, location, and more.
And more sophisticated software is only more amazing because it's more mathe-
matically complex. Computer programs are the backbone of the business world
today. Nothing is more systematic than the truths available through math.

Manufacturing

This is too easy an example of a systematic process: A product typically is acquired
or harvested from raw material, moved into a variety of stages as it is grown or
built into something practical to the consumer (production). Quality is checked. It
is then packaged (overlapping the work of the marketing department) and made
available for sale. Raw to revenue is a structured way to turn product into money
when it hits the customers' hands.

Finance/Accounting

This department's rules and practices are evident both in employee work flow and
printed documents. Their work reveals the heartbeat of an organization in that it
can clearly show how healthy a company is.

There are standard, acceptable ways to bill and acquire money.

Financial documents show management a clear picture of the status of many
key elements, including cash flow, debt, return on investment, and more.
Management reads and understands the information output (thank you, information systems) by the accounting department because of the standardized ways the
numbers are presented. In other words, an accounting professional can often pick
up a spreadsheet and tell you the story, even predict the future of a company, based
on the path revealed on those pages.

I recall an executive telling me how he had a huge quarter in sales, best ever
for the firm, but because he paid his sales team mostly based on sales posted,

not cash in, he had a rude awakening from the accountant who looked at the spreadsheet and said, "Oh, six more months of this and you're out of business." That story had a happy ending, as the executive changed the compensation payout structure (not the amounts) and told me how grateful he was that standardized accounting practices helped to quickly recognize danger lurking in success.

Customer Service

While sitting in front of computer screens (thank you again, information systems), your CS team is given rules to regulate customer interactions. Their role adds value (in fact, they often become the face and the voice of the company after the sale), prevents lost clients, and can up-sell products and services. Remove this department from the big system, your corporate infrastructure, give it to the sales reps who sold buyers in the first place, and see how the lack of a CS team disrupts the complete corporate system.

Marketing

Mini-systems exist throughout a marketing department as they seek to answer questions like:

- Who is the exact buyer we target?
- Where do we find him or her?
- Who can partner with us to find more prospects?
- What trade shows will we exhibit at?
- Will we mail, telemarket, use the web (and its diverse choices of email, blog, viral marketing, and more)?
- What lists do we acquire to accomplish these lead generation activities?
- What brochures, colors, designs, or logos will best represent the company and lead to an inquiry for the sales team?

A marketing team moves methodically through questions like these in order to best serve the company by generating leads.

EXERCISE 3.1.   Using Systems for Sales Success, Cont'd

Operations

This department, normally led by a systems master, the chief operating officer, is responsible for making sure all the systems described above work smoothly together, the ultimate goal being the same as the company's goal—to make a profit. Their work overlaps executive decisions in each department and monitors things like:

- Will the new software work across all departments, including the laptops of reps in the field?

- Is the buying team sourcing the best raw materials? Are quality control measurements being met?

- Are there ways to analyze financial data to identify how to lower costs and increase revenue?

- Can marketing reduce some activities and increase others to better generate leads?

Operations is the tie that binds departments together to ensure the company functions like a well-oiled machine (another system).

You could say that, at its simplest, a system is the application of a conditional or "if/then" formula. If prospect says X, then you respond with Y.

One of the reasons *The Ultimate Guide to Sales Training* was created is to encourage senior sales executives and training professionals to offer a selling system to their sales teams. Far too many companies, however, don't have a sales methodology in place. Okay, maybe that statement isn't entirely accurate. Far too many companies *won't enforce the use of their systems*. In contrast, many sales executives feel their hiring practices include experienced reps who don't need training in a system, and that's even more dangerous, as firms are now quantifying the costs related to losing poor performers.

As I'm writing this book, I have a client, a publishing company that is essentially in the advertising sales business. Almost 100 percent of the selling is by phone.

I went onsite for a week to monitor reps' calls as well as to meet and coach them individually. At the end of the week, each rep committed to make a specific number of phone calls each day. The average was forty.

I personally felt this number was low and told the publisher and owner so. I explained that, if three-fourths of the calls ended up in voicemail, then thirty dials were sixty-second messages—half an hour of the day's work. So ten phone calls encompassed the other seven hours? You could even make an argument that tele-marketers with more than one hundred calls on a four-hour shift, or rookie stock-brokers with more than 250 calls a day, showed how weak a commitment forty calls really is. I suggested that sixty was a more reasonable number. But the executives didn't want to stress their sales team, so they stayed at forty.

Matt was the low performer in the group and averaged six calls a day. Yes, that's six. And in spite of recommendations to release the rep, the firm feels committed to give the guy six months before they decide what to do next.

Here's where the system would work for the executive and the company. The manual says forty calls a day. "Sorry, Matt, you're not even doing the basic behavior required to succeed. Today is your last day." While I'm not giving legal advice in how to handle hiring and firing, you have a basis for saying that an individual's work is good or unacceptable. And you can act in accordance with the system in place.

How Matt was even hired in the first place is the real issue. The front end of building your sales force should include qualifying and disqualifying factors because it's expensive to make this mistake.

When you look at losses like $50,000 from hiring, training, and nurturing sales-people who leave, it's no surprise that large companies wave goodbye to millions of dollars a year from poor hiring and training practices.

To preempt this concern, you'll want to have a look at a potent new hiring tool, www.ModelofSalesExcellence.com, described at the end of this book in Chapter 33, Reps You Should *Not* Be Training. This assessment does not identify what reps *can* do, but what they *will* do. That's a world of difference, as every sales manager who hired after a great interview or good-looking resume will attest.

So we know we're surrounded by systems that keep our world running smoothly.

What about the sales department?

Implementing a sales methodology *and seeing that your sales pros use it* might be the missing link to the future of your firm. Do you want to build a superb team of sales pros? Do you want an easier job managing and coaching that team? Here are twelve reasons a system makes your life easier. Each one also addresses the perspective of the reps, so you can reinforce the benefit directly to him or her as well.

Twelve Reasons That Systems Make Your Life Easier

1. The best models aren't in the swimsuit issue of *Sports Illustrated.* It's so much more beautiful to model successful sales behavior and achieve similar successful results. Replicate how winners perform in all your organization's sales personnel.

   Rep: *You can speed up the learning curve to greater success by duplicating the activities, language skills, and brainpower in use by your best-selling colleagues.*

2. Your people will learn when to hit the road. A system defines when a sales rep should walk away from a bad buyer. This is huge. You can get your reps to invest and focus time on high-probability prospects.

   Rep: *When you learn to quickly qualify and disqualify all prospects, you'll know when quitting is a winning activity. Don't chase poor prospects and you'll spend more time with people more likely to say "yes" and give you money.* (See Chapter 12 on Qualifying and Disqualifying Prospects.)

3. "Show me the money" will get easier to say. A proven method makes sure that your reps obtain critical information during the sales call. This includes budget, decision-makers, time frame to buy, and the true motivation the prospect needs to acquire your product or service.

   Rep: *Stop getting stuck short of acquiring information you need to determine whether your offering is a good match for buyer needs.* (See Chapter 11 on first meetings.)

4. Your reps can close sales with the fast-forward button on. It speeds up the sales cycle. In your mind, you believed this might be true. It *is* true; your team can bring in more business in less time.

   Rep: *Several of the strategies you will use within your selling system will speed up your sales cycle. You can close faster by selling to your best prospects, by gathering information quickly, by setting well-defined next steps, and more.*

5. Whips can be left at home. A system sets standards that sales managers can clearly identify, control, and manage. Monitor system activity and quantify accurate appraisals of your reps.

   Rep: *You reward or punish yourself as an employee based on your behavior and adherence to the company's best-selling practices. You are managed—not by someone you do or do not get along with—but by known rules and expected behavior that you agreed to adopt when you were hired.*

6. You won't cuss at your calculator. Performance can be more easily measured. You'll know the closing rates of your reps based on number of leads generated, time invested, how much each rep earns for you, and more.

   Rep: *You must know your numbers to recognize how to move from good to great. Once you realize how small, incremental changes in activities like number of calls, increases in closing ratios, even walking away from bad prospects matter, you can bring in big money.* (See Chapter 24, Know Your Numbers.)

7. Crystal balls can be left at home. A system is predictable. There'll be very few surprises during the selling process. Your people will always know what's happening next. This eliminates prospects' propensity for hiding behind voicemail!

   Rep: *Sales pros can predict the future. They anticipate and respond to every objection. They set clear next steps after a first meeting. They know what gatekeepers are hired to do and have multiple responses to this; they uncover the budget set aside for their solution and other common selling scenarios.*

8. Train derailments are confined to movies. A system keeps salespeople on track during the selling process. As a system manager, you can easily identify where your reps stray and get them back on course.

   Rep: *It is significantly easier to coach and mentor you when a clearly defined process serves the company. Blocked by a gatekeeper? Did you respond like this . . . ? Got to the close and couldn't? Did you use language like . . . ? You get the picture. A system can help you to improve performance and income.*

9. New inventions are confined to television infomercials. Don't reinvent the wheel of selling wisdom. Just implement what already works. That's efficient.

Rep: *Whose turn is it to take out the trash? Define responsibilities. You clearly spell out the roles of the buyer and seller during the process. You can control your sales meetings, increasing your chances of success, by following your system.* (See Opening the First Meeting, Chapter 11.)

Rep: *All this talk about following a methodology might seem to mean you can't be creative when you sell. You can—by using your personality and experience to supplement the given system. Trust the company's decision to model success while being innovative within the walls formed by the strategies and technique built into it.* (See Chapter 16, The Ultimate Objection-Handling Tool.)

10. Great questions lead to greater results. When you create a book of powerful questions with which to arm your selling pros, you'll see significant progress in advancing sales dialogues closer to the close.

Rep: *One of the most significant growth areas any sales pro can improve in is his or her ability to ask potent questions—questions that get a prospect thinking about his or her solution differently. Questions that quantify, or dollarize, the value of the offering. Questions that discover how a buyer actually decides to buy. You want to have five power questions, but could easily use a dozen or more great ones to close more sales. Oh, you'll also want to use a few good questions to get referrals from your existing clients.* (See Chapter 14 on Power Questions.)

11. It is really quiet in here. "Learn to listen." That's a phrase you want to lay on your reps. Better listeners gather more information. Better listeners don't talk too much (irritating buyers). Better listeners also pick up hidden cues from the buyer. "Learn to listen!"

Rep: *Are you a good listener? Would family or friends agree with your answer? Listening is a huge skill you can improve to help you better connect with a prospect. It's no joke that people complain about salespeople who talk too much. Reduce your desire to talk, even when you have a great solution to offer, and you'll find buyers drawn to you personally (enhancing rapport) as well as your solution.* (See Chapter 15, Practicing Listening Skills.)

12. Today is *never* the tomorrow you worried about yesterday. Procrastination elimination is in place. Expectations are visible for all to see. There's no question as to the reps' planned activities. Either the reps make the effort or they're gone.

Rep: *You've heard the old saying "Idle hands are the devil's workshop"? You'll never wonder how to utilize your time. A system simplifies your whole workday because all your activities are pre-planned. You never spend time wondering which action to engage in next. This also aids in eliminating call reluctance.*

Notice the use of strong terms like *enforce, mandatory,* and *eliminate.* You know you'd like to be tougher on your reps, but fear it would be counter-productive. Let the system be the bad guy! When a rep stumbles, point to the place in the system where the misstep occurred and help him or her grow as a pro. Use the system to enforce behavior. Your rep has agreed to abide by the system (if he or she wants to play with your team), so there's no confusion about what anyone should be doing at any given moment in the sales process.

The purpose of this book is to help you define and create your own selling system. The speed at which you implement your new learning is directly related to the speed at which you can increase rep performance. Today is the day to decide you won't leave any more money on the table that sits between you and your buyers.

Remember where we started?

Great sales professionals can predict the future.

This ability defines executives, managers, reps, support personnel, even trainers. Put your system into place and you enable the whole sales team to work with an efficiency and confidence and quality that is associated with the definition of "professional." Look at all the great concepts that are affiliated with that word—elite, professional athlete, polished, expert, competitor, veteran, skilled, and more.

When will you start to build your selling system?

For more information and to help you sell your vision for your newly created (or re-created) sales system, see the Appendices at the end of this book.

Chapter 4

Competitive Intelligence and Prospect Research

In this chapter we'll discuss researching competitors and discovering data on potential buyers as well as gathering information on your industry.

I was sitting in the boardroom with the executive team of a large mortgage company in Chicago. They were rethinking their sales training approach. The company standard for their selling team was to offer nothing. That's right, no sales training. They felt they hired so well that there was no need for ongoing training.

I was there to sell them on their need for training. And I had one question to get me there. It was this prospect's power question (more on this in Power Questions, Chapter 14).

"May I see the information, the files on your competitors?"

The president snorted a "Hah! We don't do that. There are too many of them."

We were heading right down the path I'd chosen.

"Oh," I replied, "I interviewed six of your reps this past week. Each of them told me that each of the last two deals they'd lost was to another mortgage company. But they had no idea who that was or why they didn't get the sale. Would that be good to know?"

Heads nodding, I continue: "It'd be nice to know whether they had better loan terms, rates, points, fees. Be nice to know if you could adjust how you market against them. Be nice to know if your reps just lost these sales, not because they had better products, but because the other guys were better reps."

"We probably need to do that," agreed the president (note how far he's moved in thirty seconds from "We don't do that.").

How to Obtain Valuable Research Data

The story isn't about selling techniques (although they're there), it's about the value of research. During the time I consulted with that firm, I had a membership in Strategic and Competitive Intelligence Professionals (SCIP; www.scip.org). I learned to gather data, mostly with the assistance of great research librarians (your local library—still not a bad idea as a starting place when looking for information). Today SCIP has three thousand members, who have access to amazing sources of information that never existed before the birth of the World Wide Web.

Many major corporations have some of this information available to the sales team. You want to have as much detail as possible because every bit of research can give you a significant competitive advantage. However, if you're selling you don't have time to do this work, so here's an extremely valuable idea you can adopt.

Use an intern to gather this data if you don't have staff time available.

There is an emerging trend in universities today to offer sales degrees (both on an undergraduate and graduate level). These aren't simply marketing degrees with an emphasis on selling, but actual degrees focused on preparing the student for a career in sales. You'll see details in Chapter 35, A Critical Trend You Can't Ignore.

I discovered how serious this trend was when I was asked to speak at the National Collegiate Sales Competition (NCSC). Every year schools with sales degree programs send students to Dr. Terry Loe's event at Kennesaw State University outside of Atlanta, Georgia. There they participate in simulated sales calls while cameras transmit their meetings to judges observing and scoring them. (For further information, see http://coles.kennesaw.edu/ncsc/)

Individual and team champions are crowned. In 2010 the team championships went to Bowling Green State University in the undergraduate level and Texas State University for graduate level. Shantil Bryne of Colorado State University was the overall champion in 2011.

Do you think companies that hire reps out of college are taking a good look at these students? Indeed, there's a job fair that runs concurrently with the competition. Maybe your company should be sponsoring and attending this event. My apologies to ADP, the primary sponsor of the NCSC, for giving away one of their hiring secrets to the global selling world. But the future of our profession is gathering in one location every year and you need access to these men and women yourself.

Other competitions are springing up around the country as well. The common belief among employers who hire students is that they come aboard sales teams as rookies, but they have the equivalent of eighteen months of selling under their belts. This is huge when you consider the "hump" in sales is about six months. That is, a new rep will recognize within that time whether he or she likes selling, will experience some level of success, and will either decide to continue in sales as a career or decide he or she isn't fit for it and quit.

All that experience the students have gathered during their college careers translates into opportunities for your firm to hire these students as interns. Please check with your HR department and legal counsel or an employment attorney as to whether you can offer internships as paid or unpaid roles.

Where to Obtain Data

Here are three areas where you'll turn your interns loose to gather information on competitors, buyers, your industry, and customers. Of course, you'll want to check with your marketing department first, as they could have much of this data on file.

By the way, if I had to choose a single method by which to do my competitive intelligence, it'd be LinkedIn. With well over one hundred million users, you can find almost anybody from any industry. We'll revisit this master site at the end of this chapter, but think about it now: How good are you at using LinkedIn? You should be great at using this website.

Competitors

Here are some ideas for researching your competitors.

Set up a free Google Alerts account. This online version of a media clipping service can be an amazing source of information. Create several alerts with a variety of information, making sure you include the firms' executives' names, as well as their top salespeople. Why not just do one alert with the company name? Wouldn't you like to know things like "Where are my competitors serving as volunteers (like United Way)?" These good will efforts often serve as back door marketing opportunities. The more information you have, the clearer a picture you can draw of their impact in the marketplace. To set up an account, go to www.google.com/alerts.

Start a swipe file of their materials. This is a classic marketing approach to garnishing creative ideas and knowing how others are presenting themselves in the marketplace. As a sales pro, you want to know exactly what your competitors are offering and how they are using strategies like direct mail or email campaigns. You may need someone to supply you with this information. Some firms even use blind post office boxes and web-based email (not a corporate address) to gather information and leads.

Spend lots of time on their websites. Print pages off and analyze what they share publicly (and, by inference, what information isn't there). Do they brag about their clients? Those are your prospects. Do they announce trade shows at which they exhibit? Maybe you should be there. (Tradeshow attendance, even if someone is not exhibiting, is excellent information to know.) Do they list prices, offer feature/benefits lists, and more?

Here's my favorite web-based competition research strategy. Do a reverse search online to find out who is linked to your competitor's website. Use a service like http://wholinkstome.com (they identify themselves as a "reputation management" service) to discover more data this way. Also have a look at www.seomoz.org.

Monitor their key employees in social media. LinkedIn, Facebook, and other sources are rich repositories of valuable information. This strategy especially includes ex-employees. You'd be surprised what people might share after they've left a competitor.

Buy stock if they are publicly held. You'll get loads of information, including their annual report (which you can get anyway).

Buy their product. Or have someone else buy it for you. Find out what the buying experience is like. Secret shoppers do this as a business, although the companies themselves normally use shoppers to monitor how buyers interact with sellers. How good is the product follow-up? Do they up-sell? Lots of information is available by becoming a buyer that you'll never find through other means.

Finally, do a SWOT analysis on each competitor. After you've done the other work, do this. By analyzing their Strengths, Weaknesses, Opportunities, and Threats, you can paint a nice picture of how their business and selling strategies affect yours. (For those less experienced in using the SWOT process, a simple explanation is located at www.quickmba.com/strategy/swot/.)

Make your research available to your teams. It should even be a topic of discussion from time to time at your sales meetings. A thorough analysis can even be posted on your company's intranet for easy access.

Here's a quick thought on a marketing strategy I've observed based on competitive research, the competitor matrix chart. I'll tell you right now this is a brilliant strategy and the competition will HATE you for doing it. I encountered a great example of this at the 2006 Motivation Show in Chicago. I was there to observe and write about exhibitors and new products and to view companies handling this massive investment in marketing. Some do it well; too many do it poorly. At this show I met the marketing team for Creative Corporation. This company produces the ZEN Micro mp3 player. Their competition? Apple iPod. iPod owned this market with an astronomical 82 percent share in 2005, up from 64 percent the previous year. (As of mid-year 2011, their market share was still 70 percent.) How do you go toe-to-toe or head-to-head (depending on whether you're looking up or down, I guess) with this monster in your marketplace space? Design a matrix like the following sample:

Feature or Benefit	Zen	iPod
Colors	10	4
FM Tuner	YES	X
Microphone	YES	X
Battery Replace	YES	X
Charge Time	4 to 5 hrs.	4 hrs.

Prospective customers look at this and say, "What am I really buying? The big name, better budgeted company, or a product that gives a lot more for my money?"

The big name company will hate you for doing this. The trick is to line up a dozen benefits, using mostly those that the competing product or service doesn't have. *They'll look at the list and say, "But they left off this feature or skipped that benefit that we have. . . ." Too bad, life's not fair, it's your marketing piece, you set the rules.*

Now, as you happen to be a corporate sales executive and you aren't always allowed to create materials, I'd encourage you to draw up a competitor matrix chart and share it with your VP of marketing to see whether it'll work as a flyer you can use. As a sales pro, it's not a bad exercise to work through something similar to give you the language to compete. (Obviously, if you're an independent sales rep, consultant, or entrepreneur, you can easily put this chart into play for your sales work. Don't forget to place it prominently on your website as well.)

Competitor matrix—potent promotional tool—go build one today.

EXERCISE 4.1.   Create a Competitor Matrix Chart

SETUP: This is an excellent exercise for sales pros, even if your marketing department is already providing great materials to use. In fact, some firms I've worked with handed this work off to the marketing department to design a formal chart on this concept.

Choose a competitor and create your own Zen vs. iPod chart. You want to identify features and benefits and problems you solve that aren't addressed by the competing firm. That way they have a blank spot or a NO or an X in the space where your solution is charted.

EXERCISE 4.1. Create a Competitor Matrix Chart, Cont'd

	Benefit 1	Benefit 2	Benefit 3	Benefit 4	Benefit 5	Benefit 6	Benefit 7
Your Product							
Competitor's Product							

Have fun playing with this as a team and turn over your list, as large as you can create it, to the marketing team for some feedback.

Buyers

A nice bonus of researching a buyer prior to meeting is that you'll find other buyers as well. So look at this activity as a form of hybrid prospecting. Again, you can do this work yourself, or set your intern to the task once a hot lead is landed, or an appointment is set. Here are some ways to find information on your prospects.

Web research is first. This includes social media as well as a general search online. Search as well in local business journals and consumer publications like local newspapers. Is he/she a chamber of commerce member? Do they belong to trade associations? Do they attend local chapter meetings? Do they serve on the local or national board? Do you need to get involved here, if you're not?

At their website, subscribe to their online newsletter if there is one. Get thorough biographical information, then back-check the resources there like university involvement, volunteer and non-profit organization work, and more.

Look at their products and customer lists. Understanding what they sell and discussing it during a call will generate great empathy, as they have to understand they have a sales force out there doing what you do as well.

These sets of sources will give you plenty of personal and professional information.

Your Industry

Your ability to understand your business at the highest level will make you a respected sales professional. Your buyers prefer to play with the pros. They prefer to pay the pros. Industry research is critical because it not only gives you great information on your marketplace, but it can contribute to managing your personal image in the industry. By way of example, think about the association trade shows you've attended. There are always a few sales reps who are everywhere. They know everybody. They speak at events. They are friendly with clients, prospects, and competitors. You want to be that person. It will elevate you in the eyes of everyone within your business segment, and that's money in the bank.

Web surf regularly (hired that intern yet?). Consult online databases such as Hoovers (www.hoovers.com), OneSource Information Services (www.onesource. com), and Edgar Online (www.edgar-online.com). Go back to that Google Alerts account and load in keywords to get information on your industry, the trade association, vendors, and more.

Read regularly. Trade magazines are a must. This includes those published by your major associations and business publications like *The Wall Street Journal* (also available online).

Newsletters and e-zines are must-read sources of information. This includes those from industry organizations, from competitors, and your own. (I'm shocked in conversations with corporate sales reps who don't even read their own firm's marketing newsletters.)

Ask existing clients what publications they read as well as what groups they belong to. Here's another tip that serves as a hybrid marketing technique: Get invited to present at your client's industry conference, offering the client's experience implementing your solutions as a case study.

Finally, regional and local business journals are good for territory reps to find out what's really going on in their backyard.

Attend regularly. Trade associations are important. Get to the local chapter meetings and attend national and international meetings. If you can speak at these events, you'll increase awareness for yourself and your company while gaining inside information about what's happening in the industry as soon as it occurs. Work booths at these shows as well.

Your local Chamber of Commerce might or might not serve as a gathering place for information.

Networking meetings are at the bottom of this list and have limited value in gathering industry research, unless you sell locally to consumers.

One last research strategy (and a good one). Here's a unique tool that companies have used for years. Unfortunately, not enough of them are using customer advisory boards.

Customer Advisory Boards

Advisory boards are most often done with trade associations to draw off the collective brainpower of their members and vendors, but you can use this method as well.

Your customer advisory board will be composed of a variety of business professionals (and possible consumers who buy). These might include your own sales, marketing, and service people, partners, clients, respected external business professionals, retired executives from your company or the industry—and don't forget your vendors. Quick thought on vendors: Think about inviting that insurance executive. What happens when he or she has to hit you with an increase next year. A respected role on the board might just save some money.

You get the idea. Find smart people who will bring unique approaches, knowledge, and skills to the table. The purpose of the board might be to test new products or marketing ideas, to gain access to their sales forces and data, to access key decision-makers, and more.

EXERCISE 4.2. Form a Customer Advisory Board

SETUP: Forming an advisory board can be a detailed and daunting task, but well worth the effort. Most major corporations would need a champion high in the selling structure to approve this idea, so do your pre-work first and it'll be easier for your senior executives to say "yes."

1. Create company objectives to be gained by forming this board. Attain referrals; increase spending by board members; use media (like press releases) to show how this advisory board works together, creates events together, or minimally provides speaking or training programs at client events.

2. Quantify objectives by creating a dollar value to each of the objective initiatives; for example, what is a referral worth?

EXERCISE 4.2.   Form a Customer Advisory Board, Cont'd

3. Identify companies that match your target market. This includes recognizing the proper title of decision-makers. You might already have some outstanding clients who fit this profile.

4. Recruit fifteen or twenty potential members. Create a vision and craft a letter to ask these individuals for the opportunity to work together.

5. By when would you have this group in place?

The advisory group can meet at regular intervals or it might be created for a one-time event, perhaps attached to a major trade show. Be sensitive to the investment in time required and consider running the meetings virtually, by phone or webinar, even by teleconference if that makes more sense.

Here are some keys to managing this diverse population of experts: Make the experience fun and reward people for volunteering their time, energy, and brains. Hold the meeting at a nice venue with good meals and event experiences like shows, sports, and more. Send thank-you gifts to your board members. If they can't accept gifts, make sure you've identified their favorite charities and donate to them instead.

There is even an organization, the Customer Advisory Board, that will help you build a board. Check them out at www.customeradvisoryboard.org/. Download their free ten-page strategy guide on developing your board. The basis for their outstanding, yet simple approach is *align, design, and deliver.* Consider joining, too; it's a modest fee to help support their work. The tradeoff between your investment and what you gain by their knowledge is significant.

What I really like about the Customer Advisory Board's advice is the focus on sales and marketing. They even help you quantify the board's contributions to the bottom line by identifying things like the value of new leads, additional prospects, and increased spending.

Good idea? Great! When will you start to put the pieces together and form your own customer advisory board?

Last thought. Back to LinkedIn. When will you become skilled at using LinkedIn to analyze both buyers and competitors? How often do you find a resource that's both rich and free?

Chapter 5

Potent Communication Skills

Great sales pros have outstanding abilities to connect with buyers (as well as with their peers and team members). This chapter will show ways in which you can improve your verbal and written skills. You'll also see some deep teaching on the oft-ignored topic of listening skills.

Communication Skills

Just prior to writing this chapter I'd been invited to do my *Secret Language of Influence* program on communication skills in one of my favorite cities, San Diego. My audience was . . . actuaries!

For those unfamiliar with these financial "scientists," actuaries evaluate past and present insurance statistics to estimate future financial risks. On the basis of their findings, they calculate insurance premium rates and also design or modify policies to keep their companies profitable and competitive. In layman's language, they figure out when you're supposed to die.

So these men and women *love* mathematics, like those two people you remember from high school (wait, one of them hated math, but was good at taking tests). Actuaries go through an insane litany of tests, often over the course of a decade or more, in order to have the privilege to work with spreadsheets, all day long. These people are brilliant and great at what they do. As with sales pros, it's pretty easy to quickly quantify their value to the organization.

However, actuaries are about as internal a human being as you will ever meet. So much so that many people don't consider them human. Okay, that's an actuary joke I was told. They have their own jokes, just as lawyers do. The best one I heard (three different actuaries were brave enough to come up to me, a stranger, and share it) was "How do you know you've met a gregarious actuary? When talking to you, he's looking at your feet, instead of his own."

You get the picture. These men and women work with spreadsheets all day long. When an executive from their organization contacted me to speak, she said, "We're actuaries. We need help with communication skills. Will you come to San Diego?" I live in Chicago; it was winter when she called. What would you have responded?

The training ends, I walk to the door to say goodbye to one hundred attendees. There are plenty of nice comments: "I can really use this," "Thank you"; however . . . *not one person shakes my hand*.

People actually held onto their opposite wrists when they spoke to me, as if pinning their arms to their stomachs would send a clear signal to both of us that a handshake wasn't happenin'. Very strange, to greet one hundred people without a single handshake, when there are no worries about bird flu, swine flu, or leprosy.

I mentioned this to a couple of the organization's executives—not to be rude or imply I was upset, but just to make an observation about how well we do or do not connect with others.

"We're actuaries; we don't now how to connect. That's exactly why we invited you in."

Communication skills . . . how well do you connect with others? How well does your selling team connect? Connecting covers a lot of areas in the selling life. We need to better engage buyers through three communication skill areas:

- Written
- Verbal
- Listening

Written Communication Skills

OBEDIENT PROSPECTS CLOSE THEMSELVES. Read Larry's story below and watch Larry draw a blank that his prospect fills in.

> *As a certified financial planner I was proud to say I could sell myself without ever mentioning the "insurance" word. I made great money from offering policies to match my clients' portfolios.*
>
> *When I got an appointment, I would mail a letter describing what our discussion would be about. Most importantly, I included a blank chart where the prospect could write down all assets and liabilities, as well as coverage he or she had (or didn't have).*
>
> *So a two-and-a-half-hour drive to meet and assess the financial needs of a well-to-do young couple was going to be worth the trip. Of course, the tricky part is getting your prospect to do that pre-work for you. In fact, a potential client who gathers paperwork and crunches numbers before a meeting has qualified him- or herself as a very hot prospect.*
>
> *This couple shared that they had done exactly as I requested! They had organized an incredibly detailed display of information on their assets and liabilities.*
>
> *"Wow," I said, "thank you for taking the time to create this picture of your finances. It will help us structure a plan to manage your money for the short term and long haul." I was setting them up for the fact that they were probably under-insured and missing some coverage as well.*
>
> *The man and his wife both broke into broad smiles. "This was a great exercise. We had no idea of the scope of our family finances. In fact, we noticed several places on the form were blank." He paused, leaned in, and pointed to some large numbers on his personal balance sheet. "So to make your job easier, we had someone come over last night and we bought a bunch of insurance."*
>
> *I thought I would cry.*

Poor Larry—his written communication just didn't communicate very well. Larry's qualifying process should have set expectations in both directions. You explain to them what is going to happen and you describe the role of both client and rep. Larry's letter should have clearly told the prospects that they are to make no decisions until they sit down with him. A clear understanding of roles would have saved Larry both the time and the tears.

How well do you design your written communications? That would include both email and letters. We cover proposals in Chapter 7. Since much literature salespeople use is designed by marketing, we'll make this brief and to the point.

Your personal writing should include the following three elements:

1. *You focused, rather than we (or I).* Look how big we are! Here's how long we've been around! This is our plant overseas! We can make you happy when you buy from us!

   This sample is typical of too much copywriting today. The subject of each sentence is the sender, the salesperson. The subject of each sentence should be the buyer, the person with the money.

   Review and re-write all of your email and letters and invert the sentence structure to speak directly to the person reading it.

   My favorite authority who coaches this is Jerry Weissman, author of *Presenting to Win* (2008). Jerry personally advises major corporate executives how to present to potential shareholders when their companies are going public. In other words, he is helping people sell millions of dollars of stock. You should own his book. I bought it to see how I might better keynote and train. It's transformed how I write as well.

   One of his key teaching moments comes from the concept WIIFM: What's In It For Me. Jerry doesn't use this. Instead he teaches WIIFY: What's In It For You. You direct your persuasive words to the reader or listener by saying, "Here's why this is important for you" or "Why should this matter to you? Here's why . . ." or "Here's why you should take action on this now."

   Stop making yourself and your company the center of your writing attention. Focus first on the buyer. You'll then better connect and increase your chance to close him or her.

2. *Give them a reason to buy now.* The backbone of this concept comes from the old "impending event" close. In other words, if the buyer doesn't act now,

something will change—price goes up, product is bought by someone else, opportunity lost.

Each time you correspond, put some time pressure on the person receiving your email or letter. A sense of urgency could come from quantifying how much money they're losing now. It could come from how much they stand to gain quickly. It could come from shareholder dissatisfaction, lost market share, personal improvement. Give them a reason to not wait and you strengthen your ability to generate a response to your note.

3. *Give a call to action*. You could end with a distinct call to action. I'd encourage you to pepper your letter with multiple chances for a buyer to respond.

   A great example of this is built into long copy, single-page websites. This powerful model for selling online has expert testimonials, reasons to buy, tips and hints of what you'll receive, and every few paragraphs is a link to click. "Click this link" to attain all the good things described. "Click this link" and avoid the bad things that are happening now because you don't have what we've got.

   Janet Switzer is my favorite secret success story. She's the copywriting genius behind *Chicken Soup for the Soul* and power marketing genius Jay Abraham. Her best-selling book *Instant Income* (2007) is promoted at this one-page website: www.instantincome.com/iibp/. If you print out the "single page" you'll end up with eighteen pages of masterful and persuasive writing.

   You can model her structure, which I've done at the following website: www.LeadGenerationGenius.com. I encourage you, should a single webpage serve as an information tool, to model Switzer's success system for prospecting.

So there are your three pieces of the correspondence puzzle:

- Buyer-centered
- Time-sensitive
- A call to action

What do you need to work on?

In the following exercise, learners will review some documents, emails, or letters in order to decide whether they tend to focus on themselves first, rather than the recipient or prospect. Everyone who is being trained on this module should be asked to bring some recent writing for review.

EXERCISE 5.1. Practice Your Written Communication Skills

Take out and look at some recent letters or emails you've written. Are they prospect-centered with more "you" than "we"? Is there some inducement to buy now? Is there a distinct call to action? Do you want the reader to do something? You should say what that is . . . write/jot down, etc. . . . Rewrite your correspondence in order to focus on the buyer first.

Some examples:

1. "We can give you the best sales training available; find out how now."

   This becomes: "Do you have the latest persuasion principles built into your sales training? Contact us within twenty-four hours of this email to receive a free analysis of your training with recommendations on how to upgrade it and increase performance."

2. "Our company has been serving your community for over twenty years. We'd love to talk to you today about how we can help with your financial situation."

   This becomes: "Your safest decision about managing both your budget and investments is to sit down with a firm that has been serving your community for over two decades. Call us upon receipt of this letter and receive a free tax analysis that can save you hundreds of dollars on your tax return. Hurry to respond! Because of the amount of work we receive, we can only manage a limited number of these free offerings."

Again, the biggest problem with sales communications is that sellers need to re-write letters with the prospect as the subject, instead of the company, and too often a distinct call to action is missing.

Here's an actual example where I rewrote a message (thankfully, before it went out to the buyer) for a sales rep at a company where I was consulting to help the sales pros close more business.

Hey Dave—Hope you had a fantastic holiday! I wanted to put together a very small offer with you just so you could get your pinky toe in the water with [magazine]. I am very confident that once you see the metrics for yourself regarding the online exposure I can give [your company] you will be more comfortable so all I am asking for is a small shot. I will give you a Feature Banner Placement (500 × 75) for three months at just $1,500 per month with no strings attached and if I can't give you a million impressions I will buy you and the wife dinner and a movie! I would really appreciate this one small opportunity Dave

I suggested that Rob, the rep, was coming across as a bit of a beggar (noted twice within the second version) and suggested the following changes. Notice how I maintained language that was a reflection of Rob's personality. This is in alignment with my coaching that everyone should be able to "find his voice" to sell, using his own personality.

Hey Dave—~~Hope~~ TRUST you had a fantastic holiday! ~~I wanted to put together a very small offer with you just~~ YOU'LL LIKE THIS SMALL OFFER . . . so you ~~could~~ CAN get your pinky toe in the water with [the magazine].

ONCE YOU SEE . . . ~~am very confident that once you see~~ the metrics for yourself regarding the online exposure I can give [your company], you will be more comfortable ~~so all I am asking for is a small shot.~~ (Rob, DON'T ASK, you're begging!) SO YOU'LL JUST TEST RESPONSE WITH A SMALL INVESTMENT.

~~I will give you~~ YOU WILL RECEIVE a Feature Banner Placement (500 × 75) for three months at just $1,500 per month with no strings attached.

~~and if~~ When (Rob, don't say "if." Are you going to perform, or just hoping you will?) I can give you a million impressions, ~~I will buy you and the wife~~ YOU AND THE WIFE WILL RECEIVE dinner and a movie!

~~I would really appreciate this one small opportunity~~ (Rob, you're still BEGGING!) DAVE, YOU WILL BE VERY GLAD ONCE YOU REALIZE THE HIGH VALUE . . . etc.~~, Dave~~

So the final document looked like this:

Hey, Dave—TRUST you had a fantastic holiday! YOU'LL LIKE THIS SMALL OFFER . . . so you CAN get your pinky toe in the water with [the magazine].

ONCE YOU SEE the metrics for yourself regarding the online exposure I can give [your company], you will be more comfortable. SO YOU'LL JUST TEST RESPONSE WITH A SMALL INVESTMENT.

YOU WILL RECEIVE a Feature Banner Placement (500 x 75) for three months at just $1,500 per month with no strings attached.

When I can give you a million impressions, YOU AND THE WIFE WILL RECEIVE . . . dinner and a movie!

DAVE, YOU WILL BE VERY GLAD ONCE YOU REALIZE THE HIGH VALUE . . . etc.

One final fun thought: Look at these two sentences; they differ by one, single small comma. The meaning changes completely.

"Let's eat Grandma."

"Let's eat, Grandma."

Punctuation saves lives. It saves sales as well. There's even a Facebook page dedicated to this at http://www.facebook.com/pages/Lets-eat-Grandma-or-Lets-eat-Grandma-Punctuation-saves-lives/276265851258

Pay attention to grammar. Check punctuation, verb tense, subject/verb agreement, and more. Your impression in print is a permanent reminder of who you are—a pro or an amateur.

Verbal Communication Skills
Voicemail Jail

My sales manager and I had a full day ahead of us, a three-hour drive to deliver several one- to two-hour presentations, plus the return trip. We began our day anticipating the acquisition of new business.

The town we were driving to held an intriguing opportunity for us. We are accustomed to calling on the Chicago metropolitan area, but this was a small town that was probably not "hit on" by our competitors as our regular territory was. Three large companies here could use our services.

We arrived in the town and handled our first two appointments. We excitedly approached our third (and largest) prospect around 2:00 p.m. We entered the lobby, walked up to the receptionist, and announced our arrival.

The surprised receptionist informed us that our contact had taken the day off! I politely told her I would call him tomorrow and quickly hustled my sales manager out of the lobby before his "simmering" temper erupted like a volcano. He is very protective of his salespeople's time and has previously vocalized his displeasure in the lobby of a company after being "stood up."

We get back into the car and start driving out of the parking lot. After a bit of venting, we decide our next step will be to call the prospect's office and leave a voicemail saying we had been there and would reschedule the appointment. We make this call on my sales manager's cell phone using the speakerphone feature.

After I left the message, my sales manager and I both began to rant again, using some not-so-choice language and graphic detail. This went on for some thirty seconds or so, and then we heard a "BEEP!"

We realized at that moment, thirty seconds too late, that our entire conversation, with all the acid and anger, had been recorded on the prospect's voicemail!

There was absolutely nothing we could do to undo our stupid blunder! After about two weeks I called the prospect, acting as if nothing happened, to reschedule our appointment.

That was three years ago and he still won't answer the phone!

Because of the size of the opportunity, every time a new salesperson starts, the sales manager has the "rookie" call the company to try for an appointment. To this day, no one has been successful. I guess we just have to wait until that buyer with the red-hot ears leaves the company or dies!

When Teri shared her story with me, she begged that her firm and the prospect's remain anonymous. I still laugh when I think of how shocking that BEEP must have felt to our two salespeople. As my good friend (and co-author of a book by the same title) Tony Jeary (2005) says, "Life is a series of presentations."

Your communication skills send a message in many ways. Do you make the best word choices? Is there energy in your dialogue? Do you physically show strength and confidence and quality in your gestures and smile?

The focus of this section is on how to present a powerful image that shows buyers you are an outstanding communicator who is a true professional in every aspect of your business. Your buyers want to play at the pro level. They want to do business with the most professional partners, to have the most professional image, to buy the most professional solutions. They might not want to pay the pro price, but that's covered in Chapter 16 on handling objections. In another chapter (Chapter 11), we'll cover first meetings and give specifics on language choices to motivate and persuade prospects.

Here we cover vocal skills and strength, leaving voicemails, and presenting by webinar (we include PowerPoint tips). So you'll also receive some visual presentation tips at the end of this section.

Let's start with your voice. This is your instrument with which you'll orchestrate great sales conversations. Do you take really good care of it? Today, it's quite popular to hit the health club and stay in shape. Your throat, vocal chords, and tongue need care, too.

Here are seven basic rules in caring for your instrument. These are particularly critical for those of you who do a great deal of phone work.

1. Avoid caffeine, chocolate, alcohol, and milk products. The first three dry out the vocal chords, the last increases mucous in the mouth.

2. Drink plenty of water, all day long.

3. Find your perfect pitch. Hum the song, "Happy Birthday." Feel the buzzing, the resonance in your face below the eyes, down to your jaw (called your "mask"). That's your perfect pitch. In your perfect pitch you'll sound stronger, more confident, more comfortable when "playing" your instrument.

4. Practice vocal skills. Are you easy to understand? Do you speak too quickly? Even if you have an accent, taking the time to work on enunciating words will significantly improve your prospect's ability to

hear your message. There's a fun practice chart included here. Work through it regularly and you'll be pleased with improving this area of vocalization. You can also use tongue twisters for this. These are included here as well.

5. Don't yell. It's very hard on your vocal chords. Confession: I didn't pay much attention to this until I had kids. Anyone who has them, had them, or was one knows what I'm talking about.

6. Modulate your voice. Masterful presenters know how to keep listeners' attention by emphasizing words and phrases, by knowing when to increase volume, and by pausing after a key thought is expressed.

7. Smile! You're speaking to a potential client. The pleasure that sits on the horizon of this presentation, a closed sale, should cause you to smile. Smile on the phone and face-to-face; it'll show up in your voice.

Watch late night talk show hosts if you want a model for voice mastery. First, most of them have serious experience as stand-up comedians, meaning they have adopted (and mastered) all of the practices listed above (including, and especially, practicing). Next, they, like sales pros, are rewarded directly in proportion to their verbal skills. Finally, they are selling each of their words in order to get their buyers (the audience) to respond with laughter, emotion, or insights that amount to "aha" moments. Watch these performers with a new, critical set of eyes to discover what they can teach you about improving vocal skills.

Voicemail. This might be one of the most difficult pieces of the sales puzzle. We know that most people don't respond to voicemail. We also expect rejection to be a part of our daily lives, but is ignoring us here a respect issue? Are our messages boring? Too self-centered?

There must be something we can do to bump up the chances of getting a response to your phone message. Here are two options I've seen as effective for getting responses to voicemail. The first is strong, and although more traditional, it works. The second I really love. That's because it's different and unique. It's more fun to leave the message, more interesting for the buyer to hear, and gives great focus for that prospect so that he or she can easily respond. Let's look at the structure of each of the two, along with examples, so that you can build your own model from these techniques.

Strong, Traditional Voicemail Message

- Attention-grabbing

- Credibility, clients, quantify value

- Generate interest

- Close for appointment

> "John [if referred], Bob suggested I contact you. Companies like yours are finding that our solutions help them significantly increase income, some by as much as 10 percent. I'm calling to find out when you and I might sit down and discuss how that happens and to show you whether this is something you can quickly implement to experience similar results. You can reach me at [phone number and/or email address]."

You get the idea. You can name-drop competitors or clients if you choose. But remember the purpose of the call is most likely not to pitch your solutions. It's to gain an appointment. Keep your focus!

A Unique Voicemail Message

- List three specific issues you can address

- Get feedback on relevance

- Close for appointment

> "Here are the top three problems we solve for our existing clients (many of whom you know):
>
> 1. We redesign existing sales training programs so that the latest influence skills are built into reps' learning.
>
> 2. We help sales executives to improve their performance a lot by adding a little bit of change in selling behaviors.
>
> 3. We eliminate the number one problem with sales reps around the planet—they chase poor prospects.
>
> "Which one is your biggest concern? You can reach me at [phone number and/or email address]."
>
> [when you get a call-back with a positive response] "Really? Tell me more about that."

[after hearing some detail] "Let's figure out a time to talk in person so between us we can decide how to work together."

[when you get a call-back with a negative response, such as "none of these"] "Okay, so what is your biggest issue related to . . . ?"

If the buyer won't "play the game" or won't respond to your ideas, you'll want to fall back to one of several responses, such as:

"Mr./Ms. Prospect, I'm wondering why you decided to talk to me, if there seems to be no reason to talk. Did I catch you off guard with my questions? How would you figure out which issues your firm best needs to address in sales training?"

"Okay, I'm trying to help you decide how we can increase performance with your team, as we've done for others in your market. How can we figure that out?"

"Mr./Ms. Prospect, we can have a discussion about improving revenue with your team, or I can talk to someone else there about this if it's not an area you attend to."

Here's the key to this second selection (and it's a theme you'll continue to see throughout this book): You must distinguish yourself from every other sales dog hounding prospects. Don't act and sound like other salespeople!

A Truckload of Tips on Voicemail

Ten ways you can increase your chance to receive a call-back:

1. Smile! People can hear this in your voice. An old telemarketing trick is to have a small mirror in front of you to keep you aware of your expressions. You enjoy the idea that this person has money for you, right? Smile!

2. Try not to leave voicemail the first time you call, unless it's a referral or you've already connected (perhaps at a conference or trade show or networking event).

3. A better bet is to ask the screener or gatekeeper (see Chapter 13 on gatekeepers for more ideas) a good time or best way to connect with the buyer.

4. Do not leave half a message, then hang up. This silly idea is recycled every once in a while. People are too busy to be intrigued by a stranger's trick or technology problem. It doesn't work.

5. Call at odd hours and you could reach the decision-maker live.

6. Leave, within your message, the fact that you are going to call back, and when. If you give a time frame, it helps the prospect anticipate the call.

7. Be creative in your attention-grabbing first line. Voicemail is a form of phone "marketing." People love creative marketing (talking animals, talking babies, etc.). You can still be professional when you leave a line like, "I have a quiz question for you about your sales team. Do you know the number one problem salespeople face? Give me your best guess and we'll talk about how to eliminate that."

8. Use humor! If you can be funny, you'll further make yourself memorable. I've left a message like this: "Rob, I called about a revenue idea you can use, but I wanted to tell you about a hilarious selling blunder I just heard from a client who was selling agriculture insurance. He came out the farmhouse to see a huge billy goat standing on top of his brand new car. Anyway, let's talk, you'll want to know about. . . ."

9. Script your message. You can print out what you find works and mark inflections and words to emphasize. Remember, the key with a strong script is to still sound spontaneous.

10. Record yourself to find out how you really sound. This can be scary, once you hear what your voice is like on the phone. Sound resonating in your skull keeps you from hearing what others hear. I learned to record myself when I did a ton of phone selling in the 1980s. You'll learn whether to slow down, work on vocal skills, and more. Record yourself to improve your vocal "appearance" with all your prospects, the live ones as well as those on voicemail. By the way, you don't really need recording equipment; just leave your message on your own phone and listen. Better yet, leave it on your colleagues' (or mentor or networking partners) phones and ask for feedback.

Remember, you have one goal—to get an appointment. Keep your focus. Don't even think of offering literature, as it gives the buyer a chance to further stall the communication process.

Leave your email address. This can help if it happens to be the preferred way this buyer initiates relationships. You run the risk that he or she will look at your website (I hope you use a business email and not Gmail or Hotmail or a web-based service). But it's worth it to give the decision-maker another choice as to how he or she can respond.

If the person doesn't respond after several calls, you have to determine when to bail out. So know in advance how many attempts you'll make; then have a final message that says goodbye. "Mr./Ms. Prospect, last call. You're probably tired of hearing my voice and I'm sorry we haven't connected. You're too busy. This isn't a priority. I'm not sure which. You do have some numbers to help quantify how we can help improve rep performance. You also have my email, Dan@GotInfluenceInc.com. I will stop calling you at this time. Should you have someone else who could discuss what we do, I'm available. But you've made it clear there's no reason for me to continue calling. Take care." And you are done, finished. If you want to cycle back in six months, fine. But remember, your primary job early in the sales process is to qualify and disqualify prospects. You've disqualified this one. Now move on.

You had better have an *excellent* voicemail message yourself, should that person finally call back. It should be intriguing, offering distinct benefits and/or problems you solve for existing clients and a specific call to action. Mine is essentially, "Do you have the latest influence strategies built into your sales training program? If you're not sure, we should talk. It could be time to redesign! Give me a good time to call you back or email me at Dan@GotInfluenceInc.com."

Here are my three favorite techniques on leaving a voicemail that will increase your response rate:

- *Favorite Tip 1:* If you do leave a message, give a time frame for when they can call back. I often say, "You can reach me live between 2 and 3 p.m. today or the same time tomorrow afternoon." This shows you're professional, busy, and have structure to your day. Remember, showing hints of your professionalism is a key to leaving the best possible first impression.

- *Favorite Tip 2:* Do *not* use the words "only" or "just" in your message. These are known in linguistics as minimizers. They reduce the value of anything that follows. So when you say (and most of us were taught to do this), "I only want to talk about . . .," you are undermining your effort to position your solution as one of value. Instead, be confident with language like this: "You'll want to call me to discuss this, as it has a significant impact on how well your sales team can improve performance and increase revenue for the rest of this year." These potent word choices present a very distinct contrast to a minimized message.

- *Favorite Tip 3:* Pay attention to "you" versus "I" language. The subject of your conversation should be the buyer, not you. So "I want to show . . ." becomes "You'll want to know. . . ." You get the picture. This is basic marketing 101—focus first on the listener, viewer, reader. By the way, as we said earlier, your written documents should do this as well.

EXERCISE 5.2.   Practice Leaving a Voicemail Message

SETUP: In this exercise, have your team members individually write out their voicemail messages. Then the team will share and everyone will have an opportunity to rewrite their messages, utilizing the insights from the collective brainpower of the whole room.

What do you say that gets a call-back when you leave a voicemail? Remember:

- Don't use minimizers like "only" or "just."

- Use WIIFY—What's in it for you. Make it prospect-centered; don't talk about yourself.

- Start thoughts and sentences with the buyer ("You can gain. . . ."), not with yourself, "We are the biggest, best. . . .").

- Use the "top three problems" approach, if you'd like, in order to start the listener thinking about exactly how you can help his or her company.

- Have a distinct call to action, so the listener knows what is expected and has a reason to respond.

Take three minutes to create your message.

EXERCISE 5.2.   Practice Leaving a Voicemail Message, Cont'd

Let's now listen to the language each person has used to create the best voice-mail possible.

Trainer: For large group training, everyone does individual work, then receives feedback and shares only at their table. Each group can select a best message or can create a hybrid message that represents that group's best effort to share with the whole room.

GREAT TIP: Your company should create a document of the best voicemails from this exercise and have the sales professionals test each to discover which receives the best response. The messages could be switched daily or weekly, as long as you have a decent number of calls from which to measure response.

In a recent consulting project, I took over a company's sales team in order to increase their performance. Because this was a publishing company that sold recruitment advertising (to identify and hire new producers or sales reps), the sales team was collectively, on average, to make about six hundred phone calls a week. One of the first things we did was to design a potent message for the hundreds of voicemails that were being left each week. I did the exercise above to determine the best message we could possibly leave. We crafted two, including one using the top three problems solved.

This was the first message:

> *We recently conducted some industry research on recruiting and growing your business and I want to share the findings with you. This might be the most important call you have all week. This is directly related to how fast you can grow your business; call me at . . . .*

Each of the reps received about four more call-backs a day. This is significant and the company was pleased.

What was most interesting was the response we received from using the second voicemail message:

> *Here are the top three problems we solve for our existing clients:*
>
> *They are frustrated by the quality and quantity of leads to find top producers.*
>
> *They have been wasting money on advertising that doesn't work.*

They want to know how competitors like [two firms mentioned] generate over eight thousand leads annually.

Which one of these is your biggest concern?

The salespeople were shocked from day one when buyers returned calls with comments like: "It's number one, and I want to know about number three, too."

Returned voicemails increased about the same as the first message, but the conversation was completely different. There was an emotional connection with responders to the "top three" message that made the sales calls much more fun. Think of what happened from each party's perspective:

- *Buyer:* This message is about me (for a change) and I can relate to the issues described. This person knows my business and I'm going to speak with him or her to find out how we can fix some of these issues.

- *Seller:* These people really want to speak with me! There's energy on the call and it's really fun to have sales dialogues where the buyer wants to talk.

Please do not ignore the power of a well-crafted voicemail message. Put a team session together today to design your book of messages and track the increase in responses.

Now let's move on to your webinar messages. Webinars are online versions of both sales presentations and learning experiences. A "virtual classroom" is created wherein an interactive time of learning and possibly sharing is created for the audience.

Most organizations take previously designed PowerPoint presentations and speak over the images, simply taking advantage of the Internet to pitch to more people. In addition, a webinar can be archived so that those who missed the live experience can still gain information related to their learning or decision-making needs.

The problem with just dropping the PowerPoint material into the webinar infrastructure is that you won't be taking advantage of some of the amazing interactive elements available. Viewers can

- Vote (known as "polling");

- Write on the screen (each person has a different color to distinguish comments); and

- Post questions for the leader to respond to.

Presenters should

- Create handouts to share prior to the program;
- Practice using the software (get to know what it can do);
- Record the webinar; and
- Follow up by sending a link to the archived webinar (you create buzz and referrals).

An excellent resource on producing professional webinar experiences is available through the book and matching website *Webinars with WOW Factor* (2010) by Becky Pike Pluth (www.WebinarsWithWowFactor.com). Becky is a brilliant trainer who incorporates a great deal of her best practices in webinars. You'll learn to offer stretch breaks, use some fun and dynamic exercises, and create visually appealing slides (the website has about sixty slides and exercises you can download).

Your decision about producing webinars probably centers on these four major players:

- WebEx—www.WebEx.com
- Live Meeting—www.LiveMeeting.com
- Go To Meeting—www.GoToMeeting.com
- Adobe Acrobat Connect Pro—www.Adobe.com

The popular phrase "death by PowerPoint" comes from an article written by Angela R. Garber (2001). Two years later Pulitzer-prize-winning columnist Julia Keller (2003) wrote the *Chicago Tribune* article "Killing Me Microsoftly with PowerPoint." Ten plus years later, the problem remains as sales professionals continue to bore or ruin presentations.

Crafting PowerPoint slides that appeal to viewers centers on five basic rules you'll want to apply:

1. Focus on one thought per slide.
2. Use simple, easy-to-read fonts (sans serif, like Arial, Verdana, Calibri, or Trebuchet).
3. Dark slides with light colored text and images are easier to view.

4. Consistent slide design is important (too many people create a collage of looks like a third-grade art project).

5. Keep images consistent throughout. If you're using photos, stay with them. If using cartoons, use matching styles/looks.

I'll share my progression as a serious user of PowerPoint here (I'm doing sales training or keynoting multiple times every month, all year long). You can see how my design evolved from cave-man like qualities to Homo erectus in Figure 5.1.

Be sensitive to your prospect's experience. Keep it simple, colorful, and fun. Get help, even paying for good design help if you have to. Please don't destroy a selling opportunity because of your digital presentation.

Listening Skills

Recently, the Georgia Department of Natural Resources has been seeking seventy-five volunteers to be trained in listening to frogs so that the state can complete its annual frog survey. Georgia has thirty-one frog species, each with distinctive ribbits and croaks, and surveyors, after practicing detection, will monitor frog habitats to help officials measure population trends. Tracking season begins this week. (*Atlanta Journal-Constitution*, November 11–12, 2008)

How would you like to have a job where listening is your primary role?

Just as one state has thirty-one different frog dialects, each of your buyers is distinct in his or her language choices. These word selections can reveal individual and corporate decision-making strategies. They can point to how more closely aligned your language choices are (or are not) to that precious prospect. Some hints to increase your listening power are presented below.

Do you recognize whether the other person filters information visually or by sound or by touch? Visual speakers might say, "see what I mean?" or "it looks like this." Auditory speakers might say, "sounds like . . . or "hear what I mean?" Kinesthetic/tactile types might say, "We're getting a grip on the issue" or "This can build our performance." In psychology these are called representational (or "rep") systems, and they reveal how a person processes information about his or her life experiences. VAK is the acronym used to reference these proven ideas.

Figure 5.1. Progression in PowerPoint Design

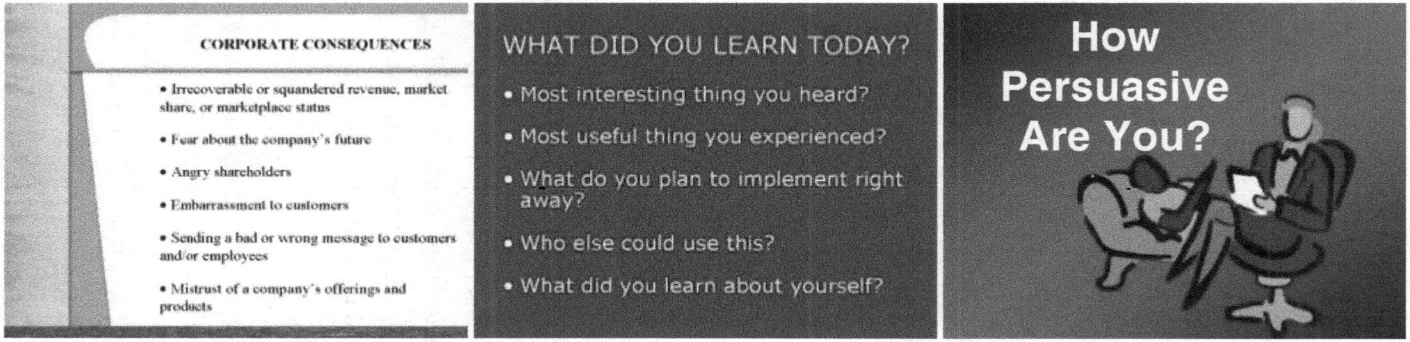

In a dialogue with someone, you want to repeat back the person's *exact* "rep" system words to show you understand his or her concerns and questions.

I know we were taught early in traditional sales training to summarize and restate, using our own words, the comments being made. This can create a disconnect if, for example, we offer back visual words to a person who processes information in an auditory fashion.

Here's what I mean. Your comment, "It *looks* like you want to *show* the company confidence," is not the same dialect. When what the person said was, "I want the company to *hear* what it's like to *sound* confident." Big disconnect—so avoid putting your own spin on others' words.

So hop to it. You don't need to recognize thirty-one croaking conversational styles to improve your listening and your performance. You just need to deal with three. Do that, and your buyers will invite you to spend more time in their habitat. And that leads to more greenbacks in the bank.

You will find great detail and exercises for using this strategy of hearing and adapting buyer dialects in Chapter 15, Practicing Listening Skills, and Chapter 9, Establishing Rapport.

Buyers' Beliefs About Communication Skills

Buyers do want to have rapport with the sales professionals across the desk or on the phone. They really want salespeople to respond, rather than react. Responsiveness implies a respectful conversation, which isn't the same as a defensive dialogue where the seller is proving his or her product's value to the buyer.

They want sales reps to *focus* on understanding the underlying issues related to the decision at hand. This is proven in the conversation when the listener gives feedback to show he or she has heard the speaker. Healthy communication works in both directions.

When a sales rep is a bad listener, it generates that "fight or flight" response. This means buyers will begin to argue, tossing out objections to show resistance. Or they'll mentally check out, just waiting to get through the sales call and end it.

You need outstanding written, verbal, and listening skills to be perceived as a true professional in your world. In addition, your ability to listen by staying curious helps you get in sync with your buyer. Keys include:

- "You" centered communication in person and in print—with a call to action and some sense of urgency
- Powerful voicemail messages that generate return calls
- Strong written "dialogues" with buyers, whether by email, webinar, social media, or other means
- Great listening skills to aid in generating rapport

Chapter 6

Buyers' Behavior and Decision-Making Strategy

In this chapter we'll cover several ways to distinguish buyers from one another, as well as ways to create a better connection with them, discussing five areas of interest, listed above.

On this day, Dan meets the World's Toughest Prospect. I'm speaking to the North American Association of Food Equipment Manufacturers (NAFEM). One of the focal points of my speech is the fact that today "Buyers are better at buying than sellers are at selling." You've probably experienced proof of this truth. There are three reasons:

1. *Many closing techniques we use don't work like they used to. Savvy, experienced buyers have heard them all, and when salespeople begin to feed them predictable lines like "this big discount is only good through today; after that you'll have to pay full price," it just gets the hackles up on potential clients. See, to us these are tactics. Once the prospect is aware of the tactic, it becomes nothing more than a trick—and nobody wants to be tricked.*

2. *Buyers can do a tremendous amount of homework online and are quite prepared before we even get in front of them. The Internet often serves us well, but can also sabotage us when buyers research the competition, customer opinions, and pricing before that all-important first meeting.*

3. *Finally, we have self-limiting beliefs that hurt our sales efforts. These include the idea that a buyer's time is more valuable than our own—so we "beg" for appointments. We train buyers to disrespect us when we respond to "mail me literature" by mailing (or emailing) information. We also chase poor prospects, using hope as a strategy when we should quickly be qualifying and disqualifying instead.*

At the end of my program, a line forms with sales managers and sales reps asking me about speaking at their companies or telling me stories or admitting they were dinosaurs (users of old techniques) or mavericks (those who "wing it" on a sales call and don't use a qualifying strategy).

Today in Orlando, I notice one tall man staying in the back of the line. He continued to step back and let others in front of him. When everyone else was gone, only the two of us remained at the front of the auditorium.

"What do you sell?" I ask.

"I don't. I'm a buyer. I've been a buyer for sixteen years." He smiles. No, he grins. It's a big Cheshire Cat grin, and he hands me his card which lists his title as Senior Buyer. I'm a sales professional, standing nose-to-nose with a professional buyer.

"So why spend seventy-five minutes listening to a sales presentation? Are you here for the entertainment piece, the selling blunders?"

> *He shakes his head and continues to grin. "I'm here to hear what new strategies these guys might be trying on me in the future. And that consequences method of yours is a good one, really good. I just wanted to tell you that professional buyers ARE doing their homework because we don't want to pay too much and we need to know that we're working with the best company we can. I'm not risking my job on some joker who isn't a professional. Salespeople need to know that."*
>
> *"Thanks," I said. "I'll share it with others when I can."*
>
> *We shook hands, and I shook my head as he walked away.*

I don't want to discourage you, but it gets worse. In that presentation I waved a four-page ad over my head. It was torn out of the airline magazine from my flight there. Dr. Chester Karrass offers his negotiation training in hundreds of locations across the globe each year. Buyers are being taught to work salespeople for lower prices, without reducing value. The good doctor is turning thousands of business-people into professional buyers.

How do we stay ahead of that curve? How do we sell when the person opposite us is already anticipating our techniques, mentally "heading us off at the pass"? We've taught sellers how predictable we can be, and that's not good.

A sales trainer from Washington, D.C., told me the following tale about the General Services Administration (GSA), which does all the buying for the federal government—paper, computers, cars, and more. If you were to call on a buyer in the D.C. office, you would be led into an office that was wildly decorated—unusual pictures on the walls, bizarre ceramic figurines, and knick-knacks cover the desk.

Ninety-nine percent of the sales reps calling on the buyer will open the sales call with a comment on one of these objects. "Cool picture." "Interesting figure; there must be a story behind that." "Is that your golf trophy?"

Unfortunately, these are not dear, collected items or family treasures. These objects are merely a source of amusement for the buyers who *bet one another, before each sales call, on what object the rep will comment on!* In other words, our predictable behavior is a source of amusement for buyers who have found a way to tolerate our often obnoxious actions.

Here is an interesting paradox: We've created this monster and we have to keep feeding this monster because it in turn feeds our families! So is it any wonder with all the bad selling going on today that buyers are suspicious or even distrustful of what we have to say to them?

The truth about the buyer/seller relationship is this: Your buyer simply needs to meet you to decide if you're the safest bet for his or her company . . . *and* the safest bet for his or her career.

One of the primary functions of *The Ultimate Guide to Sales Training* is to teach salespeople to distinguish themselves from common sales reps. This takes mental flexibility as we learn to play off the buyer's responses and understand that a sales call is really a casual conversation between two professionals who are trying to figure out how and if they'll work together. In the end, that will be a safer sales call than a hard, old-school feature-benefit pitch.

EXERCISE 6.1.   Share Examples of Tough Buyers

SETUP: These exercises serve both to note how different buyers are and to have a little fun sharing "war stories."

At your table take three minutes to share a memory of one of the TOUGHEST buyers you ever faced. Then tell your group what you learned from that memory. When I call time, pick one person who can share his or her memory with the whole group, as well as insights and learning from that experience.

Now, share a memory of one of the EASIEST buyers you ever faced. Again, tell your group what you learned from that experience. When I call time, pick one person who can share his or her memory with the whole group, as well as insights and learning from that experience.

Trainer: Ask: What do you think is the difference between easy buyers and tough ones?

EXERCISE 6.2.   Discuss Buyer Dislikes

Ask the group to share out loud on the following topic: "What do buyers most dislike about their interactions with sellers?"

Some responses might include they talk too much and are bad listeners who don't understand the buyer's real concerns, too pushy and persistent, not always completely honest.

After receiving some responses, ask, "What can we learn from having a better understanding of how buyers are frustrated by sellers?"

This chapter focuses on a variety of ways we can identify or categorize buyers so that we can more easily sell to them.

You'll learn how to adjust your sales approach based on five possible key elements. There's as much art as science in understanding others, so your organization will want to make a decision on which they prefer to use in training the sales team. The five include Gender Differences, Personal or Social Styles, Motivation and Decision-Making Preferences, How Buyers Manage Their Buying Process, and the Use of Emotion in Influencing Buyers.

Gender Differences

Perhaps you've heard this joke: Married women spend 85 cents out of every family dollar, children spend 15 cents, and men spend the rest.

In terms of relevance to selling, the biggest difference between men and women is the presence of a powerful chemical in our brains—oxytocin. And women have more of it than men. Please pay attention to some research in neurochemistry—the study of how nerve cells in our brain transmit information both electrically and chemically. Oxytocin is a chemical that creates deeper levels of bonding between two people. Simply put, since women have more of this substance than men, they tend to better connect both physically and emotionally. The most obvious way you'll note this is in facial expressions. Men tend to stay neutral, perhaps keeping a "poker face" to keep others from knowing their feelings. Women are happy to be expressive, and this outlay of emotions helps them better connect with friends, colleagues, and, most importantly for us, buyers.

You will read some significant information on evoking emotion in Chapter 14 on Power Questions. But for now let's just summarize by saying that the purpose of this book is not to be politically correct and state that genders are alike. Science shows us differently, and we need to understand that female buyers might just want a little bit more transparency in our dialogues.

At least spend more time observing the differences between men and women in conversation (you can do this much like a homework exercise). If you choose to respond differently to buyers by gender and experience better results, you've improved performance—and that's the purpose of this book.

Personal or Social Styles

Many assessments are available that pertain to the respondents' personal or social style. The key players include DiSC, Herrmann Brain Dominance Instrument, and the Myers-Briggs Type Indicator. I'll present a quick overview of these assessments and give a quick selling tip for each personal or social type listed.

DiSC

DiSC measures four behavioral "styles." Details are at www.ttidisc.com.

D   Dominance reveals how an individual responds to problems and challenges. This person tends to be confident and controlling. Leaders often exhibit dominance, so lead when you sell to this type.

I   Influence reveals how an individual persuades others. This person tends toward friendly interactions, so be engaging and likeable in order to persuade him or her.

S   Steadiness reveals how an individual responds to the pace of the environment. Slow down with this person; don't rush him or her. Establish rapport and you'll do fine.

C   Compliance reveals how an individual responds to rules and procedures set by others. This detail-oriented person is swayed by facts and figures, so be prepared in order to persuade this person.

Herrmann Brain Dominance Instrument

Here are Herrmann's four different modes of thinking. Details are at www.hbdi.com/.

Analytical thinking	Details, data, facts, and logic prevail with this type of person. Load this person up with information and he or she will be impressed.
Sequential thinking	Structure, systems, and organization are key with this type of person. Show him how your methodology will fit into his in order to sell to this person.

Interpersonal thinking	This person is very physically oriented or tactile. She is an idea people who connects well with others. So show this individual how your solution would contribute to her personally as well as to her team.
Imaginative thinking	This person is a big picture person, very visual. Cast a vision how you can creatively solve his or her problems and talk in terms of the future and long-term thinking.

Myers-Briggs Type Indicator (MBTI)

MBTI has four types, each split into contrasting pairs which form sixteen different types. Detailed descriptions can be found at www.myersbriggs.org/my-mbti-personality-type/mbti-basics/.

- Focus on outer world or inner world: Extraversion or Intraversion. Influence these types based on evidence or speaking toward their personal experience and opinions.

- Information analyzed as is or preference for interpretation and adding meaning: Sensing or Intuition. Influence this type by showing him or her data or by asking for his or her thinking on the subject.

- Decisions related to logic or the individual and his or her circumstances: Thinking or Feeling. Influence this type by reasoning or by focusing on emotion.

- Structure related to just making the decision or preference to be open to new information and options: Judging or Perceiving. Influence this type by helping the person finalize a decision or by working through plenty of possibilities related to your solution.

This isn't really about what personality or social style is better; they're each just different. The point is to understand and respect the diversity of your buyers. Don't treat them all the same. Again, being mentally flexible is the key, after considering the other person's preferred way of thinking or behaving.

The next section offers another choice based on newer psychologically sound information. You'll find the information fascinating and can be geared toward hiring great salespeople as well as better influencing buyers.

Motivation and Decision-Making Preferences

New research on motivation and decision making has revealed over forty individual strategies for decision making (see www.ModelofSalesExcellence.com). It would be crazy to try to teach all of them to sales professionals, so the five most important ones are described here:

1. *Buyers who move toward new ideas rather than away from them.* Recognize the difference and you gain the key to influencing either type using either benefits or pain. Train salespeople in how to utilize both of these strategies.

2. *Buyers who make decisions based on evidence versus personal experience.* Sell the first type with lots of testimonials, data, and conversation about what the competition is doing. The other type is sold by catering to his or her experience and personal beliefs.

3. *Buyers who love to work under systems versus those who are creative and like to "wing it."* Persuade the first type by showing how smoothly your methodology fits into his or her systems. The second type loves flexibility, so show him or her how to implement, then utilize your solution in a variety of ways.

4. *Buyers who look at the big picture versus detail-oriented types.* Show the long view to the first type, how your solution will have an over-arching impact on the whole organization over time. For the other type, show how detailed and intricate your solution is.

5. *Buyers are convinced through one of four ways: reading information or using their eyes, ears, or feelings to process information.* Send readers lots of marketing literature, white papers, and web resources to absorb. The visual person is sold based on imagery, colors, and language that uses words like see, look, or envision. The auditory person is influenced by listening to audio and language-like sounds such as ringing a bell and more. The kinesthetic person is convinced through handling product and solutions with language about touch and connecting and getting a handle on your offering. Details of these last three or VAK are available in Chapter 15.

I highly recommend assessing your sales team with this tool. You can actually create a model to match your top performers, so that you can hire people who will most likely perform at those levels. In addition, once the reps discover their motivation and decision-making patterns, it'll help them recognize the patterns in buyers.

Assessing buyer behavior and motivation is one of the most significant additions you can make to existing training. Most of my consulting work is redesigning sales training by adding these elements (and more). They form the foundation of my program called *The Secret Language of Influence*®.

How Buyers Manage Their Buying Process

Many buyers don't have a system for analyzing choices. Others have a system, but aren't aware of it. For example, think of all the pieces that need to be in place for your solution to fit an organization. Miller, Heiman, and Tuleja (1985) first pointed this out in their book, *Strategic Selling*, when they identified four different types of buyers. These included *coach* (a champion inside or outside the organization), *user* (the person or department that would be utilizing your solution), *technical* (those who fit your solution into the company's infrastructure, like adding a new software program), and *economic* (the person who signs the check). They form the acronym CUTE. It is important to be aware that you must approach each of these types differently to influence the sales process.

Since the publication of this book, a new champion of understanding buying processes has come from Sharon Drew Morgen's *Buyer Facilitation*®, a process whereby you can help a buyer identify his or her strategy and walk the person through that discovery. You can't develop a much better relationship with a buyer than this. You solve an ongoing problem, help make decisions about solutions, and see how deeply embedded you become and how grateful your new client is for your help. Look at Morgen's ideas at http://sharondrewmorgen.com/.

Use of Emotion in Influencing Buyers

Neuroeconomics is a fairly new field that focuses on how people make decisions. There are some fascinating books on this, most notably Jonah Lehrer's *How We Decide* (2009). Anyone who sells, manages, or trains salespeople should own this book. One common theme in the research has been neglected in the sales world.

That theme is emotion. There are always emotional elements during the decision-making process. We've always known that people buy emotionally, then rationalize their decision with logic. So when I say "neglected" I mean we have the knowledge that emotion is a factor, but we don't understand how to create an environment in which emotion is evident in a sales call. Great sales professionals have some proficiency in evoking emotion with a buyer. This is covered in Chapter 14 on Power Questions. I recently wrote an article on this topic. You can get additional details by asking me for it at Dan@GotInfluenceInc.com.

This chapter has offered a lot of detail, including new ideas on understanding buyers. Choose those of interest and begin to gain some knowledge, even expertise, on this topic.

Some keys to remember include:

- Today, buyers are better at buying than sellers are at selling. (Do you recall the three reasons?)

- We have to distinguish ourselves from mediocre reps.

- Great sales professionals seek first to understand how a buyer thinks and makes decisions before presenting ideas or solutions.

Chapter 7

Potent Proposals

The purpose of this chapter is to help sales professionals create dynamic proposals that help sell their services and products.

The Big One That Got Away

One of my worst sales calls, ever. Whenever I was selling sales training and didn't land a deal it was bad, but this experience made no sense. I'd been referred to a company that had two full-time sales support people preparing proposals for the selling team. That's a lot of contracts being sent out every month.

We actually quantified the value of their time. The simple, rough calculation that helped me dollarize cost of the problem was this: (support team salaries x benefits) + (sales reps' annual earnings + benefits) / percentage of time with prospects).

We measured the value (or expense or anguish) of the time sales reps put in because these salespeople had a ridiculous 10 percent of their proposals accepted!

Would you be frustrated at closing 10 percent of your proposals? This isn't 10 percent of your prospects. It's 10 percent of the buyers you'd decided deserved lots of time educating and gathering details about their needs. You trusted they were well qualified if you'd gotten this far in the sales process. Well, the answer to that cost calculation was very, very painful for the owners.

Total company cost/investment/waste = $250,000

It cost the company a quarter of a million dollars every year to prepare proposals that weren't being accepted (company perspective) or rejected (reps' perspective) or ignored (by the buyer).

My problem was that the owners just wouldn't spend $12,000 to have me train the sales team to identify a real prospect. The firm was stuck in a rut and didn't see that an investment of twelve grand would actually save the company 250 grand each year.

Excuses? The owners liked the support people, who'd been on staff for years. They didn't know how easy it would be to get all the reps together to train (really? Who's in charge of the ship?). They didn't want to offend buyers by refusing to craft proposals (buyers who cared nothing for the company for a variety of reasons, as you'll see in the top ten list that follows). Now what do you do with a prospect like this?

I had helped them identify both the emotional and logical (financial) impact of the problem. They understood that this was bad, very bad, for reps, who were quite discouraged each time they were asked to prepare documents for a prospect. They recognized that buyers were using them, simply so a high-priced proposal could be eliminated during the decision-making process.

They even accepted the fact that they were considered a joke in their industry, since competitors knew they could always beat these boys at the bargaining table.

I wasn't wasting a moment more of my time, energy, or emotional investment with these jokers. When I walked away I told myself (and later my client who referred me to them), "Sometimes, even when you have a great solution, a perfect solution, you just can't help someone who is stupid."

Now healthy self-talk is important, but isn't the purpose of this story (see Mental Health for Sales Pros, Chapter 28). The reason you're reading this tale is to warn you of the primary danger in creating proposals. That is, you'd better know you have a great shot at closing the deal, perhaps 75 to 90 percent, before you put the time into the creation process.

Do Your Proposals Allow Prospects to Steal Your Brainpower?

(Including a list of the top ten reasons why a prospect demands a proposal.)

How many of us continually invest precious sales time to draft a bid, actually pouring years of experience and expertise into this written gamble at acquiring business?

One reason most of us are so quick to accommodate potential clients is that we really do want to please people. Think of how ridiculous it would sound if you refused to provide materials to your prospect! So you and I are very likely to assume that a request for a proposal is a *yes* indicator. It reinforces our hope that we've just moved one step closer to closing the sale.

There is, however, the prospect's perspective. If we don't understand what might really be going on with that request, we could spend endless hours creating and delivering documents for people who have no intention of buying our products or services. And here's why.

Prospects love free consulting. They give you their biggest smiles and drain your brain of all its problem-solving knowledge before you understand their true intentions. And they love it even more in print than in person. If you don't have a strategy for dealing with proposal requests, you're at the mercy of every potential client. Over the past twenty years, I've analyzed many of the top sales training organizations. It's interesting to note that virtually all the great training systems have the wisdom to recognize and teach how critical it is for a salesperson *not* to give everyone proposals simply because they are requested. To help you understand the dangers of proposal writing, here's a list you'll learn from.

The Top Ten Reasons a Prospect Demands a Proposal (*The impact to you is in parentheses.*)

10. They need to keep their current vendors honest. (*What a surprise—you never had a prayer of getting the business.*)

9. They want a fair range of prices for the type of service you offer. (*Thanks for the quote. The business is going to the prospect's brother-in-law, at just below your rate.*)

8. They want to keep themselves up-to-date on the latest business ideas, processes, and technologies. (*Thanks for the education. Goodbye.*)

7. They think your product or service sounds interesting. (*But they have no intention of buying!*)

6. They need new and better ideas—to make their own changes. (*Thanks for your free consulting; that really hurts, doesn't it?*)

5. They just wonder how much it would cost. (*Wow, you're really expensive!*)

4. This request will get you off their back. (*Oops, you forgot to qualify the prospect, didn't you?*)

3. They can look good when they pass your information to the real decision-maker. (*Did you spend all that time with the wrong person?*)

2. They honestly need their problems solved. (*Too bad you don't know who sent the other eight proposals, what they charge, and maybe what they're saying about you.*) And the number one reason prospects make you pour your blood, sweat, and tears into a proposal:

1. A prospect can lie to a salesperson and still get into heaven! (*Commonly attributed to the late sales training guru David Sandler.*)

Final Thoughts on the Dangers of Proposal Preparation

Proposals are exciting. To the rep they offer assurance that their investment in the prospect is near fruition. They also offer false hope to too many sales reps. You want to ask yourself: Do you really believe that everyone asking for a customized, written solution is ready to buy?

Please, please, stop wasting your time jumping through hoops to design proposals for everyone who nods his head or grunts into your telephone. *Qualify first* (Chapter 12, Qualifying and Disqualifying Prospects), and then begin to work with your best potential clients. Your organization should have some criteria regarding what defines a quality prospect. Use them, or immediately create your own to save yourself from sales heartbreak.

If you don't quickly sort the good prospects from the time-wasters, bad prospects can sabotage your income. Set accurate, realistic expectations about who will buy from you. Showboating in print for prospects who have no intention of doing business with you is simply foolish.

Now that we have clarity on what to avoid, let's look at healthy proposal writing practices you should adopt.

Quality Contracts That Close Business

The best model I've encountered for designing proposals comes from Alan Weiss, one of the top consultants on the planet. He's one of those rare, elite business professionals whose wisdom is so profound and useful that I see him in person every chance I get. I also read anything he writes. I recommend his best-selling *Million Dollar Consulting* (2009) to anyone who sells anything. You'll find numerous references to his books in the resource section. He has several newsletters that reflect his brilliant business approaches. You will find them full of great humor and loads of aha! moments. Discover them at www.SummitConsulting.com.

Alan Weiss was gracious enough to allow us to use his model for proposals from his book *How to Write a Proposal That's Accepted Every Time* (2009).

What follows are his structures for both complex and simple agreements. Notice the use of the term "agreement," rather than proposal. Weiss assumes the close when he prepares these documents. Frame your proposal as he suggests:

A proposal is a summation, not an exploration. It confirms conceptual agreement between the consultant and buyer and demonstrates options, with attendant returns on investment (ROI).

In other words, you are not "casting a vision" as to how you and the buyer can work together. You are preparing this document because you and the buyer have decided that this is exactly how you'll begin working together. This assumes you have strong face-to-face conversation, demonstrating questioning and listening skills as identified in all the best practices of this guide.

I used to walk into large sales opportunities, casting a vision as to how we might work together. Alan Weiss mentored me directly to stop doing that. The impact on my ability (and now, I trust, yours) to close more business has been profound. Again, proposals are summaries of the working relationship, not printed pitches that exhibit your imagination and dreams about what might happen.

The proposal structure you're about to read is well detailed. Following it is a lightweight version for those who prefer a one- or two-page working document. I recommend that you always use a checklist like the sample prior to actually designing and writing up your proposal.

SAMPLE PROPOSAL CHECKLIST

☐ *Conceptual agreement reached previously:*

    ☐ Objectives: What business outcomes are to be achieved?

    ☐ Measures: What indicators will demonstrate progress and fulfillment?

    ☐ Value: What is the impact on the client organization of these objectives?

☐ All components completed:

    ☐ Situation appraisal: What is the reason for the proposal in general?

    ☐ Objectives.

    ☐ Measures.

    ☐ Value.

    ☐ Timing: What are the anticipated launch and completion dates?

    ☐ Methodology and options: What are the choices for implementation?

    ☐ Joint accountabilities: Who is responsible for what?

    ☐ Terms and conditions: What are the fees and how are they to be paid?

    ☐ Acceptance: What options are desired and will you agree to these terms?

☐ Logistics completed:

    ☐ FedEx two copies signed by you.

    ☐ Establish in the cover letter your follow-up date to call client.

Quick thought on proposals—it is most highly recommended that you offer your client three options, so their decision is which one to choose, rather than "yes" or "no" to your summary.

Sample Complex Proposal

Appraisal of the Situation

You have begun a major reorganization with the intent of improving supervision.

You are seeking to ensure at minimum a continuation of the present levels of effectiveness during the approximately six-month transition period and to improve that effectiveness still further upon completion of the new structure.

The new organization will rely heavily on a matrix management approach and will need the active support and ownership of virtually all employees at every level for ultimate success. You are seeking objective, skilled, third-party assistance to safeguard the transition and guarantee the efficacy of the approaches used during the transition period. In addition, you require ideas, insights, and proven methods used in similar situations elsewhere to deal with known dynamics such as a somewhat cynical employee base (by nature of the job), perceptions by some of diminished responsibilities, a loss of focus on the work product itself, and so on.

Objectives

The objectives of this consulting assistance include, but are not limited to:

- Adding value to the supervisory process for XXX.
- Increasing the effectiveness of supervision.
- Securing employee ownership of the changes, especially among formal and informal leadership.
- Bringing to bear world class techniques from superb organizations that have undergone similar transitions.
- Preventing problems before the more expensive and sometimes embarrassing contingent actions must be used.
- Using the opportunity to improve teamwork, prevent elitism, and build skills in matrix resource sharing and apportionment.

Sample Complex Proposal, Cont'd

- Institutionalizing knowledge and keeping turnover of needed talent to a minimum.

Measures of Success

Progress toward the objectives will be measured by:

- Feedback opportunities created for employees to inform management.
- Actual observations and anecdotal information collected by management.
- Anticipation of and responsiveness to supervisory priorities.
- Over the longer term, more effective supervision for XXX.
- Completion of the transition within a six-month period.

Value to XXX

The value of this project appears to be multifold, including:

- Improved supervision.
- Faster and more appropriate responsiveness.
- Protection and retention of key talent.
- Demonstration that major changes can be managed by existing staff without loss of focus or effectiveness on normal priorities.
- Avoidance of productivity loss by employees by focusing on the future and the job outputs, and not the transition and perceived disadvantages.
- Even greater stature in the eyes of XXX.

Timing

The transition itself is estimated to take six months, which is a reasonable expectation, barring unforeseen developments. I am able to begin within a week of your approval, provided that it is forthcoming by mid-February.

Methodology and Options

Three possible levels of interaction can be effective for this project, depending on the degree of help and participation you desire from your consultant:

Sample Complex Proposal, Cont'd

1. **Advisory.** In this capacity I would serve as your backstage resource, meeting with the small team charged with effecting the transition. The role would include being a sounding board for plans, source for ideas and techniques as well as implementation steps, devil's advocate on key moves, third-party objective review source, and facilitator of the transition process itself. We would meet as often as needed and without constraint. I would be constantly accessible by phone and email for document review and advice, and I estimate the time together to encompass about ninety days, or the first half of the transition period.

2. **Consultative.** In addition to the responsibilities and contributions of Option 1, I would also work with selected managers, team leaders, and others to help them individually with their roles in the transition and with their accountabilities as exemplars to others; recommend adjustments to systems and procedures that require modification to work optimally within the new structure; attend predetermined work meetings to evaluate the effectiveness of critical elements (e.g., resource sharing, responsiveness, honesty, equality of various elements); and be available to selected others at their request in addition to the primary team. I estimate that this involvement would last for the duration of the transition period, about six months.

3. **Collaborative.** In addition to the roles described in both Options 1 and 2, I would recommend specific work distribution changes; recommend appropriate personnel changes; provide specific skills development and/or counseling to any employees identified as requiring it by the primary team; and XXX. This option includes an audit at a future point determined by you (I suggest six months after the completed transition) to measure results against the baseline previously established. The involvement here would entail about nine months (ninety days post-transition completion) and the additional later audit.

Note that all options include unlimited access to my time and help within the parameters described.

Sample Complex Proposal, Cont'd

Joint Accountabilities

You would be responsible for internal scheduling, reasonable access to key personnel, on-site administrative support, and reasonable access to past and current documentation that would aid the project. I would sign all required nondisclosure and confidentiality agreements and would provide all administrative support off-site. We agree to immediately apprise each other of any intelligence or findings that would impact the success of the project so that rapid action could be considered. I am covered by comprehensive errors and omissions insurance.

Terms and Conditions

I never assess an hourly or daily fee, since you should not have to make an investment decision every time my assistance may be needed, nor should your people have to seek permission to spend money if they need my help. This is a unique feature of my consulting practice.

Fees for the options are:

Option 1: $45,000

Option 2: $72,000

Option 3: $126,000

These fees are *inclusive* of expenses, so long as all work required is in the general XXX area. All travel, administrative, logistical, and communication expenses are included, so there is no further amount due for any option.

Payment terms for any of the options are:

Fifty percent due on acceptance of this proposal.

Fifty percent due forty-five days after acceptance.

We offer a courtesy discount of 10 percent when the full fee is paid upon acceptance.

This project, once approved, is not cancelable for any reason, although it may be delayed, rescheduled, and otherwise postponed without any penalty whatsoever. My work is guaranteed. In the event you feel that I am not meeting the stan-

Sample Complex Proposal, Cont'd

dards described herein or based on our mutual conversations and agreements, I will refund your entire fee upon such notification.

Acceptance

Your signature below indicates acceptance of this proposal and the terms and conditions herein. Alternatively, your initial payment per the terms above will also represent acceptance of this proposal.

Please check the option you prefer: __ #1 __ #2 __ #3

For Summit Consulting Group, Inc.:   For XXX:

Signature:_____   Signature:_____

Name: Alan Weiss, Ph.D.   Name: _____

Title: President   Title: _____

Date: February 3, 20XX   Date: _____

Used by permission of Alan Weiss. http://summitconsulting.com/

EXERCISE 7.1. Practicing Proposal Writing

SETUP: Each of the elements of Dr. Weiss's proposal model are built to show the client you have clarity on his or her needs and can quantify your value, and therefore you'll have maximum impact in your ability to close a higher percentage of these printed works of art. In the following exercise, everyone should at least be able to list the language he or she would use in a simulated sales opportunity.

Sales professionals, create bullet points for each of the elements in order to understand how to build a powerful proposal. Simply write out a simulated sale, based on a recent opportunity you had. Be sure to use assumptive language, such as "when" or "as we work together," rather than weak words like "if" or "should you choose." You have fifteen minutes.

Here again is the outline of the pieces of the proposal puzzle:

EXERCISE 7.1. Practicing Proposal Writing, Cont'd

Proposal Checklist

☐ Conceptual agreement reached previously:

   ☐ Objectives: What business outcomes are to be achieved?

   ☐ Measures: What indicators will demonstrate progress and fulfillment?

   ☐ Value: What is the impact on the client organization of these objectives?

☐ All components completed:

   ☐ Situation appraisal: What is the reason for the proposal in general?

   ☐ Objectives

   ☐ Measures

Value

☐ Timing: What are the anticipated launch and completion dates?

☐ Methodology and options: What are the choices for implementation?

☐ Joint accountabilities: Who is responsible for what?

☐ Terms and conditions: What are the fees and how are they to be paid?

☐ Acceptance: What options are desired and will you agree to these terms?

☐ Logistics completed:

   ☐ FedEx two copies signed by you.

   ☐ Establish in the cover letter your follow-up date to call client.

After fifteen minutes, ask volunteers to share any one element of their proposal with the group. Everyone should take notes when they hear language that they would like to use in their own writing.

Companies should create a template from this model and use it. If you want an original source from which to build this, buy Weiss's book, *Million Dollar Consulting Toolkit* (2005). You'll find it quickly at Amazon.com.

Here's a lightweight template I promised you, for those who have less complex proposal needs.

Sample Simple Letter of Agreement Template

I'm providing a summary of our discussion of January 19, which provided the basis for our working relationship for 2005. There are to be ten areas of involvement:

1. Monthly meetings between the two of us to discuss strategy, longer-term issues, and personal growth goals.

2. Personal development for each business head, based on a series of ongoing meetings I plan with Tim, Frances, Bob, and Brittany. These will be individualized and mutually agreed on. In addition, I'll serve as a sounding board for them as they work to achieve their business goals. You will apprise them of this support.

3. Partnership with Jim, wherein I will assist him in contributing to the business as a senior manager and internal consultant, not merely as a human resource facilitator. This will be a global focus and will include improving the caliber of human resource professionals and hires. I have already established a preliminary discussion.

4. Responding to other key managers on an as-needed basis. You (or the business heads) will apprise them of this support.

5. Work with Jim to set up and facilitate the next top-level review group, to assess value-added of people and positions.

6. Specifically work with the relevant managers to establish:
    -   A succession plan and ensuing development plan.
    -   A comprehensive educational plan for the organization.
    -   Clarity of field management's role, development, and key personnel.
    -   Sales analysis tools for effectively monitoring and managing business.

7. Situational responsiveness to needs that arise that you deem require my assistance, not covered elsewhere.

8. Assistance in the preparation and delivery of the February sales meeting.

9. Working with the relevant managers to strengthen employee communications, particularly in areas of trust, credibility, and recognizing the importance of everyone's contributions.

Sample Simple Letter of Agreement Template, Cont'd

10. Quarterly meeting with Trevor to provide assistance as he sees fit, including suggestions for what he can be doing to enhance performance.

To accomplish these goals, I will increase my time allocation by about 20 percent. Historically, we've both honored schedules very well, and some months might be close to 75 percent and others 10 percent, but the average will hold.

The total fee will be $100,000, of which $32,500 has already been paid. The remaining $67,500 will be paid in ten equal installments of $6,750 from March through December. Expenses will be billed monthly, as they are now. I'll provide a monthly summary sheet of focus and results.

Let me know if I've missed anything. I've already received a call from Ron, and I'll be seeing him on some information system (IS) issues in February. I'll also be scheduling our time together with Fran in the next day or so. It's a pleasure to have somewhere to go once again during such cold weather. . . .

Cancellation Clause Templates

Note: These may be used for any event or project, from a complex sale to consulting, and from coaching to facilitation.

- This project is not cancelable for any reason. However, it may be postponed, delayed, and/or rescheduled without penalty or time limit, subject only to mutually agreeable dates and times. All payments must be made per the existing payment schedule in this agreement.

- Cancellation of this project will incur no penalty if made ninety days or more from the start date [event date, etc.]; a penalty of 25 percent if made between sixty-one and eighty-nine days from that date; a penalty of 50 percent if made between thirty-one and sixty days of that date; and a 100 percent penalty if made within thirty days of that date. Penalties are due at the time of cancellation. No services are due in the event of such cancellations.

Cancellation Clause Templates, Cont'd

- This project may be canceled by either party without penalty up to sixty days in advance of the commencement date. Subsequent to that date, if you cancel, you agree to pay a 50 percent cancellation fee up to ten days prior to the event, and a 75 percent cancellation fee within ten days of the event. If I am unable to provide the services described or must cancel within sixty days of commencement, I will provide a replacement of equal caliber agreeable to you for the existing fees agreed on, or I will return all advance payments made and we will nullify the agreement.

Additional clause for protection and comfort:

- I stand behind and assure you of the quality of my work, and will refund your entire fee if you find evidence that I have not performed in a professional and ethical manner consistent with the actions agreed on in this document.

An alternative protection clause:

- If you find that the objectives for this project are not being met according to the measures of success that we have agreed on, I will continue to work on the project at no additional fee beyond expense reimbursement until we concur that the objectives are met. Failing that, I will refund all fees paid.

These Weiss models should serve you and your organization well. Find Alan Weiss and his rich resource of articles, products, and training at www. SummitConsulting.com.

The Most Expensive Writers in the World

Tom Sant was the original designer of a software company to help companies create proposals. Automate the proposal process and you save tons of time. But every sales professional, from the C-suite down to the rep engaging prospects, should know the costs of creating his or her proposals. Remember management expert Peter Drucker's famous phrase, "If you can't measure it, you can't manage it." The text below, based on Sant's thoughts and formulas, should serve to help you measure those costs.

> *If they're doing their own letters, proposals, and presentations, your salespeople are probably among the most expensive writers in the world. And to make matters worse, they're probably not very good at it either. Typically, it takes a salesperson hours to write a proposal. That's time spent in front of a computer instead of a customer. What does this yearly investment cost?*

> *Here are three ways to calculate the outrageous cost of a Maverick's many proposals. Note: Insert your own figures into each calculation to find your "burn" rate. While this includes some simple mathematical calculations, the value of knowing what it costs to generate proposals is something you'll want to be aware of.*

> Salesperson's Salary = $100,000

> Hourly Salary Rate = $50

> (Salary/2000 hours: 50 weeks × 40 hours)

> Hours Invested per Proposal = 12

> Number of Proposals per Year = 10

> Annual Quota per Salesperson = $1,000,000

> Hourly Quota Rate = $500

> (Quota/2000 hours: 50 weeks × 40 hours)

> Value of Proposal in Sales Dollars = $50,000

Your sales people are probably among the most expensive writers in the world. And to make matters worse, they're probably not very good at it either.

1. **Costs based on salary formula:**

   Hours Invested per Proposal × Number of Proposals per Year × Hourly Salary Rate: Calculation is 12 × 10 × $50 = $6,000.

   Portion of salary burned yearly in proposal writing: $6,000!

2. **Costs based on sales quota formula:**

   Hours Invested per Proposal × Number of Proposals per Year × Hourly Quota Rate: Calculation is 12 × 10 × $500 = $60,000

   Portion of quota burned yearly in proposal writing: $60,000!

3. **Costs based on proposal value formula:**

   Value of Proposal in Sales Dollars / Hours Invested per Proposal = $4,167 per hour.

   Next: Hourly Rate by Proposal Value × Hours per Proposal × Number of Proposals per Year.

   Calculation is 4,167 × 12 × 10 × $50,000.

   Portion of proposal value burned annually in proposal writing: more than a half-million dollars! Other than Stephen King or John Grisham, nobody is making that kind of money writing!

Tom Sant is the author of the books *Persuasive Business Proposals, The Giants of Sales,* and *The Language of Success.*

Tom's company provides consulting and training to help clients write winning proposals. Find him online at www.hydeparkpartnerscal.com.

EXERCISE 7.2. Calculating Costs

Reps will take each of these three calculations and write down their personal (salary, quota, size of sale, etc.) to identify whether they're true sales pros or fiction writers.

SETUP: Here the learners will do a quick exercise to see what it costs just to craft a proposal. The purpose of this is to raise sensitivity about creating documents for buyers that are not qualified and are simply wasting valuable selling time.

A quick note on this topic, from the buyers' perspectives: Proposals give buyers a fair indication of the choices available. While they might have some flexibility in choosing based on their face-to-face experience with the rep or past history with the firm, many buyers' primary responsibility is to save their company money while choosing the best vendor. Price isn't always the key criterion. In fact, with complex proposals, there might be so many factors that price literally gets lost in the decision-making process. Here's another factor that every sales pro should know about buyers: While making the "best" choice, they also want to make the "safest" choice. That is, "safest" for their careers, their reputations, and eventually for their performance reviews (which affect income, advancement, and more). You must help buyers feel that their best interest on a personal and professional level is your highest priority.

Key Proposal Concepts

- You must have qualified your buyer before even discussing a proposal.
- Proposals are summaries, not vision-casting exercises or fiction writing.
- Offer three options when creating your proposal.

Chapter 8

Pre-Work for the Sales Call

CHAPTER OVERVIEW

Pre-Work Questions

    Exercise 8.1. Preparing for Questions

Pre-work is critical to the selling professional who wants to be prepared for any possible type of resistance, as well as to show the buyer how serious he or she is about engaging in a relationship with the buyer's firm. At the end of this chapter, you will find an excellent checklist to use prior to meeting your buyer.

Beating Sugar Ray

When I first met Waldo, he was pumping his fist in the air at a conference shouting, "I kicked Sugar Ray Leonard's ass!"

Rob "Waldo" Waldman is a friend of mine who flew F-16 fighter jets in Yugoslavia and Iraq. He completed sixty-five combat missions, went on to become a flight instructor, attained his MBA, then served as a vice president of sales for both a major software company and a mergers and acquisitions firm.

As the story goes, Waldo was being considered to speak at a sales conference. The corporate sponsor called to apologize for the bad news, saying that, instead of Waldo, they were going to hire boxing hall-of-famer, Sugar Ray Leonard.

His response: *"Sugar Ray? Are you serious? Do you know how much money he makes, whether he loses or wins a fight? He just has to show up and get paid. How's that a role model for salespeople?"*

"Well, Waldo, the meeting committee. . . ."

"Hang on! One other thing. Do you know, in combat, if I make the wrong decision what happens? I don't make it home for dinner that night—I die. I can't afford to lose. That's how you want your sales team to think. So my question is, which message would you like to send to them?"

The man said, "Good point. Let me conference call the committee and revisit this."

The next day they reversed their decision, Sugar Ray was out, and Waldo was in.

Here is a guy who has some serious consequences to his decision making. He has fractions of a second to make a choice. If he's wrong, he's the one who pays—with his life.

How's that for an incentive to make the right call the first time, every time?

Pre-Work Questions

So what distinguishes the best fighter pilots in the world from those who crash and burn? Waldo and his fellow aviators go through what they call "Mission Rehearsal." They know exactly what success looks like, but they create a contingency plan that covers multiple "what-if" scenarios:

Engine failure—At what point do you solve the problem or hit the eject button?

Weather changes—If you fly above or below the weather, it affects fuel consumption, flight time, and more.

Airfield changes—Hey, if your landing strip is bombed and you can't land, you'd better know what your second choice is and how fast and far to get there.

Plane loss—Whether mechanical or combat-related, who takes the lead when the leader is gone?

These scenarios are played out so that the pilot knows *exactly* what to do in the heat of combat.

So does Waldo rehearse doing his mission perfectly? Not much. He spends most of his time practicing for disaster. That runs a bit counter to the concept we've been taught in life—picture your success, imagine everything going smoothly and it will. Waldo rehearses the mistakes, then practices the fixes, until each possible problem is handled to 100,000 percent perfection in his mind.

Some rehearsals are done in a flight simulator. However, he does "chair flying" in his head long before doing it for real or on the computer. Waldo told me he chair-flies at his desk, in his car, even on the toilet! These preparation skills have transitioned Waldo Waldman into a tremendous success on the sales battlefield. By religiously rehearsing every possible bump in his selling road, my pilot friend is never surprised. He therefore comes across as confident and authentic. And that breeds trust, a critical tool to sales success.

EXERCISE 8.1. Preparing for Questions

SETUP: Too many salespeople wander into meetings unprepared and ready to "wing it." Some experienced sellers even brag about their ability to handle things as they pop up. This isn't in the best interest of the company or the sales representative. Additionally, it can set a poor example, which can stunt the growth of salespeople who are still in the early learning stages.

Let's think about these questions: "What goes on in your mind before you walk into a sales call? How do you prepare?"

Expect answers like "I know how to achieve rapport," "I check out their website," or "I looked the buyer up on LinkedIn."

Ask learners to share their answers out loud. Then ask the group what information is most important to have beforehand.

Every organization can vary on what it wants its sales professionals to do in preparation for a call. Here are some best practices for you to adapt those you choose to use:

- *Details on the company.* A Google search, a subscription to Hoover's, a conversation with some key employees—any or all of these can prepare you to understand current news, stock status, clients, and more. In fact, if you are serious enough about landing this client, you should minimally have printed off their marketing materials online. Better yet, get your hands on their good print matter instead. Equally potent—use Google Alerts to find out what's being said and published on the web about your prospect. (See www.google.com/alerts) (*Hint:* How about using this for competitors, too?)

- *Details about the person you're meeting.* Is it the actual decision-maker? Can you identify whether he or she will be a user of your solution? The technology implementer? An internal champion or advisor? The economic buyer? This will help you understand whether there are hidden decision-makers you need access to in order to sell to the proper prospects. You should also spend some time on social networks, such as LinkedIn to start and certainly others. Look at previous companies. Who recommends this person and why. Don't ignore some insights you can gain from more personal social sources like Facebook, if the person has a public profile.

- *How you connected.* This is the starting point for bonding, even before you utilize rapport-building skills. Is this a referral? Or a cold call? A lead generated from marketing? Be prepared to open with a comment on how you first connected: "Bill thought we should meet, and I'm glad we could match up our schedules. How do you know him?" [referrals] "I am glad you took my call and felt this was important enough to sit down over." [cold call] "You contacted us from that magazine ad. What was it exactly that made you respond?" [marketing lead]

- *Manage your mental health.* There are plenty of ideas about this in Chapter 28, such as strengthening your self-talk, focusing on what's good, and more. What type of affirmation do you say or tell yourself before you walk into that meeting? It might be a personal comment like: "I'm great at solving my clients' problems." It might be a thought focused on the meeting itself like: "This will be fascinating finding out how much this buyer needs our help." It might simply be an encouraging thought like: "I love doing this and love the people like this who help feed my family." Slap on that smile, a genuine smile. Tell yourself something uplifting and get ready to shake that buyer's hand.

- *Why you connected.* Have you written down exactly why this person agreed to meet, because that's the starting point of your conversation. "Ms. Prospect, you invited me because you said that problems with hiring telemarketing team members were lowering the quality of leads generated for the sales team. Could you tell me a bit more about that?" This gets you into the meat of the dialogue. It's about gaining a clear understanding of your prospect's situation (before pitching what you do).

- *Define your purpose.* Is this meeting to ascertain whether there's a fit, then to set the next steps? If your focus is clearly defined, it's easier to be professional and share it with the buyer. Is the meeting to figure out whether we should do an in-depth analysis of how our solution works? Is it to share some ideas with the person, so that he or she can set up a meeting with higher-ups? Is the meeting defined by the buyer's agenda? Better find out what the common goal is, then lay it out. This tests how serious the prospect is. When you tell the buyer that you'll spend forty-five minutes to determine XYZ, at which point you'll set another meeting, and he or she won't commit to the agenda, you have a problem. Getting common cause is really about early qualifying or disqualifying steps to determine whether you should pursue this person any further.

- *Prepare for resistance.* Do you have a log of the top six objections, with the responses you've determined work for you? I coach everyone I train to have this printout with them. Keep it in the car or next to the phone at all times—until you've completely memorized multiple responses to each possible objection. Remember, you want to casually and confidently respond to any resistance from prospects so you can advance the sale closer to the close.

- *Prepare your power questions.* You'll work on creating these powerful data-gathering queries in Chapter 14. Every sales pro should have five fantastic questions he wants the answers to so that buyers understand the consequences of their decisions on the deepest level. Quick example (and one of my personal favorites): "How long has this been going on, and what other solutions haven't worked in the past?"

- *Revisit the purpose defined earlier.* At the end of the call, remind the client what you agreed the next step would be. Remind the buyer right where you both are and where and when you want to be next. If there isn't a next, it means this is a "no" or a "yes." Either way, be gracious and professional. No? Then wish them good luck figuring out their solution. Yes? Tell them they made a smart decision and start the steps of your fulfillment process.

If you want to create a form to use, here's one based on the elements from this chapter. Adapt it to your needs. You get the picture.

Pre-Work Template

Details on the company		
Role of the person you're meeting		
How you connected		
Manage your mental health		
Why you connected		
Define your purpose		
Prepare for resistance?		
Prepare your power questions		
Revisit the purpose defined earlier		

I really encourage sales managers to have their team members do pre-work and do a debriefing (there's a great one in Chapter 20). Understand that every buyer would prefer to work with the most professional organization available. When a buyer's first impression of a sales pro is truly professional, there's a sense from the buyer that he or she is in a good place, a safe place. When that rep shows up with an agenda, no time is being wasted. When the rep is thorough about gathering and sharing information, mutual respect is formed. All the information is laid out, and together the rep and prospect can determine whether there's a fit between the prospect's needs and the seller's solution.

Create your company's Pre-Work Template and have your salespeople file it in their CRMs. It is a highly valuable resource for support personnel and others who will be engaged with your new client.

Part Two

Training the
Sales Pro to Sell

Part Two is where we get into the heart of sales training. Here you'll find all the expected modules for a selling system and much more. What's unique? Pay particular attention to Chapter 11 on Opening the First Meeting, which has perhaps the most important strategy you'll ever adapt into a selling system. Also Chapter 12, Qualifying and Disqualifying Prospects, will help you manage the number one problem sales pros face. The powerful Ultimate Objection-Handling Tool in Chapter 16 is the most fun work I do with clients and most highly valuable as well. You'll also find out exactly when to use pain versus when to use benefits in Chapter 17. (*Hint:* it's a question whereby the buyer identifies what he prefers to work with.) Finally, get ready to create your own quick, intense Debriefing the Call in Chapter 20 to increase learning and behavior change from sales call to sales call.

Chapter 9

Establishing Rapport

There are psychologically sound principles you can use to generate rapport with buyers. In this chapter you learn the three-step, Match, Pace, Lead model for connecting with your prospects. We'll even visit some of the ideas from the chapter on listening, because that skill is integral to attaining rapport.

Foot in Mouth Chokes Sale

Rick sells printing services, and he's probably not as good as he is persistent. It took six months of phone calls, mailing literature, and fighting with the gatekeeper to finally get into the president's office of a company that the rep wanted to sell to very badly.

He finally nailed this guy down to an appointment and, as he's led down the hall to the man's office (by that gatekeeper), Rick thought about how badly he wanted to make a good first impression. This president would look at him as either a strong, persistent salesman or a pest. The buyer would probably dispose of a pest as quickly as he could. So as Rick walked into the executive's office, he looked for a rapport-building opportunity— something on the wall or on the man's desk to use for a little opening small talk.

There it was! "John Madden!" he cried, pointing at an 8 by 10 photograph on the prospect's credenza. Every sports fan knows the 300-plus-pound commentator. He's probably the best announcer around, in spite of a fact that could stop a bus. "That's a fantastic photo! How did you get a picture of yourself with your arm around John Madden?"

Rick's rapport-building efforts crashed in flames as the shocked company president slowly answered, "That's not John Madden, that's . . . my . . . wife."

Our poor salesman, Rick, used an approach that was popular early in the evolution of selling. Are you like this at the initial contact with a prospect? Do you look for that fish on the wall, the trophy on the shelf, the picture on the desk? We're often taught to comment on these items to "break the ice."

Selling blunders like this have given me more speaking and training engagements than any creative or classic marketing effort I've implemented. Why? Because sales executives, managers, and reps themselves are constantly worried about making good first impressions.

When Rick shared this stupid mistake at a training class I was running, it was because I opened the program by saying, "Today's sales module is on rapport. What do we do when we first encounter a stranger to try to connect with him or her? Does anybody have a bad experience related to rapport?" Opening classes this way is how I've collected over six hundred of these hilarious selling blunders. Plenty more can be found to use for teaching, training, and running sales meetings at www.SalesAutopsy.com. You'll find them in video, audio, and print, even in comic book format. Each has a lesson or "postmortem" attached. Additionally, my book, *Sales Autopsy* (2006), has more than fifty of my favorite and funniest blunders, each tied to specific learning moments.

EXERCISE 9.1.   Defining Rapport

SETUP: Here we want to get the team's perception on what rapport really is. It'll give us a starting point for learning what they can do to initiate and maintain rapport throughout the selling relationship.

Answer the following questions:

- So what exactly is rapport?
- How do we attain it?
- Why is it important to do so quickly?
- Aren't techniques to imitate another person in order to sell them something manipulative?

Get feedback, then present the following answers.

What is it? Rapport is the ability to connect with your buyer on a conscious and unconscious level. Buyers' brains are always looking for a way to quickly identify whose best interests are at stake in this new relationship. In other words, their motivation is to make the best decisions, the safest decisions for their careers, their reputations, even for their performance reviews (which, of course, affect income, advancement, and more). You must help buyers feel that their best interests on a personal and professional level are your highest priority.

How do we attain it? There are psychologically sound strategies for gaining rapport, which we will learn. They are commonly used by counselors who are working to help patients change their minds and behavior. Sounds a lot like a buyer/seller interaction, doesn't it?

Why is it important to generate rapport quickly? Your ability to connect with the buyer is critical to the early steps in the sales process. In Rick's story above, I asked him what happened after the president responded to his lame ice-breaking comment. Rick said, "I was so stunned by my stupidity that I went right into my pitch, knowing in the back of my mind this guy wanted nothing to do with me. But maybe I'd get lucky and something I said would turn it around. Didn't happen. My opening words basically destroyed any shot at rapport, and I left with my tail between my legs."

The old adage "You only get one chance at a good first impression" is painfully true for sales reps. Don't do it quickly and it's costly, too. There are too many choices today and it's easier for a buyer to eliminate one than it is to say "yes." So the faster you help that buyer feel safe with you, the more likely you will be to advance the sale to a "yes" or a next step.

Can these techniques be considered manipulative or deceptive? In China there are two hundred different dialects that have their roots in the Chinese language (linguistics professors might argue about half of these represent actual languages with the rest being dialects sprouting from those tongues). If you were visiting someone in Beijing, would it be more respectful to speak to the person in the exact dialect of his or her heritage, family, and geographic location? Or would you rather use a generic Chinese dictionary or translation device? That visit (or in our case, a sales call) serves both parties best when you honor the other by communicating as closely in alignment with who the person is than who you are. That's basic selling. This belief is played out by showing the buyer you are willing to get in sync with him or her as an individual—even if your adjustments, your mental flexibility, might be invisible. When you truly want to understand the other person, these teachings will respect that desire.

Should someone on your team choose to simply fool the other person into "liking" him or her, you probably have a hiring problem. So you can use this technique to better appreciate and understand the diversity of people on our planet. Or you can use others by applying these proven techniques. My hope is that, by attaining and applying new knowledge, each rep learning this method will be a better human being first, better sales rep second. To tie into that, and to reiterate much of what's been taught throughout this book, these ideas are organic. They work at home and at work. So practice them in both locations and become a better communicator on the job and as a friend and family member.

Let's get into our rapport-building strategy. There are three steps: Matching (or Mirroring), Pacing, and Leading. These techniques were identified in the 1970s and 1980s by researchers studying successful psychologists and sociologists like Milton Erickson, Virginia Satir, and Gregory Bateson. By observing these experts' skills in quickly gaining rapport, the researchers could encode or mark the process used, in order to teach it to others. In the past thirty years, these concepts have been applied to every business setting imaginable. This includes situations like marriage counseling, police interrogations, and sales meetings for professionals like yourself.

Matching

This step in building rapport involves harmonizing yourself with the buyer. Harmony might seem like an odd word in a sales training context, but aren't we (buyer and seller) really seeking to make beautiful music together? By enjoying each other's company, you'll increase the chance of a sale. As we've been told ten thousand times: people buy from people they like. While that might not be 100 percent true, there are advantages to the two individuals liking one another. The dialogues go deeper, questions are more likely to be answered, and price becomes a bit less of an issue to the decision-maker.

We want to match the other person physiologically, verbally, and mentally. Each one is progressively more important. That is, each in turn attains higher levels of rapport.

- *Physiological matching* includes posture, movement, and gestures. First, match the position of the other person. Are her legs crossed? Cross yours. Is he leaning to one side on the arm of the chair? Lean. When she moves or gestures, you want to copy those movements as well. Here's a key to doing this right: Do not imitate the other person's physical behavior immediately. Wait ten, twenty, or thirty seconds, then casually do so. Also pay attention to facial gestures. *Important:* Match breathing to attain the pinnacle of physical rapport. You can mirror the other person's breathing by watching the rise and fall of his or her shoulders. This is very powerful in personal relationships and you can practice it with someone you care about such as a child, a friend, or a lover.

- *Verbal matching* refers to the pace, tone, volume, and energy of the person's spoken words. First, listen to how loud or soft the other's voice is. Then attend to speed and energy. If you sell on the phone, this will be your initial way to attain rapport. I can't express how valuable this technique is to anyone who works the phone. This is fairly easy to do and very easy to practice. Turn on the radio and pace a talk show host or newscaster. Do it

Table 9.1. Word Cues

Visual	Auditory	Kinesthetic
see	hear	grasp
look	listen	touch
sight	sound	feeling
clear	resonant	solid
bright	loud	heavy
picture	word	handle
hazy	noisy	rough
brings to light	rings a bell	connects
show	tell	move

on the way to work and in a week you'll be masterful at verbal matching. *Important:* Match emotion, too. Your energy, tone, and volume could be in alignment with the buyer, but your highest level of rapport occurs when you match his or her emotions as well.

- *Mental matching* means being in alignment with how the buyer processes information, both consciously and unconsciously. This refers to whether he or she is *visual, auditory,* or *kinesthetic* (another word is tactile). We will refer to these mental filters as VAK.

Table 9.1 lists words each type of person might use. These are indicators you can use to reply in kind, in the buyer's dialect.

This might seem like a lot to learn, but with some practice you'll begin to do this almost intuitively. The first two (physiological and verbal) are easier, because they're more obvious to us. They are happening right before our eyes. The mental piece takes a bit more work as we have to listen actively and adjust our language choices to match visual, auditory, or kinesthetic systems being used by the buyer. Just remember that we're gaining a competitive advantage with this increased sensitivity. So it's well worth the effort to attain expertise in these abilities. Here's a great way to raise your awareness of these individual buyer attributes.

EXERCISE 9.2. Listening for Rapport

SETUP: This is similar to the exercises and homework you will see in Chapter 15. In this case I suggest the learners keep journals to monitor how often they encounter VAK cues from people around them. Print out the VAK used previously and have learners keep it handy.

   Instructions: Get a blank notebook or journal to use to deepen your skills in identifying these VAK cues. For a full day, look for visual cues only and write them in the notebook. Do this in both personal and professional settings. Listen to word choices in others' conversations in restaurants and stores. The exercise is about a total awareness of visual language cues—much like driving and only looking for yellow cars. You might have played the kids' game Banana Split, where the first one to see a yellow car gets to punch his siblings, friends, or parents (I hate getting hit when I'm driving). That game is based on visual awareness. The next day, listen for auditory cues. One way I increased my kids' and my own sensitivity to auditory was by closing my eyes and listening to the wide variety of sounds about me. They include cars, birds, crickets, wind rustling leaves, and voices. Sounds like something simple to do? It is. On the third day, pay attention for kinesthetic cues. It might be words or it could be noticing some people who touch more than others. Sales managers should also be engaging in these exercises.

Here's how to gain feedback from a "homework" type exercise like Exercise 9.2:

- At the next scheduled sales training session, ask learners to share some of their notes.

- Ask learners to email, at the end of each day, notes on each type of person they encountered and observed.

- Create pairs at the training event and ask the two partners to have a conversation, even by phone, at the end of each day to share their learning moments.

Pacing

Pacing involves staying in sync with the buyer when he or she changes position, energy level, and more. It's fairly simple and can be practiced at home. In fact, try it with young children who are being difficult to manage. Follow the precepts you just learned about movement, language, and VAK and see how you can quickly gain rapport with a little one. Practice at play, rather than with prospects.

Leading

Leading occurs when you're in complete rapport with the buyer and can now change your behavior and language so that the buyer follows and matches you. In essence, you've reversed roles. He or she was leading you (unknowingly), and now you'll help direct his or her behavior and thinking.

This takes practice and has the biggest payoff. Here's an example from a sale I closed after I'd gained some proficiency in rapport-building and leading.

> *This buyer clearly prefers processing information through her sense of sight. She is a visual person. I'd mirrored her during about forty-five minutes of sales conversation and now felt that we were very comfortable with one another. I decided it was time to lead. (Bold words reflect her representational system.)*

> *"Donna," I say, "it **looks** like our sales training can **show** your team how to gain a **clear** advantage over the competition. Is that a good summary of how you **see** it, too?"*

> *Donna looks up a moment then says, "I want to do this for one reason."*

> *"What's that?"*

> *"I have no idea how you convinced me that I needed this sales training. And I'm willing to buy the training and see how it works, just to get the answer to my question."*

What a surprising and unusual "yes" to get from a prospect! To me this closing conversation reveals great rapport. You see, good selling is invisible to the buyer. She saw and experienced rapport combined with skill and was willing to pay to learn what happened.

That conversation, specifically that final comment of hers, is so deeply embedded in my memory that I can remember the buyer in detail—hair, eye color, dress. I even remember the stairs going up to her headquarters office and the layout of the room where we met. We became and stayed good friends.

So wouldn't it be a nice bonus if rapport worked beyond that sales call and created newer and/or deeper relationships than you'd previously experienced? The value of this learning really can go far beyond its application to your sales life.

To attain these skills you need to practice. It will also help to have a mindset that you are mentally flexible enough to adjust your behavior and words to get into sync with your buyer. This flexibility has been identified by Dr. Maxwell Maltz in his classic work, *Psycho-cybernetics* (1989). Maltz identifies what he calls the "Law of Requisite Variety." This law states that in any system (human or machine), all things being equal, the individual with the widest range of responses will control that system. In other words, any sales professional with the flexibility to make adjustments to his or her behavior can advance the sale more often than someone who is limited in his or her responses. You'll find no better proof of this than in the chapter on handling objections (Chapter 16). There you can arm yourself with more responses to resistance than you ever imagined possible. By applying your newly found verbal flexibility, you'll take charge of the buyer-seller dialogue and attain more success in sales.

EXERCISE 9.3. Practicing Different Styles

SETUP: Here's an example of how learners can increase their sensitivity to VAK.

At their tables, have reps do quick presentations of their offerings, or they can choose to do an elevator pitch, should they have one. Those listening can then identify the presenter's representational system. Group members should take turns, then practice using the other styles. For an advanced addition to this exercise, have listeners ask questions of presenters using the proper rep system while also trying to match the pace and speed of the person's speech.

There is clearly a science and specific strategy to rapport. Model what we know works, practice at home and away from work until you can easily garnish rapport with each of your buyers.

Chapter 10

Prospecting

Call it lead generation, demand generation, prospecting. Who couldn't use skills and some tricks to become a lead generation genius? This chapter was created to serve as the most comprehensive resource available for generating leads. *Note:* Should your company's marketing department provide your team with plenty of leads, you'll still want to have the salespeople spend time reading this chapter to identify ways to garnish high-quality leads from the relationships around them. Pay attention, in particular, to the first topic, Referrals. I get more complaints than you could possibly imagine from sales managers and executives about how weak their team's ability is to obtain referrals. There are some creative pieces to obtaining referrals and some nice structure as well. Next you'll find a massive list of digital and print sources. And we'll end with the dreaded "cold calling." I do have a bizarre solution to this. You'll read here *cold calling and casinos.* But no sales training book could exist without addressing cold calling. The topic is hotly argued, and whether it's wasteful or disrespectful, you can't ignore the fact that millions of sellers are using this technique every day. Here you'll discover some great, new tips on how to get buyers to respond to cold-calling efforts.

Three Thoughts on the Impact of Lousy Leads

There is a coyote alert in our neighborhood. That's suburban Chicago. It's not Montana or the hills above Los Angeles. These wild dogs are roving around town, and I've seen them. And they're pretty small—not like in the movies where animals the size of middle linebackers bark and howl at the moon. So little pooch; big, big appetite. It's no surprise that people are putting up notices for missing dogs and cats. Folks, the bad news is that your precious little critters are not coming back. *Your pets are not lost, they're lunch.*

Great sales leads can be just as frustrating to find as lost pets. Are your prospects good enough to drive sales higher than the hills? Or are your competitors lunching on the real leads—the ones that are high quality and hot?

Intelligent organizations spend as much time in their marketing efforts to disqualify bad prospects as they do to qualify the sweet ones. And like good pets, good leads are great to have around.

Here in *The Ultimate Guide to Sales Training* we'll divide our hunt for quality leads into three sections:

1. Referrals

2. Digital and print resources

3. Cold calling

This chapter is a major source of ideas and information. It's formed the basis for my work finding business over the past twenty-five plus years. I would joke in training with my clients that such a massive and valuable work should be placed in an underground bunker in Colorado, with 12-foot-thick walls that can resist almost any form of invasion, except perhaps a baseball thrown through the window.

In the end you'll probably want to create a large checklist for your selling team members. Aside from your marketing department's money being spent generating leads, you'll find these ideas to be comprehensive and creative ways to discover more business.

Ask yourself: How big, how powerful is your funnel to garnish prospects? Is your company doing everything possible to extract high-quality, hot leads from the marketplace?

Become a Lead Generation Genius

Generating Referrals

Let's be very direct in addressing this lead generation strategy. It is horribly under-utilized. In my experience working with sales managers, it is the second most neglected area of running a sales team. I won't keep you guessing about the number one problem sales managers tend to struggle with: They don't fire underperforming salespeople fast enough. So if members of your team are not regularly asking for referrals, you have issues with disrespect and disobedience. I intentionally ignore the term "insubordinate" here and go for language more appropriate to child-rearing. That is because your sales children will either follow your lead or become rebellious. These are hiring and firing issues and you'll find my ideas on that in Chapter 33, Reps You Should *Not* Be Training. Point here is this: Everyone should be asking for referrals.

Do you know why referrals are such a smart way to identify great leads? We'll give you three ways to look at referrals in order to move them up the list of topics you can use to badger both good and bad reps about. Reps should understand that it's in their best interest to constantly seek referrals—and not just from existing clients.

EXERCISE 10.1. The Rep's Perspective

SETUP: Let's look at reasons a rep should be focusing on gaining referrals.

Think about it. How is it in your best interest to use referrals as your primary source for new business?

Possible answers: Least costly source, higher chance of closing, warm (not cold) call, etc.

Trainer: As answers are offered around the room, every salesperson should be writing down reasons they need to obtain referrals.

Good sales professionals should also seek to understand their business from the buyer's angle.

EXERCISE 10.2. The Buyer's Perspective

SETUP: Now let's look at the reasons buyers might want to deal with someone who's been referred to them.

There are many reasons that we as sales pros should focus on referrals. But from the buyer's perspective, what are some reasons he or she would want to buy from a source that has been referred?

Possible answers: Some level of trust is presumed at the start, highest quality testimonial rather than reading an ad or other endorsement, etc.

Trainer: As answers are offered around the room, every salesperson should be writing down reasons he or she needs to obtain referrals.

From both the buyer and the seller perspectives, it just makes more sense to use referrals from your happy clients to identify new prospects.

SETUP: Let's cut right to the chase and *quantify* the value of referrals. This is probably the most persuasive approach to helping your sales team work harder on obtaining referrals.

Just as we help our prospects quantify the value of our product and service offerings, today we'll help our reps quantify the value of their referrals.

Here's our starting point: What exactly is a client worth? Better said, you've probably heard the buzz phrase "lifetime value" of a customer.

Do you know your number? Because when you really know that number, you might stand up and take notice of how it applies to you, the rep, and not just the company.

Trainer: Have reps discuss the importance of this concept in small groups.

When a well-known national pizza company did research on the spending habits of customers, the *average transaction* was $21.50. But when they calculated the *lifetime value* of a customer it was $50,000. So was it worth giving someone a free pizza if the driver arrived late? You bet!

We'll use the pizza example, and you'll want to identify your numbers so that your salespeople can create their own chart to know and quantify their referral value. The example below shows a *very* conservative estimate; hopefully, over a ten-year period you'd be able to get more than two referrals from just one customer!

So here we see one customer is worth $50,000. He or she gives us two new customers or $100,000. When each of *those* two customers refers just two other people to this same pizza company, we have four newer customers—worth $50,000 each—or $200,000.

Add up the lifetime value of these seven customers, the company has just multiplied its original $50,000 customer into seven customers worth $350,000 . . . just through referrals!!!!

This is a lot like that old puzzle where you put one penny on the first square of a checkerboard (okay, chessboard if we're talking about smarter reps), two on the second, and continue to double the pennies on each consecutive square. This is known as a "geometric sequence," and after sixty-four squares you'd have a total value of (get your reps to guess the answer and see how far off they'll be):

$184,467,440,737,095,516.15

Of course, you'd clearly need a chessboard the size of Donald Trump's ego upon which to fit all the pennies (one hundred coins for every dollar in that figure!). But the point is that you can play the penny game with big-time dollars by asking for referrals, then asking for more from the new clients who will give you more, and ad infinitum. The only limit to cashing in on the true value of referrals is our mortality.

To develop the discipline to ask for referrals, your sales pros first need to take on a *referral mindset.* By this we mean that you need to first *believe* that:

- Referrals are *the* preferred method (remember earlier reasons, cheapest source of leads, easier to close, warm rather than cold call).

- Prospects prefer to solve their problems and attain solutions through the safest method, a referral from a trusted source.

- Because you've learned to quantify the value of your offering(s), buyers are smart to speak with you.

- Referrals are pennies on the board. They have an exponential impact on revenue and give you more control over how much money you make.

Jesse is an insurance rep I met at a business networking dinner who really, really gets the idea of the value of referrals. He has a system whereby he contacts everyone he knows (and plenty he doesn't) to ask for leads. He has a hook to get their attention, then is quite serious about how he thanks his sources.

First, everyone who gives him a lead receives a small gesture of his appreciation. This changes, but is normally a gift card—Starbucks, gasoline, something similar. He sends postcards to everyone, and they are read because when he changes the gift people are curious as to what he's offering today. Next, he has a drawing every quarter, for a 42-inch flat-panel TV.

Would you regularly give Jesse referrals? The man has a ridiculous amount of people sending him business. When we last spoke, he was sending out several hundred postcards a month. By the time this book is published, this smart insurance rep will be spending more money on more mailings, as well as new staff to handle his growth.

A couple of things to note here: You have to make it crystal clear to everyone who a good, preferably great, prospect is. Here we are on the qualifying and disqualifying issue that will be covered in Chapter 12. But you wouldn't want to receive tons of referrals only to chase down poor prospects. Also, if you can't gift a client because it might be considered unethical, this isn't for you.

I routinely send nice gift packages to my clients after keynoting or training. But when I send a spectacular $100 Harry & David fruit, nut, cheese, and candy basket to say "Thanks!" there is more to this gesture than the write-off. They are grateful I appreciated the opportunity to speak to their sales force and it affirms further the wisdom of their decision to hire me—especially when I continue to teach them by asking, "Are your reps saying *thank you* as dramatically?" The receivers are more likely to give referrals in a follow-up call after the package has arrived.

In contrast, I've also had clients not acknowledge gifts like this. Some have even refused them. But it's the right thing to do, and you know that. So do it if your company allows—even if you pay out of your pocket, even if your VP of sales client can't accept it and gives it to the mailroom workers. Your heart for your client is what's important here.

Of course, also get advice from your accounting department on the deductibility of gifts. But don't let a financial expert tell you that it's not worth the write-off to give away gifts worth more than tax laws allow if you're generating good cash flow from the leads. You can measure some things—and others you can't.

We'll next cover how to ask for referrals from existing customers, then how to discover them within the relationships that you have with people who aren't customers.

Referrals from Current Customers

This method is again about the buyer's desire to make safe decisions. If you wanted to buy a new car, would you be better influenced by a television or print ad, a website offering, or the advice of a trusted friend?

Darin is a good friend of mine, a medical sales manager who covers an eight-state territory. When he arrived for dinner one evening in his new Lexus, I was excited to go for a ride. Then my buddy pulled over and let me drive. The experience, regardless of the seat I sat in, was like flying in an airplane. I'd never felt such a comfortable or quiet ride. I joked that this might be the car of my dreams—literally—one in which I was most likely to fall asleep driving. He suggested I was most likely to be pulled over and ticketed because you couldn't tell how fast you were traveling.

I was an owner of a Lexus within two weeks.

That potent combination of a trusted resource plus a safe bet equaled a buying decision. I could have test-driven that car at a dealership. I could have been enticed by images at a website. I could have seen a celebrity (highly paid) driving that car on TV. But nothing influenced me more than a fellow sales pro who had no agenda except to joyfully share his wise buying decision with me.

You get this. Let's assume you've adapted that *referral mindset*. You next need to arm yourself with language that will help clients share referrals with you. Every company should encourage this mindset by having available to the reps a referral script. Here's a method I've been using in training for years.

Writing the Referral Script

1. Start with an opening question or statement and state the problem you've solved or the need your product/service has met.

   - Opening question/statement: "Can I ask you a question?" or "I was wondering. . . ."

   - State the problem: "You brought us in, basically, because of your frustration with the performance of your current vendor. And your instincts and data have shown that your decision to bring us in has boosted the quality and gross profit by 11 percent. Do you feel like you've seen a good return on your investment?"

2. Check for agreement and ask for the referral. If they agree with you:

   - Then ask who they know who could use your product or service. Notice we aren't asking them if they know someone. We are assuming they have plenty of relationships they can pull from, e.g., "I'm glad to hear we're meeting your expectations. You may or may not know this, but our company is built upon relationships like yours . . . which made me wonder who you know—other companies or other executives—who could use our help? (when he or she says yes) Would you please introduce them to me?"

   - But they don't know of anyone or they don't want to refer someone to you. You want to address the elephant in the room, e.g., "Are you saying you can't think of anyone or don't want to refer anyone? Because I could ask you later for some people if you need to think about it. And if you're uncomfortable referring me to someone, I'm curious what that's about?"

- If they tell you they can't think of anyone now, then set a time for another conversation.

- If they won't refer anyone to you . . . e.g., "If you feel strongly about not doing this, that's okay, too. I am very grateful for our relationship and don't want you to feel uncomfortable here"—and remember to smile when you're saying this—smile when saying anything that's uncomfortable or tricky.

- Or they can't think of anyone at the moment, ask when you can get back to them.

- If they don't agree with you in the first place, then this is a good chance to find out what is wrong and hopefully save a customer. "Wow, let's talk about that. Would you please tell me more?"

3. Thank them and then qualify or quantify the referral.

- Your client or influencer gives you a name. When you first get that referral, qualify or quantify it with a question: "Thank you for that name. I'm curious, why do you think Mr./Ms. X would be interested in talking to me?" You'll hear some insights as to whether there's a need you should be aware of or if it's just a good connection.

4. Ask for an introduction.

- "Would you be comfortable calling him/her for me to make the introduction?" Then, after a yes (or no), "When do you think you'd be able to make that call?"

5. Thank the person. When you receive referrals, thank the source. Show gratitude by giving gifts. If that's not allowed, at least send a thank-you note. This would be a real note, not an email. Then keep the person updated on the status of your new relationship.

You can now deliver my 42-inch flat-panel TV for helping you generate loads of leads from referrals. Contact me directly for the shipping address.

It's very important to "find your own voice" when you're asking for referrals. You're obviously not going to use these examples exactly how they're written. You'll need to get the meaning across in phrases that reflect your own personality and style. So if none of these examples is comfortable for you, then edit them or totally rewrite them.

EXERCISE 10.4. Identifying Buyers for Referral

SETUP: The best way to optimize learning is to have sales team members identify buyers they're pursuing and apply the latest learning to them. Here we'll do that with clients who can share referrals.

List three current customers you could approach for referrals. Write, in your own words, how you would script the conversation. Then start using the script.

Practice with another rep. Make adjustments based on how you feel using the script, as well as advice you receive from your partner prospect/sales rep.

Sample Script

"Mr./Ms. Client (or first name), we've been working with each other and it seems like we've been able to accomplish your goal of designing a web-based marketing program that generates leads for your sales team. Is that accurate? I was wondering whether you're able to think of other business professionals in your circle of influence who might benefit from this type of help and help me connect with them?"

(I can't think of anyone right now.) "Well, it might be other business associates, customers, suppliers, you know, perhaps people you spend money on for services, etc."

(Your customer gives you a name.) "Thank you. Why do you think Mr./Ms. X would be interested in talking to me?" (Gives you an answer) "Thanks. That's really helpful information. I will contact him/her. I have found, however, that he/she would be less surprised by my phone call if he/she knew that I was calling. Would you please let him/her know that I will be contacting him/her? Thank you again."

Be prepared for some level of discomfort when first doing this. Keep in mind, too, how big the rewards are when you incorporate this as part of your regular selling practices. The key is to come up with the wording and tone that fit your personality.

Maintain That Referral Mindset!

One other tip about referrals. Some selling pros ask as early as possible for referrals. They let prospects know *before the sale* that they'll be asking for referrals *after* that prospect becomes a client.

Here's how they do it: Once they're comfortable that the sale is advancing, they'll say something like: "By the way, I wanted to let you know that we might be asking you for testimonials and referrals once you begin seeing the results from our work together."

As you begin to be comfortable asking for referrals, you can begin to use this idea with your prospects.

Referrals from Non-Customers

There are other groups of people you can ask a referral from besides your current customers. Who are they? Let's categorize them. The first group is people you spend money with. Your suppliers and vendors are in this category—those people you pay to develop and print brochures or business cards printed or purchase parts from. There are also professionals you or your company uses, such as accountants, attorneys, or bankers.

The next group is people who are influencers in your community such as:

- Community or organizational leaders—village officials, Optimists, Kiwanis, Lions, clergy, charities/non-profit leaders
- Media/press—print and online
- Professionals—accountants, attorneys, bankers
- Small and large business leaders
- Association leaders—local trade groups like the Chamber of Commerce or local chapters of national associations

Who else can you think of? How are these influencers such high-value resources? They serve as "leverage points" that give us access to large numbers of other people. Therefore, they open doors to an entirely new set of potential prospects.

EXERCISE 10.5. Searching Out Referrals

SETUP: Learners create a list of places to pursue referral sources. Encourage them to keep the list handy and be proactive about obtaining referrals. Brainstorm places you've used to meet some of these people yourself.

Possible answers:

- School events/meetings
- Sponsor local events or even sports teams (to inexpensively get in front of attendees)
- Places you volunteer
- People you share your hobby with
- Personal and professional contacts you lunch with
- Social events outside of work, friends/family gatherings
- Charity events
- Health club members
- Networking events—BNI, LeTip, local association chapters, etc.
- Speak locally—Toastmasters can help you with public speaking. Groups such as Optimists/Kiwanis/Lions Clubs need new speakers every month.
- Shopping—including retail stores, grocery, restaurants
- Home and business-based services you spend money on—heating and air conditioning, painters, phone, cable, driveway surfacing, and more

The lists people come up with can be so comprehensive that I suggest you start weekly or regular sales meetings by asking, "Does anyone have a unique way he or she discovered a good lead?" Your team will continually come up with ideas about where they can find new business—mostly because they've now adopted a *referral mindset.*

This is different, however, because these contacts are not existing clients. They may not have any idea how well your offerings can solve their problems or how good they are. How do you engage them? We all know that every selling pro should have an "elevator speech."

Here's the model I teach. It includes a variety of language approaches to crafting an elevator speech, a fifteen-, twenty-, or thirty-second response to the question: "What do you do?"

Creating Your Elevator Speech

- It's only one to five sentences; try to keep it about three.

- Answer the questions:

  - Who do you help? Who is your target audience?

  - How do you help them? What problems are solved, value/benefits attained?

- You evoke emotion by using descriptive adjectives and verbs and by having a clear call to action or question at the end.

The key concept here is to give less detail, so that the listener requests more information. You want to initiate a dialogue during which the other person says, "Tell me more" or "How do you do that?"

Here are some sample responses to "What do you do?"

- *Do you ever wonder how companies figure out which social networking sites are worth paying attention to? We cut through all the frustration and help firms build their business on the web with intelligent decisions based on, not hype, but what really works. For example, how many sites like Facebook and LinkedIn do you spend time on right now?*

- *We eliminate print confusion. What does that mean? Well, when you want to create flyers, brochures, marketing materials and more, do you just run down to FedEx/Kinko's, use a local printer, or a web-based service? Too many companies make brand and impression-related decisions based on price, rather than quality. But you probably already knew that.*

- *Here are the top three sales training problems I/we solve for my/our existing clients:*

  - *We help them to stop chasing poor prospects and discover, then close, more high-quality clients.*

  - *They significantly increase their ability to deflect and work through prospects' toughest objections.*

- *They remove mental and behavioral obstacles that can hinder personal performance.*

  Which one of these is your biggest concern?

This last example is my favorite. It also serves as a cold-calling script. It's different enough and forces the listener to think through their situation (the top three problems) as it applies to your offering. If they respond to "Which one of these is your biggest concern?" with "none," you respond, "Oh, good. What is?" And you're in a real conversation.

Here's a great exercise that really hones an elevator speech.

EXERCISE 10.6. Creating Elevator Speeches

SETUP: Reps take five minutes to create their elevator speeches. They then take turns presenting aloud to the whole group. Everyone is allowed to critique, based on the rules above. Be prepared for some brutal and humorous comments. Help them keep their focus to produce the best language that fits each sales rep's style and personality.

Again, the key concept here is to give less detail, so that the listener requests more information. Here are a couple of final thoughts on referrals:

- Be persistent in asking existing clients for their help.
- Keep that referral mindset top-of-mind and don't lose sight of the lifetime value of the new business you'll attain with these warm, even hot prospects.

To wrap up this section on Generating Referrals, I just want to remind you of the major emphasis, which was getting referrals from your current customers! If you learned nothing else, this alone should begin to increase your sales!

Prospecting Through Electronic and Print Resources

A large number of ways exist to identify new prospects. What you learn here will help you create a personal plan you might choose to use, even if your company is already sending you leads. You should check with your organization to confirm whether you are even allowed to employ some of these more creative ideas. For example, you might want to appear on a radio show, but your company's communications department might be concerned with how you'd represent the firm and what you'd say. So that opportunity might be reserved for executives who've had media coaching.

We'll divide our lead generation opportunities between electronic and print resources.

Electronic Sources

Here are three examples of electronic strategies that provide plenty of leads:

- Alex Carroll is a master at doing radio interviews to build his business, which is helping people get out of traffic tickets! Alex generates several hundred thousand dollars a year just contacting radio producers and hosts to get exposure for his company. He combines a print strategy as well, selling his books, *Speeding Excuses That Work* (2002) and *Beat the Cops* (1994). Alex has chosen the life of a true entrepreneur, rather than a corporate work environment. But he's a favorite example because I'm often telling sales reps who spend a lot of time behind the wheel to be aware of his offerings.

- SalesAutopsy.com is a training company that collects salespeople's hilarious, most embarrassing selling moments and posts the funniest ones each month through a digital newsletter. Each blunder ends with a selling tip or "postmortem." The uniqueness of this idea—and the humor—have generated a large number of leads in two ways.

  The first is clearly the advantage of an e-zine, which is its viral nature. It can be easily forwarded or passed along to associates, friends, etc. In SalesAutopsy's case, readers forwarded the stories to so many other sales professionals that now there are thousands of subscribers.

  The second way it generates leads is by catching the attention of the media. The press has written more than two hundred articles (both in prestigious print publications and online) reviewing the site—which then generates leads by people reading the article and contacting the company.

- Every business professional should have an identity on LinkedIn and Facebook. These digital hunting grounds are places where you can find people who fit your exact target audience and engage with them. Within these networks you can check out your competitors, your prospects, and potential alliance partners. Again, check with your company's policy on social media. I know some insurance firms, for example, won't let their sales reps have a presence online. This is smart in a situation when a prospect might want to connect with a rep and that rep doesn't always attend to or update his or her pages. You wouldn't want to have leads find you, then feel ignored.

Online Tips

- *Your own voicemail message.* Use your elevator speech and make an offer at the end, for example, offer a gift or discount when they contact you.

- *Your email signature line and subject line.* Make an offer, for example, a gift or discount when they contact you.

- *iPod app.* Create an application that generates awareness and referrals. An outstanding and fairly priced resource for this is www.SixVoices.com, which has several levels of service. They designed the SuperBowl App, Michael Jackson legacy App, and more.

- *Video.* Create a creative video that's viral; it could include coaching and educational tips (Do not brand with YouTube; keep this at your own site!)

- *Google.* "Link popularity check" on competitors, clients, and associate sites. www.submitexpress.com/linkpop/

- *Social networking* (Twitter, Facebook, LinkedIn).

  - Check out your competitors and your prospects and set up your own accounts to create a presence online within social networks. Which ones are good? Go to www.RainToday.com under *This Week's Sales & Marketing Content*, pick any article. Click on "Share" above the article and look at the large list of social networking sites!

  - Social networking sites have many groups where you can find a lot of potential buyers or alliance partners at once. There are sales management groups, entrepreneurial groups, top one thousand business professionals by city groups, and more. Look them up!

- *Competitors' information.* Gather your competitors' literature and review, in depth, their websites.

- *Create your own e-zine.*

- *Webinars or teleseminars.* These are inexpensive ways to show how well you work to solve problems for existing clients. Consider having some best clients partner with you to share these stories on the webinar or phone.

- *Industry e-zines.* Read what associations or influencers are sending out. You can also contribute content and/or offer gifts to their readers. Remember, always have a call to action!

- *PR/media releases.* News releases online can reach your target audience to share success stories, telling of upcoming events or awards you've won.

- *Create a "long" copy, single-page website.* This gains the attention of prospects and gives them, in depth, plenty of reasons, even testimonials, to help them reach out to you. For a great example, see *Instant Income: 101 Strategies to Bring in the Cash* at www.instantincome.com/iibp/. This powerful way to gather prospects is the brainchild of copywriting expert Janet Switzer, who's partnered with business-building experts like Jack Canfield, Dan Kennedy, and Jay Abraham. For additional details on her copywriting strategies, visit www.LeadGenerationGenius.com where I designed a website after her model.

- *Create a link campaign.* Point other websites back to your site, and offer a resources page on websites of others' resources online that your visitors, prospects, and clients might find of value.

Radio and TV Tips

- *Radio: traditional, online, and satellite.* Run ads, offer giveaways, do a talk show or host a call-in program. A simple search online will reveal plenty of inexpensive options for online radio broadcasting. Look for existing shows you can partner with or call in to, as well as places where you can produce your own show. All content can be archived, so you can build quite a body of resources to attract potential clients over time.

- *TV: cable, traditional, online.* Run ads, offer giveaways, pitch producers to appear on a talk show or call-in show. Online TV, including the use of high definition (HD), has become an inexpensive option to traditional and cable. One company, Multicast Media, produces over 4,500 live events each month. In fact, they use more bandwidth than YouTube. See www.multicastmedia.com/

EXERCISE 10.7. Brainstorming Digital Sources

SETUP: Again, everyone creates his or her own list from which to work. Have learners find accountability partners who can push them to put these ideas into play each day.

Trainer: Each rep should create a personal checklist and pick a partner who will work with him or her to make sure the lists are used to discover new business. The company should also compile a master checklist from all respondents. This can help sales and marketing management to identify places to invest time and money in lead generation.

Print Sources

Let me give you a few examples:

- This still is one of my favorite experiences doing lead generation. Twenty years ago I ran a sales force of fifteen reps with an executive search firm. We made a practice of responding to all the junk mail received. Our admin person would quickly respond with a note that said, "Thank you, we read your mail. You probably don't know how many people actually do that, but we did. And while we don't have a need for your services right now, we'll keep it handy. By the way, this is what we do, should you need help that we provide [brief explanation added]." Within six months the firm had received two new lucrative clients—from responding to junk mail! By the way, this technique led to my approach of asking anyone we spent money with for leads as well—when we'd receive a bill in the mail, say for the rent, we'd contact the real estate management company to pitch our services. We were a client of theirs and we spent money with them. Do you think they took our call the first time? Yes.

- This next example is a common strategy from the marketing world—swipe files. These are collections or files of print advertising. Use this resource to gather good . . . and bad . . . ideas to apply or avoid in your marketing literature. Everyone who is involved in lead generation should begin a swipe file. It's a fantastic way to get creative juices flowing. There are also online resources that provide similar information, such as http://creativity-online.com/.

Jim Silverman is the director of eastern sales for Vienna Beef. We met at a big food show in Chicago while I was writing this book. He'd been trying to get to a chef of a leading restaurant. So when he saw this same chef eating one of their Vienna Beef hot dogs at his booth, he took a picture with a digital camera of the guy stuffing the dog into his mouth. Jim then sent a card to this prospect a week later with that picture on the cover! It floored—and impressed—the chef, who immediately picked up the phone to speak with Jim. The ensuing upbeat and fun conversation led to the chef's commitment to begin buying from Jim. This buyer became a new customer because he'd never had a sales rep be that unique and put that type of effort into trying to capture his business before. Jim was able to send out this creative card so quickly because he used a company that sends out printed, customized greeting cards—picture, text, and all—by local post office and within a couple of days! This is a global service, too. So a sales rep in Chicago can mail a thank you, birthday, or humorous card to Sydney, Australia, in two days for the price of a card ($1 to $2) and normal ground postage! This idea illustrates how the print world brilliantly intersects the digital world. For details on this unique service and how you can this tool for prospecting, keeping in touch with current clients, and just saying thank you, visit the website I've set up at www.LeadGenerationGenius.com/. (You might notice this is the URL referenced earlier on selling through one-page websites.)

Print Resources Tips

- Business cards. Are yours boring? Do they make a call to action? Do they clearly show how you can improve the lives of your prospects?

- Magazines. Which ones are read by your target market? Subscribe to them. Can you write an article showing your successes with their readers?

- Write a book! Set aside time daily to create chapters, or get a ghostwriter.

- Publish a free booklet of tips and ideas to give away online or on the radio or at events where you might exhibit or speak.

- Publish articles locally in newspapers or business publications (and/or online).

- Send cards. This is much better than email. For cards you can customize and send cheaply, visit www.LeadGenerationGenius.com. Reps can have their own accounts so they can keep track of what's been sent to whom, which images are used, and more.

- Send your prospects articles, news items, funny content (graphical emails and letters are good). Tell them, "I thought of you when I read this and just had to mail it."

- PR/media releases. News releases sent to local TV, radio, and print publications can reach your target audience to share success stories, tell of upcoming events, or mention awards you've won.

- Publish success stories and testimonials of your best clients. This could be in your marketing literature, but also serve as a mailer.

- Use swipe files to collect good and bad print advertising, since it can inspire (or warn about what doesn't work) and give you ideas to apply to your own marketing literature. Everyone who is involved in lead generation should begin a swipe file.

- Send congratulation letters/gifts to local business professionals who receive media exposure (awards, promotions, etc.).

EXERCISE 10.8. Brainstorming Print Sources

SETUP: Here we'll again have individuals craft their own lists to target buyers. Again, we want accountability partners used as well.

Trainer: Each salesperson should create a personal checklist and pick an accountability partner to help push him or her to use the list to find new business opportunities. The company should also compile a master checklist from all respondents. This can help sales and marketing management to identify places to invest time and money in lead generation.

For a massive repository of lead generation ideas, visit the website that has been built to accompany and support *The Ultimate Guide to Sales Training* at www.UltimateGuidetoSalesTraining.com

Cold Calling

My father owned one of the largest printing companies in Central Ohio, and as a young man getting into the industry I had the opportunity to work with him.

He was an "old school" guy who believed in throwing you out of the boat to teach you to swim. Part of the training was cold calling of potential clients. I absolutely hated it and finally figured out how to make my weekly quota of calls without having to drive all over town. I would go to a business park, walk door to door, and solicit everyone in the complex. I could make thirty calls in an afternoon and coast the rest of the week.

One day my fifth stop led me into the reception area of the prospective customer's rather large office. No one sat at the receptionist's desk, so I rang a bell that went unanswered. As it was close to lunchtime, I figured I would wait. The white noise coming from the back of the building was faintly familiar, but I settled into my seat and proceeded to read a magazine and wait for the receptionist to appear.

After waiting for about fifteen minutes, I realized my precious time blowing through my cold calls was being wasted. So I peeked behind the door that led into the warehouse. There in the back were rows and rows of printing presses. I was making a sales call on another printing company to find out whether they might want to buy any of our printing services!

I slid out the door and slithered back to the office for some telephone cold calling. I never did tell my father about my stupid mistake.

When Brad shared that selling blunder with me, I figured out a scheme to completely eliminate cold calling. Traditional selling statistics reveal that cold-calling reps close about 1 percent of their contacts. This probably means nobody has a clue what the real number is, which is itself an embarrassing statement about our abilities to measure and manage behavior. But we'll get to that issue shortly.

So this funny thought pops into my head. I call Papa Blackjack, George Pappadopoulos, an expert on gambling. He tells me that an expert card-counter can gain a 3 to 5 percent advantage over the casino by using a counting system.

Here's the plan: Bring in a blackjack trainer. Teach your reps all the elements of a card-counting system. This includes three ingredients:

1. What play to make based on the cards showing,

2. How to count cards to know when you have an advantage over the casino, and

3. Money management—when to increase or decrease your bets based on your advantage (or disadvantage).

Next, spend a couple of weeks having reps practice playing blackjack. Once each rep has mastered each piece of the blackjack system, *you give them their budget or sales quota and send them to a casino to play with it.* And since they get free drinks and food, that can reduce expenses in the field. Everybody wins and your reps have never had this much fun "selling."

Three to 5 percent return versus 1 percent for an investment in cold calling? That's a smart investment, and you're already running those big sales conferences in Las Vegas anyway. So far, no company has taken me up on this to test my idea. Maybe one reader, one day, will do it. Or perhaps a corporation can test it with sales interns they've hired over the summer.

To be fair, the purpose of this section isn't to question the sanity or insanity of cold calling. It's to support the activity for firms that choose to do it. That being said, every sales executive should question and reassess each strategy he or she employs on a regular basis. So we'll address concerns with cold calling as well as techniques that work. You can choose to be influenced, either way.

Seven Good Things About Cold Calling

1. It's a great way to break in rookie reps, who can quickly find out which objections will be thrown at them, whether they can handle rejection, and whether the sales life is a path they want to set themselves on for a career.

2. You can generate lots of leads quickly. Just ask those securities reps who cut their teeth making 250 to 300 phone calls a day.

3. It's very inexpensive to use the phone today, so cheap is a factor.

4. Focus on simply one goal, such as landing an appointment, to reduce the time spent on the calls to a minimum.

5. A *great* phone conversation can work wonders with prospects.

6. If you prefer to play the numbers game with your sales reps, it's a great way to "succeed."

7. Reps who have done their homework on companies they call can gain gatekeeper respect and decision-maker attention.

Seven Bad Things About Cold Calling

1. Burnout occurs when there is poor time management and no energy management for the reps.

2. On the web, cold calling is called SPAM. (Remember when the term "junk mail" referred to printed literature?) SPAM is not a good starting place to initiate a relationship (unless the reader really is looking to enlarge body parts, receive a free iPad, pick up prescription drugs cheaply, or inherit millions).

3. Cold calling assumes the buyer isn't too busy to drop his or her work for a complete stranger (so it's perceived as disrespectful).

4. It reduces the status of the caller so that a peer-to-peer relationship (critical to high-end selling) is virtually impossible.

5. It's egocentric: "Hey, look at . . . listen to me!" This is too true about most forms of sales messaging. It's particularly bad when it's practiced hundreds of times a week by reps in a telemarketing office.

6. So many reps sound so bad on the phone that listeners label them as "telemarketers" and choose not to respond.

7. Cold calling doesn't address the value of qualifying prospects early enough, before time and energy are spent on too many bad ones.

You can surely think of more ideas to categorize cold calling as Good, Bad, even Ugly. Let's look at some ways to make this work, so we don't have to resort to a trip to the casino.

For the sake of simplicity, I'll use phone work as the basis for descriptions here. There are also plenty of face-to-face cold calls being made in business office parks, high-rise office buildings, even people's homes. The basic rules you see here apply to both types of calls.

Dan's Ten Commandments of Cold Calling

1. *It's a conversation, not a pitch.* If you sound like a parrot, spouting memorized words, you'll only earn the equivalent of birdseed in commission. If you're working off some written material, practice sounding spontaneous. Your job is to be interesting, even funny, in order to connect best with the buyer. End your opening comment with a question so it really does become a dialogue at that point. An enjoyable dialogue increases your chances of meeting your goal.

2. *It's a dialogue with one goal.* On the phone, your focus might be to gain a meeting, an appointment. It might be to set a time to call back to connect or it might be to make a site visit to the prospect. Keep your focus on the phone.

3. *Center the conversation on how you help existing prospects solve their problems or attain their goals.* Do not talk about how good your company is, how long it's been in business, or any other me-centered chatter.

4. *When engaging gatekeepers, avoid words that can undermine the value of your offering.* These include "only" or "just." In linguistics, these are called minimizers. So "I only want to talk to Ms. Decision-Maker" tells that person you're speaking with that this isn't that big of a deal, it's of minimal importance. For more information on the fascinating intricacies of language skills training, check out my book, *The Secret Language of Influence* (AMACOM, 2012).

5. *Evidence can be a powerful way to entice the prospect to listen.* When a prospect hears that his or her biggest competitor is using you to gain an edge, he or she would be foolish not to give you some time, even if it's selfish and the prospect just wants to know what the competition is up to. You can manage that concern later. Remember your goal: that appointment.

6. *Rejection is a huge part and percentage of selling.* So don't let rude gatekeepers or prospects annoy you. Laugh, literally, and move on. If this is an issue with you, if you can feel the stomach acid start sizzlin' when you are blasted off a call, review the training elements in Chapter 28, Mental Health for Sales Pros, specifically the parts on self-talk.

7. *More on helping yourself to succeed . . . smile!* It "shows" in the sound of your voice. If you want to make sure you smile, all the time, every call, put a small mirror on your computer monitor. It will work wonders. Smile joyfully, with your eyes. Pair your smile with the confidence that good things are going to happen on the phone today. You help clients in wonderful ways, and you know from the volume of existing clients, as well as in your heart, that you can serve each person with whom you connect by bettering his or her condition with your offerings. Be positive, believe positive, and smile!

8. *Skilled, advanced phone reps find ways to qualify or disqualify prospects right up-front.* This occurs best when the buyer qualifies him- or herself. You'll see how this happens in the sample conversations that follow.

9. *If you really want to attain cold-calling excellence, work hard and fast.* Most phone reps take too much time between calls. They talk with their peers: "You should have heard that joker I just got off the phone with." They just aren't good stewards of their time. Take one day and go hard to find out what your capacity is so you have a baseline for how many calls you can make on a shift or a day. If phone work is just a portion of your daily tasks, the same rule applies. Take those ninety minutes and power up into bigger numbers.

10. *Put a pencil in your lap.* This technique is for callers who are nervous or young or immature in the business. If your vocal pitch is too high, gatekeepers and prospects sense inexperience and nervousness. If you look down, your pitch goes down, too. You sound older, more mature, and confident. You can accomplish this by standing and looking down at your keyboard or computer screen, too.

11. *Bonus commandment.* This last tip is a big one for managing phone teams. I often share a story that reinforces its value. Twenty years ago I placed a sales rep on a small phone team for a very large company. Ken had a farm boy mentality. He just kept working, start to finish. Two months into the job, the president (whom he'd never met) called him in. The rookie was understandably nervous. Pages of data sat atop the big man's desk. The president waved the documents and spoke. The statistics on Ken's calling had been verified by cross-checking the contact manager with

phone records. Why? Because the new guy was making *triple* the phone calls of the other two reps combined. His new revenue contribution to the company was equally well reflected by the numbers held in the man's hand. Ken was soon a rising star, getting the chance to move out from behind his desk and on to sales calls. The other reps weren't happy. They knew their new colleague wasn't a chatty type, aside from breaks and lunches. He indirectly put pressure on his teammates to raise the bar on effort. Their sales increased, and everyone won. So this is the *big* question: Do you know what your capacity is? What can you accomplish in an hour, a shift, a day of harder, more focused cold calling?

Do you think you can (or do) follow all ten commandments? I read a funny story recently about a woman who asked her friend whether she was planning to attend church or sleep in on Sunday. The other woman shook her head and said, "I haven't gone in a long time. Besides, it's too late for me. I've probably already broken all seven commandments."

Ten! There are ten commandments. Some of you might not need. Some of you might already be using them and doing a good job. There are probably a few you really do need to follow religiously. Identify them now.

The Conversation

There are plenty of simple models for getting your message across on the phone. We address gatekeepers in Chapter 13. The key really is to closely follow the ten precepts listed above. Here are a couple of conversation options for you to use. Again, you want to "find your voice," that is, choose language you're most comfortable with in order to calmly and confidently make each call. I do not address responding to objections in the scripts, as there are hundreds of potent ways to handle resistance in Chapter 16, including the Ultimate Objection-Handling Tool.

A traditional call might come across like this . . .

Sample Conversation I

"Mr./Ms. Decision-Maker,

"I work with companies like yours that want to improve their revenue by automating their sales forces to reduce paperwork and improve access to prospects and clients. I will be in your area on Wednesday and Thursday next week. Is one of these days better for you?"

Note: I intentionally included the "I will be in your area" phrase because it's fairly common to do this. However, at one level this means the caller is just getting lined up to improve the efficiency of the rep's work day. I'd prefer to have the prospect believe I'll make a special trip just for him or her. In fact, over the past few years my initial relationships with most of my major consulting clients have started significantly better because I've told people that I'd jump on a plane to meet with them, and I have done so. How serious would the buyer be if you did that? The phone is cheaper. But the tradeoff in cost between doing it like everyone else and distinguishing yourself from everyone else is pretty good—when you close much more business.

Sample Conversation 2

"Mr./Ms. Decision-Maker,

"I work with companies like yours that want to improve their revenue by automating their sales forces to reduce paperwork and improve access to prospects and clients. For example, XYZ Company tracked that they gained an average of forty-five minutes a day from four hundred reps by implementing our solutions. What would that 10 percent increase in income do for your bottom line?"

The person responds with interest.

"Great, I thought this was important enough that you should know of it. When would you like to sit down and figure out how this could work for your team?"

Note: This is *much* stronger. You're giving evidence of success. You're helping the buyer quantify your value, so it becomes more difficult to refuse a deeper conversation.

As an alternative, I'd strongly suggest you employ the strategy described earlier in this chapter. The three-point elevator speech language is perfect for cold calling, since most elevator speeches serve as cold calls anyway.

Sample Conversation 3

"Mr./Ms. Decision-Maker,

"Here are the top three sales training problems I/we solve for my/our existing clients:

1. We help them to stop chasing poor prospects and to discover, then close, more high-quality clients.

2. *They significantly increase their ability to deflect and work through prospects' toughest objections.*

3. *They remove mental and behavioral obstacles that can hinder personal performance.*

"Which one of these is your biggest concern?"

Note: This is excellent, and it's rarely used, so the buyer is hearing a different type of sales pro. The conversation focuses on key criteria that serve to qualify the prospect, which is often a problem in cold calling because we don't know early enough whether it's worth chasing any given prospect. Also, the conversation ends with an open-ended question, so the buyer is about to start talking.

EXERCISE 10.9. Planning Cold Calls

SETUP: Here learners will write out a cold-call pitch in words with which they're comfortable. Sharing will enhance the adoption of alternative language choices.

Craft a cold-calling conversation. Take five minutes to write yours down. Then solicit ideas from as many other reps as possible before finalizing your presentation. The company should log all suggestions to publish later as a sales training tool.

Trainer: As the reps create their cold-calling conversations, draw off the collective brainpower of the team. A wide variety of ideas and skill levels exist already in your group. Make sure you write down everything that surfaces, so you can create a manual of options. This is very powerful as a way to help each rep "find his or her voice." It also serves as a great way to kick-start sales rookies coming into the organization.

The Final Piece of the Cold-Calling Puzzle

Do a quick debriefing after every call. "Quick" is critical as you don't want to slow down momentum and you don't want to reduce your number of daily calls by stopping too often. *However, there is one very important reason to debrief.* Your reps should log the objections that kept them from getting past the gatekeeper or gaining an appointment with the decision-maker.

As we address in Chapter 16, there are about six objections that every salesperson encounters regularly. Your reps' ability to calmly and confidently handle each one is a measure of their maturity in selling.

In the mid-1980s, I cut my teeth doing cold calling by logging objections on a chart. My manager could walk by, look over my shoulder, and see what I was struggling with. This provided perfect focus on coaching and role playing. At first I was nervous that my failures were being written down, tracked for anyone to observe. But when I got help on specific areas where I struggled, my attitude changed and my skills skyrocketed.

I believe this management tool was the key to my attaining individual success in selling. It's also probably the reason I became a manager and within two years was leading a team of fifteen reps myself. None of my people struggled for long on any objection. They learned fast and on the fly. We did the coaching outside calling time, of course. But you'll rarely find a better way to increase cold-calling skills than to help everyone manage and overcome resistance.

So do that debriefing, but don't take time to stop and chat. Check off the objection. It will lead to significant personal improvement as a sales pro.

You can help your sales pros to reduce marketing costs and feel better about landing new clients by creating your own comprehensive lead generation checklist and tool. When will you start?

Chapter 11

Opening the
First Meeting

CHAPTER OVERVIEW

A Psychologically Sound Strategy for Open Sales Calls

    Gain a Time Commitment

    Establish the Rules of Communication

    Set a Purpose or Goal

The *Big* Bonus When Using an Opening Strategy

Advantages of Behavior Contracts

Simply put, this might be the most important idea in the whole book. Great sales pros open strong. Weak ones don't, so they never get close to the close. This powerful strategy comes from a practice that many psychologists use to help patients change behavior. Use it and you'll transform people, too, turning prospects into clients. If your sales team is not using this three-step process to initiate conversations with buyers, you're leaving money on the table. This is the biggest addition I build into sales training programs when I'm redesigning these experiences to optimize new influence strategies.

The Opening Strategy for All Sales Calls

A man and his wife walk into a dentist's office.

The man says to the dentist, "Doc, I'm late and in a hurry. I have two buddies sitting out in my car waiting for us to go play golf, so forget about the anesthetic and just pull the tooth and be done with it. We have a 10:00 a.m. tee time at the best golf course in town and it's 9:30 already. I don't have time to wait for the drug to work!"

The dentist thinks to himself, "My goodness, this is surely a very brave man asking to have his tooth pulled without using anything to kill the pain."

So the dentist asks him, "Which tooth is it, sir?"

The man turns to his wife and says, "Open your mouth, Honey, and show him."

Sales pros—funny story, but can you really control another person? More poignantly, can you control a buyer?

One thing pounded into me when I grew up in selling was this: *You must control the sale!*

Here's the bad news about that old-school thinking—you can't control the sale. Think about this. Can you control someone? Can you control a buyer? You really can't control a sale. Good news. You can *take charge* of the sale. There is a world of difference here.

You take charge by gaining agreement on the steps you and the buyer will take as you talk and walk through the possibility of working together. This strategy of gaining agreement to begin the selling process with your buyer is the single best indicator of sales skill, or talent, I've ever encountered.

It's also the single most critical strategy I teach in sales training.

You see, too much emphasis is placed on closing. In fact, if you don't *open* strongly enough, you'll never get close to the close. You must have a method for taking charge of the buyer/seller interaction, gaining agreement as to how the two of you will "play the game" and how the conversation will end.

A Psychologically Sound Strategy to Open Sales Calls

Eric Berne (1996), whose psychology formed the basis of "transactional analysis," defined an agreement as a *specific commitment, with a well-defined course of action.* This whole field of psychology is founded on a contractual approach to each doctor/patient dialogue. Berne further describes a contract as "an explicit bilateral commitment to a well-defined course of action."

This means that all parties need to agree:

- Why they want to do something

- With whom

- What they are going to do

- By when

- Any fees, payment, or exchanges there will be

(Sounds a lot like all the information we want on the table to complete and close a sales call, doesn't it?)

Contracts need to be framed in positive words—what is wanted, rather than what is *not* wanted. When we tend to look through a negative lens, it focuses us too much on failure. As you look at the examples below and create your own agreement, try to craft them around positive words.

Berne also notes that contracts need to be "measurable, manageable, and motivational." *Measurable* means that the goals need to be tangible, that each party involved in the contract will be able to say in advance how he or she will know when the goal has been achieved. The goal must be specific and behavioral and clearly defined. The contract will also have to be manageable and feasible for all those concerned.

Enough heavy learning for now. Let's make it practical for the sales pro. This is the selling term I use that embodies a perfect example of where sound psychology intersects sound selling: Great sales pros use their own "behavioral contracts."

There are three aspects to this agreement.

1. Gain a time commitment

2. Establish the rules of communication

3. Set a purpose or goal

Let's review each of these steps and learn how to build them into your interactions with prospects. But before you take the time for that, let me give you some quantifiable reasons that validate the potency of this strategy.

A few years ago, I was asked to redesign an existing sales training program for a national financial services firm you'd probably recognize. The redesign project was to add the latest best practices as well as my own influence and persuasion strategies to the company's two-day sales training experience. You can see a model of how, exactly, to re-create your existing sales training with the CAT Scan Diagnostic Tool in Chapter 30, Redesigning Your Existing Sales Training.

We measured, then modeled the company's number one rep, Steve, who was using his own form of a behavior contract (BC) to begin conversations with buyers. The sales process typically included several meetings. The numbers are a bit intimidating (and incriminating of those who embodied the firm's average rep).

The average salesperson spent 12.5 hours with a prospect before the buyers bought or went away. Steve gained agreement right away, then determined within thirty-seven minutes whether the buyer was worth his time. He then pursued him or her or graciously said goodbye (you'll learn how to do that as well).

The average salesperson closed 15 percent of his prospects. Steve closed 76 percent of those with whom he engaged beyond the thirty-seven minutes.

Does a behavior contract really work? I could give you dozens more personal sales stories, not my own (although there are plenty there), to show this does work. Here is one of my favorite tales.

Dave was invited to attend one of my two-day training events, but had an appointment he could not change the first afternoon. That first morning he created his BC, writing it out until he could type it into a Word document later. Shortly afterward, he left for his sales call. The next morning, Dave walked up to me before class *beaming* a huge smile. I asked how the call went. He said, "I'm sitting opposite my prospect in those awkward first moments of a sales call. He knows I'm there to sell him. I know he's here to measure my honesty, my pushiness, my products, you know, all the things prospects are doing while they're also trying to get the best deal, should they buy. So I did the behavior contract, my first time ever, and when I said that we were basically there to figure out whether we'd work together, the tension just drained out of his face. His defenses dropped and our dialogue was totally safe for both of us. I was on the first call of my life where I didn't feel pressured to sell, and he obviously didn't feel pressured to buy. This BC really works." Dave went on to say he had scheduled the second meeting—a solid use of a smart strategy by a sales pro.

By the way, I always require the sales pros I train to carry their BCs with them during the day and into classes. There's nothing more important in their arsenal.

Concept: If you don't open well, you'll never get close to the close.

Let's review those three steps in detail.

Gain a Time Commitment

First, you want to re-visit the amount of time agreed on when the meeting was set up.

Establish the Rules of Communication

Then you ask permission to have an open, honest discussion. (This will include, as you will see, gaining permission to ask lots of questions.)

Set a Purpose or Goal

Finally, you gain agreement that the purpose of the meeting is simply to determine whether you should be working together, schedule a second meeting, or just part ways. In other words, recognize how this meeting is going to end. Once the prospect agrees to the three elements of your BC, you'll thank him or her and open with a leading question.

Here are three examples. The last one represents a bit bolder set of language choices. The key here is to form your own BC. You are to "find your voice" and make the words you choose a reflection of your personality. This is another reason why you want to share your BC with others on the sales team. It'll help everyone find language they feel most comfortable using.

Hint: Be sure that your prospect says he or she understands each step!

Example A

"Mr./Ms. Prospect,

"You said on the phone that we'd have forty-five minutes together. Is that still good? Great. And is it okay for us to set an objective or outcome for this time? Good. Let's do this. You'll want some questions answered, and I will, too. So let's just be candid with one another, and if it looks like you and I are just not in sync with one another, will you please tell me that this doesn't seem like a fit? And if I realize that I can't help you, I'll tell you right away, as your time is precious. Okay? Please don't worry about hurting my feelings. Just be candid, so I don't get the wrong signal and hound your email and voice mail while you try to figure out a way to ignore me.

"So at the end of our meeting together, a couple things can happen: We agree that we're not going to work together and say goodbye or we realize we need another meeting because you need to review this with someone else or I need to get some figures to you or something

like that. Should we need to meet again, we'll simply set the appointment before I go. That way we can treat this issue quickly.

"If you're undecided about what to do next, it probably means you're not comfortable with our problem solving or solutions, and we'll assume that we're not going to work together. I just want to be professional about managing our time. Again, please be candid as soon as you figure out whether we can work together or we should go our separate ways. Is that okay with you? Great, thank you.

"Now, what's the biggest concern you wanted to address during our time today?"

Or "What's the number one reason you invited me in today?"

Example B

"So we're trying to figure out whether this relationship is a good match for both of us. At the end of our meeting together, one of three things can happen:

1. *We figure out that we're good for one another and determine our next step to begin working together.*

2. *We might agree that we're not going to work together and say goodbye.*

3. *Or we could realize that we need another meeting because you need to review this with someone else or I need to get some figures to you or something similar. Should we need to meet again, we'll simply set the appointment before I go. That way we can treat this issue quickly.*

"If, after our forty-five minutes together, you're undecided about what to do next, it probably means you're not comfortable with what we offer, or our solutions, and we'll assume that we're not going to work together.

"Does that set a good framework for our conversation? Good. Now, what's the biggest concern you wanted to address during our time today?"

Example C

"How about I take a few minutes and explain how I work. Okay? This might be a very short meeting. I'm certain you have questions for me, and I have questions for you. Typically, I take some time to get a picture of who you are. Some questions might be about the personal impact of a decision to work together. Will you be okay with that?

"The purpose of this meeting is simply to determine whether we should have a second meeting. You might discover before I do that a second meeting isn't necessary. Will you be

nice enough to tell me? On the other hand, if I discover that before you do, I'm going to be very candid with you and let you know. Fair enough?

"When I'm working with serious clients like yourselves . . . you are serious, aren't you? I usually take two to three meetings. By the end of that time, most of my clients either look at me and say, 'No, this is not for me,' which, by the way, is perfectly okay with me. I'll just close your file and keep you on our mailing list. On the other hand, should you say, 'Yes this program is for me,' then we'll go ahead with the paperwork. By the end of the third meeting, if you still have to 'Think about it,' I can assure you this program isn't for you, so please just tell me 'No' outright..Okay?

"Great, let's get started."

Again: Be sure that your prospect says he or she understands each step! Be sure that he or she *agrees* to each step.

The *Big* Bonus When Using an Opening Strategy

There are basically only four ways a sales call can end. Let's look at their value to us as sales pros:

1. *Yes.* Is yes a good thing? Of course, because we've acquired a new client!

2. *No.* Is no a good thing? Yes it is! We're not going to lie in bed at night, wondering whether that person could buy from us. Remember, we don't chase poor prospects. (See how to eliminate this problem in Chapter 12.) We can cycle back to this person later, but for now we're done and on to investing time in the well-qualified, perfect prospect.

3. *Set the next appointment.* Trick question: Is "Call me next Thursday" an appointment? No! Is "Call me next Thursday afternoon?" No! Is "Call me next Thursday at 2 p.m."? Yes.

   Note: If you've ever had a prospect blow off an appointment, you should plan for that possibility. Say: "Mr./Ms. Prospect, What shall we do if I can't reach you at 2 p.m.?" The response might be, "Call my assistant" or "Try half an hour later," and so forth, so plan for surprises and you won't have any.

4. *Think it over.* Is think it over a good thing? No! It is the single worst phrase anyone in selling can hear. Your bonus on using the behavior contract is that you virtually eliminate the dreaded "think it over." If someone says,

"I'd like to think about this a bit," you gently remind him or her the agreed goal/outcome/purpose of today's conversation was to get each others' questions asked and answered and to determine whether that's enough to say "yes" or "no" or whether you'll set another appointment.

So a healthy agreement permanently eradicates the think it over disease from your sales life. Is that a good thing? YES!

To further reinforce the value of opening strongly, as a key strength to supplement closing skills, look at the double-axis grid in Figure 11.1.

Figure 11.1. Sales Pros Who Open with Agreement

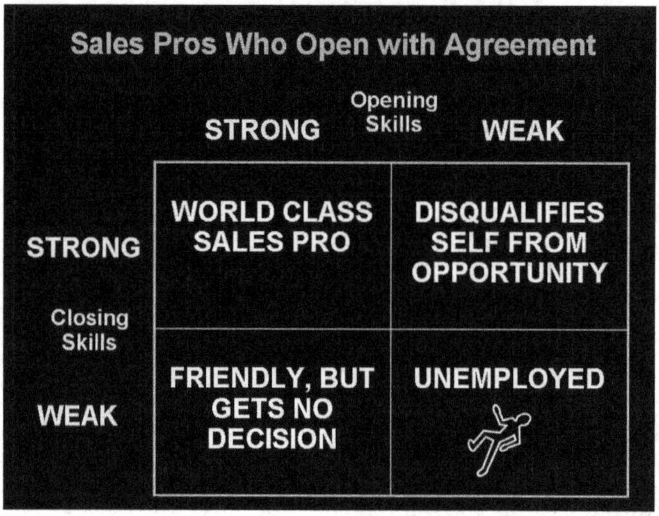

Advantages of Behavior Contracts

Again, I'd like to point out that having a behavior contract might be the most valuable piece of the sales training puzzle I've taught over the last twenty-five years. It's a bit awkward to adapt, but well worth the rep's time and energy in writing and practicing the BC strategy.

Salespeople often walk into a meeting with their personal agendas (SELL NOW!) being the primary focus. When someone comes in showing respect for my time and professionally sets an agenda, I know I can work with this person. When the meeting ends with closure and a solid understanding of status of the relationship as well as the next steps, I just had one of the most unusual and delightfully memorable experiences I've ever had in a sales meeting.

The behavior contract is a solid way to take charge of a sales call and to gain agreement from the buyer about expectations throughout the whole process. It's a truly professional way to run a meeting. It also doesn't allow for the opportunity of a "think it over" from the buyer. While it is a bit difficult to adopt, a BC might be the most valuable strategy a salesperson can use to initiate every sales call.

I *strongly* suggest your company adopt this practice immediately. Have each sales professional draw up his or her own BC, using words with which he or she is completely comfortable. Sales reps should carry these documents with them to review before all calls, until it becomes second-nature to use it at the beginning of each buyer conversation. The company should also keep documentation of as many BCs as possible, in order to share them with incoming hires and all team members.

Chapter 12

Qualifying and Disqualifying Prospects

Chasing poor prospects is trouble. This ties right into the previous section where we addressed the creation of proposals for people who had no intention of buying. In this chapter you'll learn to avoid this troublesome practice, believing everyone might possibly buy. The three-step model is simple and effective.

Do It Quickly!

"Dan Seidman," says the VP of sales, "had his name on the front page of The Wall Street Journal *this week." He pauses as the large room of realtors begins buzzing at that interesting piece of introductory information. "It was on the mailing label, but still on the cover."*

The crowd of REMAX agents and brokers explode into laughter as I bounce up on the stage of their annual sales conference.

"Thank you for that fun introduction. How's this for some more fun? I'm going to ask you a question, and the person who wins will get a fantastic gift! . . . What's the longest time you've chased a prospect . . . who DIDN'T buy?"

Maria was the last one standing. She described a beautiful house in a spectacular location and the couple who lived there. She had met and pursued them for ten and a half years before she realized they really were not going to list their home with her, in spite of a dozen plus buyers who would have fought one another to live there.

Maria receives her gift—The Sales Comic Book, a visual edition of some of my funniest selling blunders (including the appropriate real estate story where a realtor and buyer walk into a quiet house for sale, only to have a naked owner walk out of the shower).

What's not that funny is that Maria has just showed her colleagues the danger of participating in the number 1 problem that all sales professionals face. *They chase poor prospects.*

In over two decades of training salespeople, this issue easily ranks highest in concerns of both reps and sales management. In fact, each time I've mentioned this to a roomful of sales managers, I get more heads nodding than Babe Ruth Bobble Head Night at Yankee Stadium.

This is pretty simple to recognize. If salespeople are closing 10 percent of all prospects, then the other 90 percent of them are bad for business.

Concept: Don't Chase Poor Prospects!

Bad for business means we waste time, energy, money, and time with people who just aren't going to buy from us. Did you notice that time is mentioned twice? That's no mistake. We have nothing more valuable, more precious, than our time. Let's turn our focus on people deserving our time.

Smart sales pros pursue perfect prospects. These are buyers who are highly qualified, as early in the sales process as possible. Let's create a strategy that defines that perfect prospect. There are three steps.

EXERCISE 12.1. Finding Why Poor Prospects Are Bad for Business

SETUP: Here we want to help sellers recognize the dangers of investing time with people who are not going to buy.

What are some reasons why chasing poor prospects is bad for business?

Answers might include things like: waste time, makes me angry after all that work, discourages me, hate when they lie in the end, costs me money, could be working with people who are serious about our help, etc.

Trainer: Make the point: "Good answers, all. Bad news, actually. So let's be aware of how damaging it can be to keep pursuing bad business."

1. Create a Profile of the Perfect Prospect
2. Craft Questions to Determine Whether a Prospect Fits Your Profile
3. Relentlessly Turn Your Back on Those Who Don't Fit!

Here are the details of each element of this process.

Create a Profile of the Perfect Prospect

Your company might already have some of the criteria in place for qualifying prospects. If so, I strongly suggest you follow them closely. If not, here are some basic criteria you could use to begin building your own Perfect Prospect Profile.

- Financial means
- Access to all decision-makers
- Time and urgency
- Potential working relationship

Another way to identify the "Perfect Prospect" is to work backward by benchmarking your best clients. Unpack how they've matched some of these key criteria.

Once we recognize what is important to us, we want to move on to the second step.

Craft Questions to Determine Whether a Prospect Fits Your Profile

There are scores of possible questions, and you can find many more in Chapter 14 on questioning. Remember, you must have the answers to these questions. Your wording when asking them of prospects is key and should reflect the language you're most comfortable with using. Here are a few to prime the pump:

- *Financial questions.* Is there money available for our solutions? Can they share the budget?

- *Decision-maker questions.* Is the person I'm with the sole person involved, or do I need access to others? Is there transparency with these people in working to attain the best solution for the firm?

- *Time and urgency questions.* How soon is the company prepared to finalize a decision? If I can quantify money being wasted or benefits attained, will that speed up the decision-making process?

- *Potential working relationship questions.* Does this person return my calls and emails? Is there enough mutual respect that I can work on an ongoing basis with this firm or individual as a client?

Relentlessly Turn Your Back on Those Who Don't Fit!

We're cycling back to *not* chasing poor prospects here. So when you receive unsatisfactory answers to your questions, you must determine sooner, rather than later, to move on. You must say goodbye or no to these poor prospects in a professional and respectful manner. Here are some sample language choices you can use to disengage poor prospects.

- "I'd love to work with you, but it really is not in your best interest or my company's because _____ [identified disqualifier]."

- **(financial)** "You know, I'd love to work with you and as soon as you figure out the financial side of your decision, we can get together. Do you want to talk about a time frame when I can call you back, or would you like to contact me?" Then be prepared to walk away.

- **(decision-maker)** "Thank you for your time. I can appreciate how important this decision is to your company. However, I really need to continue this conversation with the person who owns the results of this decision. When he or she (or the board or team) has time to sit down, I'd be happy to re-engage. Do you want to talk about a time frame when I can call you back, or would you like to contact me?" Then be prepared to walk away.

- **(time/urgency)** "You know, I'd love to work with you, but you're not pressed to address this right away. It appears your timing isn't at a critical stage and I don't want to seem like I'm pushing you to buy any solution. That's okay. I'm here for you when you need me. Do you want to talk about a time frame when I can call you back, or would you like to contact me?" Then be prepared to walk away.

- **(working relationship)** "Thank you for our time talking. To me, it appears our philosophical differences in how each of us would handle this decision are quite different. I'm sure you have some good choices out there with whom you'd be more comfortable. Take care, and I wish you the best of luck." Walk away.

This last one is toughest to do. I learned how critically important a good working relationship is when I cut my teeth in sales as a recruiter twenty-five years ago. If a candidate for a job wouldn't listen to my coaching and take advice on how to interview and what to say, then it significantly reduced my chance to close that sale.

I believe the working relationship mismatch issue mostly comes from buyers who tend to think they're smarter and "above" salespeople. It is exacerbated by reps who beg for time and attention, then speak up to buyers, as if they are not equals or peers. In your head you must believe you are a buyer's peer. He or she needs your solution, and you hold the key to the attainment of his or her goals or the elimination of his or her problems. With your words, you must communicate your expertise as a peer. If you don't position your brain and your tongue to see that decision-maker eye-to-eye, you won't get the respect you need to attain a healthy working relationship.

Notice how most criteria end with the phrase "Then be prepared to walk away." You might be surprised when you say goodbye that the prospect has a change of heart, perhaps begins to take this decision more seriously. After all, how many sales-people can courteously say, *"Thank you, good luck with your issues, I'm out of here"*?

It is that simple. Great salespeople spend more time with better prospects and less with bad ones. Learn to quickly disqualify your poor prospects.

The following selling blunder solidly anchors the value of drawing up your criteria at the beginning of each relationship, and asking questions before investing too much time into each buyer.

Excavating Clients: Mark Attempts to Construct a Big Sale

First thing in the morning and we had a last-minute pitch to make. The president of our Chicago agency heard that a Milwaukee-based crane association was reviewing their programs, and he told me to call and ask for an appointment today—before they finalized any decisions. I called and practically begged for the meeting. I drove the two hours up I-94 completely confident that we still had a great shot at landing the business.

We'd handled loads of construction companies. I brought custom flyers and tons of testimonials with impressive pictures of earth-moving equipment. Cruise control set at 70, I smiled as I passed from Illinois into Wisconsin. There must have been six or eight crane rental companies along the highway. If you believed in omens, you'd feel pretty good about this sales call.

I pulled up to the front door to discover the association logo was a crane, the bird with the long neck. Cool idea. Some non-profit organizations really market themselves well.

The reception area was quiet and beautifully decorated. The walls were covered with cranes, hundreds and hundreds of them, that is, the birds! This association was for the preservation of, well, the other cranes.

I met the decision-maker and presented our company's offerings, but I was really rattled by our mistake. Most of my mental attention was just anger at my president. The executive director sat through the most uninspired sales conversation she'd ever encountered. I just felt stupid being there.

I left the association empty-handed with my tail feathers between my legs. I had the special pleasure of being the butt of office jokes for several months.

Now, even if I'm in a hurry, I do some homework on all my prospects.

Remember the number 1 problem sales pros encounter? Don't chase poor prospects! Define your perfect prospects, craft questions to qualify or disqualify them quickly, then walk away or begin your structured approach to close the sale.

The company should publish clear guidelines as to who is a perfect prospect and who is not. Every member of the sales team should be held accountable to abide by these practices.

Chapter 13

Bypassing Gatekeepers

CHAPTER OVERVIEW

Gatekeepers! If we won't admit it's a dirty word, at least we can't ignore how the good ones can get the stomach acid sizzling when they stonewall us from buyers who need what we have and have the money to spend on our products and services. In this chapter, you'll see seven strategies for handling gatekeepers. The first one (call at the highest level) is first because I've found it most effective both personally and with teams I've trained. But I really like the fourth one because it just seems to be unique enough to get teams I'm training passed to the right person.

Regardless of the strategy you choose, be upbeat, be persistent, and keep smiling. Great gatekeepers seem to be able to hear a smile on the phone.

Cerberus is the monstrous three-headed dog that guards the underworld in Greek mythology. He is the ultimate gatekeeper; intimidating, strong, loud, and deadly. In this sales tale, another canine caretaker gives his all to prevent a rep from reaching his man.

Screening Out Salespeople: Doug's Day Isn't All Life on the Farm

As I steered my car into the dirt driveway, a large house, barn, and silo filled my dust-covered windshield. You sure didn't wear a suit selling agriculture insurance. My plaid shirt, jeans, and sturdy work boots kept me from looking like a salesman. The agricultural market could be tricky—as building trust in conservative farm families often took a great deal of time and "small talk."

This was my first sales call on Mr. Guthrie. As I opened my car door familiar farm sounds came to me—including the sharp, angry barking of a dog. I parked the car about 20 yards from the house so anyone would have a clear view of me. I'd had my share of homeowners greeting me with shotguns in hand and was nervous about, well, making anyone nervous.

The barking grew louder, then turned to a snarl as a huge dog flew from the back of the house and charged me. This was not normal. This was not good. I froze in front of my car and waited for him to stop and just yelp noisily until his master appeared. But this vicious beast kept coming. Alarm bells rang in my brain and my heart went into hyper-drive.

The dog launched itself at me, going airborne from about 10 feet away. In my moment of absolute danger a simple thought flitted into my head, "You should have moved to the side of the car, you dummy, there is nowhere to go."

I kicked up, more out of instinct than expertise, and my boot caught the animal in the throat. He crashed into me as I threw up my hands to protect my face. The attack drove me back into my car, my right elbow shattering a headlight. I scrambled to regain my balance and the dog bounced off my body, fell to the earth, and lay still.

Wow! I had dispatched the dog with one swing of my Red Wing shoes.

Adrenaline continued to rocket through my body, and I broke into a furious sweat. Blood dripped from my elbow onto the hood of my car.

A slow drawl sounded through the swarm of thoughts stinging my brain. "You killed my dog."

It was the farmer, my prospect. "Well, if you can get by him, I'll listen to what you have to say."

It was the toughest screening job a prospect had ever done on me.

Chances are you'll never face a gatekeeper as aggressive as that farmer's dog, although you might find plenty who are equally intimidating. How are you doing when you run into someone whose job it is to keep you from interrupting the life of his or her leader?

EXERCISE 13.1. Brainstorming How to Deal with Gatekeepers

SETUP: Here we want to get feedback and ideas on how the team members deal with gatekeeper resistance.

What exactly do you say when you encounter a gatekeeper? Share ideas with the whole team. Find out what does work and what does not.

Trainer: A log of responses should be kept here to give team members choices when blocked by gatekeepers.

Are prospects' personal assistants holding you at bay? Are you saying things that work, that gain you access, or are you using words that you learned long ago, hoping the person eventually gives in and says "yes" to a phone call or an appointment?

The focus of this chapter is to give you some alternatives to what you might traditionally have learned to get past professional screeners. Let's look seriously at what has not worked for us in the past and change our behavior from now on. This is the reason we used the exercise. We know what doesn't work. Let's look at some unique ideas and some best practices, then incorporate those that *will* work for us.

As we engage in any dialogue with a gatekeeper, keep this in mind: These people are business professionals themselves. C-suite personal assistants in particular are very sharp. They have in-depth knowledge and experience with key people inside the organization. They understand the corporate structure and can be excellent resources. Show them respect and they will return it, often by helping you directly.

You should understand this key fact about the people who are professional gatekeepers. If you present your ideas or solutions as functional or operational problems, you'll be handed off to the "proper" department (so hiring goes to human resources, sales-related goes to sales, etc.). That means you could be shuttled off to lower-level decision-makers instead of having the opportunity to present to the highest quality, highest level decision-maker. The better your solutions are presented as critical to the concerns of that gatekeeper or personal assistant's boss, the more likely you are to deal with the top dog, so you want to position yourself and your offerings so well that you are given access to the true buyer.

Concept: Turn Walls into Windows

Quick thought on sending literature: I often think about how I'd like to take the first rep who ever responded to "send me some literature" by sending it and strangle him with his tie. The fact is that ties have less use every day, and this might be a good idea. The issue is that this caveman salesman began training our prospects long ago to ask for literature. He taught them they could get rid of us by requesting materials. Your job is not to mail literature (I hope); it's to get that appointment.

Please remember this as well: *You do not want to act or sound like other salespeople.* It's too easy for gatekeepers to label or categorize callers. If you're identified as a sales pest, you'll be disposed of quickly.

Gatekeeper Strategies

Here are seven tactics you can use to gain access to the true decision-maker. Remember to *keep your focus*! If your job on the call, in person, or face-to-face is to land an appointment, then all your energy, words, and behavior should work toward attaining that goal.

First Call at the Highest Level

This is your first choice because it's the smartest approach. My default phone call to a company is always to the office of the CEO. Once you have that person's assistant, ask him or her who owns the results of services, solutions, or interventions like yours. This person will want you off the phone quickly, and the best way is to give you the right information. Once he or she points you to the right executive, you call the gatekeeper and tell that person how the CEO's assistant suggested you speak with the gatekeeper's boss. You will be surprised at how often this works. You might also be surprised how you might have been heading in the wrong direction in the first place. In other words, that CEO's assistant might suggest someone you never suspected to be the proper decision-maker.

I had a funny experience when I first began doing this. The CEO's assistant of a major office products company (you would immediately recognize) recommended I speak with the North American president.

"The president's assistant is named Marianne," she offered as she wished me luck. I called and was shocked that the president himself answered his own line. My first words were (stupidly), "Oh, I thought I'd get Marianne." "Here you are," said my decision-maker, as he forwarded me to his assistant's voicemail.

It took me two months to get the president on the phone again and we had a great laugh over my mistake. His assistant had been at lunch and he was expecting another call and answered.

Call first at the highest level. It's a truly professional move that savvy sales pros use.

Ask to Leave Voicemail for the Decision-Maker

This is fairly simple to do today. But you'd better have a very potent message that incites the listener to act. Some details on this are in Chapter 5, Potent Communication Skills. Here's a unique message I most highly recommend:

> *Mr./Ms. Decision-Maker, [name of assistant] passed me over to you. Here are the top three problems we solve for our existing clients (many whom you know).*
>
> 1.
>
> 2.
>
> 3.
>
> *Which one is your biggest concern?*
>
> *A conversation about the impact of this issue would be very useful for your organization. This is (Sales Pro Name) of (Company) at 312–555–1212. I can be reached live between 3 and 5 p.m. today.*

Pitch the Gatekeeper as a Decision-Maker

When you get the sense that this person is a true center of influence inside the organization, speak with him as if he were the decision-maker. Use the top three strategies described above. Once the person acknowledges the concerns you identified (he might even know the answer), ask him for access to his boss.

Ask "Who Owns the Results of This Issue/Decision?"

You'll probably notice this phrase peppered throughout *The Ultimate Guide to Sales Training.* It is too powerful to ignore. When the gatekeeper says, "That'd be my boss," you'll respond, "Great, I'm in the right place. That's who I can help. How do I best get time with her?"

Go Around Them

Tough screener? Find ways around that person. Call at unusual times of day (or night). Find the decision-maker on LinkedIn or Facebook. (Be careful here though. Remember this is a personal social network.) Google the person using a search for the firm's email formula. So if the company's email formula is FirstName.LastName@Company.com, find the decision-maker and begin to contact him or her directly. Additionally, some voicemail messages have the buyer's cell phone number. This isn't for a pitch, but I'd consider texting the person if you leave a few messages and don't receive a response. How about a fax message? Almost everyone of stature in corporate America still has a fax number. Send the person a fax. It'll be laid right on his or her desk and might possibly be the only fax he or she receives this year.

Make 'em Laugh

You've already seen how often I use humor to communicate and coach sales pros. This works great with gatekeepers as well. This is another time to be creative and distinguish yourself from other reps.

   One of my best moves with this tactic was necessary when I had tried again and again to gain access to a CFO of a major Chicago hospital. Then I remembered the coconut! I dug into my guerrilla-marketing file and found the brochure from a Hawaiian company that mailed coconuts. That company wrote your message on them in black marker. I placed my order and sent it off with the words, "You're a tough nut to crack."

A week later my phone rang. I answered and heard nothing but laughter. "I'm sitting here at my desk and my secretary and I are dying laughing," the CFO said. "When would you like to come in?"

You can send gifts, goodies, and gags. Tell the gatekeeper afterward that you thought it'd be a nice break from boring sales reps she has to keep away from her boss all day long. Do you think that'd form a bond with the assistant?

Make 'em laugh.

Ask a Question They Can't Answer

I like this because, when you have a critical enough concern, the gatekeeper knows in his or her heart that the right thing to do is to pass you along. Here's an example:

> "Mr./Ms. Gatekeeper, have you seen the results of an analysis on how your company's benefits strategies help you recruit better employees (or hurt you)?" (No.) "Then how do we get that started?" (My boss would have to handle that conversation.)

See how this works? It's an unusual and potent approach.

Seven techniques—seven ways to gain access to the money. Which one will you start to use right away? Keep this list handy. You should also have a list compiled from your team's brainstorming session on what works and what doesn't with gatekeepers.

Companies should create a gatekeeper file and make it handy for sales pros to use. A detailed document should be part of the training manual and should also be on the computer, especially to help those selling on the phone to move past tough resistance.

Chapter 14

Power
Questions

Questions define sales pros. Good ones ask good questions. Great ones ask great questions. In this rich chapter you'll find dozens of questions to use as you navigate your way through the steps of the sale. We've broken down the topic into three areas. But the most unique element in this chapter is the focus on my favorite secret in questioning—the use of emotions to generate deeper prospecting conversations.

Using Power Questions to Advance the Sale Toward the Close

Trick question—What is your purpose in asking questions?

I'll give you a hint: In Christianity, Judaism, and Islam, there is a story about Moses and the burning bush. Moses thinks this is amazing. He is gazing at a bush that is burning, but is not burning up. Flames are roaring away and the plant remains as green as a golf course. Must be a miracle and, sure enough, God happens to be hanging around and starts speaking. Then God tosses a question at Moses. He asks, "What is that in your hand?"

As the story goes, in Moses' hand is his shepherd's staff and he thinks it's a staff, even answers the question that way. That is, until God tells him to throw it on the ground and the staff turns into a snake. It's a very exciting scene and you can look up the details for yourself.

But your job right now is to answer the question: "What is your purpose in asking questions?" Your hint was given in the story and overtly hidden in God's question: "What is that in your hand?"

Assuming that God is this all-knowing, all-powerful being, there's probably a very good chance that He knows what that stick is. He doesn't need Moses' help here. So why ask?

God challenges Moses' thinking. He asks an interview question to discover whether this prospective leader of two million people is a good fit. God asks a question so that the conversation moves in a direction that He wants it to go. That sounds to me like great selling. In other words, here's the purpose: *The question is for the benefit of the person being asked.*

Wise sales professionals know this. Great questions are not always about gathering data. Today, most data can be obtained online, aside from personal information and the specific impact of the decision. We'll use questions to discover those repercussions. You'll gather information that points to problems you can solve or benefits you offer. Develop your questions so they put your prospects on a path of your choosing.

Let's practice this concept. You're selling a car to a woman in sales:

You: Your car's all right. What made you decide to start looking at new ones?

Prospect: Just wanted to upgrade my image a bit.

You: Oh really? What is that about?

Prospect: I just got a promotion and wanted to make sure what I drive is a reflection of my success.

You: So what would happen if you kept driving the older one?

Prospect: People would probably wonder about my earnings or I'd be embarrassed to take clients out in this older car.

You: So do clients' attitudes about you affect your business?

Prospect: Yes, in the sense that they like to work with successful people, right? Doesn't everybody?

You get the idea. Your questions are leading her deeper into despair about the impact of *not* owning a new car. You could continue on by asking how it would affect her earnings or any of many other problems related to getting out of the old car and into a new one.

For another prospect, your questions could lead down a path filled with the benefits of owning: more prestige, you look great in it, fun to drive, fast ride, etc.

Learn to develop great lines of inquiry. Remember this concept:

The question is for the benefit of the person being asked.

Great sales professionals ask extraordinary questions. In this chapter you'll gain a rock-solid foundation for your questioning strategy. The learning is structured in three sections:

1. Reasons for Questions

2. Rules for Questions

3. Categories of Questions

Keep one thing in mind as you absorb this information and develop your own list of questions. You must find *your* "voice." In other words, you have to discover words and phrases that are a reflection of your own personality. Then your conversations should attain a comfort level that is close to a simple chat between friends, so you'll quickly know whether this prospect is worth pursuing or whether it's time to walk away. Remember, you're always qualifying or disqualifying (Chapter 12).

Reasons for Questions

Listed below are fifteen reasons why you'll want to learn how to ask great questions of your prospects.

1. Generate and continue to build rapport

2. Hear the prospect's needs, wants, objectives, goals, and problems

3. See how your solutions fit (or don't fit) those concerns

4. Help you gather data to quantify or dollarize the value of your solutions

5. Respond to objections

6. Give direction to the dialogue; take it down a path of your choosing in order to help the buyer see more that he or she might not be aware of (Moses' staff).

7. Assure that the buyer feels safe in his or her decision making, covering concerns such as:

    • Worry about how he or she is perceived in the organization as a decision-maker

    • How this choice will help the organization save money or obtain more of it

    • Whether he or she has made the best possible choice between options (including, of course, your competition)

8. Create candor that helps the buyer feel comfortable with you personally. When you do this, the buyer will open up and honestly share information (only happens when he or she truly believes your interest is first in serving, not closing a sale).

9. Help you up-sell and cross-sell. Discover all the issues at stake and you realize other places your solutions could serve the buyer's firm.

10. Evoke emotion through casual conversation, in order to motivate the prospect to take action. This is aided tremendously by having an air of curiosity. See this in greater detail in Chapter 15 on Practicing Listening Skills.

11. Listen first, talk last, so that you focus on gaining information

12. Keep from presenting solutions prematurely (another by-product of good listening)

13. Identify the true buyer or all the buyers

14. Nail down all the information needed to close the sale

15. Know when it's time to walk away

Rules for Questions

Five rules for questions are discussed below.

1. Evoke Emotion!

AAAAAHHHHH! I've always wanted to use that as a title to an article. I love the sound of it. And honestly, I struggled between using AAAARRGGGHHH! and AAAAAAHHHHH! and believe you'll agree that I chose the right one.

The point of that expression? The fact that it represents an emotion, an outburst of feeling. Say it again, right now. Did our title come flying off your tongue as a good feeling or as one of disgust, possibly despair?

Emotion is the first of our five rules because it's the most important, least understood, and most neglected idea in most coaching on questioning. Here's what you want to walk away with, after reading this section:

You *must* evoke emotion when you converse with prospects.

How best to do this? By crafting your questions so that they create not simply a logical, but a gut response from your buyers. How do we know this is important? How do we know it works?

The field of neuroeconomics is a combination of research from the fields of psychology, economics, and neuroscience. Researchers look at the role of the brain when we evaluate decisions, categorize risks and rewards, and interact with ourselves and others.

Almost every study on decision making reveals that when a buyer decides to buy, she or he is first driven by emotion, then validates or rationalizes the decision with logic.

Therefore, as sales professionals, evoking emotion during a sales call is key to helping buyers buy. If you neglect to create an environment in which an emotional response occurs, you'll end up with a clinical, rational prospect who decides with his or her head, not heart. If this fascinates you and you want more information, you'll be captivated by the stories, research, and applications from Jonah Lehrer's book, *How We Decide* (2009).

Corporate America understands this quite well. For example, as I was writing this chapter, BMW came out with an automobile commercial that illustrates this point:

> *What you make people feel is as important as what you make. We don't just make cars, we make joy!*

Their ad is accompanied with many images, all connected with the word "joy," a powerful emotion.

It's time for sales pros in America to intentionally adopt these practices as well. When prospects make decisions, they either choose based on benefits or good things they get, or they are motivated to take action and buy based on avoiding problems in the present or future. Our questioning strategies should center on evoking emotion first, which means we need to understand the emotional component of every benefit we offer and every problem solved by our products and/or services.

Additional details on this concept are found in Solution- Versus Consequence-Centered Selling, Chapter 17. You can develop questions that generate either positive or negative emotions. Your job is to match the emotion to the buyer's style, be it benefit-based or problem-oriented. You will find many examples in the rest of this chapter. Here are a few:

You can reinforce the power of emotion when you ask your questions by directly inserting a bit of feeling. Look at this example:

*"You had customized books ordered for your national sales conference and they
arrived at the end of the event? Oh no! What did your boss say?"*

Now you can assume, the "oh no!" shows you're empathetic to the bad experience (much like Bill Clinton's classic "I feel your pain"), but the boss question is a real rough one. Your buyer will most likely go right back to that place and time when his manager, executive, or owner just teed off on the poor person for letting this happen.

"We will never let anything like that happen to you again" (which might be your
follow-up comment) gets emotions back on track for the buyer, as he or
she will begin to experience hope, satisfaction, trust, or relief (per our list
of emotions below).

So, again, your job is to evoke emotion and form a bond with the buyer. Humor does this well, as you will see from the examples later in the chapter of responding to objections. There are literally dozens of questions you can develop for each category. I recently designed a sales training program for one financial services firm where we identified thirty-seven objections prospects were using. Read this crazy (and humorous) rep response to one:

"Aren't we too old to buy an annuity?"

"Not really, we have sea turtles older than you as clients."

Laughter (and surprise) generates a gut response that spikes emotion and bonds you with your buyer.

If you don't find your voice in some of the following five objection categories, create your own and add emotion to increase their potency in front of prospects. I've *italicized* the *words* that add emotion to the questions.

Qualifying and Disqualifying
"How fast do we want to get this *frustrating* selection made and off your
plate, so you can get back to your other responsibilities?"

Clarifying Buying Process (How They Buy, Who the Key Decision-Maker Is)
"Do you *battle* a board that helps make this decision, or will they pretty much
rubber-stamp anything you like?"

Defining Success, Goals, Problems That Require Attention

"You've had some *stressful* vendor relationships in the past, so what's the best
way to help you know you've made the right choice here?"

Finalizing the Sale

"So, I give you a proposal with the numbers we discussed and the timing that
fits and you'll be *happy* to get started?"

Follow Up with a New Client

"Is everything good? You *happy*? Can I do anything differently to make things
easier for you?"

Your emotional connection is increased by using words that help, plus facial
expressions and tone of voice to reinforce your empathy with the person's current
situation.

I coach sales pros to feel like they were talking to a best friend, to the
point where they could grab the person by the shoulders, shake him, and say,
"You've got to have this! Your life will be changed forever with a simple 'yes'!"

You get the picture—your own emotions reveal the depth of your belief in
your solutions.

Let's do a quick review before you go put this all into play.

First, the emotional component of questioning can't be underestimated.
Remember the research data on how decisions are made—they're first based on
emotions. You must build emotional word choices into your questions.

Secondly, find your voice. Make sure the questions you use reflect your personality and personal words and phrases. Make sure you ask questions with authentic
interest in the answers and use emotion in your voice and face as well.

Let's look next at another psychologically sound way to emotionally connect
with buyers.

2. Lead with Softening Statements

People's views—and buying decisions—are influenced by their personal backgrounds, experience, education, and professional roles. *Softening statements* are a
great way to not only acknowledge their experience, but also to show *respect* and
empathy for them as business professionals.

Good psychology teaches us that it helps to gain an emotional connection with
a prospect by prefacing questions with brief softening statements like these:

- "Oh, I just thought of this . . ."
- "Help me out here, please . . ."
- "I appreciate you being honest with me . . ."
- "Oh no!"
- "My goodness . . ."
- "I'm curious . . .'
- "I'm not sure exactly what you mean by that, so can you please explain . . ."

These statements lead into a conversation that sounds more spontaneous and more like two friends or business colleagues working through the decision together. This also prevents the *us versus them* dialogues that happen too often in sales. And we've all been there when a sales rep becomes defensive. Here's how it feels:

Prospect: "Your price is too high."

Seller: "Not really, when you calculate . . ." OR they say: "By how much?" OR "We have plenty of clients who decided to buy from us. . . ."

Here is the same dialogue with the sales rep using a softening statement. Take note of how this conversation feels.

Prospect: "Your price is too high."

Seller: "Help me out here, please. You're saying it's too high . . . is it too high compared to other options, or do you mean you may not have the budget for this amount?"

OR

Seller: "I just thought of this; let's work through some numbers and know for sure what the best decision is for you."

OR

Seller: "Oh no! I guess we're done talking then, right?"

Never underestimate the power of empathy during sales conversations.

Let's move on to deepening prospects' emotional response by digging deeper beneath their responses.

Concept: Evoke emotions with your questions.

3. Dig Deeper

Here's something good to know. The best questions give you not only an opportunity to evoke a deeper emotional response, but also to understand more details about the prospect's situation. Here are a few examples of areas you can dig deeper into:

- A loss of income, time, opportunity, promotion, status, business, or job
- Poor performance or poor results of self, company, co-workers
- A waste of: time, money, status

You would then follow up their answers with comments like "Tell me more" or "Interesting, what else can you share about that?" or "How has that affected . . . others, the firm, your customers, etc.?" By digging more deeply, you can take the conversation down a path of your choosing.

Notice in the questions below how the same issue can be followed up by another question that then leads the conversation down a different path:

> *"I see, so you figured out exactly how much this issue is costing the company. How much longer can you tolerate a relatively slow decision-making process?"* Path: buying process, timing

> *"I see, so you figured out exactly how much this issue is costing the company. Is this getting so expensive you might prefer a faster solution over a less-expensive one?"* Path: lost income, value

> *"I see, so you figured out exactly how much this issue is costing the company. Who's going to start holding your feet to the fire to resolve this?"* Path: decision-maker, economic stakeholder

As you identify which path you'll follow, be prepared to ask additional questions to gain clarity on the topic. For example, in the last scenario, follow-up questions could be like these:

- "So how do you equate that figure with its impact on the firm?"
- "Is it equal to losing a new sales hire each year? Or losing a point of market share?"

To conclude this point, you want to make sure that your prospect has a clear picture of the dramatic impact your solution can provide. Let's look now at identifying the types of questions to use and the time to ask them.

4. Identify the Types and Times for Questions

In this section, we're first going to show you what kinds of questions (types) to ask during the different phases (times) of the sale. We'll move chronologically through the sales process, focusing on three main elements. Additional detail on other parts of the sale can be found in the next chapter.

The first step is to qualify or disqualify your prospect.

Embedded in this step is your need to uncover whether the prospect in front of you has the budget, urgency, and authority to say "yes." Three questions for each are listed below.

Budget

- "We respect your time in working on a solution. Are there financial parameters within which we should be working?"
- "What is your expectation of the investment required?"
- "Would you be willing to share what you're able to spend?"

Urgency

- "How urgent is this issue?"
- "What is your timing to accomplish this?"
- "If you don't find a solution to your problem fairly soon, what's the impact on you?"

Authority

- "Who can immediately approve this project?"
- "Who controls the resources required to make this happen?"

- "Who ultimately owns the results of this decision?" (*By the way, this is the best question ever to use in uncovering a decision-maker or economic buyer.*)

The next phase of the sale is handling objections.

We've always been taught that the first response we receive is not normally the real reason for rejection. Here's how we discover what's really going on. Again, once you've created an environment in which emotion is present, the sales dialogue becomes significantly safer for the buyer. Try these questions:

- "If we resolve this objection, can we proceed?" (*This question respects the buyer, saying it is a legitimate concern.*)

- "Isn't the likelihood of that occurring fairly low? Please tell me how that bothers you." (*This challenges the validity of an objection that might be taking the conversation off-course.*)

- "Is that a deal killer?" (*A brave question, but a good one to use when things aren't going your way and you have rapport. It really asks, "Are you serious?"*)

The third step is gaining commitment or the close.

Three question types at this stage include getting the buyer to define what success looks like, probing for issues that might undermine the sales at the last minute, then finalizing the sale and finding opportunities to up-sell, cross-sell, and gain referrals.

Defining Success

- "How would the operation, in different departments, improve as a result of this work?"

- "What issues would be eliminated with this solution?"

- "How will you quantify or measure the value of this decision?"

Preventing Surprises

- "What might happen that could derail implementing your solution?"

- "How likely is it that we'll be working together?"

- "Do we need to discuss anything else that we haven't covered yet?"

Finalizing the Sale

- "I'll put the details into a proposal document right away. Assuming everything is as we discussed, how soon can we begin?"
- "What would you like to do next?"
- "May I start right now by preparing you to acquire this solution?"

Up-Selling, Cross-Selling, and Referrals

- "May I show you some additional options you could find of high value?"
- "Aside from your group, where else might this solution help the organization?"
- "Who outside the organization should I be talking to as well?"

Finally, every sales pro should have five power questions with which to gain the most potent information needed to close a sale. These questions represent your persuasion power.

5. Select Five Power Questions

Throughout more than twenty years of leading and training sales professionals, the five most popular questions I've heard are those below. Again, you want to craft your own, in your own words.

1. Could you tell me more or be more specific?
2. How long has that been going on and what has it cost you?
3. What have you done in the past to solve this problem? How is that working out?
4. How is that affecting you personally? How does that make you feel?
5. Have you considered just leaving things the way they are? or What would you do if you couldn't find a solution?

You must have the discipline and the skill to have your power questions answered.

Concept: Power questions reduce objections.

Categories of Questions

Described below are five categories of questions, with five sample questions in each. Brainstorm with your team and come up with ten or twelve more in each of the categories. You'll notice some overlap, and that's fine. Just make sure, at the end of the day, that your most important questions have been answered.

1. Qualifying

Remember, qualify every prospect early! Your criteria might include finding whether this person matches your perfect prospect profile. This profile should include areas like budget, access to decision-maker, urgency, and more. Do not ignore the human element here.

One issue everyone struggles with is whether he or she can work with this client. Will the person be open and honest with you? Is he or she looking at this as a partnership, or are you seen just as a vendor or, worse, a contract worker?

- "Is this a critical issue that needs urgent attention?"
- "How do you think we are a good fit?"
- "Would you share your criteria for identifying the best solution?"
- "How many other companies have you spoken to?"
- "Are you solely responsible for this decision, or are others helping to make it?"

2. Discovery

During this stage, you want to uncover who holds the money (economic buyer), who all the decision-makers are, what could go wrong, how much money is available, and whether up-selling or cross-selling opportunities exist. If you get resistance at this stage, you might consider backing up to look at whether this is truly a qualified prospect. Don't waste time speaking to the wrong person. On the other hand, this is when some tough questions have to be answered, so establish rapport and you'll get what you need.

- "Who is the real champion of this initiative?"
- "Is this part of your budget, or are the investments to solve this concern under others' control?"

- "How soon will you decide which solution to use?"

- "What, if anything, could slow up your desire to handle this issue?"

- "As you see the effectiveness of our solutions, can you think of other areas in the organization that could be helped by these solutions?"

3. Objections

Primary rule at this stage: Don't get defensive! And in spite of the old adage that objections mean there is interest, you want to decide whether resistance is really indicative of the buyer's desire to keep you in the dark. In other words, there are honest and dishonest doubters. Your purpose should be to partner with the buyer. When you're working together to help attain company goals or remove roadblocks, you'll move much more smoothly past objections and advance the sale. Notice how each response below is prefaced with a softening statement.

- "Interesting thought. What is the probability of that really happening?"

- "We can probably figure that out together. What do you think we should do?"

- "I was thinking of that as well. Do you think it's even worth worrying about, as we'll be attaining your goals in the end?"

- "Okay, great question. Rather than get into a long conversation now, can the proposal address that?"

- "Thank you for sharing that. Is it a deal killer?"

4. Vision

Help your buyer determine measures of success. Help him or her identify and quantify both goals to reach and problems to solve. Quantifying is critically important, as many buyers want to understand which metrics will prove they've made a successful decision. Additionally, great sales pros assist buyers in anticipating outcomes because buyers may be aware of wants and miss some needs. Work together to identify likely professional and personal outcomes.

- "What are some ways this solution improves your company's condition?"

- "Have you quantified the amount of money saved or revenue increased?"

- "How does this solution affect you in ways you can measure? What intangible results might you attain?"

- "What if you just left things as they are? Would it make much difference in the end?"

- "What would the perfect solution look like?"

5. Commitment

You should know this cold, hard selling fact about closing. And you should act upon it. The buyer's interest in you and your solution diminishes the moment you walk out the door. What you don't know is whether interest goes down slowly or whether it plunges like a waterfall to disappear like a drop of water in the middle of a lake. Therefore, it is important to close as quickly as possible.

- "Sounds like we've figured everything out. Shall we start?"

- "You can count on receiving my proposal tomorrow. When would you like to have it signed and start me working?"

- "What would you like me to do now?"

- "It seems as if it's in your best interest to start on this right away. Is there anything that could keep us from starting?"

- "You made a great decision to sit down with me. And it appears we've identified exactly what your issues are and how our solutions eliminate them. What would you like to do now?"

EXERCISE 14.1.   Collecting Questions

SETUP: Here we want learners to begin creating their own power questions so that they'll "own" the use of the best ones.

Trainer: Split the team into five groups, each taking one category. If there are more than five teams, excellent! Multiple groups can work on each of the categories.

1. Qualifying

2. Discovery

3. Objections

EXERCISE 14.1.   Collecting Questions, Cont'd

4. Vision

5. Commitment

Have teams write down questions for their categories and share them with everyone.

Ask: What other questions that you heard can you build into your script book that will help other reps "find their voices"?

Reps are welcome to steal ideas from other categories or other resources.

The company should log *all* questions by category and provide a list to all team members. This begins to lay the foundation for a legacy in great questioning skills.

To sum up, the keys to asking the right questions in the right way are to:

- Engage your prospect by connecting with him or her in a dynamic conversation that emulates a personal friendship or close connection.

- Evoke emotion and stay curious!

- "Find your voice" and make the questions your own.

- Identify and perfect your power questions.

- Dig deeper and take the buyer down a path you choose that will lead him or her to the close.

In the end, the number one secret to potent questioning is to use *emotions*!

Chapter 15

Practicing
Listening Skills

CHAPTER OVERVIEW

Why People Are Poor Listeners

Keys to Good Listening

What to Listen For

Exercises to Develop Great Listening Skills

A frequent complaint from sales executives is that they believe their salespeople are poor listeners. This might be because they tend to talk too much around the office, since few executives or managers are observing their sales pros in action in front of buyers. In this chapter we discuss why people are poor listeners, what makes a good listener, and exactly what your team should be listening for. A portion of this chapter replicates material in Chapter 9, Establishing Rapport. I've left it in to reinforce these potent ideas.

The man walking me into his office was quite fascinated by what I was selling. Our company offered a digital alternative to onsite college recruitment interviews. For about $5,000 a month, his firm could eliminate sending recruiters off to schools around the country.

Problems solved? Cutting quite a few jobs and several hundred thousand dollars in expenses.

Benefits attained? Quicker access to hot hires and a brand new digital solution that could position him in the role of a true hero inside the organization.

This senior human resources executive shook my hand and gestured to a chair.

I smiled and asked, "So, how did you decide to invite me in to meet with you today?" That was a bit unusual for an opening question and it took the man a moment to respond.

"Oh, I read your literature thoroughly. Then I met with my team to decide if it was worth pursuing your solution. They gave me great feedback and here we are."

Here's what I learned from that decision-maker's answer: His first approach to determining value was to read information. You might say he's visual, and that could be true (more on this concept shortly). His second strategy was to get some form of consensus from respected peers in order to decide to go through the next step.

I now knew he was persuaded in two key ways: first, by absorbing data in print and, second, through external opinions from others he trusted.

Details of this 400-level strategy can be found in my next book, *The Secret Language of Influence,* coming from AMACOM in 2012. This book is about recognizing motivational and decision-making patterns in others and is well beyond the scope of this book. Forty-eight patterns have been identified and can be used both to influence others outside the company and to manage peers and internal relationships. Sales executives who are interested in this fascinating new, psychologically sound, validated instrument can experience this too at www.ModelofSalesExcellence.com.

Because I'd been trained and spent years listening for cues, I gained a huge advantage when dealing with this executive. The sale closed for many reasons: The purchase was easy to quantify (there was a great ROI), the need was clearly there, and I was in sync with the buyer's style. (See Chapter 6 on buyer behavior.)

But what first launched the sale toward its successful conclusion was my ability to *listen* for that buyer's tendencies. This piece of the communication equation—listening—is key to setting up great dialogues with everyone in your selling circle—prospects, clients, managers, and support personnel. We've dedicated a whole chapter to it, and you'll want to dedicate some serious training time to it as well.

Frankly, here's where I get excited about the organic nature and value of training sales pros in all communication skills, including written and verbal dialogues, as described in Chapter 5 on communication skills. What you'll learn in this chapter has tremendous benefit in your personal life as well as at work. So practice at work, but also work on these skills at home.

Listening well makes others feel appreciated. It generates intimacy in people who care about one another. Listening to children helps their self-esteem and models how they should act with others. Listening will help others value you in new ways. Think about it. Who doesn't notice when someone is a great listener? After reading what's in this chapter, and with some diligent practice, you will become a great listener.

We will model what was just described, a great listener. That person is really following the Golden Rule of communicating: Listen to others as you would have them listen to you.

Use these ideas at home with a significant other as well, and don't be surprised to see your listening and persuasion skills increase faster than they would if you just worked on them in a work setting. And here's a key element to improving listening skill: Tell others (at home and work) that you are developing stronger listening skills. Create accountability toward your improvement in this area by having others buy into your growth.

Concept: Insatiable curiosity sells well.

We will wrap up the chapter with some great exercises to help your sales pros become better listeners.

Why People Are Poor Listeners

Writer Fran Lebowitz (1981) made the comment that "The opposite of talking isn't listening. The opposite of talking is waiting."

Here's how that happens: We listen at a rate of 600 to 1,000 words per minute. However, we speak at a rate of around 125 to 200 words per minute, with gusts up to 250 for professional talkers like TV and radio newscasters.

With this gap between a human's rabbit-like speed of listening and tortoise-like rate of speaking, it's no wonder the mind wanders when a seller begins to talk. So here we look at what makes *poor* listeners:

1. They think ahead about their responses to the speaker.

2. They think ahead to what they believe the speaker is going to say (this is mindreading and should be avoided at all costs).

3. They multi-task (during phone conversations, including teleconferences and webinars).

4. They begin to become defensive, often arguing mentally instead of listening completely.

5. They become distracted by things outside the speaker (that book on the shelf, ambient sounds, and more).

6. The speaker is boring—that's one scenario where both parties can share the blame.

7. They interrupt (one exception to this being a bad thing is described below).

Keys to Good Listening

Great listeners have great curiosity. This is the foundation upon which we'll build this skill set. When you're curious you won't interrupt, argue, or mentally wander. You'll be totally vested in the other person's thought processes as you wonder how he or she is developing the argument, how he's exploring an idea, how she's expressing herself. Got curiosity? You'll want to get it today. Here we look at what makes *good* listeners:

1. They stay mentally positive and neutral about the other person's ideas.

2. They mirror body language.

3. They maintain good eye contact or at least look at the bridge of the nose (not the mouth, as in some cultures a listener looking at the mouth is seen as an indicator that the speaker is lying).

4. They listen actively with verbal and nonverbal affirmation like nodding and leaning in. "Really?" "Wow, what happened next?" "That's interesting." Nonverbally, leaning in slightly toward a speaker is known as "attending" and is a very good skill to practice.

5. They listen for underlying emotion (more on this critical idea in Chapter 14, Power Questions), because responding to the emotion generates rapport and helps the buyer move toward a buying decision.

6. They recognize that it is okay to interrupt to ask for clarity or more detail. This shows true interest and, with a good question, can move the dialogue along.

7. They take notes in a sales setting, after asking for permission to do so.

8. They summarize the speaker's comments by speaking in the speaker's dialect. Remember the opening story? A reply to the executive's response might be something like: "So you read our information (Thank you. That was clearly a good investment of your time), then asked for feedback from your team. What would you like to accomplish in our conversation today?"

9. They have outstanding focus because they want to know what's really going on behind the verbal and nonverbal behavior exhibited by the speaker.

10. They are truly and completely curious about the other person's thought processes.

These keys are worth practicing, and some exercises to help you along in your journey toward listening excellence are at the end of this chapter.

If this topic really fascinates you and you want to truly master listening skills, you'll want to investigate Paul Ekman's work detecting micro-expressions in the face (and voice) to determine the emotion the speaker might be attempting to hide (Ekman, 2007). I'm a huge fan of Ekman and have his video training on my desk. It's a fascinating, scientifically sound method to understand whether a person is misrepresenting the truth. His work has recently been turned into a hit TV show on Fox called *Lie to Me*.

I've been in touch with his office for several years, attempting to find out when they'll have business training available. But his firm is paid so much money by law enforcement and government agencies that they haven't had time to attend to the general business population.

What to Listen For

Do you know how many dialects there are for the Chinese language? Two hundred. Just as China has two hundred different dialects, your buyers speak different dialects, even though we speak the same language. I'm referring to how buyers *filter information*. This occurs in one of three ways: visual, auditory, or kinesthetic (also known as tactile or physical). These "dialects" are reflected in a person's language choices.

Prospects often use words that reflect how they process information. Verbs, adverbs, and adjectives typically are selected on an unconscious level and so offer clues to the prospect's information-processing patterns. Your ability to strategically listen for word cues will help you understand how the buyer prefers to process information:

- Visually through the eyes
- Auditory through the ears
- Kinesthetically through physical or internal feelings

We refer to these patterns by the first letter of each as VAK. You want to mirror the buyer's language so that you show him or her that you understand and can communicate in his or her dialect.

Read this example of what I call a "dialect disconnect," where we offer back visual words to a person who processes information in an auditory fashion:

- Your prospect says: "That *sounds* good to me. I need the company to *hear* this proposal."
- But, you say: "Okay, it *looks* good to you. You just need your company to *see* this proposal."

You're obviously not speaking the same dialect. There's a communication gap. So, especially when you're summarizing or repeating back information to buyers, avoid putting your own spin on someone's words. Use the same exact words. This runs counter to what many of us were taught growing up in selling.

We've been told to summarize, in our own words, what the buyer just said. We now know that you're better off offering the buyer's own words to show you understand.

Take a moment to look through the following list of common sensory-based words from Table 9.1.

Visual	Auditory	Kinesthetic
see	hear	grasp
look	listen	touch
sight	sound	feeling
clear	resonant	solid
bright	loud	heavy
picture	word	handle
hazy	noisy	rough
brings to light	rings a bell	connects
show	tell	move

Here are some phrases you might use with those cue words italicized.

Visual

- I *see.*
- That doesn't *look* right.
- I need to get *clear* on this idea.
- You *color* my world.
- Get the *picture*?

Auditory

- That *rings a bell*.
- I *hear* you.
- It *sounds* good to me.
- *Listen* to this.
- Do you *resonate* with this idea?

Kinesthetic

- I've got a good *feeling* about this project.

- I need to get a *handle* on this.

- We've got to get in *touch* with her.

- You have a *solid* proposal.

- We're *up against* a wall.

Attention to and use of these three dialects will significantly increase the quality of your conversations. It will increase your ability to communicate your sales message so that it makes the most "sensory" sense to your prospect. Remember that people prefer to deal with those who are like them. Therefore, your ability to pick up as many hidden cues as possible will affect how well you gain rapport with prospects and how well you can bridge any communication gap.

Another key to great listening is to focus on the emotions being revealed in a conversation. Research on brain science confirms what we sales pros have known all along. People make decisions emotionally first, then rationalize their decisions with logic. You will find details on this idea in Chapter 14 on powerful questioning, where you'll learn how to create emotional context for your sales conversations.

Next is a set of exercises to help you increase sensitivity toward others who are speaking. Your listening skills will be tested and improved in several ways by this experience, and they will all be fun to do.

Exercises to Develop Great Listening Skills

EXERCISE 15.1.   Listening for Cues

SETUP: Here, learners will pair up and take turns talking about an area they feel passionate about. The person who is listening will listen for cues to which dialect is being used: visual, auditory, or kinesthetic.

Trainer: Give the following instructions:

Pair up and each take about fifteen seconds to think of something you are
     passionate about—a family member, a hobby, or a recent or past
     experience. Then talk for a minute or two about that topic.

EXERCISE 15.1. Listening for Cues, Cont'd

The listener should listen for the emotion behind the conversation and the mode of expression: visual, auditory, or kinesthetic.

After a minute or two, trade places and repeat the process. Don't forget the other elements of good communication: verbal and physical affirmation, good eye contact, etc.

When you're both finished, write your answers to the following questions and be prepared to discuss the experience in the large group.

- How did your partner do?
- How did you think you did?
- What do you need to work on?

Here's a homework assignment to give your sales pros.

EXERCISE 15.2. Observing Communication Preferences

SETUP: Sales team members will practice listening to conversations around them for a week and then report back on their findings.

Trainer: Give the following instructions to sales reps:

Over the next week you will listen in on conversations around you in order to increase your ability to hear which dialect people are speaking. You can do this in a restaurant (or any public setting), at your office, even at home. Focus on listening for one thing at a time during a session: visual, then auditory, then kinesthetic. All of you should simply write down words you hear in the category for which you are listening. Use the chart from earlier in this chapter to help you note which words come up in conversation, and add other words to the list to share with the group at the next meeting. During our next session, we can share the experience with accountability partners as well as the whole group.

Choose an accountability partner in this room with whom you'll share your results and talk about insights that came from listening in on conversations.

EXERCISE 15.2.   Observing Communication Preferences, Cont'd

Take one to three days to increase your sensitivity to *visual* words. Choose a variety of settings (office, restaurant, park, public transportation, theater) where you can simply listen to others around you.

Take one to three days to increase your sensitivity to *auditory* words. Choose a variety of settings (office, restaurant, park, public transportation, theater) where you can simply listen to others around you.

Take one to three days to increase your sensitivity to *kinesthetic* words. Choose a variety of settings (office, restaurant, park, public transportation, theater) where you can simply listen to others around you.

You may complete the assignment while watching a movie or television show, but be intentional and be active about your listening.

Feedback dialogue with accountability partners:

- How easy was this assignment to do?

- Did the people you listened to have conflicting word choices? That is, did one person speak visually, while the other was more auditory?

- Do you feel that you have improved your ability to identify others' dialects? In what way will you use this knowledge?

I believe it is essential to pay attention to three key things when listening:

1. What emotions are being expressed? If the speaker's style is clinical or emotionless, what emotions should exist based on the story or information shared? This might be hope or joy at the goals that can be attained. It might mean frustration or despair at the size of the problem that needs to be solved.

2. In which dialect is the speaker communicating? In other words, how does this person process information? Here we want to discover whether the individual is visual ("See what I mean?" "looks like . . ."), auditory ("sounds like we could. . ." ". . . hear what I mean?"), or kinesthetic/ tactile. In psychology these are called representational (or "rep") systems

and they reveal how a person processes information about his or her life experiences.

3. Finally, pay attention to the pace (speed) of speech, energy in the voice, volume, or anything that reveals the way this person is processing the topic.

Your job, as you respond, is to match a speaker's emotion, rep system, and pace. This enhances rapport and keeps you totally other-centered. You should also use "you" language before "I" language.

Let's assume a buyer just described a situation (you asked some great questions to get the information). He or she has offered the reasons why a solution is needed to attain goals or solve problems.

The buyer says, "I'm really sick of looking at our financial situation and seeing that we don't have enough money to go on a nice vacation. My wife and I love reading travel brochures, then seeing places from which we can watch the ocean and view museum exhibits, like a cruise ship. It's been a few years since our last trip."

Your response might be something like, "Wow, it'll be a huge relief for you to solve this concern. You've been looking at this for a couple of years? That's a bit of a wait. My job is to show you how this can happen." Your answer respects the buyer's emotion (frustration), rep system (visual, right?), pace, and focuses on "you." Here's an exercise to practice doing this now.

EXERCISE 15.3. Simulating a Real Conversation

SETUP: This exercise lets reps practice a conversation that models listening well and responding appropriately. They pair off to do this.

Trainer: Each person should speak about something he or she is passionate about—a family member, hobby, or recent experience. The listener should feed back emotion, mirror the speaker's communication mode, and end with a request for further information. Don't forget verbal and physical affirmations and to maintain good eye contact, etc.

Prior to beginning, give everyone about fifteen seconds to think of a topic so the first listener is not distracted by thinking of a topic while listening to the first speaker. Have them answer the following questions afterward:

EXERCISE 15.3.   Simulating a Real Conversation, Cont'd

- How did your partner do as a listener?
- How did you think you did?

Have them share with the group what was easy and what was difficult about this exercise.

To quote the late Bill Brooks, a brilliant sales tactician and trainer, "Listen people into buying instead of talking your way out of the sale."

Remember to get and stay curious. Be curious like a child who is fascinated by the world around him or her—new colors, sounds, words, experiences. Listen for word choices, images, and ideas. Get curious.

Great sales professionals are great listeners. They pick up nuances from buyers that others miss. Is that person visual, auditory, or kinesthetic? Practice these listening skills at home and at work in order to put them into play in front of buyers.

VAK is older than you might think. Note this quote:

I hear and I forget. I see and I remember. I do and I understand.

Confucius

Chapter 16

The Ultimate Objection-Handling Tool

Objections! Nothing hurts revenue and team performance more than prospects who have the verbal skills to put us off, to tell us "no" (or worse, "maybe"), to offer sane and insane comments that form resistance to our solutions. When I coach sales teams on handling objections, I toss out this phrase, "Shame on us when we hear an objection two or three times, but never create powerful ways to move past it and advance the sale." Two or three? How about hundreds of times a year, the same objections sticking large organizations that have thousands of sales pros? In this chapter you'll learn my secret weapon, The Ultimate Objection-Handling Tool.

An Awkward Tale

Our family goes to downtown Chicago every year at Christmas. We go just to experience the famous Marshall Field's State Street store (now a Macy's). There is always a very cool story displayed from window to window around the building. These spectacular moving works of art have included Charlie & the Chocolate Factory, Snow White, Cinderella, Harry Potter, and others. This year we also visited the Santa Claus in the store; our kids were still young enough to believe, deeply, in the big elf.

Parents and children are led down a hall that has several doors on either side. Accommodating the crowds is key to keeping the line moving, so a Santa resides behind each door. The worker elves are cautious to not walk past an open door while escorting families to the Jolly Old Elf selected for them. The strategy is, of course, totally invisible to the kids.

This year we got a black Santa.

Our kids, who are quite white, have never seen a black Santa.

Abbie, six years old, crawls on his lap and says, "I know you're not the real Santa."

St. Nick grins and says, "Why aren't I the real Santa?" He knows exactly what this child is going to say. I'm smiling because I have no other expression handy for this situation and the big black man is relishing the imminent outcome.

Abbie points at his chest and says, "The real one is at the North Pole, so you're just covering for him here." Santa's smile dissipates, but doesn't disappear; I assume that's somehow tied into his performance reviews. My smile widens and my wife and I exhale a big sigh of relief.

Father Christmas just knew what was going to happen in that conversation. However, he was wrong. But he does help to show the key concept about objection handling that we will apply to our sales training in this chapter. You need to be right when you anticipate what's going to happen on a sales call. To that end, you'll want to write this statement down. It might even be worth a tattoo on your forearm.

Concept: Great sales pros can predict the future.

This is totally true. Great sales pros know exactly what can happen and so they know what will happen. This is never more evident than it is in handling objections.

If you know every form of resistance you can encounter, *and* have prepared a response for each, you will more readily and more professionally handle anything a buyer throws at you.

To accelerate these abilities as a sales professional, I've developed the Ultimate Objection-Handling Tool. The tool works to manage buyer resistance in these ways:

1. You will identify your top six objections.

2. You will develop potent responses to each of these six objections through two different techniques.

3. You will "find your voice," that is, choose and use those responses that best fit your own personality and communication skills.

We'll continue to encourage every rep to "find his or her voice" as he or she increases the ability to persuade buyers. This chapter will help you to discover what works for you and customize your presentation accordingly. In addition, we'll wrap up with eight basic rules you should be willing to adopt whenever you encounter an objection.

EXERCISE 16.1. Identifying the Top Objections

SETUP: Here we want you to identify the top six objections encountered by sales pros. It will be the basis for everything we'll do from here on.

What are the top objections you encounter during your selling day? Gather every one you come up with, then have the sales team vote to identify the top six.

Trainer: Post objections on a whiteboard or write them on flip-chart paper posted on the wall. Then have team members vote for the six they encounter most. Use the six with the most votes to get a list from which to work.

The Top Six Objections

Every business has five basic objections that form 98 percent of all the trouble a rep will encounter during a sales call. We want to identify what they are and use them as the basis for applying the response models that follow.

Common categories could include the following:

- Price resistance

- Slowness to change/adopt new technology or ideas

- Deep relationship with current solution provider

- Need to consult another decision-maker

- Send literature/stall

Some are more serious than others. Obviously, if you keep getting "send me literature" and you can't find someone by phone or email when you follow up, you should be the one resisting—the urge to put a package in the mail.

After you have done the exercise with your team to gather all the objections they hear, you can move on to the next section on responses. Also, note the important tip on logging objections at the end of this chapter. You can use this idea to help each rep quickly improve his or her ability to move beyond whatever objections are tripping him or her up throughout the day.

Potent Response Models
Build a Book of Alternate Responses

This is a pure power play—your sales team will muscle its way through as many responses as everyone can brainstorm. It doesn't matter whether reps' comments are brief or long, just write them all down. Once you've compiled a master list, everyone can increase his or her own mental flexibility in objection handling by the sheer volume of responses available.

Start with the top six and take time to work through each one. Here's an example:

- "Your price is too high."

Responses might include:

- "Which means?"

- "Compared to what?"

- "How much did you think it would cost?"

- "Are your decisions normally driven by investing in the cheapest solution?"

- "What kind of car do you drive? So you do prefer a quality product? That's just what we provide."

- "If our competitor is cheaper, what might that say about them?"

- "So would a payment plan help manage bringing in our solution?"

You get the idea. Going through this exercise with your team will be one of the most valuable investments in training time you'll ever make. It will also be great fun. Answers for each objection will range from good to great, from insightful to incredible, from smart to sarcastic. Keep them all.

Remember the end game here is for each rep to figure out which he or she can most comfortably use. Some of the braver responses will have their place when a rep has achieved deep rapport and can get away with saying things that might normally be unacceptable. There are a couple of good examples of this in the responses above.

Break Down the Language Inside the Objection

This is an advanced strategy that I encourage everyone to use. The technique is to unpack words within the objection—words that appear to be unclear. It's easiest to show you by giving an example. You've probably heard, too many times, this objection:

- "We're okay with our current situation."

I've chosen this as an example because it occurs early in the sales process, and if you don't have an effective response, it can get you stuck or could end the call early. Look at that sentence again: *"We're okay with our current situation."*

Which words could use some deciphering? In this sentence, they include *"we,"* *"okay,"* and *"current situation."*

Here's how to craft three questions to respond to three muddled comments within the objection. I identify the focal point of the real issue in parentheses.

- "When you say 'we,' who are you referring to?" (*The conversation is going to be about decision-makers.*)

- "Thank you, but can you explain exactly what you mean by 'okay'? I'm not sure if that means things are good, great, or whether you're just getting by." (*The conversation is going to be about buyer's satisfaction with current solutions.*)

- "When you refer to the 'current situation,' it's still enough of a concern that we've decided to have this conversation, right? So what is the 'current situation'?" (*The conversation is going to be about the person's view of the impact on his or her company of the issue.*)

The words or phrases you choose to focus on will give you direction for the ensuing conversation. By asking who "we" refers to, you'll start to uncover decision-making elements (and individuals) that need to be addressed.

Here are a few additional examples where the reps ask for clarity about words within the objection:

Objection: "We're not sure whether we're going to buy right now."

Response: "What exactly do you mean by 'not sure'?" or "When you say 'right now,' do you have a time frame in mind?"

Objection: "Your pricing is a concern here."

Response: "When you say 'concern,' it means . . . ?" or "Pricing per employee or total cost? How do you analyze pricing?"

Objection: "If we did this, we'd have to have some guarantees."

Response: "When you say 'if,' does that mean you're still unsure of our working together?" or "When you say 'if,' does that mean you're pretty sure we'll work together, but need some assurances?" or "'Guarantees' refers to . . . ?"

You get the idea—find poorly defined words and ask for clarity.

Do not let buyers use phrases like *"We're okay with our current situation"* to get rid of you. When someone is intentionally vague, he or she doesn't see a need to engage you in a dialogue. Your ability to ask great questions (for more, see Chapter 14) will help you connect with potential clients.

Clarifying language is one of the truly unique methodologies I developed to use with my consulting clients. When I have a roomful of reps who first hear this concept and then start to practice it, I know I've helped elevate a team to a level of professionalism they weren't aware existed. You can almost see the light bulbs going off over heads as they begin writing their responses to break down language in their top objections. Increased sensitivity to the exact words and phrases a buyer uses is huge for anyone seeking to master the art of communicating with buyers.

In addition, the "organic" nature of this technique means you will find it useful in personal relationships as well. Practice this skill outside the office too and notice how fast and fluidly you begin to use it as you sell.

Let's briefly look at how reps can customize these methods to fit their individual styles.

Finding Your Voice

Is that objection response a reflection of YOU? Every rep knows what he or she would and could say in response and what he or she wouldn't or couldn't. The wide diversity of personalities in a roomful of reps is key to brainstorming and developing a variety in responses the team can use.

Often, in training, I'll offer a response and go around the room, asking each salesperson: "Would you say that?" Reactions can cover the spectrum from "not me" to "good one, I like it, yes" to "if I get mad enough about how the call is going." Each sales professional should write down the exact words he or she is most comfortable using when handling the top six objections.

Finally, here are some basic rules I encourage all reps to know when they encounter resistance on a call.

Basic Rules for Handling Objections

I call these rules the eight ways to stay out from behind the 8-ball.

1. *Do not get defensive.* You'll end up begging for understanding and remove yourself from the role of a peer. Ask a question instead of reacting defensively.

2. *Do not respond by telling the prospect how great your products are.* Keep your focus on a healthy dialogue, rather than feeling a need to brag.

3. *Do respond by agreeing with the prospect's thinking, then ask a question that suggests a counter-example.* ("You should probably keep working with them. You're *totally* happy with what they've done for you over time, right?")

4. *Do not exhibit lots of enthusiasm.* Nothing damages the initial image of sales reps more. You can be a pro and stay positive without working yourself into a lather.

5. *Do respond by smiling and staying both upbeat and serious.*

6. *Be prepared with three or five or six responses to every objection you might encounter.* Different prospects deserve to be treated differently. This whole chapter is about mental flexibility. How well will you prepare?

7. *Be prepared to take risks when the sale is in danger.* Do this when you have nothing to lose and are mentally prepared to walk away anyway. But remember Rules 1 and 2: Do not get defensive or pitch product!

8. *Remember, the signature on your commission checks is not from the person paying you.* The person across the desk or at the other end of the phone line is feeding your family. Keep that in mind as you interact with potential clients.

Key Tip for Managing Objections

Eric was my sales trainer twenty-five years ago. One day he sat next to me and looked at my call log. This was a print listing of each phone call with the results. (It was the 1980s, so this data wasn't yet recorded on computer.) But Eric's wisdom was timeless—as you're about to hear. One column on the page was for me to list the objection that ended too many, okay MOST, of my calls.

"Dan, do you know why we log the objections?"

Now I didn't want to talk about my struggles, so my answer was what we call in psychology "deflecting." I was putting the attention away from me, as my response went something like, "So the company can create sales training based on the most common forms of resistance?"

Like a good counselor, Eric noticed I was choosing to ignore my own issues.

"That's a smart and sharp insight. You probably think that's exactly what I want to hear or perhaps what would impress me. But it's not about the company, it's about you. We want to know EXACTLY what YOU struggle with. Because once you can handle the top five or six objections, you'll be perceived as an expert by your prospects and within our industry. And that's why you log your objections."

Brilliant thinking on the part of my mentor, and I've never forgotten that conversation. My memory of that is so pure that I can tell you the exact layout of the room and desk where I was sitting.

Now, in my training environments, I make it mandatory for phone reps in particular to log objections. Field reps can do so as well. It's just that the volume of conversations that occurs with phone-based selling makes it easier to identify and coach reps to better handle prospects' resistance.

This can be done on paper or formally on the computer—perhaps even in each contact's data record, in a searchable field so the rep and manager can see at a glance what's troubling the salesperson and slowing up progress toward a successful sale.

Decide today to identify your company's top six objections. Encourage the sales team to contribute and own all the content you develop through these models for handling resistance. Everyone should then create his or her own personal list of responses.

Also help reps keep the eight rules in mind whenever they do get pushback from buyers.

You will want to write down everything that is created from this program, and build it into your company's script book for handling objections.

Chapter 17

Solution- Versus Consequence- Centered Selling

Remember when everyone sold using features and benefits? Then a trend started where everyone began to use pain to motivate buyers to buy. Now training organizations around the planet take positions as to which approach is better. The good news and the bad news is that everybody was right. Both approaches work, but until now we didn't know exactly when to sell with pain and when to sell with gain.

The Painful Pieces of Solution Selling

Picture this: You're twelve years old and you fly into the house after school. "Mom, Dad, guess what I decided today? I'm gonna be a doctor!"

Mom is always encouraging. "Honey, that's great! Doctors are well respected. You'll make good money, have a nice spouse, and a nice house. I'm so glad you're going to be a doctor."

In contrast, how might Dad respond? "A doctor? Are you kidding me? Do you know how many years you have to go to school to become a doctor? Do you know how much money it costs? And you'll be working with sick people all day. And malpractice insurance . . ." And on and on and on he goes.

Two Distinct Buyer Types

I want you to recognize that each of these parents represents one of two basic types of prospects. Essentially, there are buyers who move toward new ideas and those who are resistant to them.

In training, I like to reinforce this concept by calling our buyers either sheep or goats. Sheep gravitate toward ideas. Goats are more likely to butt heads over something new.

So here's your sales insight in a sentence:

Concept: Buyers move TO or AWAY FROM your ideas.

This is much simpler than trying to identify buyers by using classification systems like DISC or the Myers-Briggs or the old kid's game Doctor, Lawyer, Indian Chief. (See buyers' behavior in Chapter 6.)

Let's first anchor the concept of what's known in linguistics as "to and away." Here is a quick quiz:

1. A friend describes a new business idea. You immediately:

    A. Point out some concerns he should address.

    B. Say, "Great! Go for it!"

2. You ask your spouse about buying a new car. He/she responds:

    A. "Well, there are a lot of 0 percent finance options. Let's check them out."

    B. "I'm not sure, we're talking about $30,000."

3. You get the decision-maker on the phone and say, "We can increase the productivity of your staff by 22 percent in sixty days." He/she replies:

   A. "That's sounds impressive. How do you do that?"

   B. "We're not spending money on anything new right now."

Which answer in each item is To and which is Away?

How would you respond in each case? What is your tendency, To or Away?

In psychology, a person who pushes back exhibits a *polarity response.*

So you see Mom in the opening story as a sheep—much like the prospect who moves toward new ideas. Dad is a Goat—the prospect who is going to fight you by moving away from new ideas. (*Note:* Use of gender terms is just for purposes of explanation and does not reflect the idea that men and women only think this way.)

All the sales Boomers grew up using features and benefits. We were taught to sell by saying, "Here are all the good things that will happen when you buy from us." In the 1980s and 1990s, selling started to swing in the opposite direction. Led by the late David Sandler's organization, The Sandler Sales Institute, reps began learning to use *pain* to motivate buyers to buy.

By the way, insurance reps learned long ago that they needed to sell this way: "When, not if, you die, do you have a plan to take care of your precious wife and kids?" But Sandler formalized the pain-based approach in his selling methodology, and hundreds of trainers across the United States began persuading salespeople to carry on conversations that explored and revealed the prospect's pain.

Today's sales pro has learned that one of his or her greatest assets is being able to adapt his or her approach based on the individual being sold. So once you notice a buyer's tendency to be receptive, you use benefits. When the buyer shows signs of resistance, you discuss problems your product or solutions can solve.

How to Script a Conversation for Each Type

The starting point for putting this idea in play is to create marketing copy that focuses on both To and Away. I've taught this to thousands of sales professionals and, like the reps who use the Ultimate Objection-Handling Tool (Chapter 16), the reps who use this technique begin to smoothly advance sales conversations more frequently toward the close than they've done in the past.

Most of your existing literature will center on benefits. So use that or brainstorm to create a list of all the good things about your product or service. Write them on the left side of a sheet of paper. On the right side, list opposites—problems you solve, pain they experience, consequences they're heading toward.

As you develop this script, you will want to list benefits and consequences that are personal to the buyer and to his or her organization. (There is more on this in the exercise that follows.)

As with most printed sales material, the script you write is extremely potent for phone sales reps. They can keep it right on their desks.

The following example comes from coaching a Mazda/VW dealership sales team.

You get the picture. This kind of script is clear and simple to build, and you'll sound so much more convincing when you're connecting with potential clients.

Table 17.1. Car Dealership Example

To (Benefits)	Away (Problems)
Lots of prestige in owning a nice, new car; looking successful.	Uh, I'm really embarrassed to take a client to lunch in my car.
New, unique color; nobody else has it.	This older model doesn't really send a message that I'm successful.
This is sooo fast; it's fun to drive!	I'm nervous and need a safe car, because my kids are riding in it regularly.
Super-smooth ride, handles like a dream. This is the most comfortable car I could ever imagine.	With this thing I have, I'm feeling every bump in the road. It's killing my back.
Ten-year warranty! All upkeep and maintenance is free.	I'm frustrated by it breaking down every month.

EXERCISE 17.1.   Create Your Own Script

SETUP: Using the ideas presented above, build a script for your sales team.

Build this chart now with the team. Creativity and brainstorming are the name of the game, so make it as long as it can be. (*Hint:* There's a cheat sheet for development at the end of this chapter.)

I encourage everyone who is first learning this technique to teach it to other salespeople. You can run this fun exercise in a networking group with other reps and entrepreneurs.

This slightly customized sales approach can build your income, big time, so learn to listen for acceptance or resistance and your success will be more frequent and the size of your orders will increase—guaranteed!

The Magic Question to Identify Type of Buyer

The key is to understand the differences between two buyer types—those who are motivated by benefits and value and those who are focused on solving problems. Now almost all salespeople know this in some fashion, but they don't intentionally make their pitches based on type. There are now internationally validated tools that you can experience through an assessment at www.ModelofSalesExcellence.com. Sales pros can first identify their own decision-making styles, then learn to recognize them in others, especially buyers. Once you can identify then match a buyer's decision-making criteria, he or she will be more likely to respond to the proper motivation, whether benefits you offer or problem you can solve. You want to have a couple of different approaches before you walk into a sales situation (or make a phone call). You'll want that list of benefits and a list of problems your products or services solve that you created above. Then ask the "magic" question.

The magic question is "How do you know you've chosen the right (individual or service/product)?" The person's answer tells you which type of buyer he or she is.

We'll use a financial services example: "How do you know you've chosen the right financial advisor?" Contrasting response might be . . .

"We'll get a great return on our investment." (benefits)

or

"We won't be losing chunks of our nest egg like we did with the last advisor."
(problems)

See the difference?

Two Quick Tips

1. If you don't receive a clear answer, dig a bit deeper by saying, "Can you tell me more about that?" The distinction will come out soon enough. Let's say the person says, "Oh, we'll be happier." That's a bit vague. Will they be happier because they'll make more money or lose less? "Can you tell me more?" might get a response like: "We'd be happier because we'd save for that cruise we want to go on later this year!" Clearly a benefits-oriented buyer. Or "We'd be happier because we're sick of being in the market, and a safer investment will keep us from these volatile financial swings." Okay, clearly a problem-oriented person.

2. If you are presenting to a team, a board, or a group of decision-makers, just list problems you can solve as well as benefits they can gain so that you speak to both types, because they're both probably in the room.

CHEAT SHEET FOR DIFFERENT BUYER TYPES

Phrases to Use with Away Buyers
Corporate

- Irrecoverable or squandered revenue, market share, or marketplace status
- Fear about the company's future
- Angry shareholders
- Embarrassment to customers
- Sending a bad or wrong message to customers and/or employees
- Mistrust of a company's offerings and products

Individuals

- Ruined advancement opportunity or obstruction of career path
- Reduced or lost income potential
- Loss of personal prestige
- Corporate doubt about abilities
- Inefficient work processes that increase workload and steal time from family
- Wasted efforts to close business or build business
- Family frustration over work issues

Phrases to Use with To Buyers

Corporate

- Increased revenue, market share, or marketplace status
- Excitement, hope about the company's future (perhaps reflected in stock price increase)
- Happy shareholders
- Delighted customers
- Sending a confident, upbeat message to customers and/or employees
- Complete trust in a company's offerings and products

Individual

- Great advancement opportunity with outstanding career path potential
- Increase in income potential
- Personal prestige and respect
- Corporate confidence in person's abilities
- Efficient and effective work processes that reduce workload and offer more time with the family (such as better, more frequent vacations)
- Ability to quickly close business and earn more money
- Individual and family happy with job and career

Now that you have a way to discover which type of buyer you're sitting with, you can alter your approach to match his or her type. Are they benefits-oriented or problem-solving people? *Learn to ask the magic question as early in the conversation as possible.* The insight you gain from the answer helps you focus on the language you'll use from then on.

Here's a cheat sheet to help build your ideas on To and Away.

Remember that buyers tend to be motivated to gain benefits or solve problems. Knowing which type of person you're speaking with will help you customize your conversation and close more sales.

Ask that magic question as early as possible: *"How do you know you've chosen the right (individual or service/product)?"* Practice this question in your personal life so that you can ask it confidently when you sell.

Also create a company outline of benefits and problems and make it available to everyone on the sales team.

Chapter 18

Practicing Presentation Skills

I do a lot of keynotes, so I've had years of training (and spent a lot of money) to hone presentation skills. The last few years I've been writing columns for financial services magazines and have come across a serious problem with salespeople who have to present in front of groups. Most have had no training. It shows, and it costs them money, lots of commissions. In this chapter you'll see exactly how to construct a dynamic (funny, if you choose) presentation that will wow audiences and turn some from spectators into clients. You'll find this fun and energizing as we break down the pieces of the presentation puzzle into three sections.

You Have Landed the Appointment

You made it past the initial stage, through the screening efforts of lower-level managers, and are now about to gain a promotion to the big leagues of selling.

You will present your company's solution to a team of senior decision-makers. Some will support your ideas. Others will be so set against them that you'll wonder whether they're related to the competitor that follows you.

You are understandably nervous as this is so different from an informal sales meeting. It is a formal presentation. This is where the sales pros play.

How do you get over that ripple of fear that blends with the joy of the opportunity? What if your sales manager wants to come along and observe?

You need karaoke.

Stay with me here. Singing in front of a bunch of strangers is no less unnerving than, well, singing in front of a bunch of strangers, except that with the business setting comes the possibility of plenty of money.

There is no better way to reduce or remove fear of public speaking than to do karaoke. Here's how you do that. And, by the way, you can skip karaoke if it unnerves you and go on to other solutions in this chapter.

Either take a friend or go alone, somewhere you know nobody. Pick an easy, mid-range song and just get up and do it.

What you'll most likely forget to do is to smile, so practice smiling when you practice the song before hitting the karaoke club. (You know to practice, right? You'll be receiving tips on rehearsing your sales presentation shortly.)

Even after I'd been speaking and training in front of large, small, and huge groups, I knew I needed to be bolder and take more risks with humor and unique elements of my talks and training (like hypnotizing six hundred sales reps at a global sales conference).

Oh, did I mention you have to solo? I'd done karaoke with friends where I'd stood up surrounded by six other people—that's super safe and worthless for overcoming discomfort or fear. So you solo, because you'll be flying solo on the big sales call.

I made a list of songs that I could easily sing, and enjoyed singing. I found one that was perfect for me and did it. I performed "Come Monday" by Jimmy Buffett. It wasn't spectacular, just good. I was never in danger of getting booed, heckled, or gonged. Even got some compliments and positive feedback.

When you do this, work on natural, normal gestures—no need to be dramatic, just calm and confident. And don't forget to smile. Practice smiling.

Key karaoke tip: Ask the DJ to please ("please" as in "here's $5") not put you after a great singer. There are always a few very experienced singers in these places and you'd rather follow someone who is on a dare or, minimally, on his twelfth beer.

That's it. If you can sing in front of strangers, you can present professionally, whether it's a final pitch to a corporate board or a speech at a conference.

Once you have elevated your confidence (and experience), you'll want a structure to craft the best presentation you could possibly show to that team of decision-makers. The rest of this chapter will show you how to structure your presentation, prepare and rehearse, and deliver the presentation of a lifetime so that decision-makers are more likely to say YES.

Concept: Actors and entertainers make money with great presentation skills.

Structure Your Presentation

There are three ways you can design your presentation: (1) you can use the *change formula*, a method to help organizations change strategies, change tools, and change their minds (Sounds like the focus a sales call, doesn't it?); (2) you can choose to use the flow of your *selling system*. This is what got you there in the first place, so you can be assured it has some relevance to your success so far; or (3) you can follow the structure you used when you designed your *proposal* or agreement. In many situations, the response to a quality agreement is a request for this presentation you're getting ready to do. Let's look at each of these choices.

1. Use The Change Formula

This formula was made famous by MIT Sloan School professor Edgar Schein, who received a Lifetime Achievement Award from ASTD in May of 2000. The concept was originally developed by Gleicher and popularized by Beckhard and Harris (1987).

If you understand the five things that need to be in place for change to occur, you can focus your presentation on addressing each of them. Let's first understand the formula itself.

The Change Formula

$$C = D \times V \times F > S$$

In other words, people will *change* (C) once they (1) are aware of their *dissatisfaction* (D) or frustration with their current situation; (2) are given a *vision* (V) for what the future could look and feel like; (3) are offered the *first steps* (F) to transition to that vision; and (4) realize that the dissatisfaction, vision, and first steps are greater motivators than their *status quo* (S) or their current situation.

From a selling perspective, let's look at each element:

- C is simple. *Change* means buy. The individual or organization will buy when all factors are met.

- Next, notice that the two key factors in helping change occur are *dissatisfaction* or frustration as well as a *vision* (that is, all the good things that will happen when goals are met). This corresponds with how you've learned to categorize buyers by whether they're motivated by solving problems or by attaining benefits (Chapter 17).

- *First steps* is your call to action. The buyer must make a decision in order to solve his or her problems and attain his or her goals. This is saying "yes" or signing on the dotted line or shaking your hand.

- Finally, *status quo* represents the current situation. Buyers buy when the combination of other elements is better than how things are working now. In other words, if the buyer isn't hurt or hampered by current problems, he or she is unlikely to buy. If the buyer doesn't see the vision as being big enough or good enough or lucrative enough, no sale. If we don't paint a nice enough picture of how our solution eliminates problems and offers potent benefits (and you've quantified that, too—right?), then we're unlikely to overcome the status quo.

You'll also have to recognize that the status quo also includes your competition, who are currently working to overtake you and acquire the client as their own.

It is highly unlikely that most competing firms will be this thorough in making a strong case for the value offered, so you have the advantage in knowing how the change formula works.

EXERCISE 18.1. Use the Change Formula

SETUP: Members of the sales team will understand how to use the Change Formula to construct a presentation that motivates buyers to change.

Trainer: Pick a current prospect and have your team identify each of the Change Formula elements (C, D, F, V, S) and write clear descriptions of each one below.

People will *change* (C) once they:

1. Are aware of their *dissatisfaction* (D) or frustration with their current situation

    List the source of dissatisfaction here:_____

2. Are given a *vision* (V) for what the future could look and feel like

    Identify the vision here: _____

3) Are offered the first steps (F) to transition to that vision, and

    What first steps will you suggest? _____

    _____

    _____

4) Realize that the *dissatisfaction, vision,* and *first steps* are greater motivators than their *status quo* (S) or their current situation

    Below, write down exactly what the prospect's status quo is

    _____

    _____

    _____

    _____

I'll give an example that I experienced as I was writing this book. I was coaching a senior sales and marketing executive who was having serious issues with his boss. His job was definitely in jeopardy, and I "sold" him on the change he needed to make like this (the Change Formula steps are in parentheses):

> "Rob, you admitted you're arrogant and attack others' ideas right when conversations begin. You're getting sick of fighting with the president and all the physical stress that is attached to that (*Dissatisfaction*). You want to be a great employee who exhibits excellence to the whole organization. And you want to work, somehow, to be humbler with your boss (*Vision*). I'm going to suggest you do two things: take an anger management class outside work, and within the company you'll put a sign in your office and on your computer screen that says, "SLOW DOWN!" This will keep you from responding immediately (*First Steps*). Do you think those two things are a good start to get past the trouble you're encountering right now?" (*Status Quo*)

Funny thing is I was on autopilot during that hour coaching session. When I recounted to my wife how the conversation went, she said, "Wow—you laid out the Change Formula on him and he bought it right there, no discussion, no argument." (My wife is quite familiar with change, having designed leadership training products that have netted well over $50 million in sales for the nonprofit sector.) You can find Wendy Seidman at www.GotInfluenceInc.com.

The Change Formula is used to help companies from top to bottom. It's used to complete major mergers. It's used to help departments adopt new software. You can use it to increase your sales.

2. Match Your Selling System

Should you choose to use your selling system as a formula for your presentation, you'll want to cover parts of each of these pieces of the sales puzzle:

- *Pre-work:* What company information did you discover that is relevant to your presentation and solutions? Did you uncover any buyer data?

- *Rapport:* How did you originally connect with the key prospect? Do you know some personal information or professional?

- *Prospecting:* Did the firm contact you, or did you find it?

- *First Meeting:* In your selling methodology, you learned the skills below, then used them with the prospect. Look at each and identify what information you gained when you used each. You should have notes—you got permission to take them, right?

  - *DQ/Q*—What criteria make this person a great fit for your solutions? Here's an opportunity to compare him or her to your best clients.

  - *Questioning*—What answers did you hear when you used your five power questions? Did other questions surface that gave you information that shows how well your solutions match his or her needs? Be specific.

  - *Listening*—What did you hear and learn about the buyer? Is he or she visual, auditory, or kinesthetic? This is important when you get to the final presentation. If you're presenting to a group, you'll have to use all three representational systems to cover the variety of people in the room. What emotions were expressed during the first meeting? You'll want to revisit and remind them that you recognized their (fill in the blank—frustration, joy, etc.) and feel you can support the good feelings and/or eliminate the bad emotions.

  - *Objections*—Which forms of resistance did you encounter? That is, which of your top six objections showed up? How did you handle them? Was the buyer satisfied with your ability to set them at ease? Any new objections you'll want to set aside to share with your manager and the team?

  - *Sell Gain + Pain*—Is this buyer one who moves toward a solution (benefits) or away from one (problems)? Create a list that works for either if you're presenting to one person. If you're presenting to a team, you'll want to identify about five problems you solve and five benefits they'll enjoy. Finally (and critically), did you quantify how much you'll save (away) or how much abundance (toward) they'll experience when they adopt your solution?

- *Closing*—What was shared at the end of the prior meeting(s)? Are you in the running against a known competitor? When will they decide to decide? What expectations are in place for the speed of their need for your solution?

EXERCISE 18.2.   Outline the Presentation

SETUP: The sales team is about to go deep into their selling system, using everything that preceded this chapter to outline a dialogue with a prospect.

Trainer: Pick a current prospect and have the sales team write out every possible detail related to each of the elements discussed above.

- Pre-Work
- Rapport
- Prospecting
- First Meeting
  - DQ/Q
  - Questioning
  - Listening
  - Objections
  - Sell Gain + Pain
- Closing

The sales team now has a fantastic and persuasive outline for a final presentation!

3. Match Your Proposal Structure

I trust you spent some significant time on the proposal section of this book (Chapter 7). The content comes directly from world class consultant and business strategist Alan Weiss, who generously granted permission for us to publish some of the best of his body of work. His book, *How to Write a Proposal That's Accepted Every Time* (2009), is a solid resource you should own.

If you offered your prospect a proposal that helped you acquire a meeting to present your solutions in person, you'll probably want to structure your presentation to match that document. Also consider using one of the two models above as a way to touch on other information, some of which might be new to others in the room if you are presenting to a team.

Here are the basic elements you should have in your proposal, which you will solidify by using Exercise 18.3.

- Conceptual agreement reached previously:
  - *Objectives:* What business outcomes are to be achieved? This could include problems solved or benefits attained, or both.
  - *Measures:* What will demonstrate progress and fulfillment so that the buyer can quantify value?
  - *Value:* What is the impact on the client organization? Impact could include revenue gained, money saved, or difficult-to-measure impact like personal satisfaction or better morale.

EXERCISE 18.3. Match Your Presentation to Your Proposal

SETUP: In this exercise, your sales pros will go deeper into the design of their proposals in order to match their final presentations with their proposals.

Trainer: Pick a current prospect and have sales reps cover every detail possible in each of the proposal sections when they write a presentation directed at that prospect.

Proposal Checklist

Conceptual agreement reached previously:

- Objectives
- Measures
- Value
- Situation appraisal
- Timing
- Methodology and options
- Joint accountabilities
- Terms and conditions
- Acceptance

- *Situation appraisal:* What is the reason for the proposal in general?

- *Timing:* What are the anticipated launch and completion dates?

- *Methodology and options:* What are the choices for implementation?

- *Joint accountabilities:* Who is responsible for what?

- *Terms and conditions:* What are the fees and how are they to be paid?

- *Acceptance:* What options are desired, and are terms agreeable?

Prepare and Rehearse

Prepare

This morning my client, the president of a mid-sized ad agency, Joanne, and her sales staff were somber as they filed into the boardroom for today's training. Last night they had finished their big pitch. They'd done their dog-and-pony show for a prospect they wanted badly to acquire. But a competitor they knew well had done a killer presentation.

Actually, the presenter himself was the show—smooth, cool, and sounding quite persuasive. He was English and had been hired just to do client presentations. The accent was fun to listen to (well, for the prospect). And the man was a trained actor who offered flawless gestures and moved fluidly about the room as he spoke.

Joanne was quite angry that she was most likely losing an account because her prospects were wowed by a smooth-talking James Bond–sound-alike. I started laughing when she described what had happened as the team sat silently, probably thinking this wasn't really funny at all.

"What do you find amusing about us losing this account?" Joanne said.

"It's the thought of you fixing this with a phone call. It's the vision of you getting the client. It's recognizing how powerful one thing is, that I've taught you." I paused and she gestured for me to continue. "You need to take some risks when the sale is at stake. Do you have a good relationship with the key decision-maker?"

"Yes, I do. We've known each other for years."

"Good. Here's what you'll say: 'Joe, I want to have a brief, but difficult conversation with you. This could get you upset with me, but I'm so upset myself about what happened yesterday, I have to say something.' When he tells you that he won't be upset and gives you permission to speak freely, it will be because he's now too intrigued to say no to this conversation. Did one of his people do something wrong? What is this about?

"Say, 'Joe, I respect you and the business you've built over many years and don't understand how you could be influenced by that fellow. He was a great presenter. He does this for a living. But do you think you'll ever have anything to do with that man again? He knows nothing about the advertising business. He's like a hired gun who comes into town, cleans up, takes his reward, and disappears into the sunset.'"

Joanne had a huge smile on her face. "I can see myself saying that to Joe."

And she did. And he thanked her for pointing that out. And he mentioned the insight to his team (not giving credit to Joanne as the source).

And they hired Joanne's team. They hired her, I believe, because nobody wants to be fooled. Because in the end, the client was a little offended about an actor being hired to court and sell them.

See, your presentation doesn't need to be slick. Potent is much, much better. So let's get into how to turn your outline into a powerful sales pitch.

You have chosen one of the three structures from the previous section and now have all the data, all your content laid out in front of you. How do you create the most powerful presentation possible? How do you make the prospect's experience with you and your content so strong that your advantage over competing companies becomes too obvious to ignore?

Here you'll learn how presenters persuade and sell audiences. One of the finest coaches on presentation skills is Jerry Weissman. He has helped his clients generate hundreds of billions of dollars in sales. Yes, billions. His selling success doesn't come from his skill in the performing arts. It doesn't come from his expertise in the television industry. It comes from his mentoring programs with major corporations, as described in his fascinating biography on Amazon.com.

"Jerry Weissman is the world's number one corporate presentations coach. His private client list reads like a who's who of the world's best companies, including the top brass at Yahoo!, Intel, Intuit, Cisco Systems, Microsoft, Dolby Labs, and many others.

"Mr. Weissman founded Power Presentations, Ltd., in 1988. One of his earliest efforts was the Cisco Systems IPO roadshow. Following its successful launch, Don Valentine, of Sequoia Capital, and then chairman of Cisco's board of directors, attributed 'at least two to three dollars' of the offering price to Mr. Weissman's coaching. That endorsement led to nearly five hundred other IPO roadshow presentations that have raised hundreds of billions of dollars in the stock market. Mr. Weissman's focus widened from coaching IPOs to include public and privately held companies. His techniques have helped another five hundred firms develop and deliver their mission-critical business presentations."

Don't you think you need to own Jerry's books? *Presenting to Win* (2008) and *The Power Presenter* (2009) are superb resources for anyone who speaks to single buyers or rooms full of them. As a professional speaker, I was both shocked and pleased at the information he conveys. There was plenty I found new. But the biggest benefit was for me. As someone who models sales excellence for a living, I was happy to have a new model, a *great* model of pitching success.

I mentioned one of the most valuable techniques Jerry teaches in Chapter 5 on communications. Weissman says you should use the acronym WIIFY or What's In It For You. This forces you to focus on the buyer, not you and your offerings. In other words, you'll want to avoid saying "We can do this for you . . ." Rather, say, "*You* can expect these results from our solutions." Your sentence should start with buyers, end with sellers.

He says you do this by using strongly worded comments to set up what you want to share in terms of the value and problem-solving capability of your solutions. This includes comments like "Here's why this is important for you" or "Why should this matter to you? Here's why . . ." or "Here's why you should take action on this now."

Take the WIIFY position as you start to craft language you'll use for your actual presentation. This is important because, when you speak with strength and conviction that you are the best choice available, you show serious decision-makers that their solution resides with the most confident professionals from which they can choose. Your follow-on comments will include plenty of data that supports your solutions, and you'll increase your ability to persuade others.

Next, I'd like to introduce you to another outstanding speaking coach, Carmine Gallo. He's written several books on communicating. Two in particular have special value to you as a sales professional. They are *The Presentation Secrets of Steve Jobs:*

How to Be Insanely Great in Front of Any Audience (2009) and *10 Simple Secrets of the World's Greatest Business Communicators* (2005).

Carmine's dynamic suggestions include "make numbers meaningful," "try for an unforgettable moment," and "Give 'em a show!" These three tips in particular tie into how you're being taught to sell in this book. You must evoke emotion (unforgettable moment and give a show) and you must use logic to support the emotional decision-making part of the prospect's brain. The reference to numbers (make them meaningful) uses logic to reinforce what you've learned throughout this book. Quantify decisions become easier for buyers and for life.

Carmine also says you should provide an outline for listeners, so they can track your presentation. Think how nice it would be for a team of prospects to have a single page of your highlights to review. Will the competition do this? Highly unlikely.

As you prepare your talking points, focus on the opening sixty seconds in order to put together a dynamic and memorable opening. Select one of the methods from the previous section (that is, structure your presentation after the Change Formula, your selling system, or your formal proposal). This opening might be something as simple as saying, "At the end of this presentation, you will see that we can save you $20,000 per month, nearly a quarter of a million dollars a year. That should have an interesting effect on cash flow, especially when everyone here receives his or her year-end bonus."

It might be funny, tying humor into your ideas. "A friend of mine went to prison for something he didn't do. He didn't run fast enough (attributed to comedian Damon Wayans). You've been running a long time with these issues we're here to help you solve. That's not funny. But our serious solutions can make life in this organization a lot more fun than it's been."

You get the picture: Open strong, and make it memorable.

You also want a very powerful ending. In fact, much of your rehearsal time will be spent on opening and closing your sales conversation.

Years ago I was presenting a hiring solution for sales professionals to a major corporation you would recognize. Twelve men, divisional human resource executives, were flown to Chicago to hear from three companies. The competitor before me ran forty-five minutes late. This not only turned off the buyers (respect is always an issue with buyer/seller interactions), but it messed me up because the key buyer came out to me and said, "We have to decide whether to forestall lunch and hear from you or eat lunch while you present. If you can stick to your forty-five minutes, we'll wait to eat."

So I'm twenty minutes into my talk when the doors fly open and a guy wheels in a dozen meals under cover. It had the effect of a crash cart in a hospital emergency room. Everyone's attention was now on the wagon of food, instead of me. Hunger was going to preempt my presentation. I muddled through twenty-five more minutes, constantly noticing heads glancing toward the food.

I changed my closing on the fly. In my briefcase was my afternoon snack, a gigantic red apple. I looked into my briefcase and glanced up, saying, "Gentlemen you've heard the old joke 'What's worse than finding a worm in an apple? Finding half a worm' (lots of laughter). When you choose your vendor today, make sure you select the right apple." And I pulled out mega-apple, set it on the table, and walked out of the room. The last thing I heard was someone saying, "My God, that's the biggest apple I've ever seen." Food was no longer my competitor, but a metaphor for making me a successful choice. We got the business.

Beginnings and endings are key to your time in front of your buyers. Bookend your presentation first. Create dynamic opening and closing statements. Then go through your content and do two things: Create WIIFY statements to set up each point and punch them up. Punching up refers to a writer's skill for designing dynamic word choices for books, articles, and speaking opportunities. This is done in several ways:

- Pick powerful words. Use a thesaurus, hard copy or online (http://thesaurus.com/), to find words that offer variety and strength for your presentation. One of the biggest indicators of intelligence is a large vocabulary. Your buyers want to work with the smartest option. Your word choices offer impressions that tie in to the wisdom of your solutions.

- Pick visual words. While you should use words that cover visual, auditory, and kinesthetic types (remember VAK?), visual words paint images that can be burned into buyers' brains. This is very powerful.

- Pick dynamic verbs. These are the words that move your dialogue along. They can be boring and passive—or they can be dynamic and active.

Notice how these examples distinguish weak from strong wording:

"You've been fighting this problem for a long time. Our products can help you avoid this issue in the future."

or

"This is a tough time for you. It's like scrambling up a rocky hill where you're slipping and sliding back as much as forward. (PAUSE!) You'll want a solution that keeps you from crying for help. Let's stop wasting time and money and begin to gain traction today. Let me show you exactly how you can do this." (Note that visual, auditory, and kinesthetic words have all been built into this example.)

Do you see the improvement possible with the use of powerful words and visual imagery?

Quick tip on this: Remember to pause right after you lay a powerful phrase or image on your buyers. Let it sink in. This helps you be memorable. In presentations, memorable makes money.

Important: Will you have to allow time for questions? You need to plan to either handle questions during the presentation or delay them until the end.

More important: Remember that great sales pros can predict the future? You should anticipate every possible question and have great responses for each. Work with your manager, the team, even your contact at the prospective client company, to understand any issues that might arise. These could be logistical concerns or actual objections.

There is much more on this topic in the chapter on communication skills (Chapter 5). Let's now go over some rehearsal tips.

Rehearse

You must practice to increase the power you've crafted into your presentation. Chapter 5 has some tips on rehearsing, but here are a few more you'll want to use before you put on the show.

- Use a video camera when you practice. You want to make sure you smile and are upbeat and don't have nervous gestures like putting hands in your pockets or holding them folded in front of you (commonly known as the "fig leaf" gesture).

- If you're using PowerPoint, limit the number of slides as well as the words on each. Use nice colors as a backdrop for white or light lettering.

- Write out your transitions from one segment to the next. This provides a smooth presentation that makes sense to the listeners. Even a simple review of what you just said works, such as: "These are the key benefits you'll experience when you adapt our solution. Now I want to talk a bit about some of the serious problems this will solve as well."

- Smile. It's a great opportunity to make the final cut. These people sitting in front of you will feed your family with a simple "yes." You are so good at what you do to have gone this far. Smile.

- Practice three or four or five times before your big show. Practice with others on the team and ask for feedback, too.

Now let's look at the dynamics of the presentation itself.

Deliver the Sales Presentation of a Lifetime

It's time. You're arriving at the prospect's office and are rehearsed and ready to put on the big show. Keep three things in mind:

1. You want to connect individually with everyone in the room. This means meeting and greeting each person upon arrival. You are selling a team as well as every individual. Smile.

2. You want to present overwhelming evidence that you have the best solution available in the marketplace.

3. You want a call to action. At the end, you want a clearly defined Yes, No, or Next Step.

As you begin, your self-talk should be overwhelmingly positive. "I know this content. They really want our help. Our solutions are perfect for this client. I'm the perfect resource for them. This is going to be a nice, long-term relationship."

- You've rehearsed your opening and have it down cold. Whether it's funny or serious, you want the first impression to be strong and memorable.

- Make sure you move. Don't stand still the whole time. Move forward toward the listeners as you make your key points. To the audience this is like a close-up in a movie. It says this is an important moment, so pay close attention.

- Drink water if the presentation is thirty minutes or longer.

- Pause after the most important statements. You can pause by drinking water here to further emphasize your ideas.

- Use WIIFY—What's In It For You.

- Modulate your voice and speak as if with a close friend, sometimes quietly with emphasis, sometimes loudly with energy.

- Exhibit good posture that shows authority, success, and strength.

- If you are building in time to answer questions, decide whether you'll stop for them along the way or wait until the end. Both have advantages and disadvantages. Responding during the presentation is, I believe, more respectful to the questioners, but it can break up the flow you're seeking to create through the time you have in front of them. It can be difficult to answer questions at the end because you don't want to end on a negative note, and this could easily happen with fifteen minutes of hard discussion. I personally would rather control the opening and closing, which means to answer questions as they're asked.

Again, you'll want to review Chapter 5.

Okay, you're now finished. The buyers have experienced your entertaining presentation. They clearly understand the benefits you offer, the problems you solve, the financial impact of your solutions.

It's time to close the sale.

Chapter 19

Closing

I know that a lot of readers will probably want to know right away what unique and special closes might be described in this chapter. However, it's important to understand first what the buyer and seller are experiencing as they near decision-making time. It's also critical to recognize that closing really is a natural progression that occurs beginning from that key opening conversation to rapport to questioning to handling objections and so on. We'll discuss those issues, then cover types of closes.

This Buyer Has Heard All of the Closes

Melissa collides with a very experienced prospect. Here's her story:

> *I was calling on the vice president of human resources for a large company. The size of the account would easily be the most significant sale of my career. The buyer was a soft-spoken older gentleman. I gently asked under what circumstances the prospect might move his firm's business to our company.*

"Do you think that you can beat our current insurance provider's pricing?" he asked.

"If we give you a better deal," I replied, "would you be prepared to give us your business upon the presentation of my quote?"

The quiet prospect turned red in a flash of genuine anger. He pointed a long, stiff finger at me and spat out, "Young woman, if you ever use another closing technique on me, I will throw you out of this office. Do you understand? I'm sick of all you salespeople and your tricks!"

I was so rattled I never did save that sales call. The last ten minutes of the meeting were spoken in stiff, formal terms. I did the proposal, but could not even get the VP on the phone again. I learned that some of those closing techniques you learn to hook the buyer can backfire badly.

Melissa felt terrible. She was a winner when she had actually landed an appointment with a very high-level decision-maker (essentially, she successfully closed for the meeting). Then she blew her shot at a big sale. Do you recognize the name of the closing technique that ruined her meeting? It's an oldie called the Porcupine Close: If someone asks you a "closing" question, you turn it around and stick him or her with a question that demands a commitment to buy.

We'll encounter the Porcupine Close and plenty more later; you'll even discover when to still use some of the old-school techniques.

What the Buyer and Seller Are Experiencing

Anxious feelings, from either perspective, are critical to acknowledge.

I was recently consulting with a major direct selling company. They were struggling with new businesspeople dropping out within thirty to ninety days of signing up. It seems they had been coached to contact friends, family, and neighbors to share both the products and the opportunity to sell them. They saw enthusiasm in others who were successful and were told to be enthusiastic themselves. But they had not been prepared for rejection. I pointed this out to the director of global training by sharing this story, which I made up on the spot:

Here's a beautiful, albeit painful, picture of a sales call from both the buyer's and the seller's perspectives.

Bill is fired up about his new healthy products and changing lifestyle. He bounds out of his house as he sees his neighbor Joe walking out to the car for work.

"Joe, just a minute. I want to tell you about something I'm doing that's really special. My wife and I are starting to use something and I'd like you come to a meeting tonight where you can learn about it and see what kind of opportunity exists for you as well."

Now Joe immediately recognizes that this is a network marketing opportunity. And says, "No thanks, Bill—not interested; have a good day."

(As a side note, many of these companies have never changed their initial approach, in spite of the fact that for thirty years buyers have become painfully familiar with the language, which now only warns people off.)

Bill slinks back into his house, embarrassed and humiliated. First time prospecting, bad ending—and it was a friend! At the end of the day when Bill comes home, he avoids the side of the house that faces his neighbor. In fact, he actually closes the curtains on the windows that face his friend's house, hoping that he will not make eye contact with Joe as he returns from work.

Over the next couple of weeks, when the two guys see each other, Joe quickly waves at Bill and ducks into his car. Awkward. Two months later, Bill's resistance to rejection has resulted in no new sales. He just doesn't want to be embarrassed like that again.

One Saturday, while he's working in his yard, he timidly approaches Joe and says, "Joe, I don't mean to bother you, but I wanted to tell you about what happened with that business I was trying to do. It didn't work out." And Bill proceeds to make up a story about how the money wasn't enough or it was too many hours or it was too hard for the opportunity or it wasn't what it first appeared.

In essence he's saying, "I was fooled and I almost dragged you into this and I'm sorry. Can we still be friends?" Now none of his excuses are true. But he would rather lie and maintain the friendship than make another $600 a month in his spare time.

My point here is that training rarely addresses what's going on in both parties' brains. Let's have a look at both of them.

Buyer

The reptilian brain is the part of the buyer's body that kicks in during difficult decision making. You might recall how the brain responds by choosing between "fight or flight." This means some level of stress exists and the buyer is going to (1) be difficult, offer objections, and attempt to prove you wrong (or inadequate) or (2) he or she might simply mentally check out, in essence, saying "no" without words. This is flight mode, when the buyer is disconnected and thinking about the next appointment or her shopping list or something other than the call. You experience this when she stalls or asks for literature or a detailed quote to end the conversation and send you out of the room.

Fight or flight is a result of fear about making a decision and its consequences. "Will the money be well spent?" "Will others question my decision?" "Will I choose the right product or vendor?" When these question run through a buyer's head, he will react in fight or flight mode.

Not meaning to mix metaphors, but the reptilian brain is the elephant in the room. You want to acknowledge that your prospect has a tough call to make and your intention is to come alongside and help him or her with that decision. This is why we used a Behavior Contract (see Chapter 11, Opening the First Meeting) to gain agreement, together, for the next steps to take after our discussion is over.

I like to point out the difficulties in the decision because these are the moments when you can evoke emotion and create a connection based on empathy for the prospect's plight. You might make comments like: "Tough call here, expensive decision." "Which product will best serve your company?" "We're going to figure this out together and in the end you will know you made the best call."

So for the buyer's sake and the sake of your sale, recognize and respond to the work going on within his or her reptilian brain.

Seller

As I showed in Bill and Joe's story earlier, rejection is a very real possibility in selling. Think about this. If you have a 10 percent closing rate, 90 percent of your interactions are negative. Buyers won't return your phone calls. They'll ignore emails. They'll tell you one thing and do another.

This frequent offering of "no" has deeply rooted ties to rejection from way back when you were a baby. And going forward you didn't get the car and didn't get the girl and didn't get the scholarship.

You hate "no," and rightly so.

Well, true sales pros have a strategy for when "no" arrives in the dialogue.

- You can ignore it and keep going.

- You can meet it head-on and handle the objection to advance the conversation closer to the close.

- You can pack your bags and go. (Here "no" can be good, if it's truly a no sale. But you don't want to leave at the first sign of resistance, unless you've clearly disqualified the buyer.)

- Finally, regardless of your response, you can serve yourself some healthy self-talk. This means thinking: "I'm good, I'll get the next one," or something similar.

- Don't take rejection personally. It's part of our profession.

Concept: What shall we do next?

Closing as a Natural End to the Sales Process

If you picked up this book and skipped right to Closing, hoping you'd find some nuggets of wisdom, let me clarify something that great sales pros know about crossing the selling finish line in first place.

Too much emphasis is placed on closing in sales training.

Closing should be a natural occurrence that you can count on when you've successfully completed the following pieces of the sales puzzle:

- Gained rapport and trust

- Opened professionally with agreement on a game plan for the process

- Qualified the buyer

- Worked with the decision-maker

- Handled resistance and objections

- Asked power questions that:

  - Identified buying criteria to/away, internal/external + evoke emotion

  - Quantified the value of your offering ($ saved or $ obtained)

The key, as you saw in Chapter 11, is Opening the First Meeting. As I said earlier, "If you don't open well, you'll never get close to the close."

Note: If at any point the buyer decides to buy and you haven't gone through your complete selling process, it's time to shut up and consummate the sale. However, you may be in danger of encountering buyer's remorse, where your prospect could change his or her mind. So after you've seen a signature on the dotted line, you should backtrack and verify that the buyer understands the other elements that you haven't covered yet.

An example of this, if the quantifying step has been skipped, might be a comment like: "Ms. Buyer, it looks to me like the financial value of your decision will save the company about $10,000 a month for the first year. That's my conclusion, based on what you've shared. Do those numbers make sense to you, too? (Quantify the sale) Now, what should we do next?"

This final phrase (also our key concept for Closing), "What shall we do next?" is a perfect example of how a great selling dialogue can transition naturally into a close—where both parties are on the same page, looking at how they should be working together and moving in parallel toward saying "yes" to a working relationship.

You have the framework to set the mood for the close. Let's look at some additional language choices that ask your prospect to make a decision. Remember, he or she should have agreed at the start of the process (and each time you've met) that the end of the conversation culminates in a yes, no, or next steps/appointment. You're now encouraging the prospect to do what he or she has said he or she will do.

Types of Closes

Many closing strategies been around for years. Some work from time-to-time. Others could rub buyers the wrong way, as we saw in Melissa's tale at the start of this chapter. As you read through this list, try to identify new techniques you might use. But mostly, look for language you are most comfortable with that can reflect your personality so you can wrap up the sale.

This list of closing techniques is by no means comprehensive. But it will give you an idea of ways you can dialogue with the buyer in order to finalize the sale. There's a trend in sales training to tell reps that these techniques don't work like they used to. That's only partly true.

Key: To help you identify when best to apply each close, I tell you when to use each one. Each has a description *plus* how the close works. *How* is important because you can determine which one to use by understanding the setting. In essence all of these serve as "trial" closes, or tests of the buyer's warmth toward you and your solution.

Keep in mind, these closes are not meant to be manipulative. If you can casually insert the proper close to fit the situation, you have a better chance to close the sale. If you're not in rapport with the buyer, some of them can come across as scripted, trite, and controlling. Remember that the close should be a natural progression of the buyer/seller dialogue. The best close is one the prospect offers after a solid conversation, saying something like: "Okay, what do we do to get this onboard?"

- *Alternative Choice*—Most often used in appointment setting (*Would Wednesday at 2 p.m. or Thursday at 10 a.m. be better?*), this close is the basis for good proposals. How this works: Instead of a "yes" or "no," the buyer is asked to choose A, B, or C: "This proposal offers three solutions you'll find fit, based on what you need and want to invest. Let's look at them now and figure which you'd prefer."

- *Assumptive Close*—Speak as if the buyer has already bought. (*So as we begin working together, this is how we'll implement your new solution.*) How this works: When you have great rapport, this dialogue becomes a natural progression of your conversation. "This all looks good. I'm not sure what else to cover. When would you like to start adopting your new solution?"

- *Ben Franklin Close*—Based on how the American icon made his decisions. He would create a list of all the good and bad related to the potential outcomes, drawing a line down the center of a page to separate positive from negative. How this works: Create a similar page and ask the prospect to list negatives first. This way you'll surface any leftover objections. You can actually address and eliminate them right away. When the list is overwhelmingly positive, the contrast helps the buyer recognize the wisdom of the decision. "Mr. Prospect, would it help if we listed pros and cons to help you make a decision? Let's draw a line down the middle of this page. . . ."

- *Bonus Close*—Hold back some benefit, even a financial incentive or gift, in order to push the buyer past the point of no return. How this works: Buyers who are on the fence, close to saying "yes", can often be convinced when you generously offer a no-cost, high-value incentive. "Ms. Prospect, I get the sense you're close to saying 'let's go,' so may I offer you something special to help you decide? (After a curious, 'What's that?') We'll rebate $1,000 at the end of six months together or, if you prefer, we'll donate the $1,000 to your favorite charity."

- *Calendar Close*—Set a date for the buyer to begin using your services and work backward from that date to identify when you need signatures and other actions to complete the sale. How this works: This is done when it appears the prospect is committed to working together and the conversation has centered around the time when implementation of your solution has been identified. "It sounds like the end of next month would be perfect to have this in place. So pinning down this date, the thirtieth, means we'd work backward from there and would need signatures by . . . and meetings around implementation by. . . ."

- *Emotion (or Empathy) Close*—Focus on the specific emotions your buyer revealed during the selling process. By tying the decision to feelings (attaining good ones or relieving bad ones), you can empathize and help the prospect feel better about saying "yes." How this works: You want to wrap up the sale by saying something like, "Rita, you are like, crazy frustrated, by the amount of money the firm is losing with this problem. Let's eliminate this issue now, so you can focus on running your department like you were hired to do."

- *Final Objection Close*—This assumes you're at the end of the meeting and you're asking whether there are other issues. How this works: Simply say, "Is there anything else that is keeping us from working together?" Their response tells you whether you have more work to do ("Yes, one thing") or whether it's time to move forward ("Great, let's start").

- *Free Trial Close*—Help the buyer become comfortable with your company and your solution by letting him or her experience you at no cost. This was originally called the Puppy Dog Close. ("Here, take the little dog home for a week, see if the kids like caring for him, and just bring him back if it doesn't work out.") This is extremely potent. (Who wants to pry the puppy loose from the screaming kids after seven days of play?) This used to be quite popular in automotive sales, but insurance regulations don't allow it any longer. It worked because you showed off the vehicle to friends, neighbors, and family and set everybody's expectations that you were going to own the car. How this works: Employ this when a buyer truly likes and is interested in your product, but has expressed his or her hesitance. The buyer just doesn't know what it would look like or feel like to own and experience your solution, so give him a taste of it. "You can use our software for ninety days free, including access to 24/7 customer service help. At the end of that time, you can decide whether to stay with us."

- *Getting to "Yes" Close*—This involves getting a series of yeses from the buyer which end in a final "yes" to the purchase question. Essentially, you're training the buyer to say "yes." How this works: This is implemented with close-ended questions ranging from opening comments ("Isn't it a beautiful day?") to business queries ("You're probably talking to a few different companies about solving this concern?") If you fire them off throughout the dialogue, you could come across as inflexible and too focused on forcing rapport. Use your questions carefully throughout.

- *Handshake Close*—When you can look the buyer in the eye and just know the deal is done, offer to shake hands over it. I love this technique because it assumes you are peers, equals working together. How this works: When the two of you have figured out that this relationship is a fit, but a few details need to be attended to, use this close. The personal touch of that handshake can keep the deal from coming undone should some details slow up the actual closing process (such as a CEO's or CFO's approval of the expenditure). While standing and offering your hand, say, "I'm looking forward to partnering with you on this."

- *Impending Event Close*—This is used when you want to create a sense of urgency. But the urgency has to really exist, not be manufactured to pressure the buyer. (Again, avoid anything construed as manipulative.) This close tells the prospect that if he doesn't make a decision now, circumstances will change and he won't have access to the exact solution again. How this works: "Mr. Prospect, that vehicle you just drove is our last model in the color you love, that unique Vegas gold. While we can find you another one eventually, it might be in your best interest to put a deposit down today." Said honestly and casually, it can motivate the buyer to move forward.

- *Opportunity Lost Close*—While similar to the Impending Event, this really focuses on the value or cost of not buying. It is also closely aligned to the Emotion Close. How this works: "Ms. Prospect, the $1,600 a week you're losing until this issue is resolved is equal to hiring two sales reps. You said your reps gross a quarter million dollars a year. So it appears to me that the real problem is not $1,600 a week, but half a million dollars in lost revenue a year." Again, quantifying decisions is huge throughout the sales process.

- *Porcupine Close*—We saw this backfire on Melissa in the opening story of this chapter. This close works by linking your solution to the resolution of objections. How this works: The Porcupine Close will work if you're stuck at one last objection and can suggest that, since this is the final concern, it can be connected to the purchase. "Mr. Buyer, if that's truly the last thing we need to resolve to get this solution in place, would you be good enough to go with us when we can show you how we'll deal with your concern?"

- *Reduce to the Ridiculous Close*—This is an old Zig Ziglar close, and it still works in the right situation. You want to reduce the cost of your product or service to a minimal amount, so it seems almost insignificant. How this works: "Ms. Buyer, for all the good this will do, your new solution costs less than a cup of coffee a day. That's a pretty easy call to make."

- *Summary Close*—Fire off a list of all the things the buyer is going to receive. This could include benefits as well as problems eliminated. How this works: "Mr. Prospect, let's quickly review what happens when you adapt this solution. You'll increase cash flow by $1,200 a month. You'll eliminate this distraction and can refocus your energy on running your department." Et cetera. Don't forget to use both personal as well as professional bullet points.

- *Testimonial Close*—Use a satisfied client or the referral who put you in front of this buyer to convince him or her that others have wisely decided this is the way to go. How this works: "Ms. Prospect, when Rita suggested we meet it was because she felt so convinced of the value of our solution that she said you have to have it. She was a bit overly enthusiastic, but what do you think of her opinion? Does she normally make good decisions related to running her business?" Notice in the last comment how you are aligning your buyer with the concept that good business pros make good decisions. This is evidenced by following the successes of others and not reinventing solutions.

- *Thermometer Close*—This is essentially a request of the buyer to measure his or her warmth toward your solution. This close has been popularized as the key trial close question taught by the Sandler Sale Institute. How this works: "Mr. Buyer, if you were to rate your interest in this offering on a scale of 1 to 10, with 1 meaning 'Dan, go home and leave me alone' and 10 being 'Yes, let's do this,' where would you put yourself?" A response less than optimal helps you revisit any final objections.

- *Trial Close*—Actually, most of these are trial closes when they don't work. You do want to find out how likely a buyer is to buy throughout the sales process. How this works: Be bold and ask a question like, "Ms. Buyer, do you have enough information to make a decision right now? I know both our time is precious. So what do you think?" Watch her face closely. *Caution:* If you use this prematurely you come across as a pushy sales rep, and that could undermine the rest of your conversation.

- *One Final Close*—"What would you like me to do now?" Try this when you're at the end of your meeting and feel good about the fit between your solution and buyer needs. If you did your BC properly (Chapter 11), then they can only say "yes," "no," or "set a next step."

Notice that in any close you must *Ask!* You have to ask a question to get an answer. Practice this skill at home; teach it to your kids (although they're probably hounding you already with more questions than you can stand. When you want the buyer's "yes," simply say, "Can we get started?"

Ask for the sale!

Chapter 20

Debriefing the Call

CHAPTER OVERVIEW

Seven Agenda Items for the Debriefing

1. Did you gain rapport?
2. Did you set a framework with the buyer for the meeting?
3. Did you ask questions?
4. Did you overcome the objections you encountered?
5. Did you identify needs, goals, and problems?
6. Did you quantify the value of your solution and gain agreement in terms of dollars saved or gained?
7. Did you ask for the sale?

Do your salespeople debrief after every call? Why not? This strategy is horribly neglected. I have a consulting client now who switched the third year of our contract from pure training to riding with the sales pros, then debriefing the calls. To add greater value, we do team meetings and analyze or expose the issues that surfaced in the debriefings. It's fun, it's embarrassing, and all of them are cool with the experience—even when they're on the hot seat. There is no better way to find out whether your people can sell. There is no better way to find out whether your team members are putting sales training into play. You must sit with your sellers and their prospects and find out whether they have changed their behavior based on your training. A potent debriefing is available to you by covering the following seven agenda items that include, well, everything you've already covered:

1. Did you gain rapport? (Chapter 9)

2. Did you set a framework with the buyer for the meeting? (Chapter 11)

3. Did you ask questions? (Chapter 14)

4. Did you overcome the objections you encountered? (Chapter 16)

5. Did you identify needs, goals, and problems? (Chapter 12)

6. Did you quantify the value of your solution and gain agreement in terms of dollars saved or gained? (This has been revisited throughout this book, in chapters on questioning, communication skills, closing, and more.)

7. Did you ask for the sale? (Chapter 19)

A Sales Call Debriefing

One of my first consulting clients was a law firm run by a pair of eclectic seventy-year-old lawyers. They hired me to find companies with two hundred+ employees. They would offer a private form of pre-paid legal advice as an employee benefit and make loads of money. They already had some unions as clients, so it wasn't a new product. The real reason they would make loads of money was because they wanted to sell their law firm and retire. By landing some large contracts, they could significantly increase the value of their practice.

For example, a $10,000-a-month contract would be worth not just $120,000 a year in new sales, but it would increase the value of the whole business by a factor of ten. That would be another $1.2 million above their existing value, which they could sell their business for.

Imagine getting a dozen or so similar clients over the next six months, then selling the firm for $15 to $20 million more than previously planned!

When I secured my first sales call—a large group of auto dealerships—I asked one of the partners to go with me. Who would know the service better than he? The human resources director for the dealerships showed us into her office and had great news. She had handled our firm's legal services in her previous job at one of the unions! She understood the product's value as a recruiting tool, as well as a unique benefit for her employees. We were basically there to give her some details of the service and explain pricing. It was going to be one of the easiest sales I'd ever had.

"When I became a lawyer in 1955 . . . ," began the partner. And I knew that I'd made a mistake. Forty minutes and four decades later, my "selling" partner finished. He'd contributed nothing of value to the meeting unless the HR director or I wanted a job as his biographer.

I managed to salvage the rest of our time together and we ended the meeting on a very upbeat note. She wanted the costs for six hundred employees and would immediately put it into their benefits program.

The debriefing of the call came moments after we walked out the door. "Wow!" I said as we entered the elevator outside the company's headquarters. "We've struck gold on our first sales call." The attorney looked at me for several seconds and said, "I don't want them as customers." I was stunned. "What do you mean?" I asked. My agreement had a retainer and some incentives based on the size of the clients. This deal represented a nice bonus for me. "They're automotive people. You know, car salesman, mechanics. I don't want to have those kind of people as clients." I looked at the guy in disgust and bit my tongue. Union workers' money was good, but cash from car people was not?

Back at the office, his partner agreed about the undesirable automotive clients. Shortly afterward I terminated my relationship with them.

That disappointing debrief told me one thing I'd clearly missed in my pre-sales work. I hadn't created criteria for qualifying and disqualifying my prospects (see Chapter 12). The company had some prospects they'd prefer to ignore. I'd spent time and energy targeting the wrong people.

In that too-brief debrief, I learned a lesson from the thoughts of my "boss" following that call. A quality analysis of how a sales call went needs to formally cover seven key elements of that meeting. It shouldn't surprise you that those seven elements are based on the most important chapters of this book.

Note: If your company doesn't or won't take the time to debrief, your sales professionals should be taught to debrief their calls themselves. After all, who's most responsible for their success? So even when you're flying solo, you need to make debriefing a regular practice. It can significantly help you improve your performance. I believe that a five-star debriefing means that the sales pro has covered all the elements of the pre-work as well as the selling dialogue. The pro should be proud to have applied everything he or she has learned to increase the chance of a close. To that end, using pride in their profession as the key focal point, I like to anchor what is learned on this question: *Would your mother approve?*

Seven Agenda Items for the Debriefing

I. Did You Gain Rapport?

VAK? Match, Pace, Lead? To/Away, Self-talk when you met resistance?

2. Did You Set a Framework with the Buyer for the Meeting?

Did you set boundaries and rules for the meeting? Behavior contract! Remember Chapter 11 on the first meeting! You must:

1. *Gain a time commitment.* Here you want to revisit the amount of time agreed on when the meeting was set up.

2. *Establish the rules of communication.* Then you ask permission to have an open, honest, discussion (this will include, as you will see, getting permission to ask lots of questions).

3. *Set a purpose or goal.* Finally, you gain agreement that the purpose of this meeting is simply to determine whether we should be working together, schedule a second meeting, or just part ways. In other words, recognize how this meeting is going to end. Once the prospect agrees to the three elements of your BC, thank him or her, then open with a leading question.

3. Did You Ask Questions?

Did your earliest questions seek to qualify or disqualify the prospect? Did you obtain answers to your power questions? Which ones and what were the answers?

4. Did You Overcome the Objections You Encountered?

Were they from your top six? Were there any unexpected objections? Did you handle them well? Which ones, and how did you respond? Did you get stuck on any? Which ones, and how did you respond?

5. Did You Identify Needs, Goals, and Problems?

If the buyer is To, you're working to identify benefits and goals he'll attain. If the buyer is Away, you're working to identify problems and consequences of her current or future action (or inaction). Which did you identify?

6. Did You Quantify the Value of Your Solution and Gain Agreement in Terms of Dollars Saved or Gained?

What numbers did you gain agreement with?

7. Did You Ask for the Sale?

- Yes, they bought.

- No, we both agreed this isn't a fit.

- We set a next step:

    - When *exactly* is it?

    - With whom?

    - What is the purpose of the next meeting?

With these seven questions you now have as solid a structure to debrief a sales call as you can have. I strongly encourage you to create a form designed to gather this information. Minimally, this can be handwritten or put into a Word document. If possible, build it into your CRM or contact manager. Your ability to search on each of these seven questions to find responses from past debriefings would give you a huge advantage in coaching your reps to greater success.

Remember in Chapter 16 when I recommended that objections be logged so that managers can review them and work to improve reps' skills? This is coaching and managing individual sales professionals at the highest possible level. Nothing is more valuable to improving reps' performance.

It is critical to the rep, manager, even the prospect, that a candid, truthful assessment of each sales call be done. This isn't about a rep hiding his or her embarrassment because the sale didn't close. It's about improvement and advancing the sales process. Input from other reps or managers here can actually revive situations that were deemed lost. It can also give guidance to reps and help turn warm buyers into found business. Be honest in debriefing the sales call.

Sales managers should look at debriefing as a way to:

1. Identify reps' ability to follow the steps needed to make the sale,

2. Create accurate sales forecasts, and (most importantly)

3. Disqualify poor prospects. Remember, chasing bad business is the number one problem faced by salespeople.

You met my fighter pilot friend Waldo in Chapter 8 on preparing for the sales call. He believes in the power of debriefing as well and says, "No mission is complete until you debrief."

Chapter 21

Following Up
After the Sale

CHAPTER OVERVIEW
Connect Constantly

This is simple. You landed the sale, and now have to stay connected, possibly deepening the relationship with your buyer. Check out this story and a checklist of ideas on what to do once they've signed on the line that is dotted.

I wish you could meet Denise.

She is a classic rags to riches story, having moved from a secretarial position to CEO of her own promotions firm. She was so successful that one of her company highlights was to be involved with a video shoot with Chicago Bulls hall-of-fame basketball icon Michael Jordan.

Because of her unusual path to the top, she had never had the chance to get a formal selling system under her belt. I was selling training when we met. We sat down once for about an hour to discuss having her and her key sales manager be trained by me. The meeting went well and we scheduled a second call—basically to pick up the check for her commitment to the class.

As you probably do, I attempted to discover what might un-sell her or cause buyer's remorse. I said, "Denise, what's the real reason you want to do this training? I mean, two years with me is a serious commitment."

Her answer was a total surprise and still gives me goose bumps when I replay it in my mind. "I want to be able to do exactly what you did to me. I have no idea how you sold me or what you said, and I'm willing to pay to learn how to do it." It was my ultimate compliment as a sales professional and a trainer. And I didn't "do" anything to her. I just carried on a casual conversation where together we discovered the impact of training on her firm.

But her words taught me a concept I now teach. *Great selling is invisible.* Just work alongside your prospects and apply the key elements of this *Ultimate Guide to Sales Training* and see how your sales occur with less effort. So what will you do when you land the "yes!"?

Connect Constantly

Today, you landed the big sale. What happens next? These could include:

- Getting the agreement signed and in place.
- Perhaps make introductions to the proper team members who will support your product or service.
- Saying thank you in a variety of ways—gift, note, dinner, or in person.
- Preventing buyer's remorse during any trial period so as to preclude the sale coming apart.
- Discussing how to deal with any bumps, issues that might arise down the road.
- Asking for referrals.

Short chapter here, because it's simple to identify the power of this idea.

Concept: Connect with clients constantly.

I encourage you to do what I did with Denise. Simply ask the buyer what exactly motivated him or her to say "yes." You'll learn a lot. The information you receive will help you understand some of the criteria that form a perfect prospect.

Now go share it with your manager and the rest of the team. It'll provide a great coaching moment that will help all of you sell more.

Chapter 22

Up-Selling and Cross-Selling

Companies leave money on the table for so many reasons. In this chapter you'll discover some surprising reasons to up-sell. The obvious one is to make more money. But the inverse of that is preventing the loss of a client by creating multiple exit barriers. You'll also read ways to mentally prepare to up-sell as well.

Angry Client Wanted to Spend More Money

Steve earns a very uncomfortable conversation. I'm team training a roomful of entrepreneurs. It's amazing how many brilliant business minds have little or zero sales skills.

Everyone is saying goodbye at the end of class and Mark, my partner, singles out Steve, an insurance rep. "Steve, come here please." The man walks up with a smile on his face. "Is this sales training doing you some good?"

"Yes it is, in a big way," says Steve.

As the room empties out, Mark's face changes like a light switch had been flipped. "You don't really care about me and my family, Steve, do you?" The surprise was quite visible on Steve's face. What was this about?

"Steve," Mark continued, "I was almost in a serious accident on the way here—so of course I thought of my wife and newborn and how they'd get along if I was out of the picture." He paused and forced words through clenched teeth. "You haven't sold me enough coverage, have you?"

My partner had a low-key personality, and he was clearly quite angry. Steve had sent a card when the baby arrived, meaning to discuss a program for her. But the rep had missed the other piece—the training company's explosive company growth meant there were both people and profits to protect.

Neglecting the opportunity to up-sell his trainer, who was also a client, had damaged the relationship. I stood mesmerized by the scene unfolding. Here was a sales trainer telling off a client and a sales rep missing a chance to increase earnings from an existing customer—who was also his mentor. Strange mixture of roles and role reversal going on.

Steve offered to immediately sit down and do some numbers with Mark, but the trainer said, "I've gotta go." And left the room.

Steve looked at me in shock and said, "Wow, I just learned to monitor my clients' personal and professional lives much more closely."

Tough experience, but here's the good news: The hardest sale you'll ever make is the first one.

Up-Selling and Cross-Selling

You've generated a revenue-based relationship. Now, how well will you increase the size of the sale by up-selling your product or service or by cross-selling with other members of your team who have additional offerings to enhance the life of your client?

Up-selling and cross-selling are really about asking. So when your team is not doing this well, it's similar to problems with referrals. You just have to pin down your client to a conversation about additional offerings, then begin to navigate the path toward the close.

This chapter is going to be fairly brief. The reason this will be such a short piece of the selling puzzle to address is that we're going to cover some serious reasons a company and a sales pro need to up-sell and cross-sell. You already have the selling skills to motivate this buyer to buy. So you should know whether he or she makes decisions by attaining benefits or solving problems (Chapter 17). You know how to manage the early moments of a call to give it direction and focus (Chapter 11). You have your power questions (Chapter 14), and your outstanding ability to manage objections is better than it's ever been (Chapter 16). Best of all, you've closed this person or organization once before. You really have some very good reasons that cross-selling and up-selling are important to your salespeople and your company. But here's the biggest one.

Concept: Don't leave money on the table.

So let's look at reasons why you need to use your skills to deepen the relationship with this buyer. Then we'll address the attitude you adopt when you increase the size of the sale.

Reasons to Up-Sell and Cross-Sell

1. *Generate deep, long-lasting loyalty.* Frederick Reichheld and Thomas Teal's book *The Loyalty Effect* (1996) is a must-read for anyone who needs to benefit by attaining client loyalty. These experts reveal the importance of loyalty in terms of higher profit, lower marketing acquisition costs, more referrals, and, of course, lower customer decay rates. That last is a scary term we'll look at further in Number 4 below.

2. *Make more money.* Up-sell and cross-sell if you prefer not to leave money on the table. (Notice how that's an example of To and Away from Chapter 17 in that we're trying to motivate reps who are incentivized by gaining more money or by avoiding the loss of additional income.) Up-selling and cross-selling are *critical* if you want to make more money.

3. *Gain more "share of customer."* This idea comes from the classic books by Peppers and Rogers (1996, 1999) on one-to-one marketing.

4. *Clients with deeper relationships are much less likely to leave you.* Your goal here is to create multiple exit barriers, and thus significantly reduce client attrition.

The Huthwaite Group, which offers training from Neil Rackham's *SPIN Selling* (1988) system, suggests that salespeople don't up-sell more due to three reasons:

- Risk aversion (they're nervous about rejection after a successful sale).

- Bad salesmanship (they just don't understand the value of up-selling or cross-selling as a regular selling practice).

- Flawed business logic (the salesperson just doesn't "get" all the reasons we've identified above).

Attitudes to Adopt When You Up-Sell and Cross-Sell

1. From the beginning of the relationship, focus on getting the *second* sale! There's a distinct technique to this. Seed your conversations with references to other products and services you offer beyond the current topic of discussion. When I'm training financial services pros who use seminars to generate clients, I teach them to mention, every eight to ten minutes, how a client will benefit by discussing other products. "So when you come to sit down with us for a conversation on your needs, we can cover how X and Y and Z can help you as well."

2. Stay connected, frequently touching your client by every method you can. This means, in particular, not choosing email correspondence over other techniques. Personal notes and cards are very powerful. I even like leaving voicemails after working hours. This is efficient.

3. The actual conversation (once you've landed an appointment for this purpose) is going to be a simple, casual dialogue, like "By the way, can I share something a few of our best clients have done in the past? You'll find it useful for you as well. . . ."

4. Have plenty of testimonials and stories to reinforce the wisdom they will show when they say "yes" to more.

5. Focus on them, not on you! It's not "What can I do to help?" (which is egocentric), but "How do you. . .?" And mention a problem or benefit

they're likely to attain or solve once they buy additional products or services from you.

6. Take the attitude that you are providing an extra service, not an extra sale.

7. Be proactive, not reactive, to the opportunities to sell more. Assuming a buyer will ask about additional services is foolish. You must initiate a conversation about how else you can serve each of your clients.

You'd be smart to draw from the collective brainpower of your selling team-mates to find out how to best approach these additional selling opportunities.

EXERCISE 22.1. Finding Ways to Up-Sell and Cross-Sell

SETUP: By drawing from their collective brainpower, you'll find out exactly how sales team members have dialogues with clients to up-sell and cross-sell.

In their table groups, have sales reps share language choices they use to start a conversation on additional product or service offerings.

Trainer: Have sales pros write down what everyone has said and compile these persuasive words and phrases to build into training and share with new hires.

Your company should identify buying patterns of existing clients. How many buy more? Which purchases are most likely to lead to additional sales?

In addition, your data should pinpoint:

- Which reps do this as a regular practice?

- Which reps don't?

- How much more money is earned for the individual and for the company from this regular practice?

- Does your CRM allow reps to identify critical dates and data on clients in a manner like Harvey McKay's pieces of information at www.harveymackay.com/pdfs/mackay66.pdf?

Take the time to connect your sales pros with others who support additional selling initiatives. Do they need more time with other reps who sell different prod-ucts? Do they need to meet with support/service team members as well? Create a package for each new client that lists additional offerings, then offer to spend a few minutes reviewing those of interest to the buyer.

Make a plan to introduce your company's new up-selling and cross-selling initiative. Announce that this will be an area of focus for two or three years until it becomes a regular practice for every salesperson on the team.

Part Three

Training the Sales Pro to Improve Performance

Part Three is all about the extra effort sales professionals can engage in to really boost revenue. Sadly, the most common concern I see with sales teams is that the salesmen and -women are poor stewards of their time. They just don't work as hard as they could. So we start with a ton of great personal performance improvement tips—any of which could significantly impact what can be accomplished each day. You also want reps to know their numbers so that they own the ability to control and improve them. You'll read about the power of mentors. How to work a trade show. Some deep, new thinking on negotiating skills and how to formulate a specific approach to making ethical decisions. We'll start with a boatload of quick performance tips.

Chapter 23

Daily Performance Tips

Energy management might be more important than time management. And there we kick off productivity tips, including dozens of ideas you can quickly adapt. Let's set our key thought in place right now. This chapter is as rich a resource on personal improvement as you'll find.

Concept: Are you better today than yesterday?

Tips to Push You Past the Top

Million Dollar Consulting author Alan Weiss (2009) says you can measure your true wealth in terms of *discretionary time*. This implies your most precious resource is time. Great sales pros have outstanding practices for managing their time. Throughout this chapter you will learn a couple dozen ways to increase your performance by raising your sensitivity to your daily efforts. Pay attention closely to the section on personal productivity, as it lists a great many quick ideas to improve your performance. As I've suggested for other topics, create a checklist for your sales pros and help them identify ways they can improve personal performance during their selling day.

What you learn in the next section could surprise you. It's based on recent research that suggests that energy management, not time management, should be our primary focus. We'll address this topic first.

Energy Management
Meeting Planning Misery: Joel Jumps on a Prospect Early in the Day

> As an ISES [International Special Events Society] member, our company provides event planning services for national sales conferences and yearly corporate celebrations. I had an office at home in Denver, Colorado, and this meant I was always working. I would call East Coast prospects and clients before I went to work. I would do paperwork after I got home. So I was a hermit, a recluse—none of my friends had seen me in six months. One evening I was assaulted by phone calls from everyone I knew. What was wrong with me? Had I given up on bars and all the good stuff that came inside them—music, beer, women? So with the threat of total abandonment by my buddies, I took a cab to the club. I made up for six months of alcohol abstinence in one night.
>
> It's 3 a.m., bleary-eyed and blitzed, I stagger into my home. Having programmed myself to do so—I wander right into my office. I grab my phone and call my biggest prospect—a company that spent over a quarter million dollars on their yearly sales conference. Sputtering and slobbering into the mouthpiece, I pitched him.
>
> "Oh, please, you've got to buy from me. You're the biggest company I've ever called on. I can do a great job, I swear. Besides, my commission on this project would be

beyond belief. Please use me for your event planning. We're the best. You've got to give me a chance."

I passed out on my desk. The screeching dial tone from the disconnected phone didn't even wake me up. There was only one phone call the next day. I missed it, as I didn't make it to the office.

It was the guy I had reached out to in my sorry state. "Uh, Joel, I believe it was you who called my office at three in the morning. Please don't ever call me or our company again."

I love this story. A sales rep shared it during my "confession session" at a keynote I did in a Chicago ISES event. For all the big sales meetings I've keynoted, trained at, and attended over the years, I had never thought about the reps who are selling event management services to coordinate hotels, food, and more. This story embodies the value of rest, recovery, and energy in a sales-person's life.

Jim Loehr and Jack Groppel have done extensive research on this concept at HPI, The Human Performance Institute in Orlando, Florida. These two men started by training world class tennis players, and their work evolved into teaching best practices that help business professionals attain world class skills by managing their energy.

Their foundational belief is that managing energy could be more critical to success than managing time. Energy comes from taking breaks during the business day, the week, month, and throughout the year. Their work covers how well you mentally and physically leave your work behind or "disconnect." For some great details on this concept, I highly recommend two books on this topic: *The Power of Full Engagement* (Loehr & Schwartz, 2003) and *The Corporate Athlete* (Groppel & Andelman, 1999).

Some of their tips include:

- Create positive rituals to manage your daily work effort. This includes building breaks to help you rest and recover from your efforts.

- Create a life balance that covers physical conditioning as well as emotional, mental, and spiritual facets.

- Eat properly, move around, and get fresh air, even playing (mentally and physically) to disconnect so you can rest and recover from work.

- Recognize barriers to managing energy in order to plan for overcoming them.
- Create accountability to employ the new learning and accompanying behaviors.

All of this amounts to being fully engaged in your work, because you don't want to burn out while seeking success. You can take a free "Full Engagement Profile" in five minutes at the Human Performance Institute (HPI) website: http://hpinstitute.com/assessment_profile.html.

I took The Corporate Athlete training from HPI and recognized that the "putting the pedal to the metal" mindset is good, as long as you let off the gas and get out of the car a few times a day. I disconnect during my day by getting out of my office into the sun or by watching some short videos or reading humor books (not business writing, which recycles your brain right back to what you're supposed to be leaving behind).

So gather energy throughout the workday. Eat right, move around, get that fresh air (even in winter), stop working (disconnect), and play. What do you dwell on? Take your mind to a place other than work. You can also manage energy by going to bed earlier every night.

Then recover and gain energy by getting up earlier every day. Do the numbers. Even at thirty extra minutes times 250 days a year you gain over three extra weeks of work. That's 17 percent more work, or 17 percent more commission a year. What if you woke up an hour earlier and increased earnings by one-third?

Energy management is more important than time management. That said, let's now look at time.

Time Management

Did you ever watch the *Terminator* movies? Remember when they were good? Do you think that the old fear of human beings being controlled by machines is coming to pass? Do you ever feel like YOU are being controlled by machines? They demand your attention—*immediately*—with a BEEP as an email arrives or alarm sounds. These auditory and visual stop signs make us nervous and anxious. The message? "Wait! What about me? I'm important, too!" Digital devices are a huge factor in this epidemic of urgency.

You see, if everything is a priority, nothing is a priority.

You can choose to be reactive to what life tosses at you. Or you can choose to be in control. Your ability to know what to ignore, what to worry about later, and what to attend to now will define your productivity as a sales pro.

Here's a hint on which choice to make. Do you think that spending your precious time responding to whatever pops up is really in your best interest? The answer is no. So how can you decide what's important? How do you prioritize? Divide your life into two categories. You have a professional life and a personal life. You want to find balance between them.

Because the amount of time and energy we put into our business lives can affect our private lives, we need a strategy that respects the boundaries between them. And if you don't respect the boundaries, it's probably because you haven't created them yet. So use prioritization to do that. What are some areas of focus for these two parts of our lives? The list could be quite large, but here are some suggestions:

Professional

- Closing sales
- Generating leads
- Qualifying prospects
- Finding referrals
- Servicing existing clients

Personal

- Spending time with family and friends (gaining emotional connection)
- Budgeting income for things I desire such as a new car, vacation, hobby, fun memories, etc.
- Staying/getting healthy
- Balancing work and personal life
- Engaging in personal hobbies, exploring talents, participating in activities that energize and bring joy or pleasure

EXERCISE 23.1. Prioritizing Your Activities

SETUP: Sales pros can have balance by prioritizing activities in their life. This is possibly the only time that many of your reps have done something like this.

Reps should create lists of activities in both categories that require their attention and then assign a value to each item. This is where the root of the word *priority* comes into play. "A priori" in Latin means "takes precedence."

Trainer: Have reps discuss their lists and the order they assigned to each of their priorities with partners. Assign accountability partners to help reps stay on track for a balanced life at home and at work.

It's important to understand that a higher-ranking priority doesn't necessarily replace another concern that is lower ranked. For example, if staying healthy is personally important to you and you rank the value of putting time into family higher, you still can schedule non-working time so that both are attained regularly. For example, I'm still a serious basketball player who competes overseas representing the U.S. in World Masters Games competition. To stay in shape, I'm tearing up and down the basketball court at 5 a.m. three times a week. This priority does not interfere with my family time at all. I also lift weights three days at lunch. Again, my health priorities never interfere with, don't even intersect with, my family priorities.

Work life can be a bit trickier. That's why I prefer to coach reps to block out time in their day for specific activities. It's easier to plan for a variety of levels of importance this way. Here's a sample plan:

Yesterday 4:30 to 5 p.m.	plan tomorrow's calls and workload
8:00 to 10:00 a.m.	40 to 60 phone calls, outgoing only!
10:00 to 10:10	break
10:10 to 11:45	respond to messages/return phone calls
11:45 to 12:45	lunch
12:45 to 3:00	face-to-face calls
3:00 to 4:00	outgoing calls
4:00 to 4:30	respond to messages/return phone calls
4:30 to 5:00	plan tomorrow's calls and workload

Notice that you end each day by planning the next day in detail. This is a huge time-saver. You walk into work and start to work. No buzzing about, figuring out who to call, what to do. Your co-workers will notice your strange (but productive) behavior and begin to leave you alone as they respect and eventually envy your abundant output.

This works. It's a system within your selling system. If you need convincing of the strategic value of systems, revisit Chapter 3, The Many, Many Values of a Selling System.

You now have a structure for your activities. How do you determine which activities take precedence over others? Details on prioritizing skills can be found in Chapter 28 on mental health.

One of the biggest benefits of prioritizing is that it reinforces the solution to sales reps' number one problem. Do you recall what that is?

Sales reps chase poor prospects.

When you are doing a great job of eliminating poor prospects and persuing perfect ones, you truly see the value of knowing which activities deserve attention and which need to be ignored.

Remember that 80 percent of your revenue comes from 20 percent of your customers. And 80 percent of your prospects' potential comes from 20 percent of your prospects. I really was hoping to get through this whole book without referencing the Pareto Principle (paraphrased, it means 80 percent of anything worthwhile comes from 20 percent of your efforts).

Now you have read some of my suggestions on highlighting and attending to important activities. Prioritization is the majority of the problem with time management. Now I'll give you some productivity ideas and personal tips to improve your performance.

Personal Productivity

What follows is a long list of best practices for improving personal performance. Before you read these ideas, let's make sure your POV is good.

POV or point-of-view is the perspective an author, artist, or screenwriter chooses to portray to the audience. Take this scene, for example: A shark closes in on an unsuspecting swimmer. Do we experience the swimmer's view of a beautiful ocean and skyline? Or will we see the scene from above (also called eagle-eye view) of the animal closing the distance toward its dinner? Or will we see the shark-eye view as the predator focuses on splashing feet?

You have two choices for how you view the following material on personal productivity. You can have an optimistic outlook or you can persist on pessimism. After all, you can see both the positive and negative aspects of improving yourself. Good things are going to happen when you change some behaviors, but there are still going to be some problems that warrant more change. It's never-ending. Your point of view will determine the results you get.

Daniel Goleman's (2006) classic research on optimism is quite clear (see his best-selling book, *Emotional Intelligence*). Optimists look at setbacks as temporary or confined to specific circumstances. Pessimists look at setbacks as permanent and defining incidents. It's important for us to frame setbacks in temporary language. I like to say that "You're in the middle of the story." Not the end, not the final answer, but the middle of a process that can still change/improve down the road; that is, even if it's the end of the quarter, it's not the end of your year.

I encourage you now to adopt an optimistic outlook as you read through these tips. Think positively about how you can use a few, or many, of them. Look brightly toward the increase in income that will come from following these best practices.

The tips are in no particular order, because you need to go through all of them before you can identify the ones you'll put into play and do so.

- *Email.* Only check email two or three times a day. Set times to send and respond. I personally like to work hard, ignoring email until 11 a.m. I'll revisit it at 3 p.m., then at the end of my day. This means your program stays shut. And you might as well turn off your notification sound anyway. By the way, there are few things more disrespectful to a phone caller than to hear your email beep in the background. You know the caller is thinking, "Is this person really paying attention or is he multi-tasking at my expense?"

- *Phone.* You can also ignore phone calls until your scheduled times for making calls, as you can always sneak a peek at caller I.D. for high-value conversations. In contrast, however, you might want to answer callers you recognize anyway. The time you take to pull voicemail, write down the message, and return the call can be significantly reduced if you just handle the call when it comes in. By the way, your voicemail message could also suggest best times to catch you "live." It should also give your email address and suggest that as an alternative. If the caller will email information, it could significantly reduce time spent on the phone when you have to call back.

- *Boundaries.* You can train others to respect the way you choose to work. This includes responding to email when you want and answering the phone at times you choose. See the previous section on blocking out your day to help define boundaries.

- *Lunch.* Don't eat out at noon. Go at 11:30 a.m. or 12:45 p.m. to avoid waiting in line. Consider changing your routine from time to time. How about bringing a lunch and heading to a park or forest preserve? Even sitting in your car once in a while in a nice setting will help you disconnect from the office pressures. This "disconnecting" again reinforces the concepts from earlier in this chapter on managing energy.

- *Eat right!* I have always coached reps on how to eat lunch (as well as snacks). Healthy eaters are more productive and sick less often, and they don't hit the wall at 2 p.m. every day. You can almost count on a reduction in activity and productivity around this time, every Monday through Friday. Here's what your body is doing: You will use energy to work, exercise, use your brain, and digest food. When you eat a lot of bad food, your body focuses its energy resources on breaking down that food. It prioritizes digestion at the expense of having energy available for your brain. This is why sluggishness occurs. By the way, this is also why I recommend not eating much food, mostly nutritious liquids, when sick. Your body will use energy either to fight illness or to digest food. (And remember that I'm not a doctor, so get medical advice should you choose to consider this strategy.) Why settle for these energy dips during the day? Avoid supplementing your need for stamina at work with sugar, caffeine, chocolate, and all those junky things that you'll pay for later (increased weight, huge dips in vitality, and more). Eat light and eat more often during the day to keep blood sugar levels even. You can store healthy nutrition bars and raw nuts in your desk. That being said, most bars are junk, loaded with sugar and chocolate. Go to a health food store and find the real thing (I buy organic protein bars); then order them online from discount sources. Try to eat raw nuts, as roasting (heat) ruins nutritional value. Best foods to avoid completely? Donuts, fries, chips. You knew this; time to act on it. I'm not going to shorten my time on this planet and miss the joy of my family, friends, and work because I decide, with total responsibility, to eat poorly. The good news is you can cheat to reward yourself once in a while anyway. And don't forget a healthy breakfast to launch your day. When you're ready to get really healthy, there's one source that outshines them all. Dr. Joseph Mercola is this generation's preeminent natural physician (no, it's not Dr. Andrew Weil, who is a solid resource, but sits on the fence and recommends pharmaceutical solutions as well). Dr. Mercola's website is the number one resource for information and products: www.Mercola.com.

- *Budget.* If your income fluctuates as wildly as John Travolta's acting career, you might want to have a personal budget program in place to manage those dips in income. This is huge for reps, especially rookies who don't have the cash flow or bank accounts of experienced performers. This idea overlaps many areas of your work life, too. Why not buy the Entertainment book to get 50 percent discounts on local restaurants and fast-food places for those lunches? www.entertainment.com

- *Drive time and down time.* I used to suggest (wish I could have mandated it) that reps not listen to radio news on the way to work. Almost all news is, by nature, negative. Get your brain in a healthy frame of mind by filling it with uplifting music or other fun auditory messages. Connect by cell phone (hands-free, of course) with business contacts, even friends and family. Best tip—you can always listen to learning resources on your CD or MP3 player. When I knew I had a bit of a trip ahead of me, I would duck into the local library and check out business books in audio format. Be wise in managing your time. You have the exact same amount available as your competition. What will you do to give yourself a competitive edge?

- *Work out.* If you don't have a regular practice related to staying in good physical shape, it's time to start. This could include the most basic routine imaginable. Solid health increases energy during the work day. You'll look better, too. Get help if you need it, but make working out a priority for your business and personal life. Find a partner for accountability; this is the best way to implement and continue a workout regimen.

- *Web surfing.* Don't do it during the day.

- *Increase access to buyers.* This is one of the easiest fixes in the whole book. No administrative work should be done when you have access to buyers. Your productivity and your income are both skills- and numbers-driven. You can control numbers more easily than you can increase skills. Stop doing paperwork and start accessing more buyers. No technique needed here, just better focus. Sandler Sales Institute defines this decision as being aware of Pay time vs. No Pay time.

- *Checklists.* The fascinating book *The Checklist Manifesto* by Atul Gawande (2009) was all I needed to support the idea I was doing it right when I created regular checklists to monitor my behavior. Gawande's work in the medical world has been shown to save lives in hospitals. It can save your sales life as well. Use checklists to manage your day, plan future initiatives, prioritize ideas, and more.

- *Clutter.* There's a famous Far Side cartoon with a rat sitting in a jail cell who's confessing to his cell mate, "I know I should have gotten rid of the evidence, but what can I say—I'm a packrat." Here's a simple rule: If you have no immediate use for it, dispose of it. This is just like junk food. You know you should do it, but won't. The trick is to take a pile a day and sort, then eliminate it. Clutter covers your inbox as well. Start deleting junk email, even if you subscribed to it in the first place. If you're not reading it, unsubscribe.

- *Lifelong learner.* Good news and bad news: Being a lifelong learner can be a great thing. You pack your brain with the best ideas that help you attain improvement. You can impress your friends. (Have a conversation about the links between selling, decision-making, emotion, and the reptilian brain and you can mesmerize your peers.) You can have regular, enriching, uplifting experiences through books, audio, training, or online. Bad news is that most lifelong learners never put their learning into action. So your brain clutter is about as useless as the office clutter we covered in the prior tip. You want to get a real return on your lifelong learning? Pick one to three behavior changes you'll make after each experience. That'll turn your smart decision to learn into a real investment. Start with this book. Pick three things. Now guarantee results by finding an accountability partner to kick you in the tail and make sure you're changing/adding these new behaviors.

- *Accountability.* The data here is overwhelming, too. You want real results? Find an accountability partner. I ask my trainees to identify someone to teach in order to further deepen the ideas. They are also coached to use those partners, probably outsiders to the company, for accountability to use these ideas. Who are these partners? Fellow sales reps, entrepreneurs, networking partners, etc. Interested in implementing accountability on a corporate level? Read *The Oz Principle* by Hickman, Smith, and Connors (2010).

- *Attain greatness in key steps of the sales process.* One of the tag lines I use to encourage companies to redesign existing sales training is this: *You don't need a selling system the length of a freight train to sell well.* This means you can focus on some specific elements of the sales process and improve performance by giving reps stronger skills in just a few areas. Sadly, most reps won't follow a complete and complex system. Lower your expectations about this and get them to do a few things well. Some of the key steps include:

  - *DQ quickly:* You remember our primary role with prospects is to qualify or disqualify them quickly. Do this well and you'll save tons of time by not chasing poor prospects. Read Chapter 12 and apply the learning immediately.

  - *Questioning:* Get those five power questions ready. See Chapter 14.

  - *Objection-handling:* Know your top six objections and be prepared to casually and confidently handle each one. See Chapter 16.

  - *Great first meeting:* Remember, one great opening is worth ten thousand closes. And if you don't open strongly, you'll never get close to the close. See Chapter 11.

  - *Listening skills:* This is a weak area for all of us, and you know you need to work on it (just ask a close friend or significant other). See Chapter 15.

- *Debrief each call:* Learning from mistakes is a most powerful way to improve. See Chapter 20.

- *Mastermind group.* Paul Feldman is the founder and publisher of *Insurance NewsNet Magazine*. He's also a business venture partner of mine and a good friend. Paul is a serious advocate of using a mastermind group. He spends over $20,000 a year to belong to an elite team of brilliant business pros. You can formally or informally create a group with peers whom you respect. Your team could serve one another with lead generation ideas, online advice, best personal productivity practices, book suggestions, and general tips about business creativity. I have friends who live in different states and get together quarterly. Others meet monthly.

  Start connecting with people whose brainpower and experience you trust and respect and initiate your own mastermind group. You can also do this formally and pay as Paul does (and he doesn't even hesitate to rave about the value in exchange for the money). If you want a great resource on creating a group, look at Karyn Greenstreet's website, www. passionforbusiness.com/articles/mastermind-group.htm. She is the author of *How to Start a For-Profit Mastermind Group,* available from the website.

- *Web surfing.* Don't do it during the day (second reminder).

- *Activity log.* You can better monitor your ability to manage your time by creating a log of your activities during a given week. List what you're doing start to finish of each day. You'll look at the list and feel guilty or angry or frustrated. Hey, whatever works to motivate you. Do this each quarter—to monitor how well you're making good decisions about quality use of your time.

- *Defend your time fiercely.* Piggybacking on the previous idea, you can correlate your income directly with how much work time is really work. Don't let people disrupt your money-making ability by distracting you. Don't let yourself disrupt it either. Tell people not to call during your work day, unless it's urgent. If you take a call, open it with a comment like, "I only have sixty seconds." And stick to that. Time is money, your money.

- *Collective brainpower.* Where else can you find ideas to propel your sales career into more money, recognition, and rewards? Start talking to others you respect. This might mean mentors or team members or print and audio resources. All the answers to your issues already exist. Shorten your learning curve by drawing off the brainpower of those who've trodden the selling success path ahead of you.

- *Reward.* Treat yourself for small victories as well as the great ones. It might mean buying something special or celebrating with someone who cares. And for the big wins, make your rewards memorable. I remember making a decision to compensate myself for success by deciding, for the first time, to buy a Lexus. That "prize" is a constant reminder that I can accomplish more than I have in the past. It's a symbol of growth in skills and experience and wisdom. It also makes a statement to others. An attorney friend finally gave himself the gift of his dream car, a Ferrari. Car, house, trip, toy—what will you choose? Reward yourself richly.

- *Toxic people.* You know *exactly* who they are. You're thinking of one in particular right now. Find and hang out with people who build you up. I believe my role in life is to leave people in a better place than where I found them. So be optimistic around others and choose to hang out with those who have optimistic attitudes. Avoid toxic people.

- *Fridays.* Don't buy into the fact that Fridays, especially during the summer, are fairly worthless for prospecting calls and setting appointments. If you bail on even the afternoon of this final day of the week, you're deciding to forego 10 percent of your work effort and earnings. The best reason to work harder on Friday might be the fact that too many of your competitors are taking off.

- *Book summaries.* You don't want to fast-forward through life, but you can shorten your time investment in learning by using a book summary service. There are plenty who craft summaries of complete books. You can Google "book summaries" for some choices. Here's how you best use the service: When you find a work of high value, buy the actual book and dive in for the details.

- *Must-read, cover-to-cover: Selling Power magazine.* This is the only print resource for our profession. Gerhard Gschwandtner has masterfully crafted a work of art with great articles, stories, and strategies. Buy it at a significant discount for everyone on the sales team at a website set up and run by my thirteen-year-old son. He worked Gerhard to get sales forces a great deal: www.SellingPowerFromJosh.com.

- *Smile on the phone (and face-to-face).* I learned to sell on the phone twenty-five years ago by having a mirror taped next to my desk. A quick glance showed how much I enjoyed my work. Practice smiling—a lot—when you're on the phone. Prospects sense it. You probably could smile more (even laugh more) in person as well.

- *Ask.* You're in the business of asking. Practice that.

- *Web surfing.* Don't do it during the day. (No, not again. Yes, again!)

- *Find sixty more minutes a day.* Here's how:

  - Go to bed earlier. (How about by skipping some TV?)

  - Get your morning set up the night before. This includes clothes you'll wear, perhaps lunch you'll prepare, and more. Notice how this idea matches your business practice of making the last thirty minutes of each day into the start of tomorrow.

  - Wake up sixty minutes earlier. Squeeze in your workout. Get to the office earlier before the selling hordes begin to assault your work day.

  - Eat lunch at your desk (but not too often; remember the value of energy management—disconnecting, leaving the office, and walking around).

  - Stop watching TV. Oh, did you think this bullet point was about work time? Why not quit wasting your life in front of the television. I heard a speaker once ask his audience of twelve hundred business pros for a show of hands: "How many people get paid to watch television?" Zero response. You need to have some fun, and you need to value your time. I have five shows I watch regularly. I never see them when they broadcast. I mostly catch up by watching them on the network websites at my leisure at home or when travelling. Notice how often we revisit the concept that you should value your time? TV is the second-biggest time-waster there is, right after web surfing.

  - Waiting time? Keep reading materials with you, always (especially in the car). Stuck at the airport, on a train, sitting in front of a slow-moving train? Get into your latest book or *Selling Power* magazine.

Create hand-written notes for prospects and clients. Use your cell phone to connect. Or choose to use fun, non-business materials to help you disconnect from work.

- Block out your day and measure your activities (both strategies described in detail earlier in this chapter).

- Craft your SMART goals: specific, measurable, attainable, realistic, and timely. You should have both personal and professional goals. *Write them down!* Applying your goals creates efficiencies in your work day.

- *Stop* to analyze what's working and what isn't, then make adjustments. Take a personal day every quarter (or more often if you think it helps) and do things differently.

- Have an "Attitude of Gratitude." I use a service that lets me send customized cards right from my computer. This is doubly valuable because I can put some unique and memorable images I created for *The Sales Comic Book* on the covers. This incredibly inexpensive service (they ship through the post office directly off the computer) is available over much of the world. So I can send a printed card from Chicago to Australia in a couple of days. (See details and other uses of this amazing service at www.LeadGenerationGenius.com.)

Bonus Tip: No Excuses!

There's a scene in the movie, *Blues Brothers* where John Belushi's character is confronted by the woman (Carrie Fisher) whom he left at the altar. She's packing some serious weaponry and the missing groom drops to his knees and offers her a rapid-fire litany of excuses as to why he missed their wedding: *"I ran out of gas! I had a flat tire! I didn't have enough money for cab fare! My tux didn't come back from the cleaners! An old friend came in from out of town! Someone stole my car! There was an earthquake! A terrible flood! Locusts! IT WASN'T MY FAULT, I SWEAR TO GOD!"*

Do you realize that nobody is really interested in hearing your excuses? "No excuses" means accepting responsibility for your behavior. This isn't about the rare times when the unexpected derails your ride through life. It's about knowing you need to work more, work harder, work smarter. The example I encounter most in the selling profession? You know you should get sales training, but the company won't pay for it (or worse, it's embarrassingly inadequate). So what? Who's responsible for your success? Go invest in your career and get training on your own. No excuses!

To get this toxic habit out of your system, read through this list of my favorite funny excuses heard live, extracted online, and compiled over the years:

- I have an evil twin.

- In my homeland that is acceptable behavior.

- What difference will it make one hundred years should now.

- There was a full moon or at least a pretty full moon.

- I have a fear of success.

- My underwear cut off the blood flow to my brain.

- I'm proud of what I did and I'll never do it again.

- I was adopted.

- You mean this isn't a dream?

- I'm messed up from reading self-help books.

- Who among us is completely innocent?

- I missed my naptime.

- I thought slackers were still in.

- I'll never need this in the real world.

- I have hemorrhoids.

- I was hypnotized.

- I don't get paid enough to put that kind of effort out.

- You're prejudiced against people who screw up.

- I'm nursing a broken heart.

- I haven't been the same since Elvis died.

- I drank milk past the expiration date.

- I grew up on Saturday morning cartoons.

- The altitude affects me.

- You hate me because I'm beautiful.

- I misplaced my moral compass.

- I was teased by the other kids in grade school.

- I take a lot of shots to the head.

- I was a day-care baby.

- Constipation has made me a walking time bomb.

- The psychiatrist said it was an excellent session. He even gave me this jaw restraint so I won't bite things when I am startled.

- I am extremely sensitive to a rise in the interest rates.

No excuses!

I'm now writing a book on the psychology of excuses. This is a huge problem with, well, pick an aspect of a sales pro's life. Not making enough calls is always at the top of my coaching list. I've already developed a sales training module on it. If you want to know more about the development of this program and the fascinating research behind it (I have compiled over one thousand pages of studies from around the world), reach out to me at Dan@GotInfluenceInc.com. I've already run half a dozen training programs this past year on specific strategies to eliminate excuses. Senior sales executives light up when they hear this is available.

EXERCISE 23.2. Using the List of Productivity Tips

SETUP: This was a monster checklist, and everyone going through it should be able to adapt three, five, seven, maybe ten items. Let's see how many learners are willing to push themselves to improve performance.

Trainer: Create your company's list of productivity tips. Hand it to each salesperson and set expectations that he or she will identify a minimum of three to work on immediately.

Revisit their progress in two weeks. If they've done well, have them select three more. If they haven't yet implemented all the ideas, ask them to create accountability relationships and put the three ideas into play.

EXERCISE 23.2.   Using the List of Productivity Tips, Cont'd

Remember, we're in the before and after business. If our learners don't change behavior after they've encountered our training, we have failed. Work to help them change their personal performance habits and see revenue climb. Accountability can be monitored with partners or with the sales manager overseeing his or her charges. If you digitize this list and each salesperson's selections, it'll be easier to document changed behavior.

Chapter 24

Know Your Numbers

Numbers Worth Knowing

The company might have great systems in place to track leads, monitor contacts, create and follow the sales funnel, and more. The sales pro needs to personally know his or her numbers in order to own the results of his or her performance. This chapter shows all the checkpoints at which you'll want to create awareness of numbers. That's because every place you can measure, you can manage and improve. This includes all the pieces of the sales process. It also includes a worksheet that can be used to measure and manage all these elements:

- Prospecting activity
- Phone calls per day/week/month

- Appointments landed per call
- Percent of prospects qualified or disqualified
- Frequency of objections
- Closing ratio per pitched company
- Personal and company goals
- Personal targeted earnings
- Personal incentive to hit your numbers

How Lofty Are Your Goals?

I was training a publishing company's sales team and the day's session was on backtracking from your personal goals to identify exactly what activity and behavior each rep needed to hit his or her mark.

Everyone received a worksheet (the Excel worksheet is in this chapter), and they began to do minor calculations to figure out what daily behavior they needed. After I said to start, I added, "If anyone needs help with figuring this out, raise your hand and we'll work on it together."

Joanne's hand is the only one to go up. She's an older rep who was converted from customer service to sales. As I approach she loudly declares, "This makes no sense. According to your formulas I only have to make 1.5 phone calls a day."

"Joanne," I whisper, "exactly how much in commission are you hoping to attain this year?"

With no change in her volume, she says, "I have a $25,000 base and another $5,000 would be good for me."

The room freezes like a forest full of small critters when a hawk begins to circle overhead. I look right at the sales manager, who has that wide-eyed, deer-in-the-headlights look. He had no idea (nor did I) that a salesperson could have such miniscule aspirations.

Now this story isn't about hiring problems. Nor is it about how to manage Joanne. (Although I did suggest her territory be reduced to the size of a squirrel's nest.) It is about the value of knowing your numbers.

Thank you, by the way, to the late, great Peter Drucker for helping the selling world to recognize the value of data. This is critical. Drucker said, *If you can't measure it, you can't manage it.*

Concept: Know your numbers!

I was recently having a discussion with my dear friend Gerhard Gschwandtner, founder and publisher of *Selling Power* magazine. I mentioned that I'd just done a presentation at a major global sales training conference where I addressed what's missing from existing sales training.

One of my twenty-four points was: Why don't we give personal budgeting skills to sales reps? If their income fluctuates as wildly as John Travolta's acting career, why not help them during the low times so they don't get stressed out, blame the job and quit, or do dumb things like go deeper into debt?

Gerhard said, "That's interesting you mention that. One of my award-winning sales forces (he annually recognizes best-selling teams) is Shaw Industries. They're the only organization I know that does this."

So sensitivity to numbers doesn't always mean just focus on the amount of commission you make on a sale. It could relate to any aspect of a sales pro's life, even the portion of his or her life that intersects the home.

Every sales pro should be aware of his or her own personal data like:

- Which prospecting activities are worthwhile and which are worthless?
- How many phone calls he or she makes per week:
  - What percentage reached decision-makers?
  - How many decision-makers agreed to appointments?
- How many face-to-face meetings are held per week?
- How quickly were prospects qualified or disqualified (to move forward or move on)?
- How often is each of his or her top objections encountered? If buyers keep offering resistance a certain way, it could be time to restructure the approach. Or the sales pro could count on overcoming objections with the prospect, but if so, how?

- What's the closing ratio? How often does the rep get to the finish line and cross in first place?

- What are his or her company-set goals for the team and for him- or herself?

- What are his or her personal targeted earnings for the year? How much does he or she make, regardless of individual corporate goals?

- What incentive is there to hit his or her numbers? What is the value/cost of the personal goal/reward? That is, does he or she want a new car, which one, how much does it cost?

Key questions: How much can a sales pro live on during dips in cash flow? Earlier we pointed out the value of managing your numbers at home as well. It is critical to have a personal budget. In fact, aside from the benefits of managing your home life better, anybody with aspirations to sales management, or even entrepreneurship with his or her own firm, has to be able to manage money (or, minimally, marry someone who can). Okay, that last comment is only half true, because you can count on others, but there are some things you need to have some basic knowledge about to advance your professionals skills.

How to Start at the Finish Line and Back Up to Be a Winner

Time management is founded in goal setting. You want to develop the disciplined behavior that extraordinary earners practice every day to make great money. Regardless of what level of experience you've achieved in your sales career, implement these three steps immediately:

1. Define and write down what goal you want to acquire.
2. Set a time frame for acquiring your goal.
3. Pretend you've already obtained that goal, then *work backward* to determine what activities it would take to attain it.

Here's a simple example of how to work backward to identify your success path to your goal. The bold words are fields to match with the Excel spreadsheet on the book's website, or email me, Dan@GotInfluenceInc.com.

Your goal is to pay cash for a new Infiniti automobile, which costs $60,000. You want to be driving it within one year. Follow these steps to create a professional plan for your daily work activities:

- You want $60,000 to buy your new Infiniti in one year. **GOAL**
- You make a $500 commission for each sale. **Com$**
- You need a hundred and twenty sales to award yourself the car. **SlsYr**
- This means you need ten sales each month. **SlsMo**
- You close 20 percent of your face-to-face sales calls. **ClsF2F**
- So you need to get in front of fifty buyers a month to close those ten. **TotF2F**
- You have twenty-five workdays each month, so you need two sales calls per day. **25**
- If you get an appointment with one of four phone contacts, you need to contact two hundred people to get your fifty appointments. **APPT%**
- Two hundred divided by twenty-five days = eight daily phone contacts.
- For every twenty calls you make, you get eight contacts. **TotCall**
- You need twenty phone calls and two meetings each day to earn your $60,000 car.

All this activity drives your regular behavior on the job. By employing these guidelines, you develop a professional attack on your marketplace.

Know your numbers!

Work through the steps in the exercise with your own figures to determine your daily activity. You'll be perceived as a pro. You'll feel like a pro. You'll pay yourself like a pro.

EXERCISE 24.1. Running the Numbers

SETUP: This exercise gives sales professionals a great tool that provides a snapshot of their performance. By changing behaviors, sellers can improve their performance.

EXERCISE 24.1. Running the Numbers, Cont'd

This exercise will help you to take your targeted earnings and work backward to identify individual activities needed to attain your goal. Here's the example we just used, followed by a blank chart for you to fill out.

Trainer: Go through the sample, then have everyone insert his or her own numbers and make the calculations. Lead a discussion about how changes in different places can affect how well and how much they sell. Understanding the relationship between their goal and how it is affected by daily activity is critical to sales success!

Field	Description	Figure
Goal	Dollar amount of your goal	$60,000.00
Com$	Commission earned per sale	$500.00
SlsYr	Sales needed per year to meet your goal	120
SlsMo	Sales needed per month to meet your goal	10
ClsF2F	Percent of face-to-face sales calls you close	20%
TotF2F	Number of sales calls needed to meet sales goal for the month	50
DaysMo	Days worked per month	25
ClsDay	Sales calls needed per day worked	2
Appt%	Percent of phone contacts that result in an appointment	25%
CntNo	Number of contacts needed to meet appointment goal	200
ConDay	Number of contacts needed per day worked	8
Call%	Percent of phone calls that result in a contact	40%
CallNo	Number of phone calls needed per day worked	20

You need: 20 phone calls and 2 meetings each day to meet your goal.

Now, put your own numbers in the worksheet below and let's find out about how many ways you can improve your performance, whether it's working harder or smarter.

EXERCISE 24.1.   Running the Numbers, Cont'd

Field	Description	Figure
Goal	Dollar amount of your goal	$_____
Com$	Commission earned per sale	$_____
SlsYr	Sales needed per year to meet your goal	_____
SlsMo	Sales needed per month to meet your goal	_____
ClsF2F	Percent of face-to-face sales calls you close	_____
TotF2F	Number of sales calls needed to meet sales goal for the month	_____
DaysMo	Days worked per month	_____
ClsDay	Sales calls needed per day worked	_____
Appt%	Percent of phone contacts that results in an appointment	_____
CntNo	Number of contacts needed to meet appointment goal	_____
ConDay	Number of contacts needed per day worked	_____
Call%	Percent of phone calls that result in a contact	_____
CallNo	Number of phone calls needed per day worked	_____

You need: _____ phone calls and _____ meetings each day to meet your goal.

Now let's look at how you could tweak several of these factors in order to know the impact on your performance and ability to attain the goal. What if your commission average went up to $600 from $500? Your total activity could be reduced by about 16.6 percent.

What if you decided to take off every Friday and work only four days a week? Your available days to call and meet buyers would be reduced by about 20 percent, so your workload would have to increase proportionately.

What if your closing ratio went up 20 percent? You just got better at helping buyers buy. You'd end up with your car in ten months, instead of twelve (earnings grow from $5,000/month to $6,000/month, getting you to $60,000 in ten).

You get the idea here. There are so many ways to improve your income. Stretch your brain and find creative ways to get what you want.

- Make more phone calls each day.

- Buy a used car for less.

- Negotiate a higher commission when you hit certain numbers.

- Be better at qualifying buyers, so you don't chase poor prospects.

What other ways can you alter factors that affect your success?

Create your own worksheet, or better yet, have the company create one online so the individual salespeople can work their numbers and be accountable for their commitment to specific behaviors.

When salespeople create their planning and goal-setting numbers and activities, they "own" the results and the activities required to attain those results. Know your numbers. Own your numbers.

Chapter 25

Finding and Utilizing Mentors

CHAPTER OVERVIEW

Exercise 25.1. Recognizing Past Mentors

Find a Mentor

Exercise 25.2. Finding Mentors

Be a Mentor

This chapter is simple. It shows sales pros how to speed up their journey to success by finding mentors to guide them. A method to identify and initiate a relationship with a mentor is described. There is also an encouragement to serve in the role of a mentor as well.

Everyone's a Comedian

There's an old vaudeville skit where a man comes crying to his physician.

"Doctor, I don't know what's wrong with me, but I hurt all over. If I touch my shoulder here, it hurts; and if I touch my leg here, it hurts; if I touch my head here, it hurts; and if I touch my foot here, it hurts."

"I believe you've broken your finger."

We need doctors for the same reason we need mentors. We can shorten the learning curve to success by accessing their vast experience, wisdom, and advice.

When I do training or refer to this concept in keynotes, I put a chart in my PowerPoint deck that shows all the memorable learning I've acquired in my life. This includes the very early experiences like potty training and tying my shoes. It then moves toward school-related training like driving, playing the trumpet, and basketball. And on to adult choices like scuba diving, dozens of software programs (okay, some were games), and PhotoReading (look it up).

In each learning environment a mentor encouraged me toward some level of skill. Now, when we're in the heart of our careers, we can use the same strategy to attain greater levels of abilities, skills, and behaviors as sales professionals.

EXERCISE 25.1. Recognizing Past Mentors

SETUP: To look at sales pros' past learning experiences and recognize the people who pushed them forward in any areas of their lives.

Who was a mentor in your past, whether for sport, school, hobbies, or business? In what ways did the person help you mature more quickly? At your table share something unique that you had a passion to learn.

Trainer: Ask the attendees to pick someone at the table with an unusual hobby or skill and have them tell the whole group what it is and what possessed them to attain some expertise in it. This serves a key purpose. It shows that, regardless of how odd or unique someone's passion is, there is always a teacher available to pass along his or her knowledge and expertise. How much easier, then, would it be to find a mentor in our profession? With tens of millions of people serving in selling roles, you can find someone for you.

Have some fun with the wide variety of hobbies and passions. Two of my most memorable people included a man who studied explosives to blow up rock and mountains in order to become a highly paid construction expert. A woman decided one day that it was romantic, cool, and athletic to train as a pearl diver. This experience will create some fresh bonding among the sales team as people are surprised and sometimes shocked at the odd backgrounds mixed in with the sales expertise in the room.

We want to focus now on two ways to be involved with mentoring. First, find a mentor. Next, be one. So your focal point here is a simple question: *Who's smarter than you?*

Find a Mentor

I strongly recommend that every sales professional find a mentor. Identify some people who would be ideal resources for you. Then call and ask them whether they'd be open to serving as advisors. You can do this in a variety of areas in your business life. What categories can you think of? There are people who are great organizers, great closers, great at gathering referrals, or great at finding leads.

Make sure that your passion for selling comes through in your conversation. Find out how much time you could have, how often you might connect. This could be a phone relationship or you could be buying someone breakfast or lunch once a month. Set appointments and be very strict about respecting the time allotted. Make sure you have distinct goals—areas in which you most need help.

Be an outstanding listener. Your job is to sit at the person's feet, not exercise your tongue. Ask questions for clarification and respect the person's investment in you by keeping focused on the purpose of the present conversation.

Don't forget to find out what parts of their past contributed to who they are today. Ask what books and magazines they've read, training received, associations worth joining, where they serve as volunteers. You want to try to reverse engineer their brains and experience, so you can emulate your mentors.

Debrief your session, so it's clear to your mentor that you've absorbed the learning. Give feedback to your mentor as to how you utilized his or her ideas and what happened when you did. Nothing is more satisfying to a mentor than to hear stories about how you changed your behavior because of his or her advice.

Sales managers should request that sales team members share the nature of their mentoring relationships and keep their manager updated on progress as well as learning acquired. Remember that the foundation of this training book is not about learning. It's about changed behavior. So set expectations that you'll see new behavior that turns into new revenue from the mentoring relationships.

EXERCISE 25.2.   Finding Mentors

SETUP: It's time for reps to think about who might be good mentors for them.

Who would be an ideal mentor for you today, as a salesperson? List three potential gurus. Then set a date by when you'll contact each of them.

Trainer: Everyone could be asked to be wide open in this brainstorming session. After all, they don't necessarily need someone to meet them in person for a mentoring relationship. Anyone could pick a best-selling author, a trainer, an experienced manager, or a famed entrepreneur. Also, don't be surprised if some people refuse to share their potential mentors. Some of these targeted, experienced, high-level people have limited time, and your team might not want to compete for the same person.

Once you land a mentor, don't forget to show gratitude. Thank the person often and in a variety of ways. Send notes and gifts, leave a heart-felt voicemail on voicemail after-hours.

Find a mentor today—you will pay yourself handsomely tomorrow.

Be a Mentor

She walked into my office during lunch, without an appointment. Frankly, she was quite frumpy, wearing a shapeless black dress. No makeup adorned her face. She had been standing outside our building and waited for my assistant to go to lunch; then she darted into my office. I recognized her last name immediately. It was Italian and was splashed on the sides of trucks all over the city.

"I don't want to be in the family food business," she said. "I want to go into sales."

Minutes into our conversation, something inside me was moved by how serious and brave this young gal was. I asked her to come back on Saturday morning and then spent several hours with her. I coached her on how to interview for a job and to apply some basic sales concepts to both the interview and any entry-level selling position she might land.

This girl was a great student, listening intently. Didn't take notes either. She was meek and young and had miles to travel toward sales success, but a fire had been lit, and it would provide the light for her journey. She thanked me, we shook hands, and I encouraged her to contact me when she got interviews, to let me know how things were going.

Nothing—for six months.

One afternoon this traveler wandered back into my office. She sported a light gray suit, a conservative hairstyle, and a winning smile. My student had turned her back on the bread business to become a breadwinner of her own. She had pounded the phones for several months before being promoted to an outside sales role. And while she was just doing average (for now), she LOVED her work.

What an amazing moment. It was perhaps a better experience for me than for her. My heart got bigger that afternoon. I had actually mentored someone, someone who didn't work for me. She was now part of my legacy as a sales professional. How cool is that?

I began to go to conferences and look for entrepreneurs and salespeople who were willing to honestly share their sales frustrations and hopes with me. I'd often stay up all night talking about strategy and language, in order to improve their skills and thinking about selling.

This drove my wife nuts because it was tantamount to taking in stray cats. I was spending energy with no financial return. But I was actually practicing coaching skills I would later use. And nothing compared to the feeling that came with feedback from my students. "I did this and it worked!" "The book you recommended completely changed my perspective." "You have no idea how grateful I am for the time you give me."

I had stumbled into the role of mentor/provider, and there was no limit to the supply of hungry sales children.

Everyone with any level of selling experience can mentor another rep. Even if you're a rookie, you can serve as an advocate for the profession and talk to school kids. Find a way to give back to the occupation to which we've committed our careers. Build into others.

What legacy will you leave to our profession?

Find a mentor. Be a mentor.

Chapter 26

Ten Keys to Working a Trade Show

Many companies make major investments in time and money to find leads at trade shows and industry conferences. Unfortunately, this too often results in major losses of money and time, with little return on the investment. This chapter points to ten key problems that, when eliminated or fixed, can significantly help your company identify great leads and make real money at these events. It is so rare to have, all together, a convention center of your buyers. You want to get this right.

Before we hit the list of what *not* to do, let's look at what we want to do while working a trade show: *Get a decision in the booth*.

Ten Problems at Trade Shows and the Keys to Dealing with Them

1. They Are *Sitting* in Booths!

There's a fine welcome for the prospect. The salesperson grunts as he or she pushes out of the seat, angry at the interruption of her rest and relaxation away from the office. This moment is all about first impressions. You don't want buyers to believe you're bored, tired, or resentful about being there. In my experience, many of the "sitters" are non-salespeople who have been wrangled into working the show. Then there are the others—probably reps who partied a bit too late the night before. Make sure you address behavior expectations for everyone. And those expectations should cover every one of the twenty-four hours of every single day of the show. My collection of selling blunders at SalesAutopsy.com covers a few surrounding trade shows, including drunken fights, bad gambling problems, and other unacceptable behavior that can label your company as "those guys who. . . ."

> *The Key?* Be upbeat and personable, standing at all times (so spend the money for the extra carpet padding at the booth). Visitors should feel greeted well and be treated like royalty. You should also rotate your booth personnel to better manage energy. (See number 9.)

2. They Are Standing Behind "Barriers"

Some booths are simply designed wrong. Is selling about building walls, or is it about breaking them down or going around them? If, on an ideal sales call, you want to sit next to a prospect rather than having a desk between you, why would you design a sales environment that sends the wrong message to thousands of trade show visitors? One of us must cross over into the other's territory before anything good happens. You don't want to send a message subliminally from your booth layout that means "It's us versus them."

> *The Key?* Remove all barriers; remove territories. Get out from behind the chair, table, display case, whatever. Just get nose to nose with your prospects.

3. They Are Acting Like Carnival Barkers

Salespeople shout and wave brochures at passersby, hoping that you'll stop and play with them. Now, games can be good. You want to draw visitors into the booth. "Would you like to play . . . ?" isn't a bad comment. But, "HEY! You can win a 32 gig iPod if you enter our drawing!" is a bit harsh. Notice how people are walking past, just glancing at your display as they attempt to determine whether it's something they need. They don't need to be verbally assaulted.

> *The Key?* Remember how you want to nurture a prospect on a sales call? Same concept applies in the booth. A smile, even an open-handed gesture into the booth or at a display or a drawing is safe for the visitor.

4. They Ask, "Can I Help You?"

A basic premise in selling is never to ask a question that can be answered by "no." This is a rookie mistake in retail stores. Back to first impressions. Don't start digging a hole you'll have to climb out of. Questions that generate negative responses set the buyer down a path you don't want to take them.

> *The Key?* You want to ask a unique opening question that puts the visitor at ease. My favorite is "What unusual things have you seen at the show?" or how about "What really good sessions did you attend?" Notice that these are open-ended questions that invite conversation. Once they respond you can follow up (as you learned in Chapter 14) with something like, "Really, tell me more" or "Tell me why that interests you so much." Now you have a two-way dialogue going. That's good, that's progress. Next step is to ask a smart question related to number 5.

5. They Shouldn't Be Working the Show

Someone else in the company should be. Many booth workers are technical people, assistants, or administrative people who don't understand the sales process. At that

Las Vegas show, whom did the owners want to have on the floor? "Let's get some good-looking women to draw the male buyers into the booth." I looked at the president and said, "Right, you're going to Las Vegas; good-looking women will really stand out. Please make your decision based on gaining a decent return on the significant investment in the show." A week before the show I received a call asking if I would help out. And who else could I bring to work the show? Someone had come to his senses: The women were out and sales pros were in. Put your best people in the booths. Let the rookies spend time observing the pros before they begin to "work" the crowd.

> *The Key?* You might need technical people, and if you do they should be assigned to a rep who should be part of every conversation. Remember, your job is to garnish leads. If those working the booth aren't going to discover prospects, you're missing the mission.

6. They Don't Understand How Many Show Visitors Are Time-Wasters

This is an interesting problem, the inverse of the previous issue: Don't have the wrong employees working the booth. Here, don't have the wrong attendees entering. These people have no intention of doing business with you, but they love to chat and they love whatever you're giving away. (Snickers bars get lots of traffic; a bowl of shelled peanuts does not.)

By the way, you might not realize how many of these casual visitors there really are. I attend most major trade shows in Chicago at McCormick Place because it's my local major conference center (although because of my speaking and training schedule, I'm also often at large events all over the planet). McCormick serves as my happy hunting grounds, where I can observe sales rep behavior and collect sales stories for my columns and keynotes. After years of attending every imaginable show (from both sides of the booth), I was asked to write a book for retirement-aged seniors describing how to attend tradeshows as a hobby! The book was to identify what shows would be the most fun, tell them secrets of how to get in, and list all the interesting giveaways one could collect. That book would have been profitable and fun to write, but imagine the damage to my image when I turn loose a generation of geriatric gawkers to distract exhibitors further from their mission to land business at these expensive events.

So be aware of that percentage of show attendees who are there simply for the fun of it. They are wandering the aisle where you're working. And they'll keep you from the visitor who really has money for you, but can't get your attention while you chat with Grandma Simmons.

The Key? This problem really is a qualifying issue (see this addressed in detail, Chapter 12). How quickly can you assess the value of a visitor before investing too much talk time? Back at my client's Las Vegas appearance, when visitors came to our booth, I asked the qualifying question, "Would you see yourself ordering at least a thousand of these?" When the president of the company—an inventor, not a salesperson— heard this, he became extremely upset. He felt that I was driving away smaller potential customers. He didn't realize that I was screening out time-wasters.

The serious small prospects will still want to talk about a fascinating new invention, regardless of minimum order size. They'll try to assess whether they can buy product through a distribution channel rather than direct in large quantities. The president's lesson of the day (and yours?): qualify before presenting. Sales pros quickly learn the value of this very profitable lesson. Qualify first, then present.

7. They Follow Up Too Late to Have an Impact

Worse still, some companies never follow up after a trade show. While writing this chapter I received correspondence from two separate companies I met *four months earlier* at one of the major shows in Chicago. The phone calls were identical. Each rep was surprised and a little hurt that I didn't remember him. After all, we practically became blood brothers when we met (they were getting ready for the happy hunting grounds). Of course I recalled both of them. I was testing their response to resistance. Every day is a test in selling. Your prospects are always testing you, too. I finally asked why it took so long for them to contact me. They each offered a lame excuse related to "busyness." So your company spent a small king's fortune (the fortune was small, not the king) giving you a chance to increase commissions and you got too busy to make more money. Next time, why not just take your Las Vegas tradeshow money to the gaming tables and skip the investment in an exhibit?

The Key? Have a plan for how you'll reconnect with booth visitors. If you spoke with highly qualified prospects, you should be *at the booth* setting appointments for phone calls or meetings. Others deserve attention based on buying power, seriousness, or potential as centers of influence (referrals or entrees into large organizations). Create categories, label your qualified buyers, and follow up quickly based on pre-determined activities like mail, phone, or email.

8. They Don't Focus on a Single Goal for Attendee Interactions

Focus is everything in life, sports, hobbies, and business. What is your focal point for each booth visitor? I confess this point is really a way to review bullet points 3 (carnival barkers), 4 (can I help you), 5 (shouldn't be working the booth), and 6 (time-wasters). Because even after pointing out bad behavior to avoid and good behavior to adopt, reps will still show up for shows and treat them like a working vacation: "Free Lead Day" during the day and "Show Time" at night. You'll have your fun (it really is part of the package) and time to blow off steam and relax. However, I'd put a focus sign somewhere in the booth to remind reps to keep theirs.

The Key? Focus on qualifying and disqualifying. Have handy a couple of questions that you can use to help sort prospects. You can see Chapter 12 on qualifying for ideas, but some quick ones include potential size of order, are you the decision-maker, time to purchase, etc. *Keep your focus in every single booth conversation.*

9. They Don't Schedule Booth Personnel Very Well

Standing for ten plus hours a day is VERY HARD WORK. Let's get the right people on the floor, then have them work in shifts so that their energy level stays high. What would work for you? Two or three hours at a time? All of us have seen droopy-eyed salespeople who are out of gas hours before the end of the day. How about booths where solo reps have to handle everyone (and end up ignoring most)? You're making the investment, so be smart about your image to your buying public and your impact on those buyers as well.

The Key? Control everyone's behavior to maximize their contribution to the effort. Reps at the end of their shifts who leave the booth can do one of three things: (1) go sit down and eat, (2) go outside to re-energize, get some sun and fresh air, or (3) walk the show floor to get their legs moving and relax from the tension of sales conversations. (You could even generate leads this way, as you'll see with the bonus point that follows.) Quick tip here: Rent the extra-thick carpet padding. It could be the single most valuable investment aside from the booth displays. Make it easy on your team to walk and work their space.

10. They Don't Put on a "Show" at the Show

If it's clear your team is having fun, you will attract more attention and therefore more traffic to your booth. These events become at one level a numbers game. Flood the booth with visitors, then qualify them. You want to increase buzz on the show floor by having people show off or tell others about your location. How many times have you asked someone walking the floor something like, "Where did you get that t-shirt, ice cream, stuffed animal, hat . . . ?" You get the picture. Make your space the place to visit.

The Key? There are several ways to do this:

1. Do a pre-show mailing to a targeted prequalified list of buyers to entice them to visit. You could be offering a gift, a special deal, a special experience (like a magician or celebrity).

2. Create *great* signage that pops and stops people from walking past. Booth messaging is horrible about 75 percent of the time. A giant company name "John Smith Company" tells the fast-moving attendee nothing. List the top three benefits you provide and the top three problems you solve. People will stop for strong copy and cool imagery. What ways can you graphically cause a traffic jam at your location?

3. Dress up your reps. When you have distinct clothing, you'll brand the booth before, during, and after the show. I see companies that really get this at every conference I attend or keynote. This includes wearing tuxedos, Hawaiian shirts, jumpsuits, even solid color tops and bottoms.

4. Give away good stuff. There's a whole industry built around products meant to be shared with large audiences. The two organizations that represent this business segment are The Promotional Products Association International (PPAI) at www.ppa.org and Advertising Specialties Institute (ASI) at www.asicentral.com. I write a regular

business humor column in the ASI *Advantages* magazine and find it fascinating to browse issues for new ideas. This inspired me to develop a very unique product to give away—*The Sales Comic Book:* There is nothing like it on this planet, possibly any planet. What can you come up with to get people asking, "Where did you get that?" Contact me at Dan@GotInfluenceInc.com if you'd like a copy of *The Sales Comic Book.* It could inspire you to create a similarly unique product.

5. Build something that blends into the experience of the whole show. I love this idea. Two quick ideas on this:

   • One year I had a company create badges with flashing red lights. Okay, flashy, attention-getting, but average idea. It became a superior idea when we stickered numbers to the back of the badge. There were multiple duplicates of each number. When you found someone with your number, you returned to the booth for a prize and were entered in a drawing for an electronic gift worth about $50. We gave away a dozen gifts. And I convinced the show organizers to let me give them away during a general session! Why do a drawing at your booth when you could have all three thousand attendees see you on stage? The president of the association said it was mesmerizing to see all the flashing red lights in the audience. When I got up on stage, it was a very cool picture to see the impact we'd had.

   • My other very unique engagement idea: Create a map of the show floor with a listing of all the cool things being given away by exhibitors. This requires some pre-work to connect with everyone (probably through the meeting planner or exhibit sales team). I suggested this to the American Society for Training and Development in 2009 and was pleased to see a listing of booth giveaways in the 2010 attendee materials.

   So get creative, make a splash that involves everyone at the show. You'll truly be the center of attention.

You now have plenty of ways to put a "show" into your trade show appearance. Work well ahead of time to prepare for a great experience and loads of (well-qualified) leads!

Bonus Strategy: Working Other Exhibitors

I've found that many of my clients' best leads came from other exhibitors. It should be no surprise, since everyone at the show is investing time with the identical target market. This is why I encourage booth personnel to walk the floor and begin nurturing referral relationships. This will help when you return to the booth as well. You'll better serve your visitors when you can point them to fellow exhibitors who have products or services those visitors could use.

> *The Key?* Intentionally work the show floor to identify leads, do some homework on what the competition is doing, and get other event marketing ideas on displays, giveaways, and more.

EXERCISE 26.1. Brainstorming Ideas for Better Trade Shows

SETUP: To discover some ideas in the room related to the show experience, we'll survey the group to collect their thoughts on some of the most memorable show items they've collected, as well as unique interactions in exhibit booths.

Trainer: You want your reps to brainstorm on ways they can create outstanding booth experiences. This might include things like the popular use of the Wii device to pull visitors into play. Ask to hear about some of the cool and unique things that can be given away directly or with a fishbowl and drawing. Ask them to take five minutes in their table groups to compile some ideas. Then collect their ideas and submit them to senior management as well as the tradeshow marketing team. Use three categories: interactive ideas to draw visitors in, giveaway products, and drawing (probably for a significant gift like an iPod, iPad, etc.).

So back to our concept:

Get a decision in the booth.

Your job in the booth is to get a Yes, No, or Next Step (that is, one that's clear and well-defined). Review Chapter 11 on Opening the First Meeting to revisit the language for accomplishing this.

Take your investment in a trade show very seriously. Focus first on helping your booth personnel focus on their goal, which should primarily be lead generation. Get the creative team to work on image, color, and experience for attendees. Finally, what will you give away or do to increase booth traffic?

Chapter 27

Negotiating for Sales Pros

15. Use Humor
16. Maintain Trust
17. Identify Buyers' Tactics
18. Overcome Price Objections
19. Trade, Don't Donate
20. Determine Your Initial Position Carefully
21. Establish Priorities
22. Set Goals as a Range, Not a Number
23. Choose Your Team Wisely
24. Take Notes!
25. Don't Lose Sight of the Big Picture
26. Know the Strengths and Weaknesses of Both Positions
27. Decide Whether to Lie
28. Learn to Use a Global Negotiating Style
29. Have Fun!

This is a huge chapter, both in terms of size and value. Sales pros today need negotiating skills in a big way. Whether your sale is simple and transactional or quite complex, you're going to find savvy buyers pushing you to reduce your price or give other concessions. In this chapter you'll read a review of the classic approach to negotiating, and you'll find a fresh, new structure for managing all the pieces of the negotiating puzzle. You'll also find twenty-nine great tips and techniques you can use to better manage the buyer/seller negotiation. You have enough information here to design your own model, or you can contact the designer of the 21st century model directly. Brian Dietmeyer was gracious enough to share his high-quality negotiating structure.

Tough Negotiator? Whoa, Baby!

So you thought that the old baby-swapping incident at the hospital was either a rare news item or, more likely, a soap opera plot. But the tale is actually thousands of years old.

In the time of King Solomon of Israel, two women were living together when one accidently smothers her son while sleeping. She then swaps her dead boy for the live one. Nobody reading the tale is surprised to learn that the real mom of the living boy notices the difference (the story doesn't mention the obvious trauma of waking up next to a dead boy, regardless of who the kid belongs to). So off to court they all go.

This is big news, so the case makes its way all the way up to King Solomon himself, who listens carefully to each person's version of the incident. The wisest man in the world calls for a sword and declares the perfect solution, "Cut the baby in half, so each gets a fair share." At this point, the real mother cries that she doesn't want that done, give the baby to her, pointing at the lying mother. The evil mom doesn't care about the kid anyway, so she says to go ahead and split him up. Solomon immediately recognizes that the real mother was more concerned about the life of her son than her personal desire to keep him, so he gives the living kid to the right mom.

Tradition says that Solomon lived about three thousand years ago. So we have ancient manuscripts that reveal perhaps the world's first recorded negotiation. The technique suggested by the king is known as a 50/50 compromise, whereby both parties are entitled to equal portions. In fact, today this is also known as "splitting the baby."

Ancient approaches to negotiating were wildly diverse. Often, if two camps (or cultures or enemies) disagreed, they'd return to their sides and engage in all-out war, winner take all. And while it might appear that modern negotiating has come a long, long way from this, there are still people who negotiate in order to get all they can, the hell with their opponents.

You might not ever negotiate something as critical as the life of another human being, but the ability to negotiate is a skill that many sales professionals need to master.

In my keynotes I'll often pull out a page torn from my United Airlines magazine. I'll hold up an image of one of the largest training companies on the planet, a company that sells 650 negotiating seminars a year. "This firm is teaching buyers to beat you up! And is it just a coincidence that right next to this magazine, in the seat pocket, you'll find . . . ?" And I hold up a waste bag (better known to our North American readers as a "barf bag"), to great laughter.

It is no joke that while you're diving into this book and deepening your understanding of sales training, there are professional buyers and senior corporate executives who are taking training to learn to deal with sales pros. They are learning to fire off tough objections like:

- "We can buy it cheaper somewhere else."
- "Your offering isn't any different from the competition's."
- "We don't discuss our budget, so send a proposal with your offer."

Negotiation training is big money, too. Some of the most respected academic institutions in the United States offer expensive experiences like this recent posting from Stanford University:

Influence and Negotiation Strategies Program

Program Dates: October 16–21, 2011

Application Deadline: September 12, 2011

Program Tuition: $11,000 USD

Northwestern University's Negotiation Strategies for Managers is a deal by comparison:

Maximize the Outcome of Your Negotiations

December 4–7, 2011, $5,900

Imagine multiplying that figure by the size of your sales force. Okay, that's a huge number. So you'll bring a trainer in-house, or design your own.

Let's look at content from which you can create training for your sales team. You'll read about two basic models for negotiating. Choose one to use. After a discussion of the two models, you'll find a comprehensive list of twenty-nine elements to embed into your negotiating training program.

Two Negotiation Models

This chapter describes two different ways to manage the negotiation game. You'll read an overview of some of the classic negotiation strategies. Then you'll learn a new approach that has evolved over the last ten years that significantly simplifies your ability to walk into a deal and manage it. And simplification is badly needed in this art and science we call *Getting to Yes* (from the best-selling book by Roger Fisher and William Ury).

There seems to be an intent to make negotiating a difficult, complex, even mysterious proposition. It doesn't help that some sources teach more than 150 elements you need to know. A recent book (Thompson, 2007) has pared this down to just fifty-three.

Furthermore, most negotiating tales are wrapped around ideas much more complex than Solomon and the two women used. Imagine making decisions in American major league baseball (MLB). In a room you pack all the professional team owners, league officials, and player representatives. Watch and listen as they try to navigate new agreements related to salaries, bonuses, free agent benefits, share of gate receipts, MLB logo clothing and equipment revenue, and more. These elephantine issues can loom quite large in the eyes of those inside the room, as well as those outside waiting for the conclusion.

So how do you eat an elephant? One bite at a time? Let's start with some classic techniques and knowledge you'll want to have handy in order to negotiate successfully with that well-trained, super-savvy buyer. Regardless of which model or hybrid model you choose to use, here's a fact about negotiating that will never change.

Concept: The longer your homework takes, the faster you sell.

The better you and/or your team prepares and handles pre-work, the more likely you'll be ready for any possibility in the negotiation process. This is similar to The Ultimate Objection-Handling Tool (Chapter 16), where we come to the table ready for anything the buyer throws our way.

The Classic Model

The foundation of modern negotiating is based on Fisher and Ury's work described earlier. The authors call their approach "principled negotiating." This reflects two things: (1) the collaborative nature of healthy dealings between buyers and sellers and (2) a nod to honest and ethical behavior (you'll see how serious sales professionals must take this last part in Chapter 29 on ethics).

I've chosen to use the summary here right from Wikipedia, as it's a pure, concise description of Fisher and Ury's masterful contribution to this subject.

SUMMARY

Getting to Yes describes a method called **principled negotiation** to reach an agreement whose success is judged by three criteria:

1. It should produce a wise agreement if agreement is possible.
2. It should be efficient.
3. It should improve or at least not damage the relationship between the parties.

The authors argue that their method can be used in virtually any negotiation. Issues are decided upon by their merits and the goal is a win-win situation for both sides. Below is a summary of some of the key concepts from the book. The four steps of a principled negotiation are:

1. Separate the people from the problem
2. Focus on interests, not positions
3. Invent options for mutual gain
4. Insist on using objective criteria

In principled negotiations, negotiators are encouraged to take the view that all the participants are problem solvers rather than adversaries. The authors recommend that the goal should be to reach an outcome "efficiently and amicably." The steps can be described in more detail as follows.

Step 1: Separate the People from the Problem

All negotiations involve people and people are not perfect. We have emotions, our own interests and goals, and we tend to see the world from our point of view. We also are not always the best communicators; many of us are not good listeners.

Getting to Yes outlines a number of tools for dealing with the problems of perception, emotion, and communication. However, the authors stress that separating people from problems is the best option. The keys to prevention are "building a working relationship" and "facing the problem, not the people."

Think of the people you negotiate with on a regular basis. Generally, the better we know someone, the easier it is to face a negotiation together. We tend to view people we don't know with more suspicion: Just what is "Bob" up to? Take time to get to know the other party before the negotiation begins.

Think of the negotiation as a means to solving a problem and the people on the other side as partners helping to find a solution. Ideally, both parties will come out of a negotiation feeling they have a fair agreement from which both sides can benefit.

If the negotiation feels like a situation of "you versus them," the authors suggest a couple of options:

1. Raise the issue with [the other side] explicitly . . . "Let's look together at the problem of how to satisfy our collective interests."

2. Sit on the same side of the table. . . . Try to structure the negotiation as a side-by-side activity in which the two of you—with your different interests and perceptions, and your emotional involvement—jointly face a common task.

Step 2: Focus on Interests, Not Positions

The authors use a simple example to explain the difference between interests and positions:

"Two men [are] quarrelling in a library. One wants the window open and the other wants it closed. . . . Enter the librarian. She asks one why he wants the window open: 'To get some fresh air' [his interest]. She asks the other why he wants it closed: 'To avoid a draft' [his interest]. After thinking a moment, she opens wide a window in the next room, bringing in fresh air without a draft."

The interests of the two men are the desire for fresh air and the desire to avoid a draft. The men's positions are to have the window opened or closed. The authors say we need to focus, not on whether the window in the room is opened or closed, but on how we can meet both the need for fresh air and the need to avoid a draft. More often than not, by focusing on interests, a creative solution can be found.

In this little example, each man has one interest, but in most negotiations, each party will have many interests and these interests will likely be different than yours. It's important to communicate your interests to the other party. Don't assume he has the same interests as you or that he knows what your interests are. Don't assume you know what interests the other party has. Discussion to identify and understand all the interests is a critical step in the process.

Step 3: Invent Options for Mutual Gain

The authors feel that a common problem with many negotiations is there are too few options to choose from. Little or no time is spent creating options. This, they feel, is a mistake.

There are four steps to generating options:

1. Separate inventing from deciding. As in any brainstorming session, don't judge the ideas people bring forward, just get them on the board.

2. Broaden the options on the table rather than look for a single answer. Remember the men at the library? The only option they saw was opening or closing the window in the room they were both sitting in. In fact, there are many options: borrow a sweater, open a window in another room, move to a different spot, etc.

3. Search for mutual gain. In a negotiation, both sides can be worse off and both sides can gain. Principled negotiations are not about "I win" and "you lose."

4. Invent ways of making the other party's decisions easy. Since a successful negotiation requires both parties to agree, make it easy for the other side to choose. This is where putting yourself in the other person's shoes can be very valuable. What might prevent "Bob" from agreeing? Can you do anything to change those things?

Step 4: Insist on Using Objective Criteria

Principled negotiations are not battles of will. There is no winner and you don't need to push your position until the other backs down. The goal is to "produce wise agreements amicably and efficiently."

Use of objective criteria helps remove the emotion from the discussion and allows both parties to use reason and logic. You may have to develop objective criteria, and there are a number of ways that can be done, from "traditional practices" to "market value" to "what a court would decide." Objective criteria "need[s] to be independent of each side's will."

Once objective criteria have been developed, they need to be discussed with the other side. The authors provide some guidelines:

1. Frame each issue as a joint search for objective criteria.

2. "[Use] reason and be open to reason" as to which standards are most appropriate and how they should be applied.

3. "Never yield to pressure," only to principle.

Common Challenges

Following these steps should lead you to a successful outcome, but it isn't always that easy. The authors then go on to address three types of common challenges negotiators face.

Sometimes the other party is more powerful than you:

"The most any method of negotiation can do is to meet two objectives: first, to protect you against making an agreement you should reject and, second, to help you make the most of the assets you do have so that any agreement you reach will satisfy your interests as well as possible."

To protect yourself, develop and know your BATNA: Best Alternative to a Negotiated Agreement. "The reason you negotiate is to produce something better than the results you can obtain without negotiating." The result you can obtain without negotiating is your BATNA.

"The better your BATNA, the greater your power," so it's essential to know your BATNA and take time to make sure it's as strong as it could be. The same will hold true for the other party. There are three steps to developing your BATNA:

1. Invent a list of actions you might take if no agreement is reached.

2. Improve some of the more promising ideas and convert them into practical alternatives.

3. Select, tentatively, the one alternative that seems best.

Sometimes the other party just won't play:

In a principled negotiation, you don't want to play games with the other party and you don't want him playing games with you. The authors advocate three approaches to getting things back on track in this situation:

1. Concentrate on the merits: talk about interests, options, and criteria.

2. Focus on what the other party may do: try to identify the other party's interests and the principles underlying his position.

3. Focus on what a third party can do: bring in a third party to assist if steps 1 and 2 aren't successful.

Sometimes the other party uses dirty tricks:

You may encounter a party who won't shy away from using dirty tricks. The process for dealing with this type of tactic is to follow the process for principled negotiations:

1. Separate the people from the problem.

2. Focus on interests, not positions.

3. Invent options for mutual gain.

4. Insist on using objective criteria.

5. If all else fails, "turn to your BATNA and walk out."

The authors close with three points:

1. "You knew it all the time." Much of what goes into a principled negotiation is common sense. The authors have developed an understandable framework to share the approach with others.

2. "Learn from doing." You won't become a better negotiator unless you get out there and practice.

3. Winning: "The first thing you are trying to win is a better way to negotiate—a way that avoids your having to choose between the satisfactions of getting what you deserve and of being decent. You can have both."

http://en.wikipedia.org/wiki/Getting_to_YES, accessed 08/01/2011.

In spite of the availability of Fisher and Ury's work, negotiations get crazy complex. You're reading this chapter because your selling professionals have a great deal of money at risk when consummating a sale. At the end of the chapter, I'll cover the process, the people involved, and sales skills that can be applied to the negotiating process.

A 21st Century Model

I want to begin this section of the chapter by revisiting the idea that negotiating skills are complex, difficult to learn, and require a certain type of individual to handle negotiations. This type is endowed, somehow, with the ability to handle anything, particularly the unexpected. One expert I know said that during an interview the host suggested that negotiating is like dealing with a drunk in that you have no idea what's going to happen next.

In reality and in sales, we learned the concept that "great sales pros can predict the future" (Chapter 16). This means that once we've identified every potential objection and armed ourselves with potent and persuasive language to deal with them, life will go much more smoothly on the path to a sale.

It's the same way in the world of negotiation. You really can anticipate much more than you might think. Brian Dietmeyer and his team at Think, Inc., have developed a beautiful structure for working through the negotiating process. I'm sharing it with you below, with their permission. Enjoy the language and the visuals they use to help navigate this tricky portion of the sales process.

THE STRATEGIC NEGOTIATION PROCESS*
Negotiation Strategy Coupled with a Negotiation Process

The power is in the two sides working together. A negotiation strategy without a negotiation process runs the risk of never being implemented, and a negotiation process without a negotiation strategy often results in inconsistent individual outcomes. An aligned approach will help you proactively manage your organization's reputation in the marketplace by consistently executing one deal at a time.

At its most basic level, the Strategic Negotiation Process is a step-by-step system that enables you to blueprint a negotiation, making it possible for you to see and understand a negotiation from your own perspective as well as that of your customer.

But in order to understand the process, you're going to have to start thinking differently about what negotiation really means. The traditional view of negotiation is promising, cajoling, threatening, or using any of a wide variety of tactics to get

*This material is used with permission of Brian Dietmeyer, who is senior managing partner and managing director of Think! Inc. Brian can be reached at BJD@e-thinkinc.com.

what you want from another party. Negotiation, however, begins long before you sit down with someone to work out the terms of a deal. It starts as soon as you select an account and start selling and/or managing the account relationship. This is all negotiation, and redefining it as a process is what leads to world class deal-making.

The Blueprint

Our research and global field work have shown that virtually every negotiation, regardless of who's conducting it or where it takes place, can be blueprinted in exactly the same way. This is an extremely important point, because we also found that everything that takes place in the course of a negotiation—the planning, research, and all the tactics used in the final face-to-face meeting—is ultimately driven by that blueprint. But what is this "blueprint"? It's essentially a picture of the entire negotiation revealed when each side of any deal answers the following two questions:

- What are the consequences if we do not reach agreement?
- What items are likely to be included if we do reach agreement?

In order to answer these questions, however, we must first go back to some very basic concepts about negotiating. In most negotiations, both sides have a separate "wish list" of what they would like to achieve in the negotiation. Although neither side obtains its exact list in the final deal, if the two sides do come to agreement, both have at least some of the things on their wish lists.

Whether the two parties come to agreement or not, there is a blueprint that can be applied to the situation. Figure 27.1 explains all likely outcomes of the situation.

In the middle of the blueprint are the two wish lists, and, between them, the Agreement Zone—the place where the two sides meet if they come to an agreement. There is always an alternative to both sides reaching agreement, however, which we refer to as the Consequences of No Agreement (CNA); this is shown on either side of the blueprint.

What Are the Consequences of No Agreement?

You may never have used the expression "consequences of no agreement," but chances are that you've thought about them. After all, you know that something is

Figure 27.1.   Negotiation Blueprint Agreement

blueprinting negotiation

Think! Inc.
business negotiation, redefined

Contributed and edited by Carrie Welles, vice president, Enterprise Account Solutions, Think! Inc.

going to happen if you don't make a deal. As the seller, your consequences of no agreement, your alternative to making a deal, is going to be losing the sale. Your customers, on the other hand, generally have three possible alternatives to reaching agreement with you. They could (1) go to a competitor, (2) build the solution themselves, or (3) do nothing. It's only when negotiators obtain something that's at least marginally better than their alternatives that they prefer agreement to impasse.

Understanding the consequences of no agreement, both for yourself and your customer, is the most important aspect of constructing a blueprint of a negotiation.

The reason for this is that, in any negotiation, the other side always sees your offer as a gain or loss based on its perception of the consequences of not reaching agreement with you. Simply put, if the other side believes that making a deal with you will be to its benefit, it will do it. But if the other side believes that it will be better off if it doesn't make a deal with you, regardless of the alternatives, you're going to lose the sale.

Note that we said the other side makes a decision based on its perception of the consequences. The truth is that, in most negotiations, one or both sides either hasn't taken the time to analyze its consequences of no agreement, or has misunderstood those consequences. In either case, even if one side is putting a great offer on the table, if the consequences—the alternatives to that offer—are misdiagnosed or misunderstood, chances are the two sides won't be able to reach agreement. Understanding this is the first step in blueprinting a negotiation, as well as the first step in the Strategic Negotiation Process.

What Items Are Likely to Be Included If We Do Reach Agreement?
The majority of negotiations succeed, ending in agreement rather than impasse. But in order to reach such agreement, and in order to fill in the rest of the blueprint, it's necessary to answer the second question we posed: What items are likely to be included if we do reach agreement? In the course of our consulting, we see people involved in very complicated negotiations that include a variety of items such as price, length of agreement, service, payment terms, legal terms, volume, etc. Even so, when we ask them to tell us what the negotiation is about, they often just say, "Price." Bear in mind that these are not young, inexperienced negotiators, but rather seasoned executives who may have negotiated hundreds of deals, and who still fall prey to this common mistake.

Determining what items should be part of the final deal should be a very simple exercise. Due to financial pressures, political pressures, lack of planning, and a lot of antiquated negotiation tactics, however, it's not unusual to see situations in which neither side has a clear idea of what it really wants out of a negotiation beyond one or two simple items. That's not a problem if you're negotiating over a commodity, but the less commodity-like your product or service the more important negotiation skills become, and the more opportunity there is for creating value for both sides by trading something one side values more than the other. The reality is that the heart and soul of business negotiation is trading. And in order to trade properly, a world class negotiator has to understand not only all the variables in a business deal, but also the importance of each to both sides.

Using the Blueprinting Process in a Large and Complex Negotiation

Let's try out the process on a "live deal" involving thorough analysis and effective customer questioning around the two aspects of the negotiation blueprint.

It's April 1st and you've just been told by a potential new global customer that, after all your months of trying to sell some of your machines to them, it's finally down to a choice between you and your closest competitor. The customer wants to see your "best foot forward" proposal in six weeks, by May 15th, and has hinted that your competitor is aggressively pursuing it, is being quite creative on price, and has a pretty good "product fit."

The Consequence of No Agreement (CNA)—Yours

You complete an overview of your own CNA and determine that if you don't reach agreement with the customer in this negotiation you will most likely lose the business. In this case, losing the business means you will lose about $750K in global revenue in the first year. If, however, you take into consideration potential long-term revenues from this customer, total CNA costs could be as much as $2.5M. In addition, if you don't close this deal you will lose the costs associated with the four months you've spent selling to the customer—approximately $25K for staff time, product demonstrations, etc.

You will also have some soft costs in the form of "political heat" from your vice president of global sales and the head of your product management group, both of whom have a personal interest in this sale as it impacts their bonuses, as well as yours. You are also aware that losing this sale will, in effect, fund a competitor by sending these revenues to them.

Good news for your CNA is that the market is growing—albeit slowly compared to past years. The chances of replacing this customer are fairly good and your list of other prospects for sales looks good at the moment. Also, while you have no other customers that are this large and ready to close, there are at least two or three smaller ones you feel positive about. All of them together could replace this sale, but it's always more profitable to close and service one customer than several.

Consequence of No Agreement (CNA)—Your Customer's

As always, attempting to analyze the customer's CNA is trickier. In this case, you know their CNA is to go to your major competitor, and, as they've hinted, pay less. What's tricky, though, is the total analysis—that is, determining the positive and negative effects—of their choosing the competitor over you. The first thing you do is pull together a team from your side. You invite one of the company's account managers who worked for your competitor on this deal, a guy from engineering who just came to you from the customer's organization, and some additional product experts. You give them an overview of the situation and ask them to help you brainstorm all the elements the customer may be considering when comparing your offer to their CNA.

After brainstorming, you ask the group whether, from the customer's perspective, each element is positive or negative compared to choosing you. The team breaks down the analysis in terms of design of the solution, delivery and installation, ongoing maintenance, output, and long-term upkeep. They also suggest doing an evaluation of comparative terms and conditions. The results of their analysis suggest the questions that must be addressed are:

Design Elements

- Whether or not there is an off-the-shelf solution that fits the customer's needs;

- How much "ground up" design is needed to build and test custom aspects; and

- How much time/commitment is needed from the customer for design.

Delivery and Installation Elements

- How long will it take?

- How long will the customer's operation be down while the machine is being installed? and

- How labor intensive will it be for the customer?

Maintenance Elements

- How often does the machine break down?

- What are the service hours and fees? and

- How difficult will it be to train the customer's team to run it?

Output Elements

- How many units per hour will the machine put out?

- What is the customer's machine's defect rate? and

- Can the machine be run "24/7"?

Upkeep Elements

- What do maintenance costs look like in years two, three, and four?

- How easily upgradeable is the machine? and

- What is the machine's expected service life?

Terms and Conditions Elements

- Lease versus buy;

- Flexibility of contracts;

- Payment terms; and

- Short-term product price.

In regard to design, you've determined that your competitor does have a pretty good "off-the-shelf" machine, while yours would require some customization. Your customization, however, would be free, and would require very little customer interface.

In terms of installation, your engineering department has just found some independent studies showing that easily customizable machines—like yours—are also relatively easy to install, and therefore end up taking about as much total time to install as less flexible "off-the-shelf" machines.

As far as maintenance is concerned, the folks in your engineering department and, especially, the engineer who just came over from the customer, say you have a huge advantage in terms of your machine's reliability. Of course, customers aren't likely to tell you that, but it's one of your strengths.

In regard to output, you and your competitor are pretty close. Their output may be a bit higher than yours, but since your machines run a higher percentage of the time, it probably makes up for the difference. In terms of upkeep, because of how they've been engineered, your machines break down much less frequently and, as a result, last longer.

Finally, in regard to terms and conditions, you and your competitor both offer lease or buy options, your industry contracts are all pretty much the same and payment terms are usually 25 percent at signing, 25 percent on delivery, and 50 percent when running. Your "price" is a bit higher, but you've determined that because of the reliability and flexibility of your machines, they have less downtime, easier long-term upgrades, and longer shelf life. As a result, not only does your return on investment get better after year one, but your product is less expensive to own in years two and three.

In answering the questions about each group of elements, you've determined that there is a value proposition gap between what you have to offer and the customer's CNA (your competitor) in all but one of them (Output). Based on that, you feel good about this negotiation; however, the problem is that either your customer doesn't have all the data on its CNA that you do, or it's bluffing.

Wish List—Your Side

You've pulled together your product manager, pricing manager, and someone from the legal department for this estimation and, after much wrangling, have prioritized your wish list of trades as follows:

Wish List—The Other Side

With the help of the account manager who used to work for your competitor and your pricing manager, you've estimated the types of trades this customer has looked for in the past and come up with the following educated guesses for its wish list.

You know exactly what the customer's CNA is, and you've done a pretty good job of analyzing its positive and negative elements. Now, in order to learn how your customer sees its CNA, and to educate the customer on it, you prepare the following questions:

- Have you determined how much customization the two machines will need for installation?
- How do you see the impact on your facility during installation?
- Do you have a certain amount of time budgeted for installation?
- What are your expectations in terms of machine downtime?

- When the machine breaks down, how quickly do you expect service?

- How much staff retraining do you expect you'll need?

- Do you have a figure in mind for year one maintenance costs?

- Do you have figures in mind for costs in years two through four?

- How would you like to handle future upgrades?

- Do you complete total cost of ownership analyses or just compare acquisition price?

Having developed questions to validate your customer's CNA, you now develop questions to validate its wish list items, as follows:

- I understand you will be looking to negotiate price, service, upgrades, length of contract, volume, and man hours to install. Is that right? Is there anything missing? Is there anything that should be deleted?

- What would you rank as your lead priority? That is, what should we focus on most? How about second, third, fourth, etc.?

- Do you have any specific targets you'd like to hit for each item?

You now send out an email to the head buyer, vice president of manufacturing, vice president of finance, and all the other people you've been selling to, asking them if you can have fifteen minutes of their time to better understand their needs for the upcoming negotiation. If they ask for them, you can send the questions in advance. When you get together with them, whether on the phone or in person, you ask the easy wish list questions first to get the ball rolling, then go on to the CNA questions. You also bring someone else from your account team with you to record the customer's answers.

Having had meetings with your buying influences on several levels to validate your assumptions, you now feel that, even though the customer didn't answer all your questions, you were able to tighten up your estimations. You also feel that you succeeded in educating them on many aspects of their CNA as well as on many of the items to be agreed upon in the negotiation. Now, taking into account your interest in length of contract, price, and volume, and the customer's in price, service, and upgrades, you devise three customized offers, equal to you (in that you would accept any one of them), but very different to your customer.

Now it's May 7th and you're ready to make a presentation—a full week before the customer's due date. You invite the customer's head buyer, vice president of manufacturing, and vice president of finance, and bring along product and technical support people from your side.

You open the presentation by thanking the group for taking the time to answer your questions a few weeks earlier, and let it know that doing so went a long way toward helping you customize three different potential relationships. You also tell the group that you realize that if they don't choose you they will choose your nearest competitor, and admit that your competitor has a pretty good off-the-shelf solution as well as pretty good output. You also note that during your earlier conversations, the buyer and the vice president of finance put a lot of emphasis on price, and that the vice president of manufacturing talked a lot about "up-time," that is, the reliability of machines. This is the point at which you present the value proposition gap you found in your CNA analysis, specifically:

- Your machines are higher in short-term price (year one);
- Your machines are X percent more reliable than your competitor's, resulting in:
  - Higher output (which manufacturing was concerned with); and
  - Less maintenance cost (which the buyer and finance department wanted).
- The combination of higher output and lower maintenance makes your machines cost less starting late in year one, then drop by X percent in years two and three.

You tell them that based on their needs and the value proposition of your competitor, you've put together three different relationships that you highlight on a flip chart or PowerPoint presentation. You briefly overview some key elements of each, then offer everyone a handout containing the details and go through them. You now ask them to rank the three offers in terms of their preference. They quickly agree that the short-term option is the least preferable, but there's a lot of internal negotiation among them over which of the remaining options is most preferable. It's obvious that neither is quite right, so at this point you begin the trading to come up with one solution that fits their needs. They keep telling you that you're more expensive; you keep going back to total costs. They try to push you for concessions; you continue to trade using both wish lists. In the end, you settle on this deal:

Final Agreement

Length: Three years

Price: $255K per machine

Volume: Three machines

Service: Five days x 24 hours

Upgrades: 25 percent discount

Installation Support: 300 hours

Negotiation Strategy Coupled with a Negotiation Process

The power is in the two sides working together. A negotiation strategy without a negotiation process runs the risk of never being implemented, and a negotiation process without a negotiation strategy often results in inconsistent individual outcomes. An aligned approach will help you proactively manage your organization's reputation in the marketplace by consistently executing one deal at a time.

Brian Dietmeyer, the author of this piece, is senior managing partner and managing director of Think! Inc. Brian can be reached at BJD@e-thinkinc.com.

Tips and Techniques for Negotiating

This long list of twenty-nine items should give you plenty of content to develop your own training for the sales team. Pay particular attention to the two pieces at the end of this list: Global Negotiating Styles and Lying While Negotiating.

1. Identify the Other Party's Style

G.R. Shell offers five styles in the book *Bargaining for Advantage* (2006). Knowing the other person's style and adjusting your sales approach is 100 percent in alignment with one of the key purposes of this book—to teach mental flexibility in order to elevate sales skills. Shell's five styles are:

- *Accommodating:* Individuals who enjoy solving the other party's problems and preserving personal relationships. Accommodators are sensitive to the emotional states, body language, and verbal signals of the other party. They can, however, feel taken advantage of in situations when the other party places little emphasis on the relationship.

- *Avoiding:* Individuals who do not like to negotiate and don't do it unless warranted. When negotiating, avoiders tend to defer and dodge the confrontational aspects of negotiating; however, they may be perceived as tactful and diplomatic.

- *Collaborating:* Individuals who enjoy negotiations that involve solving tough problems in creative ways. Collaborators are good at using negotiations to understand the concerns and interests of other parties. They can, however, create problems by transforming simple situations into more complex ones.

- *Competing:* Individuals who enjoy negotiations because they present an opportunity to win something. Competitive negotiators have strong instincts for all aspects of negotiating and are often strategic. Because their style can dominate the bargaining process, competitive negotiators often neglect the importance of relationships.

- *Compromising:* Individuals who are eager to close the deal by doing what is fair and equal for all parties involved in the negotiation. Compromisers can be useful when there is limited time to complete the deal; however, compromisers often unnecessarily rush the negotiation process and make concessions too quickly.

2. Determine the Buyer's Experience

Determine which of the following you are facing and adjust your strategy accordingly:

- Professional buyers (purchasing agents) who buy as a full-time job

- Executives and managers who buy as part of their roles

- Consumers, entrepreneurs, and less savvy businesspeople who buy infrequently, based on need or an urgent need to address (A car is totaled in an accident, so it's time for that once-every-five-years decision.)

3. Identify Strategies Being Used

Anticipating the ways your buyer is working the negotiation is very important. You can prepare responses to objections you anticipate. You can even call the other party on unfair tactics. Is she taking a problem-solving or an aggressive bargaining approach? Remind her this is supposed to be a collaborative effort.

4. Establish Balance of Power

Even in collaborative efforts, one party might have an upper hand. It could be that the buyer has multiple options, so chooses to take a hard line. The seller could have a solution that can be implemented faster than a competitor's, quickly eliminating a major problem the buyer is facing. This is known as "situational power." Be aware of this, as it can change throughout the negotiation. In a collaborative setting, forms of power (such as position or expertise) can be pointed out so that both parties understand what is happening during the negotiation. This can't eliminate the source of power, but it can help limit unfair use of power.

5. Clarify Specifications/Offerings

How flexible is the buyer when creating a request for proposal? Your role as a sales professional is to help the buying organization understand how well your solution fits their needs. Can you start a discussion from the very beginning to help them understand how important changes to the RFP could be?

6. Understand Competitive Options

Who else is under consideration? This is where selling skills come into play. How do you distinguish your product and service offerings from the competition, without being disrespectful? This is most easily done with potent marketing literature that can be handed to the buying team. Do you have a colorful, persuasive chart showing you're the best choice? Are there external data and evidence to support the information?

7. Prepare the Buyer

How much data has the buyer accumulated about his impending decision (within the firm) as well as his external choices for solutions? A well-prepared buyer has more leverage and is more likely to bargain aggressively. In addition, he or she is more likely to have enough information to aid your collaborative efforts to find new solutions.

8. Estimate Speed of the Decision

This tip is related to the balance of power, but a buyer close to a deadline is more likely to accommodate concessions or make bargains. If the decision isn't imminent, you could be in for some frustration as a salesperson since there is not any pressure to decide.

9. Remain Flexible and Open to Options

This whole book is about staying mentally flexible yourself. You can learn to encourage flexibility for the buyer if you offer options that open up the possibility of new solutions. Creative options enhance the win-win relationship like nothing else in the whole negotiating experience.

10. Develop Outstanding Language Skills

If your language skills are superior, you can disagree and argue, even fight with the buyer or buying team. Your ability to do this in a healthy, respectful manner is key to maintaining the relationship with your client. Watch out for inflammatory language, that is, words and phrases that are either too strong or too weak.

11. Deal with Your Emotions

It is important to maintain control. Most advice about negotiating suggests that emotion has no place at the table. But do ask yourself whether the value of understanding and mirroring emotion to the buyer is important to building rapport and a clear understanding on their part of the need for your product or services.

12. Discover the Other's Perspective

Direct questions are powerful ways to gain clear understanding of the buyer's feelings, even policies about reaching a decision. Don't be afraid to model open, honest dialogues right at the beginning of the relationship. For a pure and potent strategy on how to do this, see Chapter 11 on opening sales calls.

13. Do Your Homework Well!

A well-prepared seller has already identified options, objections, lowest negotiable price, and more. He or she collects data on competitors, market-related information, and more. Anticipate what could occur and you'll be more confident when resistance arises.

14. Know When to Stop Talking

If the meeting is running long, late in the day, and people are tired, it's smarter to stop and return to the table energized and rested at another time. You don't want to be in a place where you make mistakes or where tempers might run hot. Pick up cues from the buyer. If you see fatigue, say something like: "I think we could use a break or some rest before we start throwing staplers at one another." Sleep is the ultimate energizer. And your unconscious can work during your dream state to identify new solutions for the next foray into consummating the big sale. You can also use breaks to obtain feedback and advice from others who are not at the table, even non-business confidants.

15. Use Humor

Humor is a healthy way to blow off steam and deflect difficult conversations. Can you keep smiling, perhaps by keeping your eye on the prize, and be good company? Stories and a sense of humor can help maintain an upbeat atmosphere in what are often difficult negotiation meetings.

16. Maintain Trust

Trust is truly the key to a great process. Think about how people you care about and trust stick with you during disagreements, big and small. Honesty and transparency will help gain and keep trust at the negotiating table.

17. Identify Buyers' Tactics

You did your homework; now you're having a live conversation. Recognize the strategy or objection or reason behind the questions he or she is asking and you'll go far toward seeing how the buyer is working his or her end of this deal. You might even want to identify a tactic by name, if it's underhanded or manipulative: "Susan, you're not threatening to walk just to gain one last concession, are you?" Your counter-tactics can keep the discussion on a professional, peer-based level.

18. Overcome Price Objections

You gained the skills to manage objections by using the Ultimate Objection-Handling Tool in Chapter 16. It's time to revisit this superb suite of strategies. You prepared for price resistance during the homework phase of negotiating. Are you ready to handle resistance on the fly, when the topic arises during bargaining talks?

19. Trade, Don't Donate

Never give something up unless you receive a concession or trade in exchange. Simply conceding a point to the buyer will train the buyer to keep asking for more, with no consequences to his or her position. Take the attitude that you are willing to concede points, if they do so in kind. My four years of schooling in the Latin language has finally paid off as I recognize the power of the popular phrase *quid pro quo* or "this for that." Own it yourself when your buyer asks for a concession.

20. Determine Your Initial Position Carefully

Your initial position gives the buyer his or her first impression of you and the potential deal. Start too high and you can antagonize the buyer. Start too low and you'll end up losing money for your company.

21. Establish Priorities

Set your priorities and keep them in mind so that you can rank the value of any trade or concession you'll be asked to make.

22. Set Goals as a Range, Not a Number

Remember that you can be more flexible in working toward a mutually optimistic solution when you have a range within which to work. This technique works well when you wisely combine it with Numbers 19, 20, and 21.

23. Choose Your Team Wisely

Because the combination of skills and personalities during negotiations can be toxic or powerful, be aware of how other people on your team can affect the balance, based on how each relates to the buyers. If your approach is careful, cautious, and firm, then a team member who acts like a bull in the china shop, regardless of his or her seniority, can crash a deal. Be sensitive to the players on the other team as well and work toward a match of styles.

24. Take Notes!

Someone must document the complete negotiation process. This is critical to eliminate confusion and create a history of conversations and concessions. You could choose to share your notes with the buying team, if desired, or you can keep your notes as a reference, should things become difficult or if contradictory beliefs about past discussions arise.

25. Don't Lose Sight of the Big Picture

As you work together, each party to the negotiation will see a different big picture. Don't set yours aside during the heat of the conversation. You have something they want or possibly need or else you wouldn't be at the table right now. They in turn have something you want. How will you work together so both parties are happy with what they see?

26. Know the Strengths and Weaknesses of Both Positions

You have to be aware of your own weaknesses and strengths as well as theirs. A wide variety of factors can limit your ability to negotiate successfully, and the balance of power can shift at a critical juncture. What happens when you are close to a deadline (as in a pro sports team's start of the season)? Things change. Your list of limitations and strengths might have to be adjusted as you sit at the bargaining table.

27. Decide Whether to Lie

While researching this chapter I struggled with whether to reference one of the biggest players in the negotiation training arena. Dr. Chester Karrass and his organization have a distinct anti-sales-professionals approach to coaching their clients. This can be noted simply by reading the tips listed on their website, www. karrass.com/kar_eng/tipofthemonth.htm.

Repeated calls, emails, and website contact forms were filled to interview Melvin Klayman, executive vice president, or Keith Money, managing director, at Karrass, which were ignored. This was even when I made it clear that this was about as significant a book at this is:

> "I'm finalizing the first draft of major work on sales training for Pfeiffer Publishing. This book of best practices will hit the market next year, selling to senior sales and human resource executives, as well as entrepreneurs. . . . Please let me know if you're interested in gaining exposure through this product, *The Ultimate Guide to Sales Training*."

However, there are plenty of good bits of information at their website. But much of it centers on the idea that it's "them versus us." This classic, old-school mentality is thinly masked by stating that this leads to win-win negotiating. It's really not, because they're teaching hardball, win at all costs techniques.

One example of this is what they call the "bogey." This is, in essence, a bold lie to set the seller on his or her heels. And you're taught to lie with a smile on your face, as described from this tip:

> "When a buyer says, 'I love your proposal and really want to work with you, but I have only so much money to spend,' most salespeople will respond in a positive, friendly fashion. How can you be hostile toward someone who likes you and your proposal? The salesperson sees this as an opportunity to get involved with the buyer to find ways to solve the 'problem' created by the bogey."

Greg Williams' insights are brilliant for parties on either side of the bargaining table. Every sales professional should understand what motivates buyers to buy, and this is found out by using great questioning skills. In addition, great sales pros can respectfully challenge a buyer who seems to be misleading the discussion or bending the truth.

This can be done in many ways, one of which is to just state to the effect that, "Well, if that's true and we're this far apart, I can't imagine any way we can work together. So this appears to be our final discussion." Then shut up and be prepared to walk away.

This could be a disqualifying issue, a point at which you realize it's too expensive to deal with someone. Or worse, you might not want a client who's this difficult to deal with.

This is also the point in your reading at which you might say, "Dan, you're crazy. It's a three-million-dollar contract. My commission is $150,000. If I have to, I'll work this prospect until I drop."

As long as you respect the value of your time and feel that this sale is real, keep with it. But this is like negotiating with terrorists. We are training others, by our responses, that it's okay to keep using manipulative strategies. We all finally get smart when we've been beaten up enough, then pissed off enough to no longer tolerate tricks.

Again, are your intentions and actions both honest and ethical? And are your insights into the use of lying accurate enough to identify the basis for the prospect's use or misuse of truth-telling techniques? And can you negotiate skillfully using the truth to create a win-win atmosphere in which respect leads to the best deal for both parties?

28. Learn to Use a Global Negotiating Style

Global economy? Enough said. We need to be aware of the differences that other cultures bring to the negotiating table. This requires some specific training, but anyone who has travelled to another country has experienced some of these distinctions:

- *Meeting/greeting.* How do you greet someone? Do you shake the hand of someone of the opposite gender? Is a weak handshake symbolic of weakness? A strong shake equal to aggressiveness? Would you use first names or more formal language?

- *Eye contact.* North American, and even Arab, cultures make eye contact to provide a sense of trustworthiness. In contrast, Asian cultures view lack of eye contact and looking down as a sign of respect.

- *Space and touch.* Members of Asian cultures don't normally touch unless they are family or close friends. In fact, four feet is a normal distance between two speakers. In the Americas and Arab countries, the opposite is true, as physical connectedness is a sign of affirmation and friendship.

- *Time orientation.* This is one of the most interesting and confusing factors in intercultural connectivity. Basically you can divide the world into two types of people: those who are known as *monochronic* or those known as *polychronic.* Monochronic people are linear in orientation and focus on one thing at a time. They want attendees on time (not doing so is disrespectful). They want clear starting and ending points to meetings. Dialogues are specific to the topic at hand. You would find this orientation most common in the United States, Germany, and Japan. Polychronic people engage in simultaneous activities, with many people. They are flexible in meetings, whether beginning or ending, and often take breaks randomly. Locations where polychronic orientation prevails include Latin cultures and some European and African nations.

To complicate this further, there are also time orientations toward past, present, and future. If you are interested in details and research on this, check out *The Time Paradox: The New Psychology of Time That Will Change Your Life* by Philip Zimbardo and John Boyd (2008). They even have a self-assessment you can take to identify your personal orientation toward time. Fascinating stuff.

- *Male/female identity.* Are women nurturing or task-oriented? Japanese and Latin American women tend toward assertive behavior. Scandinavian and Thai women are more oriented toward nurture and cooperation. Do your homework before making mistakes when engaging male and female counterparts at the negotiating table.

Many of these factors are morphing as businesspeople spend more time outside their borders and begin to adapt practices of other cultures. It's still good to be sensitive to traditional practices when encountering other nationalities at the bargaining table. One of my favorite books on this topic was the eye-opening research and fascinating writing of Fons Trompenaar (1997), *Riding the Waves of Culture: Understanding Diversity in Global Business.*

In addition, Dr. Geert Hofstede introduced research on cultural paradigms ten years ago. If you're interested in tackling a book with more than six hundred pages, you'll want to read *Culture's Consequences: Comparing Values, Behaviors, Institutions, and Organizations Across Nations* (2001). Other academic experts have taken alternative approaches to cultural definitions. Another resource that could serve you well is *Beyond Hofstede: Culture Frameworks for Global Marketing and Management,* edited by Cheryl Nakata (2009).

29. Have Fun!

Your negotiating work will expose you to a large variety of personalities and cultural backgrounds and techniques. Few people have the opportunity to learn from others in this way. Believe in yourself, prepare well, and you'll enjoy even the most complex of sales scenarios.

Use the material in this chapter to identify which type of approach works for your company. I encourage you to, at least, share some of the twenty-nine tips and techniques with your team right away, perhaps even run some sales meetings focusing on them. Then go to work developing a structured approach to negotiating with buyers. Remember the point we have made from the beginning of this book—the value of selling by way of a system.

Chapter 28

Mental Health for Sales Pros

This chapter covers critical information and learning for you, the sales executive or manager or trainer, as well as for the rep. You've often heard the idea that sales pros should distinguish themselves from the competition. That's exactly why I love this chapter so much. It covers content that is rarely, mostly never, taught to sales organizations. Here you'll find ten fascinating areas that can significantly improve performance, just by attending to the mental side of sales. The last section, Ethics, is so critical (dare we say, criminally critical?) in today's society that the next chapter contains a detailed structure for ethical behavior in our profession. Let's look at the following ten ways to manage the heads and hearts of our sales team.

1. Rejection
2. Balance
3. Priorities
4. Goals
5. Attitude
6. Self-talk
7. Resilience
8. Procrastination
9. Optimism
10. Ethics (see the Lambert material in Chapter 29)

Head Health, the Power of Self-Talk, and Much, Much More

So much of mental health is about self-talk and how we verbally, *inside our heads,* manage rejection and trouble, as well as the good. This content could have been placed in Chapter 5 on communication skills, but there we talked about how we use the muscle inside our mouths, the tongue. Here we'll work on the muscle above our mouths, the brain.

The mental piece of the selling puzzle is virtually missing from training, until today. Okay, it might surface somewhat in a pre-hiring assessment, and some of that information is helpful before the reps are brought on board. But you can coach all reps to change their self-talk, just as you can teach them new language skills in questioning, handling objections, and more.

In the rest of the chapter, we'll cover ten different ways to help improve or purify your sales reps' head health. As you look at the ten ways, some might not seem to fit. But they do, as things like balance and goals and priorities are only improved after a person decides mentally to make the changes needed to improve them. You'll also notice overlap among the ten. Blend them together, eliminate some if you choose, to add new training of real value to your sales team.

Concept: Embrace a healthy head; reject rejection.

1. Rejection

I was invited into a meeting with a team that headed up global sales training with one of the largest sales forces in the world. It was a network marketing organization. Because their salespeople were typical consumers, virtually none of them had any selling experience. Of those with sales experience, the percentage with training was tiny.

I directed the discussion to the sales dialogue: "What happens when the newborn seller (yes, they are truly babies to our profession) talks to his target market? The first contacts (much like a new insurance sales rep) are friends, family, and neighbors.

"So picture this: You're the new rep. You talk to your next-door neighbor. It's awkward for a dozen different reasons (your newness means you have no idea what's going to happen, how he'll respond, etc.) and you slink back to your house embarrassed. No, that's not a strong enough word. You're humiliated (but hopeful).

"Next day you see him leaving for work and offer a feeble wave. He nods his head and quickly ducks into the car. After work you don't even walk near the window that looks on his house.

"Maybe your coach who signed you up has some tips and encouraging words. But you then call a family member, who chuckles and says, 'no thanks' to the meeting you desperately want people to attend.

"So eventually someone says 'yes,' perhaps even a few do. But nobody buys. Or maybe one or two will, but this selling stuff is HARD!

"Thirty days later you walk boldly up to the neighbor. 'Hey Bill! I'm not doing that network marketing thing anymore, I don't have enough time, but the products are great and we still use them. When did you want to get out like we talked about and see that new sports bar across town?'

"What you're saying to Bill is that you want to move beyond the rejection you received when you put him in a bad place a month ago.

"But what's really happened is that you might have failed, unconsciously or otherwise, in the business because you'd rather maintain relationships than make more money. Or rejection is so hard on you that you get rid of it by falling away from your business opportunity, in spite of the evidence that plenty of people are successful and make good money doing it."

Back to our meeting with the sales training team: So I ran this scenario by them, asking the question alluded to above: "What if a large percentage of people fail— perhaps on purpose—simply because they are unprepared for rejection? They have no strategy, no self-talk to move past it. And they'd rather be in relationships with others than in business with them."

Awkward (but to me, very interesting) silence.

Here's a key concept: If you don't prepare sales reps for rejection and failure, those negative experiences can color their view of selling so darkly, they might lead to the rep rejecting sales as a career.

Let's be realistic; 90 to 95 percent of our selling interactions are negative—phone calls and emails ignored, gatekeepers fiercely protective of the decision-maker, sales calls with constant prospect resistance, sure sales lost for unknown reasons. Five or 10 percent closing ratio? What a relief to have some happy moments scattered about our days.

It's been my experience that the "hump" in selling for rookies is six months. Get your new reps over the hump with enough success to generate a desire for more of it and you're building a potential champion in the field or on the phone.

This number was confirmed recently when I was asked to speak at the National Collegiate Sales Competition (NCSC), run by Dr. Terry Loe from Kennesaw State University (http://coles.kennesaw.edu/ncsc/). The school's Coles College of Business has students engage in simulated sales calls for both a product and a service. Each competitor is viewed remotely by video and scored.

I arrived early to help judge and was surprised at the size of the job fair filled with sponsors. Dr. Loe told me the sponsors always came back (Who wouldn't love that at an annual event?), as the feedback he received was that schools putting out graduates with sales degrees offered students with education, training, and internships that gave them the equivalent of eighteen months of selling experience before their careers started. They were well over the six-month "hump," and most had plenty of job offers to choose from. How many graduates can say that today?

By the way, the NCSC was a *great* experience, led by a man with a passion for the future of our profession. I encourage any organization that hires reps to contact Dr. Terry Loe and support his work. His investment in this unique event makes so much sense when you realize that over 50 percent of college graduates go into some sales-related work. That begs the question of why more universities aren't offering degrees in selling. Support our profession, get into the NCSC job fair, serve as a judge, connect with these students who have made a career decision to sell.

Sales reps get into selling because of the earning potential or glamour or because someone sold them on the vision described in Chapter 2 on selling the value of a career in sales. But how do you prepare sales reps, regardless of experience, to deal with the dark side of the selling world—rejection?

For more than twenty years many managers and trainers have taught a simple phrase to teach sales pros when rejection occurs. It's this:

Yes, no, next . . .

- Got the sale, the YES? Good, move on—next!

- Got the NO? Good, move on—next!

- "Yes, no, next"

This is potent self-talk (more on this follows) for your reps to use. If that is a bit simplistic or you have reps who are a bit longer-winded (even when talking to themselves!), teach them a phrase they're most comfortable with that points to a positive future:

- "I'm getting the next one."

- "That's fine. I'm great at what I do. One miss doesn't mark me."

You get the idea; look up at life, not down.

> **EXERCISE 28.1.   Listing Comebacks for Rejection**

SETUP: Let's get some quick feedback from reps about rejection.

Trainer: Ask the reps what they say to themselves when they lose a sale, particularly when they thought it was in hand or thought they had a great shot at the business. Then have them work in pairs or small groups to decide what they *should* say. Have them share their answers while you make a master list for later reference. You'll get some good laughs, much of it from foul language, but get into this because you want to reinforce reps' ability to quickly move on.

2. Work/Life Balance

> *John is a good friend of mine. We're both competitive athletes who had the good fortune (and hard work ethic) to enjoy sports careers beyond college. Our kids are the same age and work out together. John is a money manager and is in one of the most stressful jobs you can find.*
>
> *One afternoon he called me after the stock market closed to say a client was angry because John lost him $200,000 that day. Now the investor is worth hundreds of millions of dollars. And the mistake was actually the client's, who didn't respond to a request to approve a stock play that day until after a dip in the market.*
>
> *I asked John how he handled the anxiety related to his work.*
>
> *"Dan, do you know the average person who does what I do doesn't make it to the age of fifty-eight?"*
>
> *"That's your answer? You handle it by dying at fifty-seven? You mean people make a conscious decision to die early, but prior to that they enjoy extraordinarily high earnings?"*

Death. There's the ultimate sacrifice for job-related stress. This issue is exactly why many major corporations, led by the insurance industry no less, have mandatory vacation policies in place for executives. Most of this massive emotional and physical strain comes from our inability to disconnect our personal and professional lives.

Our primary time to separate from work both mentally and physically comes during vacation. However, the United States offers the lowest number of days to disconnect. The following table lists nine countries and the average number of paid vacation days per year employees receive in each country.

Paid Vacation Around the World	
Italy	42 days
France	37 days
Germany	35 days
Brazil	34 days
United Kingdom	28 days
Canada	26 days
Korea	25 days
Japan	25 days
U.S.	13 days

Source: World Tourism Organization (WTO).

I'm not suggesting we change company vacation policy. But we can influence up, by sharing some of the research on work/life balance. At the least, we can help our sales professionals be more serious about taking time off. Everyone on your selling team needs to make a conscious decision to create separation and balance from work. This shouldn't happen only when on vacation.

In Chapter 23 on daily performance tips, you'll discover how the Human Performance Institute teaches business professionals to disconnect regularly. This means escaping mentally and physically during each month, each week, even during the workday. The energy gained is significant. In a fascinating story you'll see how the basis for this teaching comes from research into world class tennis players.

For now, let's look at a solution for stress offered by the prestigious Mayo Clinic. As long as you're working, juggling the demands of career and personal life will probably be an ongoing challenge. Use these ideas to help you find the work/life balance that's best for you:

- *Track your time.* Track everything you do for one week, including work-related and personal activities. Decide what's necessary and what satisfies you the most. Cut or delegate activities you don't enjoy or can't handle—or share your concerns and possible solutions with your employer or others.

- *Take advantage of your options.* Ask your employer about flex hours, a compressed work week, job sharing, telecommuting, or other scheduling flexibility. The more control you have over your hours, the less stressed you're likely to feel.

- *Learn to say no.* Whether it's a co-worker asking you to spearhead an extra project or your child's teacher asking you to manage the class play, remember that it's okay to respectfully say no. When you quit doing the things you do only out of guilt or a false sense of obligation, you'll make more room in your life for the activities that are meaningful to you and bring you joy.

- *Leave work at work.* With the technology to connect to anyone at any time from virtually anywhere, there may be no boundary between work and home—unless you create it. Make a conscious decision to separate work time from personal time. When you're with your family, for instance, turn off your cell phone and put away your laptop computer.

- *Manage your time.* Organize household tasks efficiently, such as running errands in batches or doing a load of laundry every day, rather than saving it all for your day off. Put family events on a weekly family calendar and keep a daily to-do list. Do what needs to be done and let the rest go. Limit time-consuming misunderstandings by communicating clearly and listening carefully. Take notes if necessary.

- *Bolster your support system.* At work, join forces with co-workers who can cover for you—and vice versa—when family conflicts arise. At home, enlist trusted friends and loved ones to pitch in with child care or household responsibilities when you need to work overtime or travel.

- *Nurture yourself.* Eat healthy foods, include physical activity in your daily routine, and get enough sleep. Set aside time each day for an activity that you enjoy, such as practicing yoga or reading. Better yet, discover activities you can do with your partner, family, or friends—such as hiking, dancing, or taking cooking classes.

  Source: www.mayoclinic.com/health/work-life-balance/WL00056/
  NSECTIONGROUP=2

The organization also suggests you should seek professional help when your ability to manage these issues becomes too much for you and you feel a loss of control over them.

EXERCISE 28.2. **Committing to Change Work/Life Balance**

SETUP: Deepen the discussion about boundaries by having learners check off which areas they're doing well and which they're not doing well.

Trainer: Ask your sales team to look at how well they manage boundaries, based on the Mayo Clinic checklist above. Ask each of them to mark where he or she is on each of these seven points.

Topic	I do this!	Sometimes	Never
Track your time			
Take advantage of your options			
Learn to say no			
Leave work at work			
Manage your time			
Bolster your support system			
Nurture yourself			

Next, have team members share in table groups the things they need to work on. Have them write their specific goals to improve on at least one of them, then name an accountability partner who can work with them over the next thirty days to implement this change. The partner could be in the room or it could be an outsider, such as a friend, family member, or spouse. If the partner is not in the room, the rep should write down the person's name and when he or she will commit to a conversation on this topic.

Increase your sensitivity to work/life balance. The benefits are sitting right in front of you. The problems that come with a lack of balance can wreck families. For a spectacular resource on this topic, I highly recommend visiting and subscribing to Tim Ferriss' blog posts: www.fourhourworkweek.com/

Remember what we're in the game for—it's to enjoy our earnings with people we love.

3. Priorities

Picture this: You're at Sea World and a whale trainer says she needs three volunteers to help feed Shamu (a punch line here about "you get to feed him to the sharks" would be funny, but the editors probably would feel it's a distraction). Great, thanks for leaving that in.

Three thousand hands fly toward heaven, accompanied by screams of joy, anticipation, and hope: "PICK ME!" "ME FIRST!"

As one guest is selected, the other 2,999 become even more frantic for your attention. After all, their chances have just been reduced by 33 percent.

When number 2 is chosen, only one spot is left. The noise could deafen a submerged whale.

You get the image, the idea. Those shouting heads are just like every personal and professional activity rioting for your attention. Why should we prioritize? How will you prioritize? What will you prioritize? Me! Me! Me!

Why Do We Prioritize?

If we don't rank the value of our activities, we function by default.

Imagine how dangerous it would be to make decisions this way. To operate our lives, every day, by reacting to the loudest voice behind the highest hand. So who runs your selling life? Whatever you choose to react to? Basing business decisions on responding to pressure is not necessarily in your best interests!

Prioritizing has clear benefits to the sales professional. It:

- Eliminates procrastination
- Gives great focus during the work day
- Helps you attend to your strengths
- Teaches delegation of low-level tasks
- Keeps income-related activities at the top of the list

What other reasons can you think of that make prioritizing a priority?

How Do We Prioritize?

You're looking at your day's work and trying to figure out what's first, what's most important, what's going to make you the most money (and fastest). How do you teach reps to prioritize their workload? First, every task should serve a greater goal. In selling, most activities should support generation of revenue. Of course, there are support and follow-up activities as well. Just be conscientious of the true purpose of everything you do in your work day.

There are many ways to learn how to prioritize activities. Not all of the traditional categories apply to sales professionals. Of those listed here, you'll find a description as well as cautions related to each.

- *Urgency or due date*—The most obvious way to prioritize as deadlines cry for attention. Be cautious of the value here. Does completion lead to revenue? If not, can the deadline be extended? Can it be delegated to others?

- *Volume or weight of the work*—Heavy loads can be chunked daily to chip away at the large task. Again, don't let this workload function as a mountain summit whose sheer size cries for your attention. What can be delegated? Can you climb it more slowly? How about later?

- *Persistent pressure*—Don't be shamed into attending to others' needs. Keep your focus, learn to manage those relationships, and let them know that you'd love to help (if true), but your concerns take precedence.

- *Ease*—Prefer to knock off some simple tasks and feel better for having eliminated "to do" list items? Here's a hint: If you have energy problems during the day, work through the easy activities at this time. (Find more help on energy issues in Daily Performance Tips, Chapter 23.)

- *Difficulty*—Or do you prefer to remove hard tasks in order to feel relief at knowing they're behind you?

- *Problem popping up*—Digital or not, sometimes things cry suddenly for immediate attention. Can you ignore it? Can you delay responding? Just because it's a problem doesn't mean it should derail the plans and priorities of your day.

- *Passion*—Is it just more fun to work on something you love to do? Just be aware that this category can serve as a distraction from more important issues.

EXERCISE 28.3. Practicing Prioritization

SETUP: To practice the concept of using some best practices in prioritizing, sales reps will choose some sample activities in a work day and identify their importance.

Trainer: You will want to give team members copies of the following chart and say, "Let's work on prioritizing some of your sales activities according to the principles listed below. Choose three behaviors you have to engage in during a normal day. These could include phone calls for prospecting, phone follow-up with clients, meeting with team members on new clients, face-to-face sales calls, coaching meetings, or calls.

"List your activities; then rate each by High, Medium, or Low priority for each category."

Priority	I	2	3
Urgency or due date			
Volume or weight of the work			
Persistent pressure			
Ease			
Difficulty			
Problem popping up			
Passion			

Reps should discuss their reasoning at their tables. There aren't necessarily any right or wrong answers. But feedback from colleagues might help them hone in on what should take precedence in their selling lives.

What Do We Prioritize?

Priorities can be based on the acquisition of money, how much time and energy they take (don't underestimate energy!), how they help attain goals (both personal and corporate), whether to attend to interruptions, and, perhaps most importantly, the development of our time management skills (see Chapter 23).

Every task should have a deadline, even if you have to create one yourself to see it to completion. Setting priorities simply mirrors goal-setting concepts. Sales pros who prioritize are less likely to procrastinate if they focus on income-producing activities first.

Another key concept that can help you frame prioritizing and planning is time management in Chapter 23, Daily Performance Tips.

4. Goals

Read about a sales colleague whose most embarrassing sales moment (from www.SalesAutopsy.com) has been titled:

Ghost of Dale Carnegie Comes Back to Haunt a Sales Pro

It started out so smoothly. I had generated a good lead and called on the company to discuss handling their insurance needs. The office manager really had her act together, giving me all the information I requested to submit to insurance carriers and get the quotes. I drafted the proposal and went to meet the woman business owner to present her choices.

Everything continued well. My numbers were good, and the prospect was giving me good buying signals. I had been aware of her unusual last name and decided to add in my Dale Carnegie "How to Win Friends and Influence People" strategy.

You might be familiar with the fact that Carnegie wrote that people's names are the most precious thing in the world to them. Questions about people's names can be quite flattering. There is often a story behind them. Perhaps the family came to America from a foreign country. Maybe a famous person was an ancestor.

"I have a friend, my very best friend in the world, with the same unique last name as yours. Could you two be related?" I asked. My big smile invited her to share some personal information.

She glared at me. "That is my husband's ex-wife."

In my mind alarm bells rang, lights flashed, and a voice whimpered, "Oh no."

Across the desk a voice said, "We'll get back to you."

And of course she never did.

Poor Carol. She basically said: "Hey, my best friend used to sleep with your husband. Wanna do business with me?" And there she was, in first place, goal line in sight, and she stumbled over an old technique. Now I'm not saying that it doesn't work, but too many salespeople have the wrong goals when they encounter buyers. The whole "rapport thing" can really muddle a relationship if one's focus is on some feeble attempt to connect with the other person. This, by the way, is exactly why I have given you the highly valuable Chapter 11, Opening the First Meeting, which gives you three distinct goals at the start of your conversations.

How good are your goals?

This is a tricky place to train. You've hired upbeat, optimistic people and they probably have higher expectations than they'll attain. But that's a good thing. It's lower expectations that are bad. When you have a simple formula that each rep will individually work through, they own the details of their goals. That bears repeating a third time.

> Let the reps work out the details of their daily activity in order to own the behavior needed to attain their goals.

Owning the details, often called "chunking down," helps sales pros in several ways, mostly by having them pre-plan all their daily activities so that they can start work when they get to work each morning. If you feed the numbers, the information to them, the data can lose its power to motivate.

Here's an exercise to see exactly how that works.

EXERCISE 28.4. Committing to Goals

SETUP: Here we want team members to identify and create commitment to specific goals for each workday. This serves the company in a big way—by getting more selling activity from each person in the room.

Let's discuss and then identify what you believe to be reasonable goals for each day of your selling life. This simple activity can help you become significantly more productive, which in turn turns into more income. Write down how many phone calls you should be making each day. Write down how many client or prospect meetings you should be having. Write down which administrative activities you need to do each day (remember *priorities*!).

Trainer: Have them discuss their lists and numbers at their tables. Who's a bit high, perhaps unreasonable? Who's too low? How can they stretch themselves to get more done in a day? Have them write down their final goals and commit to completing them.

If you were looking to revisit standard advice on goal setting, there are benefits to using SMART goals. As you know, that acronym stands for Specific, Measurable, Attainable, Realistic, and Timely. Build that language into your training here, if you choose. It might fit into a single phrase like, "By December 31, 20XX, I will earn $75,000 in commissions above my base salary in order to have enough money to buy that new Lexus hybrid SUV."

This brings us to the other part of goal setting, casting a vision for attaining something beyond work. You earn money to spend on people and places and things. So your reps should have a visual reminder, a picture of that car or that vacation spot posted where they see it regularly—go for it.

The smart thing about a visual reminder is that everyone else who sees it can reinforce the rep's desire to win it by encouraging and asking and pushing the rep to get the prize.

EXERCISE 28.5. Picturing the Prize

SETUP: To talk about "prizes," what reps want to do with the fruits of their labor. Picturing outcomes or goals is key to attaining them.

Trainer: Lead a discussion, asking them to dream of a "prize" and share it with the team. Ask: "What picture should sit in front of you every day?" Urge them to draw a picture, print one out, or take it from a magazine or website.

5. Attitude

A sales rep's attitude is the foundation of his or her interaction with the world. It colors how he or she views prospects, how he or she works with co-workers, and how he or she dialogues with family to start and end each day. An organization can be enervated by great attitudes. In contrast, one sour attitude can spoil a meeting or a day.

One of the finest ways to help your sales pros adopt a healthy attitude is to have them focus on gratitude. To set up teaching for this, share the following story:

Poorly Paid Insects

> *According to an article in* The New Scientist, *an entomologist at Cornell University has worked out that the annual value of insect services in the United States is around US $57 billion. Insect services include crop pollination and land cleaning.*

*This means that, outside the awareness of over three hundred million Americans,
insects are working for the U.S. economy, and not getting paid. And they're doing
it without our permission. So aside from the fact that some scientist at an Ivy
League school probably got paid a few hundred thousand of our tax dollars to do
this speculative research, there's a lesson here for salespeople and it's related to the
theme of being grateful for what others are doing for us.*

Here's the lesson, in a question: "Who is helping in the background?"

*Go beyond the obvious. It's not about the sales assistant or marketing team or anyone
you're closely aligned with in your selling day.*

*Let's make it about the other people with whom you have limited contact who support
you. Internally, it might be accounting/finance and HR people. Externally, it
might be suppliers or the actual manufacturers of the products you sell.*

EXERCISE 25.6. Showing Gratitude

SETUP: A way to focus on gratitude is to start the conversation about attitude.

By yourself, identify who is in the background, contributing to your success.
Don't miss people from the past who've contributed, too. Then thank them.

Send a note, flowers, goodies to eat, something that says "you're important to
me and I want to acknowledge you." Write down the individual(s) and what you'll
do—a phone call, letter, gift. Set a date to complete it, too. Next share with your
tablemates the reason you're grateful.

Trainer: Point out how healthy and uplifting it is to dwell on these relationships.
Tell the team you'd love to hear about responses to the salespeople's experiences
reaching out to people with expressions of gratitude.

Watch energy soar around the office. Listen to the difference it makes when
attitude improves, even for a day. That should give you something to anchor on,
to recognize how valuable an upbeat attitude can be within an organization.

But what about on an ongoing basis? How do you keep attitudes elevated each
day?

One of my favorite training experiences was a day of call coaching with World
Vision. This fundraising organization is recognized as one of the finest charities in

the world, with almost 90 percent of their donations going directly to service the needs of under-resourced people around the planet. Here's some copy from their website at www.worldvision.org/content.nsf/about/why-donate:

> "In addition, we continually strive to keep our overhead rate low. In 2009, 89 percent of our total operating expenses were used for programs that benefit children, families, and communities in need."

Because World Vision keep costs so low, many of the phone callers are students, grads fresh out of school, and part-time workers. So you'd imagine this could be an area where youth and inexperience can seriously affect attitudes. Imagine making forty to sixty phone calls a day and getting rejected constantly—even when calling existing donors. A tough economy is especially hard on fundraisers as well as donors.

I recognized this and built this exercise into the training day at World Vision.

EXERCISE 28.7. Creating Heart and Head Check Self-Tests

SETUP: This is a powerful way for workers to visualize the good things in their lives. Create a simple Heart and Head Check Self-Test.

Trainer: As this sample is based on World Vision, you will want to use your own industry or company to create the self-test and then print out the results for reps.

On a piece of paper, create positive responses to your feelings about . . .

The economy

> *Things are hard now, but people really do have more money than they need. If someone gives up a case of Coke a month, they can help . . .*

Fundraising industry

> *Tough economy is hard on our industry. But fundraisers do good work, helping people who have much less than we do.*

Your company

> *I work for one of the most prestigious, respected, and ethical organizations on the planet and am proud of it!*

EXERCISE 28.7.   Creating Heart and Head Check Self-Tests, Cont'd

Donors' perception about World Vision

> *They trust that 10 cents of every dollar goes to running the organization, while 90 cents helps the people they see on our website and in TV commercials.*

Your office

> *My work environment is bright and easy to work in, with fun employees, newer computers and phones.*

Your boss

> *Larry is easy to work with and really cares about me personally as well as my work role.*

Your job

> *I get to interact with interesting people from all over the country and from all walks of life. It's a cool reflection of God's diverse creation, all experienced on the phone.*

Your self

> *I landed a job here! It's a lot of work and fun, too. Every day I try to contribute a little more than the day before.*

Notice how healthy responses found light at the end of every tunnel. For example, the *fundraising industry* response was about people being served, rather than the tight wallets of today's donors.

Print the responses to your survey, put them by the desks on the walls, and see how uplifting this is for anyone walking into the work area. You just branded healthy attitude inside the company. Reps on the road? They can create and take their lists with them and peek at them often as needed.

Of course, your checklist will be different. It'll refer specifically to your industry (such as financial services), your company (by name), and "buyers'" perception (rather than donors).

Here's something else to try with this exercise. Email the blank document to each of the reps, have them rewrite it for their marriage, for kids, for family, or anyone they connect with. Remember, the best learners become teachers as soon as they come across new knowledge. Have them run this exercise at home or teach other salespeople or entrepreneurs or association and networking colleagues.

So change attitude by focusing on gratitude. And change it forever by giving them printed evidence of all the good they encounter and offer each day.

6. Self-Talk

I'm coaching the base paths on my son's little league team. We have runners on first and third when our batter hits the ball to the pitcher. The boy on the base in front of me breaks for home plate and I yell, "Stop, come back!"

The pitcher turns and stares. There's this big, collective "Oohhh!" from the crowd as parents realize, just as my runner realizes that . . . he's running home from first base!

I have no idea how the little nerve synapses misfired in little Matt's mind, but I do know this—he was heading in the wrong direction and disastrous consequences were about to result. The boy is tagged out sliding into home and walks back to the dugout, fighting back tears.

I waved off his dad, who was walking over from the stands, immediately sat next to Matt and asked him what he said to himself when that happened. This, by the way, is what I recommend everyone do with anyone they care about. Kids, loved ones, friends—ask them what they say, in their heads, when things go poorly. Managing this is HUGE for children's self-esteem. You want to catch it early, with both kids and sales reps.

Matt says, "I really suck at baseball. I can't do anything right." This thinking is pure poison for a kid and sets him up for future failure. My response (and you'll see next how it fits the model for dealing with self-talk) is this: "Matt, you just hit a single to get on base, right? You're one of the team's best fielders. You're fast and everyone loves you as a teammate. Let's look at your experience with baseball in a different way. Can you do that?"

Matt says, "Uh, I did get a hit and I scored twice last game. And mom and dad said I was so good last time, they treated me to three scoops of ice cream afterwards. I guess sometimes I'm good at this."

"Great!" I reply. "Whenever you come to bat or run the bases or field a ball, I want you to say to yourself, (I point to my head) 'I'm great at this game.' You keep saying that, instead of negative things. Can you do that? Let me hear it now."

"I'm great at this game."

"Really, Matt. I believe it. Do you? (he's nodding) Tell me again."

"I'm great at this game."

Strong self-talk can set anyone on a path of encouragement, hope, and positive beliefs about their abilities. For a nice example of this, tied into the baseball story, look at this online video: http://video.answers.com/how-to-play-baseball-positive-self-talk-5149919

This short video shows how to replace negative talk, fear, or hesitation with a simple phrase like the one chosen by all-time-baseball-hitting great Pete Rose: "See the ball, Hit the ball"

EXERCISE 28.8.   Learning to Use Positive Self-Talk

SETUP: Let's talk about self-talk when things go south for salespeople.

On a piece of paper write down what you say in your head immediately when you lose a sale or when something you hoped/expected to have happen does not. Be honest, the exact words.

Example: *I hate when people say "no." Either these prospects are stupid or I can't communicate well enough to persuade them to switch.*

Now, what can you say instead that leads to positive thoughts and upbeat behavior?

Trainer: Ask for feedback and ideas from others at the table, then in the room, and move from person to person for their self-talk examples.

Martin Seligman, father of "positive psychology," has focused on differences in success and performance for optimists versus pessimists. His groundbreaking work *Learned Optimism* (1998) (and later, *Authentic Happiness,* 2004) teaches us that negative thought patterns can really limit our present and future potential in both professional and personal relationships.

I start my training module on this (of course, after a story) by saying, "Today we'll learn to undo what Seligman refers to as 'catastrophic thoughts.' Could someone define that term, please?"

This has huge application for your friends and family, too. So pay close attention, as you'll discover how to work this psychological magic on your kids and others. In fact, I use this when coaching kids in sports. Let's say one of my players (but not my son) strikes out. I immediately sit him down and ask what he said in his head when he was called out. Managing this is HUGE for children's self-esteem. You want to catch it early, with both kids and sales reps.

Fixing negative self-talk requires going through a process whereby we learn to *argue with ourselves*. This makes for memorable and potentially long-lasting learning.

Three Steps to Healthy and Potent Self-Talk

1. The first step is to recognize an idea that resounds in our heads that shows disgust or despair.

   I hate when people say "no." Either these prospects are stupid or I can't communicate well enough to persuade them to switch.

2. Then check it against real evidence or facts.

   These prospects run very successful companies, so they can't really be stupid. And I communicate great at the office, at home, and with the excellent clients I already have.

3. Rewrite your self-talk to show accurate, logical facts that affect your ability to sell, or at least give you a healthy perspective on reality. By arguing this way, you separate beliefs from facts and can mentally rewrite them based on logic and evidence.

The power of positive self-talk. Let all members of your sales team find their voices in determining language to use, in their heads, when they encounter anything—both good and bad—in their selling lives. They'll move quickly past success and failure, whether large or small, and keep working on the next prospect, the next proposal, the next win.

7. Resilience

I opened my mail and there was my Costco Connection *magazine. The one thing I read is a regular column, Debate. It's really a survey on opinions: Are hybrid cars good? Should the government provide healthcare? etc. Each month's letters to the editor contains reader responses to the prior month's Debate topic.*

There it was! My letter to the editor I'd written on last month's column, the topic "email spam."

"Dan Seidman writes: I love reading my spam. How thoroughly entertaining it is to read about:

- *My inheritance of $200 million, which awaits my response to acquire.*

- *My ability, for a few dollars, to increase the size of body parts (some of which, as a male, I don't even possess).*

- *My increase in training skills (this my favorite spam of all time) that would come from attending Effective Strategies for Classroom Behavior Management. The 'expert' trainer had worked in the school system of Mississippi, a state that's ranked forty-sixth in the country. I found this data about the state:*

  - *Overall State Grade: D+*

  - *Chance of Student Success: D+*

  - *School Finance: D+*

  - *K-12 Achievement: F*

"Yes, I want to sit at this expert's feet!

"Spam is good. It distracts me and forces me to slow down, to disconnect from my work. It gives me a needed breather from the pressures of the day."

Now you know the editor saw my email and said something like, "Look at this nutcase; let's print it and see who gets mad at the guy."

Here's the reason I wrote a letter I knew would be published. It wasn't because spam is a good thing. It wasn't because I'm a purveyor of spam. It was because I choose to be optimistic about everything that comes my way (and I saw an opportunity to gain exposure in the magazine, but that'd fall under Chapter 10, Prospecting).

Great sales pros can stay positive throughout anything, and that is a rough definition of the word "resilience." Resilience is a critical characteristic for selling pros. What would you think are some types of thinking and behavior that are evident in resilient people?

Factors That Identify Resilient People

- They move on quickly. (See "Rejection" in this chapter, and Chapter 12 on qualifying and disqualifying.)
- They are flexible (smart) enough to change when necessary.
- They know what their beliefs are and stand by them.
- They have a strong sense of right and wrong.
- They are not swayed by the crowd.
- They remain optimistic.
- They focus on completion of their goals, success—not perfection.
- They are open to criticism, but not necessarily swayed by it. Nor are they hurt by it.
- They rely on the belief in their entire body of work as assurance, not the most recent success or failure.

(An outstanding resource on this topic is Alan Weiss' book *Thrive!* (2009). I highly recommend it. Its content focuses almost solely on coaching the mental part of success, and in the most practical ways.)

EXERCISE 28.9. Checklist for Resilience

SETUP: Let's look at how the team proves itself resilient.

Let's check how we're doing on the idea of resilience. Check the box as it applies to you for each of the factors, then discuss with your table group what you do well and what you struggle with.

Trainer: Make copies of the following form for your group, then create a master for future reference.

EXERCISE 28.9. Checklist for Resilience, Cont'd			
Factors That Identify Resilient People	**I do this**	**Sometimes**	**Never**
You move on quickly.			
You are flexible (smart) enough to change when necessary.			
You know what your beliefs are and stand by them.			
You have a strong sense of right and wrong.			
You are not swayed by the crowd.			
You remain optimistic.			
You focus on completion of your goals, success—not perfection.			
You are open to criticism, but not necessarily swayed by it. You are not hurt by it.			
You rely on the belief in your entire body of work as assurance, not the most recent success or failure.			

Resilient behavior ties in tightly to self-talk. If you need to create written language to support your desire for more resilient behavior, write down your self-talk. Get feedback and ideas about language choices from your tablemates.

8. Procrastination

"My mother, from time to time, puts on her wedding dress. Not because she's sentimental. She just gets really far behind in her laundry."

—Comedian Brian Kiley

Research shows that procrastinators are bad decision-makers, bad planners, and, as our comedian might note, they could smell bad as well. Many sales pros put off tasks they find difficult or distasteful (like paperwork!). Perhaps they lack confidence in completing some activities. They are attracted to bright, shiny objects—that is, they are easily distracted.

Teach your reps to follow a system for blocking out daily activities and to stick to it. Crafting a daily list of priorities is key, so get back and revisit that section, if you need to.

Every sales executive should explain that procrastination is completely unacceptable in his or her organization. You have a commitment to the company to accomplish your sales activities and generate as much money for yourself and the firm as possible. Procrastinators never discover their true potential, because they never give a full day's work back to their employers.

Bottom line: Procrastination creates big problems for a company, and slow-to-respond reps can send a bad impression to buyers as well. Post this sign in the office for all sales team members to see:

9. Optimism

Long ago someone told me that I should hang out with positive people. Now he might have given that advice because he thought I was deficient in positive attitude and it might rub off, or it was simply good advice.

But you know this from experience. Not a lot of new learning is going to convince you of the value of optimism. Here's my summary of some data from Dr. Martin Seligman's (2004) research that you'll find interesting and worth sharing with the team:

- Optimists significantly outperform pessimists.
- Optimists and pessimists look at similar experiences and come to different conclusions.
    - Good experience? Optimists look at it as a permanent indication of what they get and deserve. Pessimists, however, see good things as temporary or lucky.

- Bad experience? Optimists look at it as a temporary condition. Pessimists, in contrast, see bad things as indicative of their permanent state.

- Optimism can be learned. (See the self-talk section of this chapter on adjusting negative thinking to positive by "arguing with yourself.")

Note: Pessimism isn't all bad; the ability to anticipate negative things will help us respond better to objections. Pessimism will help predict some problems we need to be aware of and respond to ahead of time. You just want the main focus of your selling pros' thoughts to be optimistic.

Here are three key elements to teach selling pros to generate optimism in their daily lives:

1. *Choose to compliment rather than complain.* Focus on the good that can be found and, as you do that more, you'll do it more easily.

2. *Hang out with positive people.* Eliminate negative influences in your life. This is tough. It might even mean walking away from long-term relationships that are so hard on you that they poison your mind and your words; they darkly color your days. Assess who in your life looks at the bright side and spend more time with him or her. It might even mean spending more time with small children who don't know anything more than joy, playfulness, and happiness.

3. *Recognize that your job is to build others up.* Leave them in a better place than you found them, even if they don't buy! Even if they're not work relationships. This advice is as organic as it gets. Practice it at home and on the job.

Share these three ideas with your team and see what a difference it makes fairly quickly.

One way I've trained reps to start their day optimistically is to tell them this: *Don't listen to radio news on the way to work.* News by nature is negative. Fill your mind with upbeat, healthy things. Listen instead to music you love, or to a great audio recording of a favorite book or selling ideas. But use that time to prepare for the day in a healthy way.

You can also post positive quotes around the office or send them by email. Try to avoid, by the way, the common ones like "light at the end of the tunnel," "the glass is half full," or "every cloud has a silver lining." You can Google and find more positive quotes than you'll ever use.

You'll think of other things.

Optimism—it's a great way to create an upbeat atmosphere and lift company morale.

EXERCISE 28.10. Checking Your Optimism

SETUP: Here's a quick check on some basic optimism principles for sales reps.

Let's look at how you do on three positive suggestions to help you become a more optimistic sales pro.

Trainer: Have your sales pros quickly check off this list and get feedback from the team as to the accuracy of their perceptions.

Optimistic?	I do	Sometimes	Never
Choose to compliment rather than complain			
Hang out with positive people			
Recognize that my job is to build others up			

---

10. Ethics

I'm not mentioning the man's name here, as he's still a respected and fairly powerful Chicago businessman. But I worked for this shrewd man years ago when one day there was quite a buzz about the office.

Our biggest competitor was coming in to discuss merging. The competitor was an entrepreneur, one of the first companies into our market, our "space." He wasn't too sophisticated a businessperson and was clearly outmatched by our firm's growing sales team and well-funded company.

Hours later, the man was gone and our owner called a sales meeting. We sat around the boardroom as he stood, unsmiling, a stack of papers in his hands.

"This is a list of Mr. X's clients." He tossed the papers onto the table. "Get after them, right now." Evidently, the merger wasn't necessary.

> *I refused to work on leads, claiming I was too busy with hot prospects to start on some fresh ones. In reality, I was embarrassed to be put in that place where I had to make an ethical decision about my job. And I suddenly wasn't confident enough in my successful selling role to directly challenge the integrity of our executive order.*

World-renowned philosopher Vincent van Gogh once said, "Conscience is a man's compass." Okay, he was a painter, but he probably had plenty of time to think while he was staring at blank canvas. Let's address our moral compasses.

This brief treatise on ethics has been expanded masterfully in the next chapter, where you will find Brian Lambert's thinking on the topic. So I encourage you to read what is presented here now and decide later how and with whom you can create a basis for ethical sales decision making and behavior for your firm.

And yes, mental health is concerned with ethics. Everything about ethics is founded in the principle that decisions are pre-made. What better place to train on ethics than *before* our sales pros meet their buyers? This is a constant process, identifying throughout your selling day which behaviors are both healthy and ethical. From your pre-work through your debriefing, you want to make sure that all your questions, comments, and activities are beyond reproach. For example, you don't exaggerate the value of your solutions by quantifying them with numbers that are not realistic.

Ethics begins by identifying what is right and what is wrong. This moral basis for how people treat one another is formalized in society by the creation of rules and laws. An ethical decision-maker not only knows what's right, but he or she chooses to do the right thing as well.

It would serve your organization well to identify ethics as a business discipline, to require every person on staff to abide by the company's ethical standards or code of conduct. Some reasons for this are listed below.

Five Reasons to Have a Code of Conduct

1. It ensures a good image in the marketplace.
2. It helps staff people hold one another accountable for proper behavior.
3. It keeps corporate policies "legal" by seeing that the firm's actions follow guidelines related to hiring practices, sales strategies, management policies, and more.

4. It aids employees in decision making by setting boundaries for acceptable behavior.

5. It sets values as a positive focus, rather than stressing the negative consequences of misbehavior.

The good code of conduct covers behavior related to many things, including dress code, discrimination, respecting company secrets, and more.

The following six pillars of character provide a good foundation around which you can wrap your company's policies:

1. *Trustworthiness:* honesty, integrity, promise-keeping, loyalty

2. *Respect:* autonomy, privacy, dignity, courtesy, tolerance, acceptance

3. *Responsibility:* accountability, pursuit of excellence

4. *Caring:* compassion, consideration, giving, sharing, kindness, loving

5. *Justice and fairness:* procedural fairness, impartiality, consistency, equity, equality, due process

6. *Civic virtue and citizenship:* law-abiding, community service, protection of environment

   Source: from the "Six Pillars of Character" developed by The Josephson Institute, http://charactercounts.org/sixpillars.html.

Notice how some of these ethical standards cover actions that might be voluntary by nature (community service, giving, sharing, compassion). I believe this is a key to sales professionals, who need to understand that they serve their marketplace and their buyers, even when those buyers do not become clients.

EXERCISE 28.11. Questioning Ethical Standards

SETUP: This is more food for thought than an exercise, but it's good to get your sales team thinking about ethical approaches to work and life itself.

Trainer: Ask them to answer the following two-part question honestly and share with partners:

Are you sensitive enough to ethical issues that you're bothered by decisions related to them? Or has your conscience been battered about and

EXERCISE 28.11.   Questioning Ethical Standards, Cont'd

compromised so much over time that you shut off the switch in your brain and heart that says, "Stop!"

If you thought too long about this, you probably answered "yes" to the second part. Find an accountability partner or mentor to create healthy checks and balances for your business dealings.

The chapter that follows is a comprehensive study on developing an ethical framework for your organization's sales team. It includes a contract you can adapt for each individual to sign.

Chapter 29

Ethics for Sales Pros*

*A major portion of the material in this chapter was written by Brian Lambert for inclusion in this work and is used with his permission.

The Company Ethical Code
Ethical Challenges and Case Studies
  Introduction
  Scenario 1
  Scenario 2
  Scenario 3
  Scenario 4
  Scenario 5

The information in this chapter, which comes largely from Brian Lambert, can help your organization create a structured and powerful approach to ethical behavior in the marketplace. The information needs to be studied, then handed off to someone else who can create your own ethical framework. If the details here read like a graduate-level manuscript, it's also a work of art, as these are all the elements of Brian Lambert's "Ethics for Sales Professionals."

> *First grade and I'm walking to school with my twin brother (back when you could be six and walk to school). As we pass the little local grocery store, the owner isn't in sight. Somehow this makes each of the bananas on the cart outside much riper and bigger. So I grab one and, with a jerk of my arm and a twist of my skinny little wrist, a perfect banana snaps off into my hand.*

> *I remember taking three strides; one . . . two . . . three . . . when a monstrously strong hand slams into my back, crushes my shirt as it grabs a fistful of cotton, and jerks me around. I stare wide-eyed and terrified at the store owner, who snatches the banana back with his free hand.*

> *My brother reveals the instincts of a tightly knit family (after all, we're twins) and sprints away in the direction of the school. I'm left alone with this huge man. I later remember being relieved that I'd used the bathroom right before we left the house.*

> *"We're going home to tell your mother what you've done."*

> *And I bolt, too. Lunging away from his grip, I don't head toward school, but back to my house, where my mother is surprised to see me walk in the door.*

"I don't feel well, Mom." This is totally true as the stomach acid sizzles inside my gut.

I spend a sick day away from school. Today, I look back at my crime and realize that, as a kid, I didn't even rationalize my behavior with things like, "It's only one banana" or "He makes plenty of money and won't miss the three cents."

I knew what I did was wrong.

Don't you wish corporate misbehavior was so clearly and easily defined?

The material in this chapter, provided by Brian Lambert, is critical for sales organizations because it gives overwhelming evidence and a detailed structure for the need to develop your own ethics statement. And you should consider creating an ethics contract for each of your reps to sign as well.

The content that follows is as solid a foundation as you'll ever find on the concept of ethics and its specific application to selling. It was developed by Dr. Brian Lambert of Forrester Research. Brian is one of the few people on the planet who have studied professional selling at the Ph.D. level and also been a bag-carrying salesperson and sales manager. He has worked to advance the status of the sales profession for more than fifteen years. (More about him at the end of the chapter.)

I met Brian when he founded the international competencies organization, UPSA. The United Professional Sales Association was his vision for creating standards of excellence for sales professionals around the planet. I was honored to serve on the board of this prestigious organization until it was merged into ASTD, the American Society for Training and Development (www.ASTD.org).

Brian developed this work on ethics in 1999, prior to attaining his Ph.D. based on his extensive research on our sales profession.

The Need for an Ethical Selling Framework

Salespeople must continue to be proud of their role as the revenue generation engine of the company, and the revenue generation engine for the country in which they reside. In fact, the global economy would surely fail if companies could not sell their goods and services to each other. But the absence of an ethical code in what could arguably be called the world's oldest profession has been detrimental to the growth and acceptance of salespeople as true professionals. The role of the sales profession in global commerce requires an embracing of an ethical code—voluntarily.

Corporations, by charter, are designed to last forever. To attain their objectives, corporations have multiple relationships. It is important to remember that corporations do not buy or sell their solutions. People buy or sell solutions on behalf of companies. There is a human element to corporations, and with that human element comes the ability to make mistakes. Most business people understand that the potential for revenue generation depends on:

- Customers with needs

- The size of the target market

- The ability to persuade

Large firms such as HP, Procter & Gamble, IBM, and Coca-Cola will probably be around one hundred years from today. Therefore, it is not good business for people to hurt their companies in any manner. But many people have done just that in recent years by hurting the very source of their revenue—the customer. A smart business will help all customer-facing professionals remember to not lie to or cheat the customer. More importantly, a smart business will hold their employees (all their employees) accountable to this charge if only for the very reason that the press becomes enamored by stories about corporate dishonesty (aka people dishonesty). In recent years, the business world has been rocked by a handful of individuals who have brought a premature end to their businesses through unethical behavior. These include:

- Enron

- WorldCom

- Arthur Andersen

Does a business need to end in order for a dishonest action to be deemed bad? The answer to that lies in the hundreds of business examples where dishonesty, impropriety, or scandal have rocked the business enough to hurt customers, shareholders, or other key stakeholders. Some recent examples include:

- Ogilvy & Mather over-billing the government's Office of National Drug Control

- Five bankers fired from Barclay's of London for spending $62,200 on dinner—for themselves

- The CEO of Savvis Communication totaling up a six-figure strip club bill and paying for it on a corporate credit card, and then refusing to pay for it

What is going on in these situations? Perhaps people don't know about or don't care about business standards or ethics, or perhaps people are greedy. A better question would be: "Why do good people go along with unethical behavior in the first place?" Perhaps they believe that "no one will know" or they believe that if the person acting in this manner stops, then someone else will surely pick up where he or she left off.

A Definition of Ethics

To properly frame the discussion of sales ethics, let us first establish a definition of ethics in the broader, non-professional sense.

> *eth·ics*—*plural noun* (1) (*used with a singular or plural verb*) a system of moral principles: the *ethics* of a culture. (2) the rules of conduct recognized
>
> in respect to a particular class of human actions or a particular group, culture, etc.: medical ethics; Christian ethics. (3) moral principles, as of an individual (His *ethics* forbade betrayal of a confidence). (4) (*usually used with a singular verb*) that branch of philosophy dealing with values relating to human conduct, with respect to the rightness and wrongness of certain actions and to the goodness and badness of the motives and ends of such actions.
>
> *eth·i·cal*—*adjective* (1) pertaining to or dealing with morals or the principles of morality; pertaining to right and wrong in conduct. (2) being in accordance with the rules or standards for right conduct or practice, esp. the standards of a profession. (It was not considered *ethical* for physicians to advertise.)

As you can see, there is a strong connection between ethics and the concept of right and wrong, or morality. Even when focused through the lens of professional ethics, the dictionary definitions focus on rules and standards.

As we have discussed earlier, the sales professional is frequently asked to weigh whose rules and standards should take precedence in a given situation. Regardless of the existence of true ethical challenges, the requirement to decide whose best interest to act in occurs in sales situations every day.

If we give the client a break on the price to help him or her stay under budget, are we harming the company we work for by denying them maximum revenue? In the same scenario, are we harming ourselves and our families by reducing the amount of commission we will make? It is the need to make these decisions on a regular basis, and the apparent flexibility in which salespeople make those decisions, that helps contribute to the perception that salespeople are unethical.

Assuming the definitions above are accurate, what are the behaviors that some salespeople exhibit that perpetuate the belief that our profession is unethical?

Non-Buyer-Oriented Behavior

- Pushy
- Hard sell
- Fast-talking
- High pressure

Deceptive Behavior

- Exaggerate
- Withhold information
- Deceive with half-truths
- Bluff

Illegal Behavior

- Misuse company assets
- Defraud
- Con
- Coerce

None of these items is unique to salespeople or required by our profession to perform our job functions or be successful. It would be fair to say that these traits exist in individuals all over the world, regardless of profession. It is only logical then to draw the conclusion that it is the combination of the frequency that ethical issues arise for sales professionals and the public-facing nature of our jobs, which leads to the high level of perceived unethical behavior.

Why Sales Ethics Are Important

Ethics are standards of conduct and moral judgment. In other words, it is the system or code or morals of a particular profession. The sales profession is as demanding as any other profession, perhaps even more demanding. Like other professions, selling has its unique requirements—the knowledge, attitudes, skills, and habits that an individual must acquire to achieve superior performance. All of these attributes require an ethical and moral foundation. Unfortunately, criminals typically rationalize their behavior with the last action they took instead of analyzing the entire situation.

There are many reasons why a person in business may act unethically, including:

- A strong tendency to bow to authority and follow orders: "I'm just following orders." Anyone who gives up individual free will and autonomy and turns his or her conscience over to someone else is not a professional.

- A strong tendency to do what peer group does—social pressure and conformity: "Everyone does it." Anyone who gives up free will and autonomy and hands over individuality to a crowd is not a professional.

- An absence of clearly defined and communicated standards: "Nobody told me." Organizations must create and communicate ethical standards to trump the "nobody told me" cop-out. A professional knows and understands what he or she is supposed to do—no excuses.

- Rewards to salespeople often unwittingly reinforce doing the wrong thing:
  - Compensation systems often reward getting orders regardless of what is best for customers.

- Contests often reward non-customer-centric behavior.

- Bonuses for making budgets regardless of what is reasonable.

- CFOs or top management sometimes recommend accounting practices that *preserve a company's assets.* Too often they have the wrong assets in mind.

- A company's and a salesperson's most precious asset is an excellent reputation. Protect this reputation by always doing the right thing.

The Case for an Ethical Code

It is because of the very existence of the above-mentioned climate that a clearly defined and publicly available ethical code is essential to the future of sales as a profession. Ethical challenges will arise. Salespeople require the resources and training to handle them when they occur. Additionally, a clearly articulated ethical code allows the profession and its standard bearers (corporate human resources) to single out as rarities, and take action against, violators of the ethical code. The punitive function is present in the other major professions in the world, and the fear of action often keeps representatives focused on the ethical implications of their actions.

Furthermore, salespeople are often left on an island with little or no immediate supervision or readily available checks and balances. Decisions are often made in the field with little time for reflection or to contemplate the long-term effects of each of the hundreds of decisions a salesperson makes each day. An easily referenced ethical code becomes one of the many tools a top-level salesperson can use to guide his or actions to ensure consistency, honesty, and fairness in dealing with clients and potential customers.

Now more than ever is the time to follow Peter Drucker's sage advice:

"It is more important to do the right thing than to do things right."

Areas of Responsibility in Selling

As previously mentioned, the buying-selling process, by its very nature, provides a multitude of opportunities for ethical challenges. Generally speaking, there are five areas of ethical responsibility in the selling context.

Responsibility to End-Users

- End-users are the individuals who use the product or services.
- In some businesses (retail, utilities, transportation, for example), the purchaser and the consumer are the same.
- In other businesses (media, advertising) they are different.
- Audience/readers/subscribers = end-user.
- Advertisers = purchaser.
- Put end-users first.
- Don't lie to them.
- Don't sell them shoddy products.
- Don't sell unsafe products.
- Don't accept advertising for products you wouldn't recommend to a relative.

Responsibility to Their Consciences

- Doing what's right according to one's own moral standards.
- "There is no pillow as soft as a clear conscience."
- Doing the right thing increases self-esteem, self-image, and self-confidence.
- Greed is a cancer that will kill a person's and a company's reputation and eventually kill the organism.
- Their own reputation and the reputation of the company
- Some people are unethical because they believe they won't get caught, but they are playing an ethical lottery with the odds of losing extremely high.
- Doing the right thing every business day is the only sure way of not getting caught and of maintaining a reputation and the self-esteem that goes along with it.

Responsibility to Their Purchasers

- Purchasers typically don't buy from people and companies they don't trust.
- "Under-promise and over-deliver."

- Don't sell purchasers:
  - Something they don't need
  - Something they can't afford
  - Something that doesn't work
- Don't market or sell in a manner:
  - That is in bad taste
  - That hurts a customer's image
  - That is misleading
- Salespeople should not:
  - Give kickbacks
  - Use bait-and-switch tactics
  - Let customers feel like they lost a negotiation
  - Reveal information before it's supposed to be released
  - Give competitive information before a product launch
- Salespeople should not:

  - Promise what the product cannot deliver
  - Promise what the company cannot deliver
  - Promise results, as there are too many uncontrollable factors
  - Promise something they can't deliver:
    - Promotions
    - Merchandising
    - Tickets
    - Position
  - Placements

Responsibility to the Community
- This means the global community, the world community, society
- "Do no harm"

- To maintain faith in the free-market system
- Investors, regulators, general public
- "Suppose everybody in business did this?"
- An industry community
- The advertising-supported media
- Americans get their news and often their values, beliefs, and attitudes from the media
- The media altered people's view of the world and their prejudices because they were free of government and special-interest group control
- Salespeople have a responsibility to keep the media free by fueling it with advertising
- Protecting democracy
- A local community
- Don't foul your nest or cheat your neighbor
- Broadcasters get licenses to serve the community

Responsibility to Their Companies

- Salespeople represent their companies to advertisers
- Especially with intangible products, a salesperson is the surrogate for the product
- The salesperson is the company in the eyes of a customer
- A company's credibility depends on the salesperson's credibility

Named Stakeholders in the Selling Context

Numerous stakeholders have a vested interest in the impact of the company commerce cycle. A stakeholder is any individual, group, or organization that will have a significant impact on, or will be significantly impacted by, the competency level of a salesperson. Sales professionals serve multiple stakeholders, such as the buyer, the buying organization, the selling organization and its employees, colleagues, the global economy, etc. A well-implemented selling model will serve all of its stakeholders. Good selling models and methodologies also address morality and ethics when dealing with stakeholders, especially in the buying and selling relationship. The company serves four types of sales stakeholders:

- *Absolute*—Stakeholders who are held the most accountable for the success and failure of the sales professional or who have the most to lose or gain by their success or failure (including themselves and/or their families). Absolute stakeholders are always the "highest ranking" people the sales professional must answer to.

- *Indirect*—Stakeholders who are affected by the sales professional's performance and who support the sale by providing the product or service once it is sold. Indirect stakeholders (such as customer service, production, and R&D) help create loyal customers by servicing them after the sale as well as creating products and services that work as promised.

- *Direct*—Stakeholders who interact with the sales professional daily as well as those who are directly tied to the sales professional's success in competitively positioning the selling organization in the buyer/seller relationship. They are often the closest stakeholders to the sales professional in their work environment.

- *Limited*—Stakeholders who are affected by the sales professional's abilities, but only after several layers of removal from the point of sale. Limited stakeholders such as the global economy and society at large are often affected by the cumulative effect of the entire sales profession.

These stakeholders exist within the context and environment of selling as well as within a local or global economy (depending on the organization), as shown in Figure 29.1. As such, each stakeholder has a different political and technological view of the world; therefore, political interaction is concerned with the interaction between sales stakeholders. The technology could be IT, special written documentation, or other proprietary information and knowledge.

Figure 29.1. Stakeholders of the Sales Process

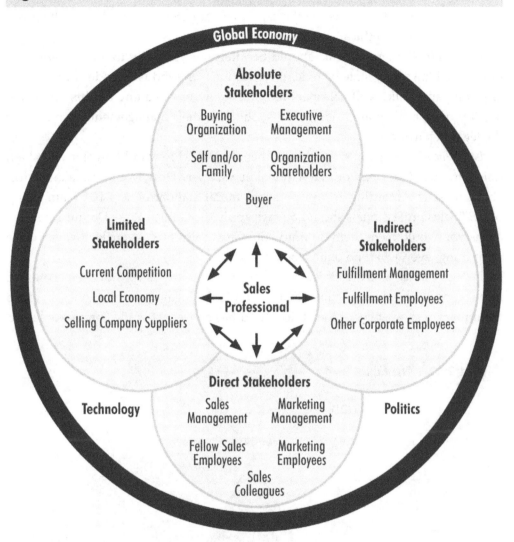

Source: Brian Lambert. Used with permission.

The Ethics Triad®

The ethics triad is defined as the three-part test of determining whether the given decision or action is ethical, shown in Figure 29.2.

Is it legal? The term "legal" should be interpreted broadly to include any civil or criminal laws, any state or federal regulations, any industry codes of ethics, or any company policies. If salespeople don't know or have any doubts about the legality of what they are doing, they should ask their management team and/or the legal department.

Is it ethical? Salespeople should ask themselves: "How would I feel if what I am doing appeared on CNN or in a national newspaper? How would it make me feel about myself? According to my personal moral standards, is what I am doing okay?" Sales professionals should always apply the Golden Rule: Do unto customers as you would have them do unto you. Great sales professionals always do the right thing, even when no one is looking.

Is it economical? A truly ethical salesperson must always consider the economic implications of his or her actions in addition to the legal and ethical ones, because the impact of this aspect of the ethical triad has an impact at the commerce level.

Figure 29.2. The Ethics Triad

Source: Brian Lambert. Used with permission.

Salespeople must remember that economic decisions have a domino effect through all the various stakeholders. A decision that makes short-term economic sense may not make sense for the long-term health of the business. An outcome that is economically advantageous to the company may not be so for the client or to the salesperson's livelihood. These types of decisions are complicated, even more so if the financial pressure of hitting a quota or supporting a family are included.

A salesperson should always strive to examine the potential economic implications and, in the event of an ethical question, ensure that any decisions are best for all parties involved without unduly burdening any stakeholder with the brunt of the economic decision.

To shed light on the rationale behind the Ethics Triad, it is sometimes helpful to think of the following questions in relation to a specific selling situation:

- "How would I react if I were the customer?"
- "Would I stake my professional reputation on the decision I make?"
- "Is this legal, ethical, and economically sound?"
- "Who, if anyone, will be hurt by my decision?"
- "Is it fair to all? To both sides, to the consumer, to the salesperson, to the various stakeholders, and to the company?"
- "What if everybody did this?"
- "Would my loved ones be proud of me if they knew what I was about to do?"

Building Trust and Credibility in the Selling Context

Trust is based on one's reputation. Trust comes from your customer's experience with you over time, from knowledge that what you say is true and in his or her best interests. If you want the customer's trust, you have to earn it, because it is built on honesty and an obvious commitment to your customer and the success of his or her business. Since this is the case, this person is relying on you to help him or her achieve some goals. Often, the fate of the person's job will rest in the decision to trust you. From an ethical perspective, then, the establishment of trust between you and your customer precludes any form of dishonesty, even those seemingly harmless white lies used to save face or avoid uncomfortable or embarrassing situations.

Trust develops when a salesperson is seen as:

- A buyer's advocate
  - The extent to which a salesperson values and protects the interests of his or her customers.
  - The salesperson truly cares about the partnership. The salesperson will go to bat for the customer.
- A candid professional
  - The extent to which a salesperson is honest and up-front with others, especially with regard to issues/factors that may impact those others.
  - The salesperson is honest in his or her spoken word. The salesperson's presentation is fair and balanced.
- A dependable colleague
  - The extent to which a salesperson consistently and predictably follows through on commitments he or she makes to others.
  - Buyers can rely on the salesperson. The salesperson keeps his or her promises.
- A likable business partner
  - The extent to which a salesperson's behaviors, actions, and personality are consistent with and/or appreciated by his or her customers.
  - The buyer likes doing business with the salesperson. The buyer likes doing business with the salesperson's company.
- A competent expert
  - The extent to which a salesperson possesses relevant knowledge and capability.
  - The salesperson knows what he or she needs to know.
  - The salesperson and his or her company have the ability and resources to get the job done right.

Credibility comes from performance, not talk. Many people have heard the phrase "actions speak louder than words." This is especially true in selling. To build credibility means possessing and displaying a belief in the selling organization, its products or services, and the way it does business. It means having a thorough knowledge of the solutions a company provides and understanding how to apply that knowledge. It also means displaying a willingness to learn about customers and their unique problems and needs. Credibility comes from a track record of successes and an ability to apply any lessons learned along the way. It's at the heart of true professionalism. Like trust, credibility takes time to build and depends heavily on your professional reputation.

Legal Concerns of Sales Stakeholders

Because of the nature of professional selling, salespeople must understand important elements of good business practices. Most salespeople are charged with negotiating in good faith and are also responsible for representing their own organizations to their buyers. Because of this, salespeople must understand what constitutes an illegal business practice (especially in the United States). U.S. salespeople are subject to U.S. laws such as the Foreign Corrupt Practices Act, which makes it illegal for U.S. companies to pay bribes to foreign officials.

One specific example of illegal business practice is price discrimination. Price discrimination is defined as *a seller giving unjustified special prices, discounts, or services to some customers and not to others.* The Robinson-Patman Act forbids price discrimination in interstate commerce in the United States.

Any differences in price require justification, such as:

- Legitimate differences in the cost of manufacture, sale, or delivery
- Legitimate differences in the quality or nature of the product delivered
- An attempt to meet prices offered by competitors in a market

Price discrimination is an important consideration, but it is not the only consideration salespeople should make. The following actions would also constitute illegal business practice (in the United States):

- *Business defamation:* This occurs when a salesperson makes unfair or untrue statements to customers about a competitor, its products, or its salespeople.

- *Reciprocity:* The special relationship in which two companies agree to buy products from each other.

- *Tying agreements:* When a buyer is required to purchase one product in order to get another product.

- *Conspiracy:* Agreement between competitors before customers are contacted.

- *Collusion:* When competitors work together while the customer is making a purchase decision.

It is important to remember that cultural differences and legal differences depend on the country. Value judgments and laws vary widely across cultures and countries. Salespeople have a responsibility to understand what constitutes acceptable and non-acceptable business practices. These should be discussed internally by the salesperson's management team so there is no confusion.

Some examples of these gray areas include:

- *Lubrication:* Providing small sums of money or gifts, typically made to low-ranking managers or government officials, in countries where these payments are not illegal.

- *Subordination:* Paying larger sums of money to higher-ranking officials to get them to do something that is illegal or to ignore an illegal act.

Gray areas do exist *concerning the right way to conduct business* when selling. One such example is around the area of interfering with competitors. A salesperson should always manage his or her behavior in a way that supports doing business the *right way.* Illegal interference may occur when a salesperson tries to get a customer to break a contract with a competitor by using overly harsh or confrontational language or statements that may not be true (opinions). Another example of this would be tampering with a competitor's product or overtly disrupting a competitor's market research by buying merchandise from their stores.

To reduce the chances of violating laws governing sales practices, salespeople should adopt the following guidelines:

- Be sure that all specific statements about a solution's performance are accurate.

- Be sure that all specific positive statements about performance can be supported by evidence.

- Remind buyers to pay attention to warnings and operating instructions.

- Caution buyers on how the product/service should be used if they are contemplating using product inappropriately.

- Assess a buyer's experience and knowledge and let him or her know of any areas for improvement that would help in the operation or use of the product/service.

- Don't make negative statements about a competitor's product, service, financial condition, or business practices.

A suggested framework for professional ethics is provided below.

Professional Ethics Framework

Introduction

Company employees and contract workers should consider the principles set out in the Ethical Selling Framework (ESF) as the basic principles they should follow when performing their work. In the event of a complaint being made against a representative, failure to comply with the appropriate principle within the ESF will be taken into consideration in deciding whether his or her actions constitute a case of professional misconduct requiring further investigation by the company. Disciplinary proceedings, however, are not restricted to matters set out in the principles.

As individuals engaged in the profession of selling, company employees and contract workers pledge to uphold and abide by the following code of conduct at all times during the pre-contract and post-contract phases.

Company Code of Conduct

- I will maintain high standards of integrity and professional conduct.

- I will accept responsibility for my actions.

- I will continually seek to enhance my professional capabilities.

- I will practice with fairness and honesty.

- I will encourage others in the profession to act in an ethical and professional manner.

The Professional Buyer's Bill of Rights

As a buyer dealing with a representative of the company, you are entitled to the following rights during the pre-contract (pre-sales) phase of our relationship:

1. The Right to Information

    a. I will furnish you information about the product or service in a manner that you request.

2. The Right to a Fair Price

    a. I will make time to work with you and demonstrate my product and services according to your schedule.

3. The Right to the Facts

    a. I will provide you with the benefits and drawbacks of the solution(s) I recommend without exaggeration or withholding.

    b. I will advise you on each product and/or service I sell as it relates to your organization's business requirements, financial capabilities, and usage requirements.

4. The Right to Respect

    a. I will uphold my duties of buyer loyalty, obedience, confidentiality, disclosure, accounting, and due care.

5. The Right to Confer

    a. I will respect your right to obtain advice from others on your buying team as well as others within the company whom you trust.

    b. I agree to help you through the due diligence phase of your purchase by providing requested documentation and buying support (if requested).

6. The Right to Objective Advice

    a. I will make recommendations to you based on your needs as a buyer.

    b. I agree to make every appropriate solution available to you that meets or exceeds your stated needs and wishes and which my organization sells.

    c. I will offer solutions that are within reach of your organization's financial ability and comfort level.

7. The Right to Confidentiality and Disclosure

   a. I will keep information about you and your organization confidential.

   b. I will disclose potential conflicts of interest to all relevant parties.

8. The Right to Professional Competency and Integrity

   a. I will act in accordance to the Ethical Code and Code of Conduct at all times in our buying-selling relationship.

   b. I will do everything I can to make the transaction go as smoothly as possible for you.

9. The Right to Expedient Service

   a. I will return calls and contact requests diligently, and I will keep you informed.

   b. If requested, I will give you a proposal of the actual deliverables and scope of our engagement before you make an offer to purchase it.

10. The Right to Comfort and Confidence

    a. It is my desire that you be comfortable and confident in my ability to serve you at all times.

11. The Right to Exit

    a. Therefore, if you at any time want to cancel this relationship before the contracting phase, I will honor your wishes.

This is my pledge to you as my buyer.

The Company Ethical Code

The ethical code sets out the professional standards expected of a representative; it reflects expected best practices and points out what is not permissible. As it has the force of a company ethics council regulation, its contravention is a disciplinary offense.

It is not practical or possible to establish ethical requirements that apply to all situations and circumstances representatives may encounter. The objectives as well as the fundamental principles of the ethical code are of a general nature and are not intended to be used to solve a representative's ethical problems in a specific case. Representatives should consider the principles set out in the ethical code as the basic principles they should follow when performing their work.

In the event of a complaint being made against a representative, failure to comply with the appropriate principle will be taken into consideration in deciding whether the action constitutes a case of professional misconduct requiring further investigation by the association. Disciplinary proceedings, however, are not restricted to matters set out in the principles. The following pages contain the Company Representative Code of Ethics in its entirety.

Representative Standards of Conduct

1. These ethical standards identify those principles that should be followed by all representatives of the company as set forth in the bylaws of the association. Accordingly, for the purposes of this code and the disciplinary rules, the word "representatives" refers to full- and part-time employees, interns, contract workers, and others who represent the firm's products and services to the marketplace. A representative who contravenes the code may be guilty of professional misconduct or of acting in an unprofessional manner. In that case, a complaint may be made against him/her under the company's disciplinary rules.

2. There are representatives of the company engaged in different aspects of the profession (i.e., customer service, pre-sales, tele-sales, inside sales, outside sales, solution selling, commodity selling, etc.). Some are self-employed either on their own or in partnership; others are employed by affiliated corporations and partnerships. The principal object of these Ethical Standards is to serve as the professional body for those engaged in a wide variety of professional selling disciplines.

3. Throughout these standards, masculine pronouns are intended to refer to members of either gender.

Fundamental Principles Governing Conduct of a Representative of the Company

1. Integrity, which includes:

   a. Avoiding conflict between the individual's private self-interest and that of his/her employer or clients;

b. Serving his/her employer or, where applicable, his/her professional clients, honestly and in good faith;

c. Acting honestly and in good faith toward all those outside his/her own organization (in addition to those mentioned above) who deal with him or her;

d. Fulfilling the duties of trust owed by reason of the actual appointment or appointments held by him/her; and

e. Upholding, in whatever way is appropriate to the sales profession, the standards of integrity and fair dealing required for the honest conduct of business and for the effective functioning of the financial markets in which the representative or his/her employer(s) play a part.

2. Independence in making professional judgments and in giving opinions and statements with the best of intentions—and with the client's or prospect's best interest at heart.

3. Quest for true understanding of the needs, goals, and problems of a client or prospect.

4. Courtesy and consideration to all with whom he has contact in his professional work.

5. Professional competence, which includes:

a. Compliance with the technical and professional standards expected of him not only as a representative of the company, but also by virtue of the seniority and responsibility of his position;

b. Carrying out his duties with reasonable care and skill, particularly where his failure to do so could adversely affect members of the public; persons, including corporate executives, dealing with his employer; or, where applicable, professional clients or prospects;

c. Never prescribing a solution without completing the due diligence effort to fully understand the client or prospect;

d. Confidentiality, which includes refraining from using for his own purpose, or for some other improper purpose, information obtained in the course of his employment or in the performance of his duties, or which he knows to be of a confidential nature; and

   e. Compliance with the codes and rules of other professional bodies to which the representative belongs.

Relationships and Duties

1. A representative who engages in the selling function has duties derived from the fundamental principles set out in the above section, to a number of different classes of people.

   - The first such class is his or her own employer. The nature of the sales professional's employment can breed conflicts of interest, especially when other parties place special trust in the integrity of the sales professional by virtue of his role and professional standing. The representative must avoid misleading those parties not only by misstatements, but also by omitting material information. Where this type of conflict of interest causes difficulty, the representative should seek legal advice or request guidance from the company.

   - Another class of people to whom a duty is owed is members of the public or others likely to read and act on documents the representative prepares for use outside his own organization. Examples are an offer document, a proposal, a disclosure letter, an email, or an article in a newspaper.

   - A third class is represented by corporate executives and other authorizing buying agents and others with whom a representative deals on his employer's behalf in the course of his duties. Here too his professional duty is to honor the trust that such outside parties may reasonably place in him or her as a representative and by virtue of his or her appointment. Whenever this causes conflicts of interest, he or she should ensure that the outside parties understand his or her position clearly, and, if he or she thinks it appropriate to do so, seek legal advice or guidance from the company.

   - A fourth class is his or her fellow employees, and particularly his or her junior staff (if applicable), who look to him or her as a person of professional integrity. Particular care should be emphasized with fellow employees in the customer service, sales management, sales support, marketing, and/or fulfillment or production areas.

2. The duties described in the principles above should be complied with, so far as applicable, by individuals working as sales professionals who are not representative, or others engaged in selling activities, support, or training. All representative of the company must comply with the principles above.

3. Representatives who are employed but who are not engaged in the activities covered by the above will have analogous relationships. They too must conduct themselves in those relationships in accordance with the principles and duties contained in the above paragraphs.

4. Representatives of the company must comply with:

   - The rules of any other profession to which they belong; and

   - The normal standards of a professional in practice, including courtesy toward competitors, care on behalf of their clients' interests, safeguarding clients' proprietary information entrusted to them, and maintaining the respect in which the public holds their profession.

   - In addition, every representative has a professional and collegiate relationship with his fellow representatives.

5. He or she must avoid any impairment of his or her integrity and independence of judgment, especially in the choice of parties to deal with on his or her employer's behalf.

6. He must ensure that his employer is aware of, and has agreed to, any personal business that he may conduct with parties who also conduct or seek to conduct business with his employer, and disclose any benefits thereby received or to be received by him.

7. Representatives not engaged in professional selling should follow the same principles where analogous issues arise.

Ethical Challenges and Case Studies
Introduction
The following section includes ethical challenges based on the real experiences of salespeople all across the United States. They are presented in a format not to suggest a right or wrong answer but to assist the reader in understanding the type

of ethical challenges that salespeople face and the subtleties that often accompany them. Most importantly, readers should always ask themselves "why" they would make a certain decision and balance their thinking against the principles presented in the ethical code, the buyers bill of rights, and the ethical triad discussed earlier in this chapter.

Scenario 1

In the normal course of business a potential customer mentions that your other main competitor is taking him and his wife to the Super Bowl as a guest in their luxury suite. He does not come out and say that you must offer up a similar option, but the implication is clear: His business is for sale to the company who wines and dines him the best.

The deal size is significant; you would clear your quota for the year on this one deal alone. Additionally, this is a big-name client whose name would command respect from other potential clients. While entertaining customers is common practice for your company, outings of that magnitude are far outside the understood limit. Your gut tells you that if it would close the deal your management might approve a significant expenditure.

Based on your understanding of the ethical triad and code of ethics, what would you do?

Additionally, consider the ethical stance of the customer and your competition.

Scenario 2

You are in the last week of the quarter and your sales manager tells you to do what you have to do to close the McClatchkey deal. The company needs the revenue to report earnings and he's authorized you to give the customer a significant discount to close the deal this week.

This is a deal you have spent a lot of time on and have worked particularly hard to win the trust and respect of the decision-maker. Based on your knowledge of the client's timetable, you had not forecast the deal as ready to close until late in the next quarter.

What are some of the ethical considerations you should take into account in deciding your approach to the situation?

Scenario 3

You have just walked out of a great first sales meeting with a prospect. She has provided you with several strong buying signals, and seems ready to choose your solution. This is a surprise given that your service is fairly complex, and usually multiple meetings with various departments are required to ensure adequate resources are available and that the service provides the expected results. Quick close deals have often worked out fine in the end, but there are also potential pitfalls that could pose significant cost and time frame implications in the future.

Should you move immediately to closing the deal? What are the potential ramifications if something does go sour with the deal?

Scenario 4

You are one of two finalists for a high-dollar contract. You know the other competitor and their product well. In your estimation there is no appreciable difference between your two products, as far as this customer's needs are concerned. Your price structure is equivalent to theirs and you know that either company can deliver a solution that would benefit the customer.

Through a friend in the industry, you hear that one of your competitor's top engineers has left the company and is bad mouthing his former employer. While the engineer's departure may or may not affect your competitor's ability to perform, you are confident that if the client knew this information it would swing the deal to you.

Should you share the information with your prospect?

Scenario 5

A fellow salesperson in your company has recently left and joined a competing firm. One day the receptionist transfers a call to you from one of this salesperson's long-term accounts. The receptionist tells you that this person asked for the former representative by name, but wasn't told that he had left. Because your team often answers the phone for each other, you suspect you could just take the order and make a sale. However, if the client knows that the former rep is at a new shop, they will likely seek that firm out due to the relationship they have with the other representative.

How would you handle the situation?

Brian Lambert's content in this chapter is critical for companies as well as the individual who feels the need to set the bar high, in order to avoid ethical breaches in the marketplace. Again, I encourage you to develop your own printed ethical standards and agreement for all members of the sales staff, including support personnel and outside contractors.

Here are some details on Brian.

Brian Lambert is a senior analyst with Forrester Research serving technology sales enablement professionals. He came to Forrester from the American Society for Training and Development (ASTD), where he created content, tools, and resources to help improve salesperson performance within client organizations. Before joining ASTD, Brian founded the United Professional Sales Association, where he led the global effort to define sales competencies and certification programs for high-performing salespeople in complex/consultative selling environments.

Before joining corporate America, Brian was a captain in the United States Air Force, where he served as a logistics officer and director of group training, managing new-hire and ongoing development programs and human performance improvement initiatives.

Brian has authored four books on professional selling, including *World-Class Selling: New Sales Competencies* and *10 Steps to Successful Sales* published by ASTD Press in 2009. His latest book, *Sales Chaos*, was published by Pfeiffer and ASTD early in 2011. He has received winner's circle awards for sales performance and Air Force medals for leadership. In 2006, Brian was recognized by *Sales & Marketing*

Management magazine as one of the most influential people in professional selling. He has a master's of science in human resource and information resource management from Central Michigan University and a Ph.D. in organization and management from Capella University.

You can find Brian Lambert at Forrester Research (blambert@forrester.com), (703) 584-2632; fax: (703) 894-2784; mobile: (703) 447-5865; www.forrester.com/rb/analyst/brian_lambert.

Part Four

Re-Creating Your Training Experience: Key Concerns

You might have purchased this massive book for one of three reasons. You're probably thinking:

1. We need to see whether anything is missing from our existing training program.
2. We know our training isn't as good as it could be, so I found a resource with outstanding strategies and exercises.
3. It looks really great on my bookshelf.

This is where I caution training professionals and sales executives about the dangers of being a "lifelong learner." Remember from the beginning I shared that the focus of training is not just learning, but changed behavior?

This part of the book is designed to drive you to the place where you can see how to redesign your existing training (Chapter 30). It includes a format to do that and it also offers the option to buy other training from the many sources available in the marketplace (Chapter 31). Don't miss some great research and insights on sales contests—from a true authority on that topic (Chapter 32).

You'll want to know, as well, which reps you should be spending a dime on to train (Chapter 33). There's a new Model of Sales Excellence you can use as a resource to help you identify who you should be hiring and training.

You'll see a few things I've listed as missing from the book and why I chose to leave them out (Chapter 34).

Finally, your executive team needs to know about a key, critical trend you can't ignore in our profession (Chapter 35). That is the push in the academic world to get university students to consider sales as a career. There is some unique data here, as well as some organizations you need to connect with.

Please, consider your next step with this content. Design your own call to action. What will you do with what you now know?

Chapter 30

Redesigning Your Existing Sales Training

When I began using the unique content in this book for my clients, I realized my work fit into two categories.

1. Companies that had no formal training (We'll just hire good people)

2. Companies that have "okay" training programs and know there's a better source out there to improve sales team performance

For the first set of clients, I just went in and offered my training. And the good thing about great training is that, when it changes behavior, it is quite obvious to the company that they made a wise decision to bring me in. For example, I'm working with a small client right now. They want to hit $2.5 million in sales for 2011. At this writing we're four months into the year and the company is at $2.3 million. Now I've gone beyond training and am coaching and overseeing the sales team, but the point is that my focal point is changing behavior, not just giving good experiences to the company's salespeople.

For the second set of clients, those that needed changes in their training, I have developed a formal structure to analyze existing training.

You'll find that structure, the CAT Scan Diagnostic Tool, here. The tool covers Content (what this book is about), Architecture (how you design for behavior change, not just learning—the model you'll see here is based on a model that has sold close to $50 million in training product), and Trainer (how good, how great are your sales training professionals?). The Trainer part is the most difficult to analyze, simply because it means I have to observe (live or by video) what trainers' skills are really like. Enjoy the deep insights into the heart of training presented here that really works to improve performance.

The CAT Scan Diagnostic Tool

A senior sales training executive from a major global corporation described his frustration with what he labeled *the sales training game*. "We spent $2 million on a selling system a few years back and our reps won't put it into play. So we're looking to drop another $1.5 million on a new sales training program."

I'm not mentioning the selling system that he's dumping. It's one of the big ones, prestigious, proven, and I know it works.

Can you relate to this scenario? What was really happening here? What was the real problem (or problems) that this company was ignoring—at the cost of millions of precious training dollars?

- Did the classroom content fall short of what that organization needed to increase sales performance? That might mean the wrong knowledge, skills, and attitudes (KSAs) were taught (or neglected) during the training.

- Did the training design bypass continued reinforcement of concepts and skills, so that the learning was not effectively implemented across the sales team? That might reflect how well (or poorly) the training experience was architected by the designer.

- Did the training experience fall short of burning the new knowledge into the brains of the reps? That might reflect on the individual abilities (or lack of them) of the trainers.

Simply put, we as training professionals are in the "before and after" business. If there is not a distinct difference between our attendees' performance prior to and post-training, we have failed. Or to put it another way, sales training is the most easily quantifiable training investment a company can make. Does the sales team adopt and apply the new learning, then increase performance and revenue? Then the training worked. If not, we're back to asking *what really happened* with our training investment.

I created the CAT Scan Diagnostic Tool to give focus to sales executives, managers, and trainers in defining the three key elements related to training that improves rep performance. These are

1. *Content.* Will you include the most critical components to help your sales team increase earnings? Should certain content be given less initial attention, perhaps because that content is not as useful as it was in the past? Are you aligning rep approaches with their buyers' purchasing processes?

2. *Architecture.* Is your training program crafted to enhance learning and acquisition of skills and behavior? Does it include the latest techniques based on what we know now about adult learning skills?

3. *Trainer skills.* Do your trainers have dynamic delivery skills that engage learners to increase adoption and application of the content?

Let's look in detail at each of these components of the model.

Content

"In early January, when a national deep freeze extended even to the Florida Keys, iguanas fell into their natural hibernation-like torpor, and some compassionate Floridians, unaccustomed to seeing iguanas that appeared nearly dead, took them indoors to warm them up, which is a mistake. The owner of the veterinary clinic in Marathon said one 'sweet lady' called him about the five-footer she had dragged inside. 'When it woke up,' said the vet, 'she couldn't understand why it seemed to be coming after her. When they warm up, they go back to being a wild animal.'"

Keynoter (Key West), January 7, 2008

If you facilitate or oversee sales coaching and education, here's a question for you: *What are you dragging into your training house that doesn't belong there?*

Too much of traditional sales training is based on strategies that are no longer as effective as they were in the 1970s and 1980s. You know this is true, too. Prospects have heard all of our closes, and when we offer up some of these common comments, they come across as pre-planned, perhaps even manipulative.

Simply put, today's buyer is better at buying than sellers are at selling.

We need newer techniques. Techniques that work because they are psychologically sound. Techniques that work when a counselor has a patient on a couch. A psychologist and a sales pro both need to accomplish the same thing. They need to *inspire change* in the behavior of those who sit across the desk or on the other end of the phone line.

Selling is about change. How do we create motivation or help our prospects to change? How do we get them to change products, change vendors, change their buying strategies, *change their minds*?

Well, we now know a great deal more about buyers than we knew in the old "blast 'em with features and benefits" days. ("I'm praying one thing on this laundry list of benefits will strike a chord and cause that guy to buy.") Today's sales training professionals recognize that when we discover how a prospect makes decisions, we can align our sales strategy with that decision-making process and increase the chances of closing new business.

But what else *should* you be dragging into your training house that can enhance sales rep performance? There's a garage full of new things that are being built into great training programs. For example, we also know more about health, nutrition, and, more importantly, energy. In fact, with sales teams I've managed or been hired to train, I even teach them how to eat lunch! Think about it. Do you want reps crashing around 2 p.m. every day, tanking productivity and diminishing morale in the office or out in the field?

You can re-visit Chapter 23, Daily Performance Tips, and build a few of the ideas into regular, required practices for your sales team members.

How about storytelling? You loved stories as kids. Every TV show or movie you experience grabs you through the magic of story. You even live your life out in a sequence of stories every day. Sales pros who use stories artfully and intentionally can mesmerize prospects. In fact, the sales call itself is a story of two intersecting people who are made up of various belief systems, career paths, and decision-making strategies. People resonate with stories. They learn and adapt and buy because they gain rapport, together, through stories.

These are just a few of many ideas you can use to truly enhance the sales training content you offer your team. So drag those old, five-foot lizard-like ideas out of the house. Replace them with smart new strategies that increase the quality of your training, the quality of your sales team, and the quality and quantity of your earnings.

Define your top three concerns that can most quickly increase team performance if fixed and that can be covered by sales training.

Do it quickly before your sales continue to hibernate.

Architecture

"My mother, from time to time, puts on her wedding dress. Not because she's sentimental. She just gets really far behind in her laundry."

Comedian Brian Kiley

Training pros (married or not), what do you need to do that you've been putting off?

It just might be re-creating your training experience. An enormous and embarrassing amount of training is based on the ways we learned growing up. That is teachers teaching in school. Talking, talking, talking, and tossing a few questions here and there.

Because so much of success in the selling life is based on dialogues with others, it is critical for a potent sales training program to employ lots of skill-based role play. This is a key method that distinguishes sales training from many other forms of learning. In addition, because each conversation needs to reflect the personality of a rep, exercises must accommodate language choices with which a salesperson is comfortable. This makes mental flexibility a high criteria for the selling pro and the trainer. For example, I often provide a twelve-page document of responses to the pricing objection ("Your price is too high"). Somewhere in those pages, each rep will find words he or she is most comfortable using to move beyond this objection.

I was recently asked to redesign a sales training program for a financial services firm with 350 reps. The trainer (a highly successful rep who was moved into the role) literally spoke for two days straight—and that was the complete training experience!

Now this is a bit extreme. Most of us today are seeing the value of adding some exercises and interactivity to our training. But having a methodology for structuring our content is both a relief and a blessing to training and sales departments that are dissatisfied with the results of their instruction. This trainer, because he didn't transfer learning to the learners, was inundated daily by reps calling from all over the country to ask additional questions and to see whether they might even fly in to shadow him and watch him sell. This represented tons of extra hours of work, simply because the training experience wasn't effective.

Again, we're in the before and after business. We need that change in behavior to get our selling pros going after new business (and closing it), before we go out of business.

The quick and simple six-step process presented here is based on a highly successful model used by Wendy Seidman, former executive director of content development/training for the Willow Creek Association (WCA), one of the largest Christian leadership training organizations in the world. She was the first hire when the WCA was formed, having previously worked with Shell Oil Company in training and development. Wendy has over two decades of quality training experience. Her award-winning training products have been translated into many languages and put into use across the planet. These tools have been validated in the marketplace through $45 to $50 million in sales.

Overall, our purpose remains as clearly and originally stated: We are in the before and after business. And training must help people do something differently as a result of the learning experience. Look at the chart below for the differences between how some companies behave now and how they should behave with regard to training.

How to Develop Training Presentations That Work!	
How Most of Us Approach Training	**How We Should Approach Training**
What am I going to *say*?	What are the participants going **to do**?
How can I make it interesting?	Which activities will have the most impact?
Will I have enough material to fill the time? Or do I have too much material?	Will they accomplish the goal in the time allowed?
Instructor-oriented	Participant-oriented
Knowledge-based	Action-based

Designing Your Training Session

Designing your training session is similar to creating a roadmap. First, you need to know where you're going—the goal. Next, you need to know where you're starting from—the target audience. And finally, you need to give them directions or steps to reach that goal.

The six-step process I'll describe below is just the Design phase from the ADDIE structure (Analyze, Design, Develop, Implement, Evaluate). For more information on ADDIE, look at any resource you've ever browsed on the production of a training experience.

In sales training, it makes the most sense to create the steps to match the selling process your learners will move through to complete a sale. In other words, the training is designed to chronologically match the sales professional's experience finding, conversing with, and closing a buyer (with all your critical content elements laid in between):

1. *Identify the Desired Response/Goal:* What should the participants be able to do when they get back to their jobs? For example, how will the sales rep be able to handle the top six objections he or she encounters with prospects?

2. *Determine the Target Audience:* Who are they? What is their experience with your subject?

3. *List the Steps:* How do you get to the desired response/goal? What's the process or roadmap? List the steps sequentially. They need to be in order.

4. *Identify the Activities:* For each step you listed, what do you want the participants to do in the training session to ensure learning occurs?

5. *Develop the Content:* What information do the participants need to know, feel, and/or experience before they do each activity?

6. *Select the Delivery Method:* Decide which teaching method to use for each step, and write them in a chart like the one earlier.

In addition, your architectural design should include post-training elements to deepen the learning transfer. You're probably familiar with the concept referred to as "spaced repetition" or "intermittent reinforcement." Those are mushy academic words. Let's give it a name with power: trailing impact.

Trailing Impact: Architect Post-Training Elements

Continued reinforcement of the training experience can further transfer learning and embed skills. Reinforcement might include:

- Accountability through coaching or mentoring programs
- Role plays at sales meetings
- Job aids
- Refresher courses
- Creating commitments—in print—to apply learned behaviors
- Webinars or tele-seminars
- Computer-based or email reminders
- Audio reinforcement with CDs or MP3s
- Contests or competitions that immediately follow the sales training experience, which offer a fun and effective way to gain both mental and physical buy-in for the new learning

We are married to this wonderful business. Please don't neglect the real reason a successful relationship thrives. You have to work continually on building into the other person. You build continually into your learners but don't leave them at the altar after your training experience. You stay connected by building trailing impact into the tie that binds—that bond between trainer and learner.

For a sample of this trailing impact experience, visit *The Ultimate Guide to Sales Training* website at www.UltimateGuidetoSalesTraining.com

Trainer

An amateur photographer was invited to a dinner and brought a few photographs.

The host looked at them and commented, "These are very good. You must have an excellent camera."

Later in the evening, as the photographer was leaving, he turned to the host and said, "That was a delicious meal. You must have some excellent pots."

A question for trainers and those who manage them: How great (or not) are your skills in front of an audience of learners? Sales training is not just about the tools, the job aids, participants' guides, the PowerPoint, and the props (that is, the cameras and the cookware). It's also about your ability as a facilitator and communicator (and at times, entertainer). Great sales trainers have persuasive personalities.

We have continually described this learning as a sales training *experience*. When we use the term "experience" it puts responsibility on the trainer to exhibit entertaining and persuasive platform skills, to perform and engage attendees, to enhance and embed the learning. So, just as good training puts attendees out of their comfort zones, trainers themselves can improve personal performance by moving beyond their comfort zones and gaining the platform skills of outstanding actors, speakers, musicians, and comedians.

I was recently consulting with a highly regarded train-the-trainer company that had two major clients you would immediately recognize. This international sales training organization recently realized the value of trainer platform skills and has invested significant money in train-the-trainer work. This is being done just to get their people to give learners a richer experience from the front of the room.

The final piece of our CAT scan diagnostic process is all about two things great trainers do to offer learners a memorable and high-impact experience: (1) they prepare as professionals and (2) they perform as professionals.

Prepare as a Pro

Preparation involves an ongoing investment in your career. When a trainer adopts practices that help make the training experience dynamic, the event is made memorable to learners. Learning is more deeply embedded by replacing boredom with entertaining and engaging moments. This is not about getting silly during a session, but about keeping the experience upbeat, fast-moving, and fun. Here are some key practices for top-notch training performers:

- Do not read your material. Know the content cold.

- Rehearse your presentation. Do this in front of a mirror (to eliminate bad gestures or nervous physical habits), in front of a camera, or in front of a group of peers.

- Chunk down your material to manageable pieces for your practice sessions. This is also the time to add personal stories, appropriate news items, and humor to support your content.

- Write out your transitions from one segment to the next. Transitions form the glue that holds your training experience together. This is neglected far too often by trainers (and designers). Good transitions make for a smooth ride through the training day.

- Know your audience. Review their profiles, if available, to understand experience levels with the content.

- Gather your own personal stories to give concrete examples to the learning. This also lends credibility to the trainer. Sales audiences often walk into a room wondering why they should listen to you. *Note:* If you are a non-salesperson who is training, you have two options: use supporting stories about how salespeople sold you, or interview some sales reps or managers for stories they would use that are relevant to specific training modules. A comment like "Janet Smith, your regional sales manager, told a tale that perfectly supports this point . . ." offers a powerful message that reinforces learning.

- Dress professionally. Your first impression on learners is critical to credibility, so pay close attention to your looks. Biggest problem here? Guys with unpolished shoes.

- Practice smiling.

- Practice vocal exercises. Some focus areas for your voice include developing *strength* and *stamina* for half-day and longer sessions, clear *enunciation* of words, *emphasis* on specific words and phrases, *pausing* after important statements, and *variety* in volume and *emphasis* (to eliminate a boring monotone).

- Do some warm-ups before you practice and before training. A trainer's voice is an instrument that makes him or her money. Take good care of it and it will never let you down.

- Review speakers and entertainers you admire. Late-night talk show hosts have incredible skills connecting with audiences and individuals. Study their gestures, facial expressions, vocal variety, and movement.

- Avoid caffeine and milk products, which stress the throat (up to twenty-four hours prior to training). Sorry, but chocolate falls into both of these no-no categories.

- Know your room and your equipment.

- Critique yourself. Videotape your training sessions: (1) watch the video with sound off and notice gestures and movement; (2) listen to the sound without video to critique your vocal skills.

- Optional, but smart—get acting training privately or at a local university or through coaches with www.nsaonline.org. Get vocal training as well.

- Smile!

Perform as a Pro

Performance is all about your time on the platform. Much of that time you are both an educator and an entertainer. Your "performance" breathes life into the content:

- Smile! When you are enjoying yourself, you set the framework for the whole audience to do so.

- Connect with your audience. Meet and greet attendees as they enter the room.

- Your first two minutes are critical. Open with an insightful observation, a promise, or a humorous anecdote that supports the day's training (for example, "You made a great decision to be in this room today. Just the fact that you're open to new learning means you can adopt what you'll experience and go back to your jobs and use this investment to make more money as sales pros").

- Engage in positive self-talk. ("This is going to be a great experience, for me as well as for my learners.")
- Move! Don't stand in one place. Walk into and connect with your learners, even sit at times.
- Make eye contact constantly. When you are speaking, your eyes should stop on a person for two to five seconds. When someone else is speaking, give him or her your complete attention.
- Smile! (This point is not repeated by accident.)
- Affirm comments and questions. Build learners' contributions into the experience by encouraging interaction (for example, "Great comment! Thank you for sharing that insight with us").
- Breathe.
- Remember to make eye contact for two to five seconds, and Smile!
- Put into play those movements and gestures and facial expressions you've adopted.
- Modulate your voice. Speak as if with a close friend, sometimes quietly with emphasis, sometimes louder with energy.
- Drink lots water.
- Relax and Smile!
- Use WIIFY—What's in it for you. I like this much more than the old WIIFM (what's in it for me).
- Connect constantly with their learning experience by affirming the value of the content. Do this by following a teaching point with a comment like, "So what is the real value of this to you? It's this. . . ."
- Exhibit good posture that shows authority, success, and strength.
- Move forward on points of great importance to the learners.
- Pause, a lot.

- Have fun!

- Be yourself! Banter.

- Read humorous material in order to stimulate your sense of humor. Find places for some funny lines during your program. (Remember your rehearsal time, when you embedded humor in the spot you felt it fit?)

- Smile!

- All that being said and done. . . . Relax, it's not about you. It's about the learners' experience. So be yourself.

Trainers, like all professionals—business, academic, even sports—need to hone their skills to give their audiences the best possible experience while accomplishing their mission to change behavior.

You're not yet done with this . . .

"The mind, once expanded to the dimensions of larger ideas, never returns to its original size."

Oliver Wendell Holmes

It's time for you to cook up the new you. Time to revisit some of the concepts you looked at in this chapter on the CAT Scan Diagnostic Tool. As you think about changes that might be beneficial to your influential role as a senior sales executive, manager, or trainer, you'll want to look at what you can do to give your sales team their best shot at success in the field. Decide that you will set new standards for sales training excellence. Decide to leave a legacy for your organization that will live long beyond your current role.

I'll wrap this learning up just as I end all my training experiences (and keynotes).

Please answer and act on these three quick questions . . .

What did you find interesting, fascinating, useful?

1.

2.

3.

What did you learn about yourself?

Some information here probably affirms that you're already doing things right. Other advice points to concerns that need to be addressed. List here what you learned related to your experience and where you need to grow.

1.

2.

3.

Who will you teach this to?

The best learners teach others immediately after acquiring new knowledge. They realize that by helping those others, a teacher quickly becomes an expert. List here the people you know who would love to hear some ideas, even some you felt were useful from this chapter. After their names, list exactly what you want to share with them, and when you'll do so.

1.

2.

3.

Congratulations on your move toward sales training excellence!

ASTD has an Info-line that supports these concepts—Sales Training that Drives Revenue, available at http://store.astd.org/Default.aspx?tabid=167&ProductId=19830

For more information on how I can help your organization analyze existing sales training, my contact information can be found in About the Author at the end of this book.

Chapter 31

Buy It, Don't Build It

CHAPTER OVERVIEW

Yin and Yang Selling

How Effective Is Your Sales Approach?

    Part 1: Why Companies Do Not Have a Sales Approach

    Part 2: Assessing Your Company's Current Sales Methodology

    Part 3: Assessing the Sales Training Currently Provided to Your Team

---

In this chapter you'll hear from one of the great selling experts on our planet. You'll also find a checklist of pieces of the sales process you might want to use to critique any selling system you choose to buy. Here I'll introduce you to a resource you can use to view plenty of training company choices, all thoroughly critiqued by that expert you're about to meet.

Yin and Yang Selling

I'll never forget answering my phone to hear Dave greet me and say that he'd found a college professor on the West Coast who had "borrowed" all the sales training and business humor content from my website, www.SalesAutopsy.com, placing it on his university website as his own. He had stripped all reference to me off the pages, but had used my meta tags to increase my web traffic to his site. The man was a marketing professor who also taught ethics classes (go figure). A conversation with the dean of the business school led to what I'd imagine were some very uncomfortable conversations. And the problem was resolved.

Who is Dave, this all-seeing, all-knowing sales authority? Dave Stein is more than a good friend. He is also one of the elite—a rare authority on every aspect of the sales training profession. His company, ES Research Group, Inc., was formed to help corporate sales executives make difficult decisions related to *which sales training companies to hire*, which systems might make a perfect match, out of all the choices in existence. In contrast, *The Ultimate Guide to Sales Training* was created to help you *redesign your existing sales training*.

You might call us Dave and Dan, the Yin and Yang of the sales training universe.

Dave agreed to share his model for helping sales executives analyze the sales training decision in this book, because at any time during the life of your company, your team might just switch systems. Perhaps you'll move from your own sales training creation to an existing model like Miller Heiman or Huthwaite or any of the scores of high-quality providers. Or maybe you'll abandon an existing system to craft your own sales training methodology. Either way, this chapter will serve to introduce you to the services Dave Stein and ES Research offer.

What follows is a detailed description of Dave's process by which you can analyze your existing sales training. I encourage you to use this process as a filter through which you can make your sales training decisions.

ES Research Group (ESR) is an amazing resource of intelligence and advice on sales effectiveness, sales productivity, offering technologies, and tools. In addition, they carry comprehensive information on a variety of sales training companies, which is exactly why they serve us well as an alternative to building our own selling methodology. ESR's approach is to align these sales training organizations to best fit the needs of companies seeking to improve sales productivity.

As professional matchmakers between training providers and buyers, ESR gives guidance through an often-confusing array of choices.

How Effective Is Your Sales Approach*

Few companies have the right approach to selling. Some have no approach at all. This is apparent not only from a recent ESR survey, but also from one-on-one interviews with many managers and executives who direct and support sales organizations. In the first part of this special ESR/Insight™ on sales effectiveness, we will examine why companies do not have a sales approach. In the second part, we will provide a checklist that will enable you to make a quick determination of where you stand from a methodology perspective. In the third part, we will do the same for sales training. We expect that this ESR/Insight will provide a solid foundation for a self-appraisal of your current sales methodology/training situation.

Part 1: Why Companies Do Not Have a Sales Approach

In a 2005 survey across a broad sampling of industries, ESR found that 41 percent of respondents did not use any formal, institutionalized sales methodology at all or, alternatively, employed a "style" of selling rather than an institutionalized set of processes. Generic consultative selling and solution selling are some examples. Fourteen percent provided unique names of methodologies that their companies used that no other responded listed. Some of those were actually titles of popular and not-so-popular books about sales. This signals an abundance of opportunity for companies without a formal sales approach (actually companies like that employ many sales approaches—perhaps as many as one for each salesperson), and for the sales training/consulting providers who might have the right solutions to help those companies achieve new levels of sales effectiveness, leading directly to increased and predictable revenue streams.

This survey, as well as a look at the fifteen leading sales training/consulting providers, indicates that there is no prominent leader in the sales training market. Companies that were clear leaders in the past have been acquired or have shrunk in size due to a number of reasons, including losing their best talent, who left to form their own companies. With no market leader, and so many diverse providers all telling a different story, many companies that would invest in sales effectiveness solutions are confused and have become immobilized.

ESR's research shows that only 18 percent of the VPs of sales, HR managers, chief learning officers, and training directors had a formal process for ongoing assessment of their sales training requirements. Even fewer—8 percent within that 18 percent—specifically measured the effectiveness of their sales training initiatives.

That leaves many corporations with sales teams that must fend for themselves whenever a new competitor appears on the scene, when their customers begin buying differently, or if there is a dip in the economy.

Why Companies Do Not Have a Formal Sales Approach

Companies that do not have a rational, funded, and consistent sales approach are usually not rewarded with consistent sales performance. There are many reasons why that may be true, such as having inferior products, those whose price the market will not bear, or company viability issues, to name a few. But there are far too few companies executing at a best-in-class sales effectiveness level. Let us start by looking at why some sales VPs do not invest in what it takes to build and employ even a basic, formal approach. Here are some of the reasons derived from interviews with sales managers and vice presidents:

- Those managers and executives think they do have an approach, but it is not relevant to their current selling environment, not comprehensive enough, or not being used by the people who sell.

- The managers are not process-oriented and therefore believe that processes inherently inhibit productivity, rather than enhance it.

- They do not believe sales training works, since they themselves were never trained to sell as part of a well-founded, comprehensive sales effectiveness strategy.

- They cannot allocate budget for sales consulting or training because they are unable to present a credible business case that includes a target ROI.

- They will not invest in training because they are compensated on operating income, and training is seen as a large expense potentially impacting their bonuses.

- They will not allocate the time to have their salespeople trained, feeling it takes away from selling time.

- They believe they hire top salespeople who do not need training. Anyone who does not make quota is replaced by another top performer, so, sales management concludes, there is no need to train.

- They have no idea how to select or engage with a sales training company and, out of fear of failure, they do nothing.

- They have invested in a CRM system and feel that is all the process their salespeople need.

- Their salespeople tell management that they have been through all the training they need and that it is just a disruption.

Methodology Comes First

ESR believes that the right sales approach has sales training supporting a company's sales methodology and related processes. When companies do decide that sales training is a step in the right direction, they do not always proceed forward for the right reasons, in the right order, or in the right way.

We have found that when companies do select a training company without first building or adopting a sales methodology, they do so because:

- They have no clue on how to go about "building or adopting a sales methodology" and therefore are bringing in a sales training and consulting firm to help them shape one as well as to train their sales force on it.

- They are now facing, or have been facing, obstacles in winning against a specific competitor or group of competitors and they have waited too long to take appropriate action.

- Customer buying patterns have changed and their sales teams have been unable to do what is required to close business. In effect, what worked then does not work now.

- A weakness in their company's product or service cannot be overcome by the salespeople .

- The company is not the lowest priced vendor and finds itself only in price-sensitive deals.

- They feel that training is something that "should" happen, or their salespeople complain that they need training, so they bring in a trainer to fill a day during the annual or quarterly sales meeting.

- They have new products or services to sell and their salespeople are not trained on how to accomplish that.

- Sales forecasts are missed, good sales talent leaves, management no longer has the ability to lead the team in an effective way, so sales training is looked at as the universal elixir—a last-ditch effort to save a dysfunctional organization.

- Sales management feels its people need to be motivated, not necessarily educated, so a trainer is brought in to rally the troops.

How Many Training/Consulting Providers Are Found

When companies do engage with a sales training/consulting provider, our research reveals the following about those companies:

- They engage with a training provider with whom they have worked in the past, even though the company's situation may be very different from what it was in the past.

- They obtain a referral from someone in another company who has engaged a sales training provider, even if the other company's requirements may be very different from their own.

- They hire a company that has the hottest new approach, or a trainer who wrote a book with what is purported to be a solution to what the company believes its problem is.

- They attend a promotional event (webinar, sales leaders' conference, or public training event) and are impressed with the quality and style of the trainer.

- They search the Internet until they find a trainer whose offerings are appealing based on what is represented on the trainer's site.

- They receive a recommendation from a top sales performer from within their group.

As you can see, there are many reasons why sales managers and executives whose responsibility includes building or maintaining a sales methodology and securing appropriate training for their teams either do it the wrong way or do not do it at all. (You can start using the right approach by referring to these ESR/Insight briefs: *An Introduction to Sales Training Requirements Definition and RFPs; Criteria for Evaluating Sales Training/Consulting Solutions (Part A): A Two-Tiered Evaluation Strategy;* and *Leading Sales Training/Consulting Providers—Part A.*)

Part 2: Assessing Your Company's Current Sales Methodology

ESR believes that the right sales approach has sales training supporting a company's sales methodology and related processes. (See ESR/Insight *Is Your Selling Methodology Aligned with Your Customers' Buying Methodology?*)

Understanding that readers represent companies in diverse industries and of different sizes, here is a series of questions that will provide you with a basic understanding of whether your company has an established sales methodology and whether your sales team is effectively employing it.

Your Team

Do you have a documented set of processes and tools that:

- Facilitate your understanding and the recording of the qualifications (skills, traits, past performance, behaviors, etc.) required of any and every person who sells for your company?

- Enable you to consistently find and hire salespeople who consistently deliver?

- Compensate your salespeople fairly while advancing your business goals and objectives in the right direction?

- Motivate your salespeople to perform, work as a team, and do the right things the right way (other than just monetary compensation)?

- Deploy sales and corporate resources optimally and strategically across your portfolio of opportunities?

- Assist you in organizing and managing your team for maximum sales effectiveness?

- Provide metrics to track individual and team performance based on financial considerations as well as required skills development against predetermined skills models?

Demand Management and Generation

Do you have a documented set of processes and tools that:

- Enable your salespeople to identify who their target customers are, by geography, by industry or market segment, by company name, and by job title within those companies or agencies?

- Educate your salespeople with the trends, issues, enablers, and obstacles for their customers' success in those markets?

- "Warm" those targeted customers through effective, ongoing lead generation, branding, and other forms of outbound marketing?

- Provide alternative, proven mechanisms for your salespeople to reach those targeted customers, for example, cold-calling scripts, event marketing, and email campaigns (if that function is not provided by your marketing organization)?

- Provide questions to be asked of their potential customers that will build credibility and at the same time evoke responses revealing customer pain?

- Arm your salespeople with clear, concise, compelling, and differentiated value-oriented messages to be delivered to each key evaluator, recommender, decision-maker, and budget holder within your target customers' organizations?

- Provide your salespeople with the information they need or the tools to obtain information about your target customers and markets?

- Lead your sales team through an ongoing, objective, qualification process, preventing them from pursuing business that is not winnable or not worth investing the time and money into winning?

- Enable your salespeople to easily capture and track the progress of sales opportunities from first contact as well as collect, store, and retrieve critical information about that potential customer and the opportunity?

- Provide guidance to your salespeople regarding how your customers typically buy, step-by-step?

- Provide the ongoing ability to measure progress against hard and soft goals and objectives?

Opportunity Planning and Management

Do you have a documented set of processes and tools that:

- Encourage your salespeople to effectively plan their sales campaigns, including every meeting, presentation, and other event?

- Encourage your people to use the methodology, processes, and tools, since they know that if they do so, their sales performance will be enhanced?

- Provide your salespeople with guidance so they can devise an effective sales strategy based on the unique circumstances of that opportunity?

- Clearly delineate responsibility and ownership (executive management, product marketing, engineering, customer care, etc.) for the many tasks and activities required to pursue an opportunity?

- Enable your salespeople to develop a business case for acquisition of your product or service by your customer, including a credible and accurate ROI if appropriate?
- Continually refresh and dispense a dynamic set of "talking points" for effective management of customer objections?
- Provide live or online, on-demand knowledge-based coaching for salespeople who are facing tough competitors or buyers or other challenging situations?
- Assure that opportunities are being accurately assessed so that management has an ongoing, realistic picture of the sales pipeline and forecast?
- Give your salespeople clear direction, boundaries, and positioning techniques with respect to negotiation of prices, fees, and terms and conditions of sale?
- Smoothly transition a newly acquired customer to your post-sales support team or account executive?
- Provide salespeople who work with existing customers with resources to resolve issues so they can focus on selling?
- Objectively determine the real reasons opportunities are won or lost?
- Provide the ongoing ability to easily and accurately measure progress of an opportunity against the plan?

Ongoing Account Management

Do you have a documented set of processes and tools that:

- Provide you with the ability to accurately assess the potential long-term value of your customers so that your time and resources can be optimally invested and managed?
- Enable your senior account executives, who manage your virtual sales teams (sales, executive management, marketing, customer care, etc.), to build and manage mutually beneficial long-term relationships with your key accounts?
- Provide accurate indicators of customer satisfaction to reduce the likelihood of competitive advancement and expand sales potential?

- Facilitate your ongoing understanding of any potential gaps that exist between the value your customers believe they should be receiving from your products and services and what they are actually receiving?

- Ease communications between customer executives and your executives so that your business plans going forward reflect the future needs of your customers?

Sales Support

Do you have a documented set of processes and tools that:

- Provide your salespeople with the assistance and support they require to efficiently and accurately respond to RFPs (requests for proposals), demonstrate products, design solutions, construct proposals, create presentations, build prototypes, or produce customer references, among other things?

- Support ongoing feedback from sales to marketing regarding customer requirements and the ability of your products and services to meet those requirements?

- Provide a mechanism for salespeople to record what they learn about the competition, so that it can be collected, analyzed, and distributed back to them in a usable fashion?

- Offer salespeople up-to-date, objective information about their competitors' companies, products and services, and sales strategies and tactics, with clear and precise recommendations on how to use that information for competitive advantage?

- Enable communication to and from members of your team about critical issues and news (good and bad) that will impact them, such as wins and losses, and provide suggested positioning statements for use with customers?

Partners

Do you have a documented set of processes and tools that:

- Provide your salespeople with a full understanding of the relationships your company has with business partners and how and when to best gain their cooperation and assistance?

- Allow your salespeople and those of your most important partners to share common terms, process milestones, strategies, and tactics?

Process Improvement

Do you have a documented set of processes and tools that:

- Enable you to monitor progress and adjust your methodology and processes as deficiencies or changes in your selling environment become apparent?

Part 3: Assessing the Sales Training Currently Provided to Your Team

ESR believes that the right sales approach has sales training supporting a company's sales methodology and related processes. (See ESR/Insight *Is Your Selling Methodology Aligned with Your Customers' Buying Methodology?*)

Understanding that our members represent companies in diverse industries and of different sizes, a bit later there is a series of questions that will provide you with a basic understanding of whether your sales team is receiving training that will provide them with the skills and capabilities they need to win.

Again, Your Methodology Comes First

Before we begin any discussion of sales training itself, ask yourself this question: Do you have a formal, documented sales methodology that is relevant to your business situation, designed with your customers' buying methods in mind, and supported by processes and tools?

If the answer is no, we recommend that you stop any training initiatives at this point and design or adapt a sales methodology. If you commence or continue training your salespeople at this point, you will most likely be wasting your money.

Sales Training Supports Compliance with Your Methodology

If you do have a sales methodology in place, the main purpose of sales training is to support and encourage the use of that methodology. For example, a qualification process should be a component of your methodology. That process should provide your people with the qualification criteria appropriate to your selling environment. You may delineate your selling process into four phases. For each phase there should be qualifiers that must be met in order for your salespeople to continue pursuing that opportunity. When all criteria are met in one phase, the opportunity progresses to the next phase. When all the criteria in the final phase have been met, one would expect that your company will have been selected, or a contract will have been signed.

To further this example, the qualification module of an effective sales training program would:

- Present the qualification process to the participants.

- Provide explanations of why it is necessary.

- Provide examples of situations in which the criteria were met and those in which they were not met.

- Provide the salespeople with what information needs to be obtained to determine whether a criterion has been met.

- Provide real-life examples of how salespeople in the past have obtained that information.

- Provide the opportunity, through a workshop or role playing, for the salespeople to practice the skills they just learned.

- Provide the capability for management for post-program follow-up to make sure the salespeople are employing those skills.

- Provide a method for tracking improvement in qualification across the team as well as for individual salespeople resulting from the training.

- Provide a mechanism for ongoing improvement of the qualification process itself through feedback from the field. (This is more a process function than a training function, but it does need to be mentioned.)

With that being said, it is important that the type of training you provide your salespeople is appropriate to their needs. In our ESR/Insight brief, *Not All Sales Training Programs Are Created Equal: A Guide to Understanding the Type of Sales Training Your Salespeople Need*, we delve into the five types of training that are appropriate for different requirements:

1. Basic Selling Skills
2. Advanced Selling Skills

3. Opportunity Management Education

4. Account Management Education

5. Sales Management Education

Let's look a bit more deeply into whether your salespeople are getting the right training.

First, at the Highest Level

- Does your sales methodology dictate the content of your training or is the reverse the case? The framework of your training programs should support the understanding and use of the sales approach that has been defined and implemented through your sales methodology. You do not want training that is in contention with your methodology, either in concept, terminology, or practice.

- Are the objectives of the training you provide based upon development of specific skills that have been identified as weaknesses among the sales team, either through independent assessment or formalized performance reviews, or do they address new skills they must learn in order to sell effectively?

- Answer these questions: What precisely will your salespeople be able to do at the conclusion of the training program? and What impact will that have on your business?

- Is the training strategic? To put it simply, do you know the next three training events you will be holding, what will be taught and accomplished, and when those will take place?

- Have you benchmarked current performance in the area(s) where training is being targeted? Are there metrics in place that will enable you to readily measure the return on that training investment?

- Is sales and executive management educated about and supportive of the training that is taking place? Do they participate? Do they adhere to the processes that constitute your sales methodology?

- Has tailoring (minor adjustments) or customization (considerable modification to meet the specific needs of the audience) been done to tune the training to your requirements?

- Have you carefully selected a training provider based on your specific requirements?

Next Take a Look at the Program Itself. Here Are Just a Few Questions

- Are the objectives of your programs clear to you and the participants?
- Do the participants know what is expected of them coming into the programs?
- Are there pre-program assignments that prepare the participants and enable them to bring value to the program?
- Is the post-program follow-up designed to support, reinforce, and measure?
- Are the programs the appropriate length to meet your requirements? For example, a one-hour program covering opportunity planning is inadequate for sales teams selling $100 million outsourcing solutions.
- Has the program been designed with enough interactivity for thoughts to be provoked, questions to be answered, and experience of the participants to be leveraged?
- Has the program been designed using established educational design standards?
- Does your program have an equal balance of "what to do" as well as "how to do it"? Many programs ESR has reviewed contain an over-balance of the former. Even experienced salespeople need examples of how to execute what it is you are requiring them to do and practice in doing it.

About the Instructor

- Is the instructor effective? Are instructors credible in front of your team? This applies to internally as well as externally sourced instructors.
- Does the instructor understand the different ways people learn and incorporate these into their style of program delivery?
- Does the instructor maintain momentum throughout the program so that he or she keeps the attention of the participants and maximizes the impact?

- Does the instructor use real-life examples that the participants would identify with to illustrate their points?

- Does the instructor understand your company, what they sell, and the obstacles and challenges your people face, even if those are not the immediate subject covered in the program?

- Has the instructor taken the time to understand the commonalities and differences among the group, such as experience levels, job responsibilities, and performance levels?

About the Program Materials

- Are the participants provided with materials that accurately represent what is being taught during the program?

- Do the materials contain in part or summary the key components of your sales methodology for reference purposes?

- Are the materials logically organized and clear to read?

- Are additional resources provided, such as articles, bibliographies, checklists, lists of tips, charts, and other take-aways?

- Are there any inconsistencies in the materials that might confuse a participant, such as wrong terminology or undefined terms?

Post-Program Follow-Up

- Do you understand in advance of any program what follow-up there will be once the program has concluded?

- Will the instructor be available to answer questions?

- How will the effectiveness of the program be measured?

- What mechanisms are in place to assure that the next program has improvements based on feedback from the last one?

- Are participants provided with assignments to assure that they are applying what has been learned during the program?

About Venue

- Is the facility at which your training takes place conducive to learning? World class sales trainers tell us that a noisy room, one that is too hot or cold, or too large or small can seriously hinder learning, even with the most committed and well-intentioned instructor.

- How conducive is the location to meeting the real objectives of the training? For example, are you certain that a resort one hundred miles from the closest major airport is right for your training program? Maybe a day of golf is not what's important.

To the Point

Now is the time for sales managers to demonstrate their leadership by taking an approach—the right approach—for achieving sales effectiveness within their organizations.

1. Stop the excuses. Establish a formal sales approach suitable for your company.

2. Objectively assess your current situation. Engage with outside resources if necessary.

3. Define your requirements and build or adopt a sales methodology before embarking on sales training.

4. Select a sales training provider that best meets your requirements, referring to ESR assessments of individual providers.

As you are analyzing ideas on the hows and whos and which and why of your sales training decision, I encourage you to contact Dave Stein, P.O. Box 1356, West Tisbury, MA 02575 (info@ESResearch.com); (508) 313-9585; fax (508) 629-0210; www.ESResearch.com.

Chapter 32

Sales Contests Connected to Training

Budget Considerations
Clear Benchmarks for Program Success
Ongoing Observation/Analysis
Post-Program Evaluation
Cash vs. Non-Cash Awards
Cash Awards
Advantages of Non-Cash Awards
Common Mistakes with Incentive and Recognition Programs
Setting the Budget First
Insufficient Funding
Overly Aggressive Objectives/Goals
Contests vs. Campaigns
Incentive? It's Called a Paycheck
Too Many Objectives
Silent Programs Fail!
Energized Incompetence
Not Knowing Your Audience
Exaggerated Promises from Performance Improvement Companies

You'll never find a deeper, more thorough analysis of how to run a successful sales contest than what you read here. (Just try to find a recent book on this topic.) With his deep research, insights, stories, and charts (for example, What about the choice between offering cash or other incentives?), another expert in his segment of the selling industry, Jim Micklos, has contributed this outstanding content.

How to Build a *Great* Incentive Program for Your Sales Pros

This chapter is very important for three reasons:

1. One of the best decisions you can make is to run a contest immediately after a sales training experience. This can really embed new learning and language usage your sales pros need to adopt in order to truly improve performance.

2. Companies building these programs have loads of questions. Do you know how to best reward your team? Money, trips, prizes, recognition? All of these, a blend? How do you get spouse or significant other or accountability partner buy-in in order to kick your sales pro in the tail to win?

3. Try to find a book on this topic anywhere. There is simply not enough detailed information on choices you can make in designing your sales contest or incentive and recognition program in order to make it highly effective. Here are statistics, case study references, and more to help your initiatives succeed.

Jim Micklos, who created and is sharing this information, is a brilliant strategist with over twenty years' experience designing incentive programs. You'll want to use this data to build an outstanding incentive program for your next national sales competition. I like the phrase used in his bio, which states: "Jim focuses on delivering incentive and recognition programs that have predictable and measurable results with *extraordinary ROI*."

Incentive, Recognition, and Performance Improvement Programs

In this chapter, we will review the different types and aspects of performance improvement programs. If properly structured, these types of activities should be viewed as an investment rather than an expense. The question then becomes: When is the right time to make this investment? The answer is simple but not obvious given the many different circumstances in business. When growth is taking place, you want to operate a performance improvement program to ensure you are gaining more than your competition. When business is flat, an added spark of incentives can make growth occur when it otherwise would not. In declining markets, this type of investment can really pay dividends into the future by stealing market share from the competition. Because they are effective in all business climates, performance improvement programs should always be considered when formulating any business strategies.

Incentive, recognition, and performance improvement programs are powerful tools that should operate on and reinforce key principles of effective leadership:

- Setting clear expectations

- Making expectations credible

- Rewards following positive performance or improvement

- Compelling consequences following poor performance

When properly conceived, designed, applied, and operated, such programs will deliver predictable and measurable improvements in the results you obtain from a variety of participant groups. Internally, sales teams and non-sales employees all can be motivated to provide significant improvements in revenue and profits, productivity, morale, and a variety of other important areas. Externally, these programs are highly effective with manufacturer sales agencies, distributors, dealers, and even customers.

Two fundamental aspects of these programs are

- There are no simple formulas

- There are very few hard and fast rules

Human motivation has been studied extensively for many years, and these studies have yielded two primary conclusions:

- Motivation isn't easy

- Motivation is much different from one individual and situation to the next

Effective programs are a balance of art and science, both of which benefit greatly from experience. Many companies hold fast to a do it yourself ("D-I-Y") mentality. Even though some D-I-Y programs appear to produce the desired results, most deliver far less than they could, and few deliver measurable results that show a clear and positive return on investment. Similar to other specialized consultants, the experts in performance improvement can be a vital addition to your business resources.

The information in this chapter reflects decades of experience in the design and operation of every form of incentive and/or recognition program across all industries and for companies of all sizes.

The key topics covered in this chapter include:

1. Differences between incentive and recognition programs
2. Benefits of comprehensive performance improvement systems
3. Key elements of successful programs
   - Measurable program objectives
   - Realistic program objectives
   - Specific program period
   - Carefully selected participants
   - Significant award opportunities
   - Appealing awards
   - Clear rules
   - Frequent program communication
   - Performance reporting
   - Budget considerations
   - Clear benchmarks for program success
   - Ongoing observation/analysis
   - Post-program evaluation
4. Cash vs. non-cash awards
5. Common mistakes
   - Setting the budget first
   - Insufficient funding
   - Overly aggressive objectives/goals
   - Contests vs. campaigns
   - Incentive? It's called a paycheck
   - Too many objectives
   - Silent programs fail!
   - Energized incompetence
   - Know your audience
   - Exaggerated promises from performance improvement companies

Whether you manage your efforts in-house, allocate some elements to outside suppliers, or utilize the services and expertise of a performance improvement company, this chapter will provide clear and specific direction.

Incentives vs. Recognition

To understand the differences between these two types of efforts, we first need to identify that your potential participant group (employee group, sales force, dealer or distributor network, customer base, etc.) can be divided into five distinct performance groups (very similar to the academic grade levels). The groups from which you typically realize the most improvement are B and C groups. (See Figure 32.1.)

- **Group A**, approximately 9 percent of any participant group, consistently performs at high levels. These are the self-starting, self-managers who are obsessed with performing at their best. Point them in the right direction, give them the right tools, and watch them deliver excellent results. A significant factor that improves their exceptional performance is personal recognition (that is, being acknowledged as the best).

Figure 32.1. Typical Performance Distribution Within a Participant Base

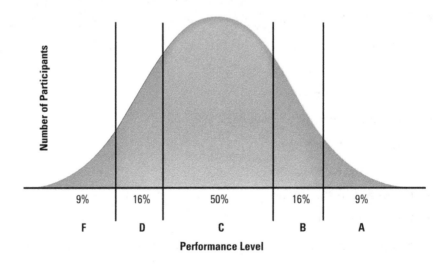

- **Group B**, the next 16 percent, perform at above-average levels. For the most part, they perform as directed and work to the level they deem necessary to maintain their positions. Some may lack the necessary knowledge, experience, skills, or coaching to excel. Nearly all are capable of significant improvement when those weaknesses are addressed. Most of this B group may see themselves as future top performers; some don't believe they can be among the very best.

- **Group C** are the average performers and comprise 50 percent of all participants. They perform their jobs every day and then go home. They are not fully engaged and require something to influence them to step up their performance. They do have the minimum necessary skills and knowledge to perform their jobs, but lack the internal drive to increase their performance.

- **Groups D and F**, 25 percent of any participant group, function at below-average levels. They may be new hires, those approaching retirement, in the wrong job, or individuals who don't want to perform better. Many of these individuals will never deliver enough performance (regardless of program) and should be terminated. The power of a properly designed incentive program can elevate some to much higher levels.

In summary, the vast majority of potential improvement will be from Groups B and C. Group A may improve some with recognition because they want to be the "best of the best." Group B can become members of the lower end of Group A with outside influences that make up for lack of internal drive. Group C can improve to become members of Group B through increased influences on their behavior (although they likely will never become members of Group A because of shortfalls in their skill sets). Some of Groups D and F can improve their performance, but the bulk of these groups are headed for termination for one reason or another. Understanding where participants are in performance levels and who can actually improve their performance are critical in identifying the primary targets when designing performance improvement programs. Groups B and C represent significant potential and should be the program focus.

The most common form of recognition program is designed to reward the top performers—the elite 10 percent of a group who attain the highest levels, as seen in Figure 32.2.

Figure 32.2. Impact of a Typical Recognition-Only Program

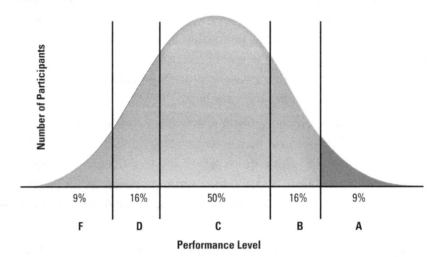

- Recognition-only programs offer attainable rewards to approximately 10 percent of your participant group. Although the rewards may be considerable (glamorous group travel, expensive and luxurious merchandise, praise, and impressive trophies), the qualifications for recognition, while theoretically attainable by many, are perceived as unattainable by nearly everyone outside of group A and a very small portion of group B.

- Ninety percent of your participant group won't be recognized. They know that going in and receive no motivation from the "opportunity." As far as they are concerned, there is no opportunity. In some cases, this group is irritated that the program is even in place.

- Recognition-only programs do not drive significant growth. They do stimulate competition among the high-performance group, but most are already very close to their full potential and have limited potential for further improvement. More importantly, many of them know they can achieve recognition status simply by maintaining current levels of performance.

- A recognition program fulfills the important role of defining and recognizing excellent performance. It does little to drive the vast majority of your participant group to improve their performance.

The goal of any program is to produce a significant improvement in performance. It is critical that your program impacts the majority of your participants. Everyone must feel that the program is fair, that they can earn significant rewards for improved performance and the rewards justify the extra effort required. Combining Recognition and Incentive allows you to positively impact almost all performance levels. The advantages, seen in Figure 32.3, include:

- A performance-based incentive program offers potential rewards to nearly all of your participants

- Individual rewards are based solely on individual performance

- Individual rewards are proportionate to individual incremental results delivered

Figure 32.3. Impact of Incentive/Recognition Combination

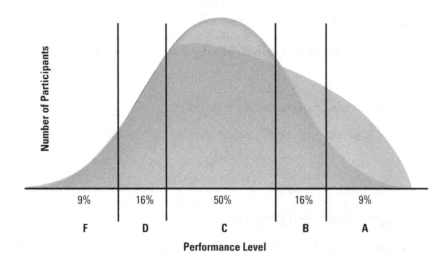

- Virtually every participant perceives a real opportunity to be rewarded
- Most of the performance curve is shifted

Group A high performers improve to earn extra rewards as well as top performer recognition. Groups B and C see and respond to a realistic reward opportunity. Those in Groups D and F with the potential to improve perceive the opportunity to earn rewards for moving up to average performance.

A Comprehensive Reinforcement System

Incentive and recognition programs are not a replacement for a sound compensation system/benefits package. They are enhancements to your existing compensation plan that go far beyond basic expectations and stimulate extraordinary effort and results.

Delivering maximum performance requires three separate components: Compensation, Recognition, and Incentives as shown below.

Compensation

- Basic
- Attracts and keeps good people long-term
- Long-term, stable
- Private
- Meets basic needs
- Should be 95 percent of the individual's total potential reward for work

Recognition

- Establishes levels of performance excellence
- Maintains and rewards peak performance
- Long-term
- Extremely public
- Meets higher needs, ego gratification
- Should be 1 to 2 percent of the peak individual's total reward for work

Incentive

- Drives growth with specialized focus
- Accomplishes specific objectives and changes specific behaviors
- Short- and long-term
- Private and public
- Creates extra motivation
- Injects fun into the work environment
- Should be 3 to 5 percent of the individual's total reinforcement

Key Elements of Successful Programs

Several key elements are essential to success. From creating excitement and generating the proper focus to changing behaviors and maximizing results, these key elements must work in perfect harmony. Following are brief explanations and examples for each element.

Measurable Program Objectives

In order to reward success, you must be able to measure it. The performance improvement expectation must be clear, specific, and credible. That means that both you and the participant group have a shared understanding of the outcome. For example:

- "Increase sales" is too vague.
- "Increase revenue 20 percent over the same period prior year, including 5 percent anticipated market growth and 5 percent estimated price increases," allows precise setting of participant goals and specific post-program evaluation.

Realistic Program Objectives

It is critical that the objective be realistic. Nothing kills the effectiveness of a program more quickly than setting unrealistic goals. A 20 percent increase in revenue may sound great, but if the current economic conditions are tough, no one will believe it is possible and therefore most won't even try to reach it. The goal should be a stretch that is realistic to attain and produces enough incremental revenue to justify the cost.

Any business improvement that can be obtained through increased performance may be a valid objective, provided it:

- Is realistic/attainable

- Can be clearly measured

- Will provide sufficient returns to justify your program investment

- Is measurable on a regular basis

Non-quantifiable objectives, such as improved morale and increased teamwork, are also frequently valid and critical to success, despite their subjective nature. Although they may not be as easy to quantify, you can identify indicators for improvement. You must have a shared understanding of exactly "how" you will measure success before you start the program. Any short-term gains will be jeopardized if your participants don't understand "why" they won or lost.

Specific Program Period
There are two time factors to consider—when to start and when to finish.

- Your start date must be early enough to allow attainment of your objectives yet still allow sufficient time for program development and launch. The overall length usually ranges from three months to twelve months. It is difficult to maintain momentum for a program longer than twelve months.

- To support an effective return on investment, your program needs to be long enough to generate sufficient incremental revenue to fund meaningful awards, recover the fixed investments made in communications and performance reporting, and deliver additional incremental profit. Other factors to consider when determining the correct program period are length of sales cycles, timing of relevant training initiatives, cultural changes in process, seasonality of sales, major changes in work processes, and new product introductions.

A specific end date is also essential. It:

- Defines the length of the award opportunity,

- Creates a sense of urgency,

- Allows for effective results evaluation, and

- Gives you the opportunity to discontinue or revise any aspect of the program.

Many companies plan major campaigns to last a full calendar year or run an entire fiscal year; that way, the program results and expenses both impact the same fiscal year.

Carefully Selected Participants

When planning a program, you want to choose the people who will have the most direct impact on the results you want to achieve.

While the answer may seem obvious—the targeted employee group (the sales team, the service team, the call center staff, the delivery staff, the collections area, etc.) may not be the only people who impact the success of the program. You should identify others who impact the core participants and therefore can influence the outcome—either positively or negatively (for example, immediate managers, support departments, etc.).

Everyone in the "delivery circuit" related to your program objective should have an opportunity to earn. Including everyone usually creates a push/pull effect and ensures maximum performance. For example, using a two-step distribution model, consider the following:

- A sales incentive for the manufacturing company's sales force

- A purchase incentive for the distributors' principals

- Sales incentives for the distributors' outside sales, inside sales, and counter sales staffs

- A frequent purchase incentive for the distributors' customers

You always need the appropriate managers to support your program. Giving them a stake in the rewards is the best way to ensure that.

While you might not provide the same incentives or rewards for the support team, you do want to make sure your efforts are not deliberately or unintentionally influenced by outside forces.

Significant Award Opportunities

Awards must have a perceived value sufficient to justify the effort required to earn them. Typically, a participant (an employee of the sponsoring company) who performs well should be able to earn an award valued at 3 to 5 percent of his or her regular compensation. If the participant is not an employee of the sponsoring company, say a salesperson in a distribution channel, the potential award value should be 7 to 9 percent of his or her regular compensation.

A combination of individual and team awards can multiply motivation and increases cooperation and collaboration within the team. Individuals who may not have a real shot at the big individual awards can still win with their teams. This program design encourages stronger performers to help lesser performers, thereby increasing the performance level for everyone.

Appealing Awards

When you evaluate potential awards, consider two important facts:

- Non-cash awards are much more effective than cash.
- A group travel experience is the most appealing award you can offer.

Following is key information supporting group travel:

- No award is more requested by potential participants.
- Travel memories build over time and often last a lifetime.
- Group travel provides the ideal forum for information exchange and relationship building.
- The experience should include spouses/significant others, which adds to the perceived value of the award. Spouses/significant others provide constant reinforcement during the qualification period, helping maximize results.

Group travel usually requires a commitment to a substantial award budget as well as significant individual award values. In some situations, your gain from individual performance improvement cannot support the expense of the travel award, thus potentially negatively impacting the program results/ROI. The rules should be written to ensure enough incremental performance is attained to justify the award.

Group travel may not be the most effective award for some participant groups. Lower income, second income, or less sophisticated individuals may find it overwhelming or in conflict with their personal values. You do not want an award to be intimidating; you want it to be a positive experience.

The time off the job to participate in the travel award can sometimes be problematic.

Merchandise awards allow greater flexibility and provide broader appeal than group travel.

- Award points redeemable for merchandise awards allow you to issue award values that are consistent with a variety of results/gains.

- Your participants periodically earn award points that can be accumulated over the life of the program for a high-value award, several lesser value awards, or any combination of merchandise.

- An extensive award catalog creates the most effective offering possible:

  - It offers something for everyone.

  - A wide variety of awards with high-profile items encourages goal setting and drives performance.

  - A broad catalog relieves you of the burden of sourcing, selecting, and purchasing award items as well as managing the delivery of those awards.

Clear Rules

"Do this, get that" is the objective when developing the program rules. You want the rules to be simple, clear, and easy to understand so there are no questions about what behaviors you desire and what will be rewarded. Use terms with which your participants are familiar.

- Limit award opportunities to the key results and/or behaviors.
- Offer the greatest award value for the most critical performance.

- Offer additional awards for focus elements (sales to target accounts, higher margin items, featured supplier items, new products, greatest improvement, etc.).

- Require sufficient improvement to fund meaningful awards.

- Make sure the goals are challenging yet attainable.

- Make sure the program is perceived by your participants as fair, attainable, and realistic.

- Consider both national and localized recognition.

Frequent Program Communication

Frequent communication is critical to maintaining excitement and momentum. The longer the time period, the more communication needed to ensure the participants remain focused on the program goals.

There are three phases to the communication process—the program launch, ongoing communication during the program, and the announcement of winners.

Program Launch

- Consider launch kickoff meetings, webinars, and/or DVD presentations, etc.

- Include a custom theme and logo that depict the goals/awards, complement your overall image, create a brand identity for the program, and drive excitement.

- Announcement materials must be exciting and complete.

- Display the awards prominently.

- Provide all the information participants need in easy-to-read designs.

- Include a message from top management reinforcing the importance of the program.

- Include promotional items useful in the workplace or at home, or representing the travel award destination, imprinted with your program theme logo.

Ongoing Communication

- Ongoing communication should be frequent and informative. It should highlight progress updates and provide coaching direction.

- Use the communication plan as a great opportunity to refresh recent training or emphasize other messages that support the behavior that leads to success.

- Communicate at least monthly for programs that last three or more months.

- Weekly communication is best for shorter programs.

- Take advantage of existing vehicles (such as team meetings, newsletters, bulletin boards, etc.).

- Use print and electronic media.

- Include dimensional items when appropriate.

- Use a mix of public and individual updates/messages.

- Alternate mailings to both business and home addresses.

- Include mailings targeted at the spouse/significant other.

Announcement of Winners

- Make the announcements fun, entertaining, and memorable. This is a special moment for the winners and they deserve the appropriate public recognition.

- The process can be formal, such as annual award dinners or annual company meetings. It can also be an informal gathering of the team for fifteen minutes at the beginning or end of the day. Either way, consider the following:

  - Invite a senior manager to make the announcement.

  - Plan for the event; make sure the participants know the date and time in advance so they can attend.

  - If done during work time, plan for coverage so everyone can attend.

  - Make the presentation dramatic.

- Encourage the award recipients to talk about how they achieved the new, higher standards (which will inspire and educate others).
- Include family/spouses if possible.

Performance Reporting

It is critical to keep participants posted on their progress to goals and awards with "performance statements" (either printed or online).

- Update statements at least monthly during a six- to twelve-month program, more frequently for shorter durations.
- Include current period and program-to-date performance and earnings.
- Include details on competitive standings when appropriate.
- Show progress to goal and whether they are on track to attainment of goals.

Provide each manager with individual and summary reports of their subordinates' performance. Format reports to highlight top performers and those who need assistance in reaching their goals.

Budget Considerations

When setting the budget, here are some things to remember:

- Project potential levels of improvement and resulting revenue/profit increases.
- Define acceptable, preferred, and ideal results.
- Estimate all program expenses by category.
- Merchandise awards:
  - In a performance-based program, these are usually variable and proportionate to the improvement realized. Estimate such award expenses based on your acceptable/preferred/ideal performance projections.
- Travel awards (per person cost × number of travelers):
  - Include all land and projected air costs.
  - Air travel expenses are almost always estimates until the itinerary is actually booked.

- Recognition awards (trophies, crystal, plaques, certificates, etc.):
  - Communications (including shipping and handling).
  - Performance reporting.
  - Internal labor and costs for any D-I-Y elements.

Items, quantities, travel inclusions, etc., will change during the program. Any item that changes during the program from its initial design up to and including operation must be tracked to accurately account for any differences between the initial budget and final expenses/results of the program.

Clear Benchmarks for Program Success

Pre-established benchmarks, in more detail than your program objectives, are vital to evaluating program success and determining how to make your next program more effective. While these should be established prior to program launch, experience has shown that your benchmarks will be more accurate if you define them after all other program elements have been finalized.

- Set specific targets for program results.
- Include historic seasonality in your performance projections.
- Define acceptable/preferred/ideal projections and budgets.
- Include key support milestones (communication mailing dates, timely/ accurate monthly reporting/feedback, etc.).
- Define how attainment of non-quantifiable objectives will be determined.

Ongoing Observation/Analysis

Most programs begin with a significant increase of performance in the initial weeks or months. In addition, there is almost always a spike in performance during the final months of any program as participants work harder to meet their goals, and maximize their awards.

- Perform periodic reviews of performance and expenses to date as well as projected results and final expenses.
- The reviews should occur quarterly for a twelve-month program, bi-monthly for a six-month program, and monthly for programs of shorter duration.

- Analyze participants who are up, and especially those who are down.

- Gather success stories and share solutions to problems.

- Be cautious of making severe overall decisions or massive changes to the program based on early results.

- Use these reviews to make minor modifications to the program, direct efforts toward improving weak performance, recognize and publish examples of outstanding performance to date, and avoid any surprises late in the program.

Post-Program Evaluation

This is the final version of your periodic reviews, comparing actual results and expenses with your original budget.

- Include post-program participant surveys, anecdotal evidence gathered during the program (for example, a dealer who inquires to see how much more he has to order to win a travel award), and any other subjective feedback available.

- Variances from original budgets and benchmarks should be investigated to determine why they occurred. Use this information to modify the program in future years.

Cash vs. Non-Cash Awards

Ask your participants what they want most and the vast majority will answer "Cash." In reality, cash award programs actually reduce the overall impact and personal value of a program. Parallel studies have consistently shown that results from non-cash award programs are significantly greater than those that offered cash awards.

Following is pertinent information regarding cash versus non-cash programs.

Cash Awards

Cash is compensation, not an award. With the best intentions, managers often think the employees will spend the cash bonus on a luxury or special item. Research from Wirthlin Worldwide Research (www.wirthlin.com) shows that isn't the case:

- 29 percent went to pay bills.

- 18 percent did not remember how it was spent.

- 15 percent said they did not receive it.

- 11 percent purchased gifts.

- 11 percent bought household items.

- 11 percent put the money into savings.

- 5 percent went on vacation.

Some other points include:

- Cash can be used as a discount. It allows participants to stop short of their potential/your goal.

- Cash incentives can become income.

- If you change direction or stop the program, it has the same effect as a pay cut.

- Cash turns into an entitlement.

- Cash incentives are "non-public"—they are personal income and cannot be promoted as reward examples.

Advantages of Non-Cash Awards

Using non-cash awards can bring many benefits, such as:

- Non-cash awards generate family involvement in the beginning and throughout the program.

- Merchandise and travel awards encourage goal setting.

- They (1) create an emotional commitment (engagement) to the performance increase required and (2) motivate and deliver higher performance in order to earn the award.

- Very public recognition of achievement and presentation of awards.

- Rewarding yourself or your family is guilt-free.

- Provide trophy value—long-term remembrance of sponsoring company and accomplishments.

- Rewards are more subjective and have a higher perceived value.
- Non-cash award programs can be changed to address current business issues without causing hardships on the employees or customers.
- Memory value of the award builds over time.
- Non-cash awards give bragging rights to winners (it is perfectly acceptable to brag about your achieving President's Club and your upcoming travel experience in Hawaii).

Concrete Evidence

- The Performance Improvement Industry (non-cash incentives) has been in existence since the 1940s because it works.
- A head-to-head comparison in tire dealers in a real-world example proved it works.
- The fact that non-cash rewards drive greater performance than cash rewards has been proved through independent studies at the University of Chicago, Northwestern University, and Wirthlin Worldwide Research.
- Behavior theory and psychological theory both support tangible reinforcement of non-cash incentives.

Common Mistakes with Incentive and Recognition Programs

Setting the Budget First

Often, companies determine their budget and develop a program to fit the budget. The proper approach is to identify the desired performance, calculate the improvement required to earn awards, define the results/costs, and then confirm a budget.

Insufficient Funding

A common mistake made, especially by first-time users, is trying to cut corners within the budget.

Ensure sufficient budget for communications and performance tracking/reporting. These fixed expenses range from 10 to 20 percent of typical programs.

Your potential for success is severely reduced without effective support in these areas, so every dollar cut from these budgets jeopardizes your return.

Overly Aggressive Objectives/Goals

Another mistake people make is to set overly aggressive goals. Here are some considerations to counter this tendency:

- The key to setting objectives and goals is challenging, yet attainable.

- Goals that are too aggressive will discourage participants instead of motivating them (the result is they will give up early in the program).

- Goals should be based on a combination of prior performance, market expectations, planned price increases, and any product, channel, or go-to-market changes that could affect growth potential.

Contests vs. Campaigns

Contests offer two benefits:

- Fair competition encourages incremental performance.

- Contests allow you to stretch your award budget. A $200,000 award budget for one hundred sales reps creates an average award of $2,000. Divided among twenty contest winners, the average award becomes $10,000, sufficient for an exciting group travel experience.

Contests also have one major disadvantage—they create losers!

- In the above example, for every winner you'll have four losers. Some of them will have worked hard to win, will have nothing to show for it, may be very irritated, and likely will not engage during the next contest.

- The solution is to offer an award to every participant who meets the assigned program goal (perhaps $2,000 each), with the travel award going to the top performers. Everyone who meets his or her goal and helps attain your objective earns an award recognizing his or her contribution.

- A common mistake is to reward only the largest volume participants. This automatically favors those who were largest in the past. Conversely, medium and smaller volume participants will see themselves excluded from the start.

Campaigns offer award opportunities to every participant. Each person who exceeds his or her performance goal is rewarded. Everyone stays engaged throughout the program, as people control their own destiny.

Some further points about contests are outlined below.

Incentive? It's Called a Paycheck

This is a common argument against including some participants (such as managers) or even running a program at all.

- It's pure nonsense.

- Salary, commissions, and benefits determine where someone works. Incentives influence how hard and smart they work when they are there.

- Non-cash incentives provide the motivation required to deliver positive incremental results.

Too Many Objectives

Having too many objectives leads to failure.

- Keep your program focused. Avoid trying to improve too many areas at once. More than three program objectives are probably too many.

- Performance improvement programs are specialized tools and extremely effective in accomplishing specific objectives if they are designed and used properly for that job.

Silent Programs Fail!

People have to know what's happening.

- Frequent and effective program communication is essential.

- Timely and accurate performance reporting/feedback and management information are critical to success.

- Communications ensure your participants will work hard to deliver the results you want so they can earn their awards.

- Participants have plenty of other things on their minds and, no matter what awards you offer, you have to fight for mindshare—communication is the answer.

- Develop a detailed, frequent schedule and system for communications and performance reporting.

- Follow the schedules and budgets.

- Your communications need to be high-impact, brief, informative, and entertaining, always highlighting the potential awards.

Energized Incompetence

Within your planning to improve performance, you will be designing a program to ensure that motivation is maximized. Make sure you keep in mind the complete performance model:

Performance = Ability × Motivation

Without the ability to perform, you will have a highly charged and excited group of participants in a state of *energized incompetence*.

- Be certain your participants have the knowledge and tools, as well as the coaching, to do what you are asking of them. Make certain your organization has the necessary tools as well.

- Lack of product information, sales techniques, reporting/feedback mechanisms, and a host of other elements can kill a program before it starts.

- Product, skills, and sales training elements can be an effective element of your program communications.

- Small bonus awards for passing quizzes and answering surveys will add an insignificant expense to your budget while dramatically increasing participant capabilities and interest in your program communications.

Not Knowing Your Audience

Any program must be developed with the audience in mind.

- Differences in perspectives and reality between the top and the bottom are often the greatest dangers in any management initiative.

- Be sure you have a true understanding of the challenges you are presenting and the effort it will take to meet them.

- Share your ideas with middle managers and some front-line participants to ensure they'll interpret criteria the same way you do.

- There are people in every organization who will respect your confidence and keep your planning confidential. Find them and listen to them. They'll become the champions of your program in the field and they'll add power to your program.

Exaggerated Promises from Performance Improvement Companies

When evaluating potential suppliers to help you, watch out for "packaged programs," inexperienced suppliers, and companies in which performance improvement is not their core competency.

- Your organization, situation, needs, objectives, and challenges are different from those of any other company. A pre-packaged, self-contained, ready-to-go program is highly unlikely to address all of your needs. If it doesn't, results of your program will be diminished.

- Ad agencies, sales promotion agencies, and premium vendors are not performance improvement experts, no matter how vehemently they insist otherwise. There are some apparent similarities between their primary business and some elements of performance improvement programs. They may even be long-trusted suppliers in their specialized areas who already possess intimate knowledge of your company; however, they are not performance improvement experts, any more than a performance improvement company is a qualified advertising agency.

As you evaluate options to growing and improving your business, keep in mind that "What gets measured and rewarded, gets done!" With any objective that involves the performance of people, incentives and recognition should be part of the strategy. Custom performance improvement solutions are an integral part of any strategy that seeks to maximize measurable results.

The best place to start is with a full-service performance improvement company. Let them bring their intellectual capital to bear on your business challenges. They have experience with many companies, industries, participant groups, and metrics. They have expertise in management reporting, communications, and award selection. They know what works and what does not work. They will become your *trusted advisor*. You will end up with a true win-win scenario:

- WIN for your business
- WIN for your participants

Jim Micklos is vice president of business development for FUSION Performance Marketing, a full-service performance improvement company. FUSION specializes in developing highly creative custom solutions to clients' sales and marketing challenges. Jim focuses on delivering incentive and recognition programs that have predictable and measurable results with extraordinary ROI.

Jim is an industry subject-matter expert in performance improvement with more than two decades of experience in sales and sales management. Much of the experience Jim has gained throughout his career has been built in developing go-to-market strategies for his clients, designing performance improvement programs, and working with clients with varied distribution channels.

Prior to working in the performance improvement industry, Jim held executive positions with American Hospital Supply, Belden, and Combibloc, Inc. Jim's background includes sales operations, client services, and cross-functional training positions in finance and manufacturing management. Jim utilizes this deep and varied background in the development of numerous sales and marketing initiatives for his clients, always with a keen emphasis on delivering results. When you're ready for a fascinating conversation, you'll want to sit down with Jim.

My most recent meeting with him was to introduce him to a client of mine. The company wanted to create a competition for the sales team that would culminate in a trip to Costa Rica. This unique location includes beaches, volcanoes, rainforest, and more. Hearing Jim describe travel options, choices between world class hotels versus budget-based choices, and how to get the spouse/significant other involved was a fascinating experience. He just has all the answers. And great leaders have always surrounded themselves with people who offer expertise they don't have.

You can contact Jim at (312) 929-3901 or jmicklos@fpmglobal.com.

Chapter 33

Reps You Should *Not* Be Training

CHAPTER OVERVIEW
Training Is Not Always the Answer
Assessment of Sales Aptitude

This chapter will offer you a new resource to analyze your sales team. It will show you how to create an amazing model of excellence from which you can transform your hiring practices. With many old assessment tools floating around, it shouldn't be a surprise to find that something better has been developed. What I like best about this instrument is that it can tell you the difference between what salespeople *can* do and what they *will* do. Most tools measure ability, but if the person won't put his or her ability into play, you have a bad hire who won't take and adapt training into his or her daily behavior.

300 (Not the Movie)

My client has one of the largest sales forces in the world. They wanted to speak about a project to analyze their top performers. They had identified the three hundred

*best salespeople and were sending them a twenty-question quiz in order to figure
out what made these men and women tick.*

*"I have a question about this," I said. "It's been my experience that very few top
salespeople know themselves what makes them great. You ask them and will hear
things like 'I have good instincts' or 'I work harder than my competition.' So I'd
look for a psychologically sound, validated instrument to measure and model
your reps."*

Training Is Not Always the Answer

There's an old adage in sales training, "Training is not always the answer." Briefly,
this refers to situations in which training cannot address the concern. This might
include situations like using a simple job aid to address some needs or realizing
that there are some reps who lack motivation to perform up to your company's
expectation. It's an unfortunate fact that too many training dollars and training
hours are invested in the wrong reps.

If I can offer a basic metaphor, it does no good to train a dog to moo. He'll simply
get trampled underfoot while trying to communicate with company that has no
interest in his existence.

There are also sales reps who aren't fit to be in the company of your prospect
and buyers. Fortunately, there are plenty of pre-hiring assessments that can help
measure personality fit and other factors you'll want to match your hiring
profiles.

Assessment of Sales Aptitude

However, here is something new of which you want to be aware. It's an assessment
that determines decision-making patterns. These motivational and attitudinal patterns, or MAPs, can help identify how a person filters past experience and uses it
to make decisions. If you recall, in the Introduction to this book, I share a story of
a woman who blows up during a sales training program, based on her interpretation of one of my PowerPoint slides. Her personal history (or baggage) caused her
to put herself into a state of anger over a simple cartoon.

You want to focus on the purpose of assessments: *Identify how a person filters past
experience and uses it to make decisions.*

Imagine the value of each rep becoming aware of his or her personal patterns, based on experience (and honestly, I freaked out when I had this assessment done. It was scary accurate and showed me things about myself I absolutely knew as truth, but of which I'd never been aware).

This means that a company can actually measure, then model top reps. You can create a profile from this model to use during the hiring process that will keep you focused on candidates who are most closely aligned to your premier performers. But wait, there's more.

Imagine the power of a company and each rep becoming aware of his or her individual buyer's tendencies to make decisions. This can enable sales pros to adjust their presentations (by phone or face-to-face), in order to maximize speaking in a dialect that matches the buyer's decision-making patterns.

This is very powerful because it can be tied directly into newer influence strategies embedded in the assessment. A few of these patterns are outlined in this book. One example is Chapter 17 on determining whether to sell using benefits and goals or consequences and problem-solving language. As your intrigue with this new knowledge grows and you want more details on these patterns, they are discussed in my upcoming book, *The Secret Language of Influence* (2012).

To use the assessment, interpretation, and coaching model with your sales team, visit www.ModelofSalesExcellence.com for more information. Several white papers are available with greater detail on the assessment, and I have arranged for senior sales executives to have themselves assessed for *free* in order to experience this amazing tool.

One final thought: You should also know that MAPs are not indicators of intelligence or personality or ability. They don't represent what you *can* do, but rather what you *want* to do. Therein lies the answer to a confusing question about why some of the best potential lies untapped in your sales force.

> *"Can" versus "want" means people can have measurable ability to sell well, but they simply choose to put their energy into non-productive behavior.*

You want to hire, manage, and coach sales pros who *want* to do what's necessary to attain personal success. Then you can optimize revenue with maximum productivity from your selling team.

Spend some time at www.ModelofSalesExcellence.com and have your assessment done. You'll be grateful that options exist that can help you model successful hiring and then build a successful selling system to increase rep performance.

Chapter 34

What's Missing
from This Book

Covering content related to sales performance can put one in a position to expand this book into areas not critical to sales training–related performance. Some of these topics are training programs I offer for special situations, that don't apply to everyone, like using humor to sell or the elimination of excuses (although that's getting rave reviews this year). By the time this book comes out, I'll have done the program at least a dozen times. So here's a quick overview of ideas you'll need to procure elsewhere.

What's Been Left Out

I've left out any discussion of CRM systems and other training (like new product launches) that aren't related to skills that impact the prospect/seller relationships.

Territory management isn't covered here, as it's a bit too narrow a topic, is limited in how many choices there are to intelligently manage it, and doesn't relate to enough of the selling population at large.

Use of social media or Web or Sales 2.0, 3.0, or whatever iteration will exist by the time this book is published, is also not discussed. In a world where options appear and disappear quickly, it'd be a bad call to have you invest time in reading about a solution that might not even exist or whose offerings might be so different six months from now that they don't deserve space here.

Sales management is not a sales training topic, so it is not addressed here, although I hope a wise sales manager will read enough of the key selling ideas here that he or she can better motivate his team to apply them.

Strategic account management is not addressed, as you'll find the richest resource on this topic to be the SAMA association at www.strategicaccounts.org/. You will find a list of other digitally based resources in Appendix 2, such as LinkedIn's variety of communities you can access under the category of Sales.

Additionally, I'm doing some very unique work on three topics that are just a bit too far out there to be included in a manual on sales training, but I'll discuss them a bit below.

Three Unique Topics for the Future

1. Storytelling for Sales Pros

The power of story has been documented for thousands of years. Why aren't we using it more when we engage in dialogues with buyers? Even something as simple as a metaphor to frame your solutions can be potent: "Remember when your company changed its communication methods by getting rid of typewriters, then word processors, then basic computers? I recall what a relief it was to upgrade from inefficient tools to the next version. And in contrast, how efficient and dynamic are today's digital choices for your business? Our solutions represent the latest and best choices in the area of . . . for you today."

My PET model for storytelling covers the use of elements that are **P**ersonal, **E**motional, and **T**each the buyer to view you as the best choice he or she can make.

2. The Use of Humor for Sales Pros

Who can resist sitting with someone who is witty and fun company? Your ability to generate humor is a huge addition to your ability to engage prospects. Everyone can be better company by using humor. This skill can be taught, regardless of the wide variety of personalities represented in your selling team.

3. The Elimination of Excuses for Sales Pros

There is some highly unique information available on the psychology of excuse-making. In a program I call The Excuse Elimination Diet, you can teach your sales pros to first identify how and why their brains come up with excuses (It's insidious!). They can then learn to manage and attack these excuses in order to eliminate the impact of this weak and worthless self-talk on their productivity. This is a fascinating and powerful learning experience that every sales executive I've encountered needs badly. I'm writing *The Excuse Elimination Diet* book right now on this topic, drawing from over fifty intriguing research studies.

You can contact me directly when you feel it's time to attend to any or all of these topics.

Chapter 35

A Critical
Trend You
Can't Ignore

CHAPTER OVERVIEW

The trend you're about to read about is pretty much a secret in the business world (why that's true in a moment). It's the push in academia to get students to consider a sales career. This includes some serious internship work, which can speed up the learning curve to selling success. And that's why your business colleagues and competition aren't telling you about their secret. They're tearing down the doors of schools to hire reps who aren't really rookies. Read the research on this trend, provided by Howard Stevens of The Chally Group Worldwide and his Sales Education Foundation.

Simulated Sales Calls

A few years ago I had the pleasure of being invited to keynote the National Collegiate Sales Competition (NCSC). This event is held each spring at Kennesaw State University in Georgia, USA. Dr. Terry Loe brings in students who have set their sights on the selling profession. They come from universities that offer sales programs in their business departments.

A series of simulated sales calls, of both products and services, form the experience. Student sellers and "buyers" are observed on video and scored based on criteria that are used to identify quality salespeople. Winners are announced, and throughout the three days of the event a job fair runs. I was shocked at the exhibitors' aggressive pursuit of these students. Dr. Loe told me that hiring companies felt that the experience and internships of these graduates amounted to the equivalent of eighteen months of sales prior to starting a new job.

I immediately recognized the value of hiring these students. In my experience, six months was "the hump." That is, when rookies were about six months into their first selling jobs, they either knew that they could sell and would enjoy the career choice or they'd bust out and seek another job. Sales reps arriving with eighteen months of experience meant they were well trained, fairly seasoned (at least with handling rejection), and well worth any salary being offered. At the NCSC job fair, plenty of those job offerings did not include entry-level sales salaries.

This academic movement is well documented through the work of Howard Stevens, chairman and CEO of The Chally Group Worldwide. The Chally Group is a talent management, leadership development, and sales improvement corporation. I asked Howard for some information, including statistics I could provide for the readers of this book.

Howard has formed The Sales Education Foundation, a component fund of The Dayton Foundation, to gain the support of corporate sales executives. You'll see references to it below. And I will encourage you to become involved with that organization, for all the reasons you're about to read. Here is the information provided by Howard Stevens and USEF Executive Director Jeanne Frawley.

The Greatest Challenges and Opportunities for the Sales Forces of the Future:* Executive Summary

The First Challenge**

Companies spend billions annually on training salespeople ($7.1 billion in U.S. companies alone) so that their average salesperson can spend more than thirty-three hours per year in training. In technical markets, the costs associated with the development of just one salesperson are often in excess of $100,000 (US), and it may take as long as two years before any profit is realized from that new sales hire. Why is "sales force" training the largest employee investment most companies must make? There is no other alternative!

The Second Challenge***

Thirty-nine percent of the customer's selection of a vendor is based on the added value the salesperson brings to the relationship. Unfortunately, customers care less about salespeople with the "traditionally trained sales skills" than a salesperson's:

- General management skills and ability to understand their business
- Effectiveness at customer advocacy to protect their interests within the vendor
- Ability to diagnose and design applications

*From The Sales Education Foundation, a component fund of The Dayton Foundation. Used with permission.
**Johnston, Wesley J., *Journal of Personal Selling & Sales Management*, Summer 2005.
***Achieve Sales Excellence, and the 2007 Customer Selected World Class Sales Research Report.

- Accessibility

- Problem solving and innovativeness

The Solution: College Trained Sales Professionals Who Are Both Educated and Trained in Competencies Like:

- Business acumen and P&L analysis

- Computer literacy and information technology

- Account management and process "disciplines," such as supply chain management

- Interpersonal and relationship building skills

- Market analysis and product/service promotion and distribution

The Benefits

- Sales grads "ramp up" 50 percent faster. And are 35 percent less likely to turn over.****

- They already have demonstrated the aptitude and desire for sales.****

- They are more focused and in-tune with the numbers and the processes designed to get the numbers; and they are more aware of what they need to do.*

- Sales grads are offered positions at a significantly higher rate than non-sales grads. According to the National Association of Colleges and Employers (NACE), only 39 percent of college graduates were offered jobs upon graduation in 2010. Sales programs report over 85 percent placement at graduation.

The Professional Salesperson of the Future

The changing dynamics between buyers and sellers are being driven by larger societal trends that are affecting us all. The proliferation of information, the mobility of the workforce, the ease of communication, and the globalization of markets—these and other trends have altered the way we live. Similarly, they have altered the way we work. The overriding requirement for today's salesperson, simply

****Quotes from HR Chally corporate sponsor survey 2007.

stated, is: "Be the outsource of preference." The basic priority, therefore, is to add value to the customer's business.

The Problem

Too many new products do not match customers' priorities or are too difficult to understand or use; sometimes they are simply not needed. Salespeople who are rewarded for quarterly profit, for example, have little likelihood of investing the time needed to develop "customers for life" relationships or partnerships. The focus must change from product to benefit or business result. Grandiose products and services with more capacity, features, or options are often just seen as over-priced. Additionally, products and services must be simple to use and manage, either in their own right or because the salesperson simplifies the complexity as part of the sale. The focus must also change from price and delivery to ease of use, not only of the product but in doing business with the seller. The salesperson of preference will take responsibility for managing the relationship or, as sometimes defined, the "partnership" between seller and customer. This requires the role of the salesperson, and consequently, the role of educators, and, eventually, on-the-job sales managers who train and develop the salespeople to change.

Changing Customers

To put the changes in perspective, think of how differently you yourself purchase things now than you did in the past. Recall how you might have purchased a tele-vision in 1992, the year that HR Chally began benchmarking world class sales forces. Without the Internet and easy access to information, your search for a TV probably began with the Saturday newspaper and a trip to an electronics store. When you encountered a retail salesperson, you were likely early in your buying process. You were probably still in "education" mode and wanting to learn about the products that were available. By the time you encounter a salesperson today, you have probably already educated yourself on the alternatives and begun to narrow your choices. And with the increased complexity of the products (high-definition formats, flat panels, etc.), you have probably also amassed a long list of technical questions that you will expect the salesperson to answer with great authority and confidence. Compared to 1992, you are a much more sophisticated buyer. Consequently, you are a more demanding buyer. You are less tolerant of the typical deer-in-the-headlights salesperson who is no more useful than the tag on the retail display that you can read for yourself. You expect salespeople to be skilled, knowledgeable, and, above all, value-added. If salespeople cannot demonstrate in a very brief amount of time that they can understand and resolve your concerns, you will quickly discard them and move on to another salesperson or to another electronics store.

These are the trends that all sales forces face today: increasing product complexity, increasing customer sophistication, decreasing access to buyers, and decreasing customer loyalty. These factors all combine to create a selling environment that is more challenging now than ever before. The power has clearly shifted from the seller to the buyer, and buyers are using that power to turn up the heat on the salespeople who court them. As any sales executive will recognize, this is the bad news. But there is good news, too.

Changing Salespeople

The good news is that these changing customers expect salespeople to transform themselves into professionals who are deft at identifying and satisfying their new buying needs. But they don't believe in any individual salesperson until that new professionalism has been demonstrated.

Today, the dubious reputation of salesmen, sometimes earned, permeates our popular culture in books, movies, and jokes of every kind. So it isn't surprising that much of the general public—not to mention a great many business executives—have failed to view sales as a legitimate profession, let alone a desirable career. Instead, over many generations, business people have come to think of sales as a kind of "necessary evil," unavoidable in commerce—yet more tolerated than appreciated. Given this, it's not surprising that many perceive sales jobs as something one takes until a better opportunity comes along. Add to this a persistent belief that guile and charm are more common in salespeople than learned skills, and it becomes increasingly obvious why a comprehensive approach to sales training, and the overall professionalization of sales, have been slow to develop.

The emerging effort to have higher education play a leading role in sales training is critically needed. While sales management degrees have been available since the early 1900s, degrees specifically devoted to sales itself have been virtually nonexistent. Today, there are fewer than a few dozen such programs across the globe, out of more than four thousand colleges and universities in the United States alone.

While these programs differ in the details of their approach, all seek to help train sales specialists who can combine an expert knowledge of sales strategy with a parallel expertise in a targeted field of business. The idea is to create a new breed of sales professionals who are prepared for business even before they are trained by an individual company. The programs benefit both business and students by aligning educational goals with the realities of the employment market.

The Opportunity

Fortunately for industry, opportunities abound to benefit from and to support these programs. Preliminary findings from Chally's research indicate that students from formal sales programs ramp up at a rate of up to 50 percent faster than candidates from other disciplines. This, coupled with the increased tenure of such employees, yields a significant cost savings for employers.

When The Sales Education Foundation, a component fund of The Dayton Foundation, began in 2007, approximately two dozen colleges and universities had established formal sales programs. Today, more than fifty colleges have embraced the trend, with multiple tier one institutions joining the ranks.

To ensure that such opportunities increase for industry, it benefits employers to sponsor the university programs. Since not all companies have a connection to one local institution, Chally has made it possible for organizations or individuals to sponsor the efforts on a grander scale. The Sales Education Foundation provides scholarships, career selection tools, and experiential learning opportunities to students pursuing professional sales programs.

Here is the description and mission statement of the Foundation:

Today, more college graduates will become salespeople than all other careers combined. Yet only a few dozen of the more than four thousand colleges and universities across the world have established a formal sales program. To address this need, The Sales Education Foundation was established as a non-profit foundation to promote the profession of sales through colleges and universities with verified sales education curriculums. The USEF is working with a variety of industry professionals and academic trailblazers to establish and support effective university sales programs throughout the globe.

Our Mission and Goal

The overall mission of The Sales Education Foundation is to promote the profession of sales and its role as the driving force to the global economy. Our goal is to increase the number of schools that offer Approved Professional Sales Education programs yearly by 10 percent.

I encourage you to stop right now and contact Jeanne Frawley, the executive director of The Sales Education Foundation. Join, volunteer, attend their job fairs, contribute to the next generation of sales pros!

The Sales Education Foundation

www.saleseducationfoundation.org/

(800) 776-4436

Part Five

Appendices

In the appendices to this book I offer some resources, including websites and blogs you will find of use.

Appendix 1

The Ultimate Sales Training Website/Blog

You'll want to spend some regular time visiting: www.UltimateGuidetoSalesTraining.com

Because of the massive amount of information in this book, we've created a website to support and reinforce these ideas.

Please register online to get deep into this content, where you will be able to print out the exercises and checklists.

You'll find sections dedicated to each chapter, and we want feedback about your experiences using these ideas.

Do you have an opinion or question? Disagree with some concept? Get online and give us your thoughts.

www.UltimateGuidetoSalesTraining.com

Appendix 2

Websites of Books, Companies, and Associations in This Book

Adobe Acrobat Connect Pro: www.Adobe.com

Advertising Specialties Institute (ASI): www.asicentral.com

Alan Weiss: www.SummitConsulting.com

Becky Pike's *Webinars with Wow Factor*: www.WebinarsWithWowFactor.com

Brian Dietmeyer: BJD@e-thinkinc.com

Brian Lambert: www.forrester.com/rb/analyst/brian_lambert

Chally Group Worldwide: www.chally.com/

Chester Karrass: www.karrass.com/kar_eng/tipofthemonth.htm

Creativity: http://creativity-online.com/

Dan Seidman, author, Got Influence? www.GotInfluenceInc.com

De Bono, E.: www.debonoconsulting.com

DISC: www.ttidisc.com

Dr. Mercola: www.Mercola.com

Edgar Online: www.edgar-online.com

Effectiveness Solutions Research Corporation: www.ESResearch.com

Entertainment coupon book: www.entertainment.com

Facebook: www.Facebook.com

Fisher and Ury: http://en.wikipedia.org/wiki/Getting_to_YES

Full Engagement Profile: http://hpinstitute.com/assessment_profile.html

Gerhard Gschwandtner: www.SellingPower.com

Go To Meeting: www.GoToMeeting.com

Google Alerts: www.google.com/alerts

Got Influence? www.GotInfluenceInc.com

Harvey McKay: www.harveymackay.com/pdfs/mackay66.pdf?

Herrmann Brain Dominance Instrument: www.hbdi.com/

Hoovers: www.hoovers.com

How to Start a For-Profit Mastermind Group: www.passionforbusiness.com/
    articles/mastermind-group.htm

Janet Switzer: www.instantincome.com/iibp/

Jerry Weissman: powerltd.com

Jim Loehr and Jack Groppel: http://hpinstitute.com/assessment_profile.html

http://procureinsights.wordpress.com/2010/08/30/
    you-dont-get-what-you-deserve-you-get-what-you-negotiate/

Jim Micklos: www.fpmglobal.com

Karyn Greenstreet: www.passionforbusiness.com/articles/mastermind-group
    .htm

Link Popularity Check: www.submitexpress.com/linkpop/

LinkedIn: www.LinkedIn.com

Live Meeting: www.LiveMeeting.com

Myers-Briggs Type Indicator: www.myersbriggs.org/my-mbti-personality
-type/mbti-basics/

National Collegiate Sales Competition: http://coles.kennesaw.edu/ncsc/

National Speakers Association: www.nsaonline.org

OneSource Information Services: www.onesource.com

Sales Training That Drives Revenue: http://store.astd.org/Default.aspx?tabid=
167&ProductId=19830

SAMA association: www.strategicaccounts.org/

Selling Power magazine: www.SellingPowerFromJosh.com

Sharon Drew Morgen's *Buyer Facilitation®:* http://sharondrewmorgen.com/

"Six Pillars of Character" developed by The Josephson Institute: http://
charactercounts.org/sixpillars.html

Strategic and Competitive Intelligence Professionals: www.scip.org

SWOT analysis: www.quickmba.com/strategy/swot/

The Customer Advisory Board: www.customeradvisoryboard.org/

The Human Performance Institute: http://hpinstitute.com/assessment
_profile.html

The Josephson Institute's Six Pillars of Character: http://charactercounts.org/
sixpillars.html

The Promotional Products Association International (PPAI): www.ppa.org

The University Sales Education Foundation: www.saleseducationfoundation
.org/

Thesaurus: http://thesaurus.com/

Tom Sant's *Persuasive Business Proposals:* www.hydeparkpartnerscal.com

web-based competition research: http://wholinkstome.com or http://www
.seomoz.org

WebEx: www.WebEx.com

WIFFY: What's In It For You: powerltd.com

World Vision: www.worldvision.org/content.nsf/about/why-donate

www.fourhourworkweek.com

www.GotInfluenceInc.com

www.LeadGenerationGenius.com

www.mayoclinic.com/health/work-life-balance/WL00056/
     NSECTIONGROUP=2

www.ModelofSalesExcellence.com

www.RainToday.com

www.SalesAutopsy.com

www.UltimateGuidetoSalesTraining.com

www.worldvision.org

Appendix 3

The Most Interesting Man in the (Sales) World

One of the key concepts in selling is to find your center of influence. This is the person who seems to know everybody, who seems to have access to your perfect prospect, who seems to be ageless and timeless in his or her knowledge about your industry, marketplace, and profession.

One authority magnificently fills this role in the sales profession. The Most Interesting Man in the (Sales) World is Gerhard Gschwandtner, founder and publisher of *Selling Power* magazine (www.SellingPower.com).

Gerhard was born in Austria and has made his mark in the United States and globally over the past thirty years by growing a four-color direct mail piece into one of the most beautiful magazines you'll ever hold in your hand. *Selling Power* has covered every possibly sales expert from the great ones like Zig Ziglar and Neil Rackham right alongside corporate and entrepreneurial masters you've never heard of, but need to know about.

Gerhard's skill with the written word and artwork, and even his personal skill with the camera, combine to form a publication that every salesperson should be reading. I feel so strongly about the quality of *Selling Power* that I always recommend to other publishers I write for (a couple dozen excellent magazines) that they review his product as a model for both visual and content appeal.

The company's website has thousands of pages of resources. The firm runs events throughout the year and publishes books. *Selling Power* even offers webinars, CDs, DVDs, and more.

If you are serious about your profession, you should be subscribing to *Selling Power.*

Gerhard even has a special arrangement with one of the youngest sales pros on the planet, who can have a copy of the magazine sent to the home of everyone on your sales team for a yearly rate that is 20 percent below the lowest available price.

Check this out at www.SellingPowerfromJosh.com.

Statement of disclosure: When you arrive at this website you might see video and photos of a very young salesman who looks like the author of this book. It is my thirteen-year-old son, Joshua.

Here's a tip on using the magazine: Get your sales pros to select some ideas that had the greatest impact on them each month and run a portion of your weekly sales meeting by having your salespeople discuss their favorite strategies and learning from the magazine.

By now you have enough information to realize the wisdom of subscribing to this rich resource. *Selling Power* plus The Most Interesting Man in the (Sales) World. Add them both to your intellectual property today.

References

American Psychological Association. (2000). *American Psychologist*, *55*, as quoted in Mercola.com.

Beckhard, R. (1969). *Organization development: Strategies and models*. Reading, MA: Addison-Wesley.

Beckhard, R., & Harris, R.T. (1987). *Organizational transitions: Managing complex change*. Reading, MA: Addison-Wesley.

Berne, E. (1996). *Games people play: The basic handbook of transactional analysis*. New York: Ballantine Books.

"Can't get no satisfaction." (2006, December 4). *New York* magazine.

Carroll, A. (2002). *Speeding excuses that work: The cleverest copouts and ticket victories!* Santa Barbara, CA: Gray Area Press.

Carroll, A. (2005). *Beat the cops: The guide to fighting your traffic ticket and winning*. Santa Barbara, CA: Gray Area Press.

Ekman, P. (2007). *Emotions revealed: Recognizing faces and feelings to improve communication and emotional life* (2nd ed.). New York: Holt.

eRoi. (2006). *Email deliverability survey*. Portland, OR: eRoi.

Families and Work Institute. (2001). *Feeling overworked: When work becomes too much*. New York: Author.

Family Matters! survey. (1998). Washington, DC: The National Partnership for Women and Families.

Ferriss, T. (2009). *The 4-hour workweek* (expanded and updated). New York: Crown Archetype.

Fisher, R., & Ury, W.L. (1992). *Getting to yes: Negotiating agreement without giving in*. New York: Houghton Mifflin.

Gallo, C. (2005). *10 simple secrets of the world's greatest business communicators*. Naperville, IL: Sourcebooks, Inc.

Gallo, C. (2009). *The presentation secrets of Steve Jobs: How to be insanely great in front of any audience.* New York: McGraw-Hill.

Garber, A.R. (2001). "Death by PowerPoint." www.smallbusinesscomputing.com.

Gawande, A. (2009). *The checklist manifesto: How to get things right.* New York: Metropolitan Books.

Goleman, D. (2006). *Emotional intelligence: Why it can matter more than IQ* (10th ann. ed.). New York: Bantam Books.

Greenstreet, K. (n.d.). *How to start a for-profit mastermind group* (2nd ed.). www .passionforbusiness.com/products.

Groppel, J., & Andelman, B. (1999). *The corporate athlete.* Hoboken, NJ: John Wiley & Sons.

Hickman, C., Smith, T., & Connors, R. (2010). *The Oz principle: Getting results through individual and organizational accountability.* New York: Portfolio Trade.

Hofstede, G. (2001). *Culture's consequences: Comparing values, behaviors, institutions, and organizations across nations* (2nd ed.). Thousand Oaks, CA: Sage.

Jeary, T., Dower, K., & Fishman, J.E. (2005). *Life is a series of presentations: Eight ways to inspire, inform, and influence anyone, anywhere, anytime.* New York: Fireside Books.

Karrass, C.L. (1993). *The negotiating game* (rev. ed.). New York: HarperCollins.

Karrass, C.L. (1995). *Give and take: The complete guide to negotiating strategies* (rev. ed.). New York: Harper Paperbacks.

Karrass, C.L. (1996). *In business as in life, you don't get what you deserve, you get what you negotiate.* Palo Alto, CA: Stanford Street Press.

Keller, J. (2003, January 5). Killing me microsoftly with PowerPoint. *The Chicago Tribune.*

Lambert, B. (2009). *10 steps to successful sales.* Alexandria, VA: ASTD Press.

Lambert, B., Ohai, T., & Kerkhoff, E. (2009). *World-class selling: New sales competencies.* Alexandria, VA: ASTD Press.

Lebowitz, F. (1981). *Social studies.* New York: Random House.

Lehrer, J. (2009). *How we decide.* New York: Houghton Mifflin.

Loehr, J., & Schwartz, T. (2003). *The power of full engagement: Managing energy, not time, is the key to high performance and personal renewal.* New York: The Free Press.

Maltz, M. (1989). *Cyber-cybernetics: A new way to get more living out of life*. New York: Pocket Books.

Miller, R.B., Heiman, S.E., & Tuleja, T. (1985). *Strategic selling: The unique sales system proven successful by America's best companies*. New York: William Morrow.

Moine, D., & Lloyd, K. (2008). *Ultimate selling power: How to create and enjoy a multimillion dollar sales career*. Franklin Lakes, NJ: Career Press.

Nakata, C. (Ed.). (2009). *Beyond Hofstede: Culture frameworks for global marketing and management*. New York: Palgrave Macmillan.

Ohai, T., & Lambert, B. (2011). *Sales chaos: Using agility selling to think and sell differently*. San Francisco, Pfeiffer and Alexandria, VA: ASTD Press.

Parinelli, T. (2005). *Getting to VITO (the Very Important Top Officer): 10 steps to VITO's office*. Hoboken, NJ: John Wiley & Sons.

Peppers, D., & Rogers, M. (1996). *The one to one future: Building relationships one customer at a time*. New York: Currency/Doubleday.

Peppers, D., & Rogers, M. (1999). *The one to one fieldbook*. New York: Crown.

Pluth, B.P. (2010). *Webinars with WOW factor: Tips, tricks, and interactivities for virtual training*. Eden Prairie, MN: Bob Pike Group.

Rackham, N. (1988). *SPIN selling*. New York: McGraw-Hill.

Reichheld, F. (1996). *The loyalty effect: The hidden forces behind growth, profits, and lasting value*. Cambridge, MA: Harvard Business School Press.

Sant, T. (2003). *Persuasive business proposals: Writing to win more customers, clients, and contracts*. New York: AMACOM.

Sant, T. (2006). *The giants of sales: What Dale Carnegie, John Patterson, Elmer Wheeler, and Joe Girard can teach you about real sales success*. New York: AMACOM.

Sant, T. (2008). *The language of success*. New York: AMACOM.

Seidman, D. (2006). *Sales autopsy: 50 postmortems reveal what killed the sale (and what might have saved it)*. Chicago: Kaplan Publishing.

Seidman, D. (2012). *The secret language of influence*. New York: AMACOM.

Seligman, M. (1998). *Learned optimism: How to change your mind and your life*. New York: The Free Press.

Seligman, M. (2004). *Authentic happiness: Using the new positive psychology to realize your potential for lasting fulfillment*. New York: The Free Press.

Shell, G.R. (2006). *Bargaining for advantage: Negotiation strategies for reasonable people* (2nd ed.). New York: Penguin Books.

Switzer, J. (2007). *Instant income: Strategies that bring in the cash*. New York: McGraw-Hill.

Thompson, L.L. (2007). *The truth about negotiations*. Upper Saddle River, NJ: FT Press.

Thull, J. (2010). *Mastering the complex sale* (2nd ed.). Hoboken, NJ: John Wiley & Sons.

United States @ work study. (2000). New York: Aon Consulting.

Trompenaar, F. (1997). *Riding the waves of culture: Understanding diversity in global business* (2nd ed.). New York: McGraw-Hill.

Weiss, A. (2005). *Million dollar consulting: Step by step guidance, checklists, templates, and samples from "Million dollar consulting."* Hoboken, NJ: John Wiley & Sons.

Weiss, A. (2009). *How to write a proposal that's accepted every time* (2nd ed.). Peterborough, NH: Kennedy Information.

Weiss, A. (2009). *Million dollar consulting: The professional's guide to growing a practice* (4th ed.). New York: McGraw-Hill.

Weiss, A. (2009). *Thrive! Stop wishing your life away*. East Greenwich, RI: Las Brisas Research Press.

Weissman, J. (2008). *Presenting to win: The art of telling your story* (rev ed.). Upper Saddle River, NJ: FT Press.

Weissman, J. (2009). *The power presenter: Technique, style, and strategy from America's top speaking coach*. Hoboken, NJ: John Wiley & Sons.

Zimbardo, P., & Boyd, J. (2008). *The time paradox: The new psychology of time that will change your life*. New York: The Free Press.

About the Author

Dan Seidman is one of America's top speakers, coaches, and trainers on *influence*. He is the author of the number one business best-seller, *Sales Autopsy* (Kaplan Publishing, 2006). Therein Dan reveals the top seven traits that distinguish world class sales professionals from the rest of the selling world.

Dan is a World Master's athlete who has three gold medals playing on the U.S. basketball team. He has been selected as one of the "Top 12 Sales Coaches in America" in Dr. Don Moine's *Ultimate Selling Power* and runs the award-winning website SalesAutopsy.com.

Selling Power magazine selected the Sales Autopsy Training Experience as a finalist in its 2006 Sales Excellence Awards. Dan's columns reach more than 1.5 million readers a month, both online at Monster.com and in print at *Agent Sales Journal, Independent Agent, Advantages, Insurance NewsNet Magazine*, and more.

Dan Seidman lives in Barrington, Illinois, with his princess bride, Wendy, and son Joshua. Twin girls were recently discovered at his residence. They're being called Abigail and Rebekah.

Contact Dan today at (847) 359-7860 or Dan@GotInfluenceInc.com to determine when he is available to help improve your sales team's performance.

Got Influence?

Does your sales training program contain the latest strategies on motivating buyers to buy, sales influence, and persuasion, and—most critically—does it change behavior, rather than teach ideas? If not . . .

It's time to re-design!

Dan Seidman's body of work covers much of the latest and best practices in sales training.

Here Are the Top Ways He Can Help You Improve Sales Team Performance

1. By analyzing your existing sales training program using the CAT Scan Diagnostic Tool (found in Chapter 30 of this book) in order to re-design it and quickly create a boost in revenue.

2 Share Secret Language of Influence® content to upgrade existing training. These psychologically sound strategies are based on the latest working knowledge in persuasion, motivation, and decision making.

3. Create a Model of Sales Excellence to analyze your top performers and copy their behaviors for others to follow. This new influence tool is better than any personality assessment in the world today.

4. Perform a Week of Maximum Engagement exercise, which will immediately push your team to new revenue heights in five days. If you can't wait to re-work your sales training, you'll want a conversation with Dan on this one.

5. Keynote your national and regional sales conferences with insights, experience, and plenty of humor from his collection of 600+ selling blunders.

Dan's clients have included such companies as:

Million Dollar Roundtable

Advertising Specialties Institute

American Banker's Association Sales Management Conference

American Society for Training & Development

Ameriprise

Amway International

Association of Accounting Marketing

Ball State University Sales Symposium

Banta Global Sales

Blue Cross Blue Shield

Christian Management Association

Discover Card International

Karl Storz Global Sales

National Association of Food Equipment Manufacturers

National Association of Health Underwriters (NAHU)

Profiles International Global Sales

Publishers Marketing Association

Society of Certified Property and Casualty Underwriters (CPCU)

State Farm Insurance

Willow Creek Association

World Vision

Unique Programs and Keynotes
The Ultimate Objection-Handling Tool

Bring your six toughest, most frequently encountered objections and leave with 48 to 60 or more great responses! You'll want to take serious notes and create a script book for both experienced and new sales professionals. Everyone on your team, with a wide variety of personalities and skills represented, will be able to "find his or her voice" and utilize working words that help all of them move beyond prospect resistance.

Secret Language of Influence: Your Passport to Persuasion Power

Your words are gold coins. Language coaching is the most neglected area of sales skills training today. You should be sensitive of which words to adopt (and which to avoid) with prospects and clients. Great sales pros are flexible enough to adjust their approach to the individual buyer. (See Dan's book on the topic coming out in 2012.)

Excuse Elimination Diet

Excuses killing productivity? Excuses offering lame rationalization as to why your people aren't closing more sales? Excuses making you sick? This wildly unique and useful program is based on more than one thousand pages of fascinating research on how the brain accepts and validates excuses. Dan will teach your sales pros how to eliminate excuses that are ruining sales and keeping your people from attaining high performance. (*Note:* This has application for everyone's professional and personal lives.)

Lead Generation Genius: Wise Ways to Find Buyers by the Boatload

25+ years of guerrilla marketing, research, and creative tactics for seeking, finding, and closing your perfect prospect. We'll draw off the collective brainpower of attendees as well.

The One Sales Test You're Guaranteed to Fail

1. Who are you REALLY competing with?
2. What is the number 1 PROBLEM encountered by anyone who sells anything?
3. What is your RESPONSIBILITY on a sales call?

(*Hint:* Face-to-face or phone calls, the answer has to be correct *100 percent* of the time.)

World class sales professionals can answer and ACT upon each of these. . . . How will you respond? How well will your sales team respond?

A Week of Maximum Engagement

Dan's best-kept secret for his best-kept clients. This unique program will identify the true capacity of each member of your selling team. This strategy is the single best way to bump sales performance in a short time. Big AHA! moments contained within for senior sales executives and corporate officers.

Each of these programs (and others encompassing every piece of the selling puzzle) teaches your sales professionals to have the mental flexibility to create customized conversations that motivate buyers to buy!

Contact Dan today at Dan@GotInfluence.com and request one of these insightful articles:

One Sales Test You're Guaranteed to Fail

The 800 Pound Lie of Guerrilla Marketing

Aaaahhhh! (The use of emotion in sales dialogues)

Index

Page references followed by *fig* indicate an illustrated figure; followed by *t* indicate a table; followed by *e* indicate an exercise.

CPSIA information can be obtained
at www.ICGtesting.com
Printed in the USA
BVHW010239030621
608725BV00012B/334